ARMS CONTROL
TOWARD THE
21st CENTURY

ARMS CONTROL

TOWARD THE

21st CENTURY

edited by

Jeffrey A. Larsen
Gregory J. Rattray

LYNNE
RIENNER
PUBLISHERS

BOULDER
LONDON

Published in the United States of America in 1996 by
Lynne Rienner Publishers, Inc.
1800 30th Street, Boulder, Colorado 80301

and in the United Kingdom by
Lynne Rienner Publishers, Inc.
3 Henrietta Street, Covent Garden, London WC2E 8LU

Library of Congress Cataloging-in-Publication Data
Arms control toward the 21st century / Jeffrey A. Larsen and Gregory
   J. Rattray, editors.
      p.   cm.
   Includes bibliographical references and index.
   ISBN 1-55587-561-0 (alk. paper)
   ISBN 1-55587-584-X (pbk.: alk. paper)
   1. Arms control. I. Larsen, Jeffrey Arthur. II. Rattray,
Gregory J., 1962– .
JX1974.A6745   1996
327.1'74—dc20
                                   95-26188
                                   CIP

British Cataloguing in Publication Data
A Cataloguing in Publication record for this book
is available from the British Library.

This book was typeset by Letra Libre, Boulder, Colorado.

Printed and bound in the United States of America

The paper in this publication meets the requirements
(∞) of the American National Standard for Permanence of
Paper for Printed Library Materials Z39.48-1984.

5 4 3 2 1

Contents

Foreword

Ronald F. Lehman

How should we think about arms control? Should we pursue it as an ideology or a methodology, a goal or a tool? Is it a field of science or a practical art? Is arms control a new way of thinking, or is it simply diplomacy and war by other means? Although basic answers to these questions were clarified by the arms control revolution, which occurred at the end of the Cold War, definitive answers are still evolving.

Arms Control Toward the Twenty-First Century will help provide further answers. This important new survey of arms control issues gives students of arms control the latest and best synthesis of lessons learned from the Cold War. More important, it points the way to a new millennium.

Of course, efforts to control arms are not new. Proposals to ban specific weapons or to limit the scope of military activity can be found early in the history of diplomacy, law, religion, technology, and warfare. Only in the twentieth century, however, has arms control emerged as both an overarching concept and an academic and professional specialization.

It is not surprising that arms control is multidisciplinary. Analytically, the subject is complex; substantively, its impact is broad, affecting politics and economics as well as national security. The scope of arms control itself has grown. The term *arms control* is sometimes used narrowly to mean only negotiated limitations on military weapons and forces. In recent usage, however, the term encompasses far more—disarmament, negotiated constraints, nonproliferation, export controls, confidence- and security-building measures, unilateral declaratory defense policies, aspects of diplomacy, international law, defense conversion, and certain activities related to international peacekeeping. In this wider context, arms control issues are often discussed with issues of the political economy and the stressed ecology of a shrinking globe.

This complex definition reflects the political dynamism of the ongoing arms control process. Certainly, the golden age of arms control treaties was intertwined with pivotal events in the East-West competition and was frequently a catalyst for growing cooperation. The pursuit of arms control, however, did not begin with the modern Cold War, nor has it ended with it. The dynamism continues. New priorities have arisen, even as many Cold War issues and ideologies remain.

As we approach the twenty-first century, uncertainty continues to accompany the process that led to the two strategic arms treaties (START I and START II), the Chemical Weapons Convention, and even the nuclear Non-Proliferation Treaty. Global economic development, nuclear ambitions such as those we have seen in Iraq and North Korea, and turmoil in nuclear-capable states threaten to accelerate the spread of the knowledge, technology, materials, and skilled manpower necessary to acquire weapons of mass destruction and their means of delivery. Also, ethnic violence in Europe calls into question the viability of new structures for peace, such as those codified in the documents of the Conference on Security and Cooperation in Europe.

Thus, arms control will remain a major theme of foreign policy and national security strategy for many years. The heightened centrality of arms control during the Cold War often seemed temporary and artificial, but contemporary study of civil-military relations and political-military affairs would be shallow without a strong arms control component. Fear of the spread of weapons of mass destruction into regions of intense conflict will keep arms control issues salient well into the post–Cold War era.

The authors of *Arms Control Toward the Twenty-First Century* examine arms control goals in light of changing policies. They illuminate how arms control often seems like a regulatory process, constraining in one area only to see the arms competition move to new arenas. They give examples of the asymptotic phenomenon that as we get closer to some of our goals, achieving final success can become more difficult.

Arms control is often about technologies: comparative, competitive, and even cooperative. Thus, the authors have not neglected the hardware of arms control. Nor have they neglected other technical and legal aspects of arms control, but they have placed them in the broader context of foreign and defense policy. The authors have correctly highlighted the important role of geography in shaping negotiating issues and assigning value to military forces. And they have elaborated on how arms control influences and is influenced by domestic political and economic events.

The approach taken by the authors is grounded in reality and never becomes too abstract. They draw from the history of arms control to illustrate their findings. The reader will appreciate the details given of the considerable recent arms control accomplishments. Many will be surprised by the scope of agreements, the network of constraints, the magnitude of the reductions, and the intrusive verification measures to be implemented. The important role that arms control played in promoting political change, the costs of implementation, and the less tangible prices paid to reach agreement will also be of interest.

This text's greatest contribution is the help it gives us in thinking about the future. Superpower arms control remains important, but multilateral issues now dominate. Some are global, some are regional. Many are designed to further tighten the constraints on the military capability of nation-states to wage war. More needs to be done to address the problem of subnational and transnational violence. One can imagine arms control addressing the problems of lower levels of conflict, but more innovative approaches will be necessary.

In this period of massive implementation of agreements, monetary and other types of costs of the ever-expanding web of constraints on states, particularly nuclear weapon states, will have to be contained if arms control is to spread further. In addition, further arms control regimes will be of limited value, or even counterproductive, if the international community does not strengthen responses to violations of agreements.

I hope that this book will help the reader to think through the implications of arms control as an end and a means. Perhaps a better understanding of sound principles of arms control will emerge. Understanding the foundation and context of arms control should help differentiate between trends and trendiness. Above all, the important interface between arms control and political change will become clear.

As technology spreads and the global economy becomes ever more interdependent, we could find ourselves choosing between economic growth and national security. To advance both, far greater political reform—democracy, the rule of law, and openness—will be necessary around the world. Arms control properly implemented can help with this as well.

That the U.S. Air Force Academy and the Institute for National Security Studies have brought this book together has enhanced its quality and has also given it special meaning. Military organizations and equipment are usually the subject of arms control, and military personnel have provided key skills for the resolution of arms control challenges. More symbolically, the establishment of the U.S. Air Force coincided with the age of nuclear weapons, which has also been the age of arms control. My father flew B-17 bombers in World War II and B-29s in the Korean War, but the B-36 bombers that he flew, which carried nuclear weapons, were never used in war. The U.S. Air Force has demonstrated that arms control and military capability can work together to promote peace, and with its support of this volume it continues in that direction.

Acknowledgments

The editors wish to thank the contributors to this work for their efforts and diligence in meeting tight deadlines and tough restrictions on chapter topics and length, yet still coming up with masterful original work. We were pleased to be able to work with many old friends on this project and to develop several new ones. This has been a real team effort, from the genesis of the original concept in early 1994 through the final production phase. Thanks to Lynne Rienner for believing in the idea and for her support throughout the tough early days finding authors that met all of our requirements, as well as to Ambassador Ron Lehman, who also supported this project from the beginning. We are especially grateful to the National Security Negotiations Division, Directorate of Plans, Headquarters U.S. Air Force (AF/XOXI), for its financial sponsorship of this effort through the USAF Institute for National Security Studies (INSS).

Special thanks to T. J. O'Connell, who came to INSS mid-project as our executive officer and saw us through the authors' workshop and draft manuscript. His steadfast good humor and tireless efforts were invaluable to the success of this project and to nurturing and maintaining contacts with our contributors. T. J. was responsible for gathering most of the data found in the appendixes. Another major contributor to this effort was Timothy J. Krein, our INSS Air Force reservist. Tim read many of the early chapters and was instrumental in doing the final formatting of the revised manuscript. Valuable help was also provided by Diana Heerdt, our INSS secretary who prepared the manuscript for final review; Sheryl Holt, who offered secretarial support when we needed help before Diana was on our staff; Robert "Bo" Dunaway, who designed the maps in Chapter 6 and Appendix 2 and, along with Mike Jessop, helped us with some aggravating computer problems; and Rich Cadis and Judy Thurlow, of the academy graphic arts section, who designed the timeline in Appendix 1.

Finally, thanks to Cyndy Larsen and Francesca Rattray, who supported us on those late nights and weekends in the office because they recognized the value of the project, and its importance to us.

We dedicate this book to students of national security facing new challenges at the turn of the millennium. We hope this volume proves valuable to your efforts at understanding arms control and its role in international relations.

Jeffrey A. Larsen
Gregory J. Rattray

Introduction

Gregory J. Rattray

This book provides students of arms control an examination of the underlying principles of the topic, as well as a vision of where arms control is going as we approach the twenty-first century. Given the changing international system and uncertainty about how states will achieve security in this environment, we believe a fresh look at arms control is both timely and necessary.

Historical Background

Humankind's efforts to control the consequences of the possession and use of weapons followed quickly upon the heels of weapons development. History records negotiations between the Greek city-states of Sparta and Athens concerning limitations to fortifications in the fifth century B.C.[1] During the Middle Ages, the Catholic church issued canons proscribing violence against clerics and women, banned jousting tournaments (which tended to turn into battles), and attempted to ban weapons such as the crossbow.[2] Early in our country's history, the United States and Great Britain signed the 1817 Rush-Bagot Agreement calling for the virtual removal of armed warships from the Great Lakes. The potential for devastation inherent in the armed might of newly industrialized countries prompted the 1899 and 1907 Hague Conventions to outlaw weapons such as dumdum bullets and asphyxiating gases, hoping to thereby mitigate the impact of future wars.

World War I fully exposed the horrors and totality of modern interstate conflict and the limits to controlling arms through agreements. Pres. Woodrow Wilson called it "the war to end all wars." Attempts to prevent the recurrence of the use of poison gas prompted the 1925 Geneva Protocol to again prohibit the use of chemical and, additionally, biological weapons. The 1928 Kellogg-Briand Pact, signed by 63 countries, went even further by attempting to completely abolish aggressive war as a legitimate right of states.

1

In more focused negotiations, such as the Washington Naval Conference of 1922 and the London Naval Conferences of 1930 and 1935, treaties were made in an effort to balance the naval strength of the major powers. These agreements constrained the size of the fleets of the United States, the United Kingdom, Japan, France, and Italy.

The limitations of such efforts were again made clear by the outbreak and massive scope of World War II. As this conflict concluded with the dropping of the first atomic weapons on Hiroshima and Nagasaki, humankind faced an even more insistent challenge to control the possibilities for violence and destruction unleashed in the pursuit of weapons and national security.

Arms Control During the Cold War

These efforts to limit the pursuit and acquisition of weapons became known as arms control. Despite the failure of early efforts to control the nuclear genie, arms control during the Cold War eventually assumed a high priority on the national security agenda as a way of managing the superpower nuclear rivalry. The new importance of arms control was a reaction to the bipolar structure of the international system and the new and, many argued, revolutionary nature of nuclear weapons. Later portions of this book discuss the Cold War arms control record in depth. Generally, these negotiations were limited in scope and focused on increased strategic nuclear stability between the superpowers. The Strategic Arms Limitation Talks (SALT) and the Strategic Arms Reduction Talks (START) held center stage during this period. Other important multilateral negotiations and agreements occurred that limited nuclear testing and deployment, particularly the Non-Proliferation Treaty (NPT). Efforts were conducted in other areas, such as the Biological and Toxin Weapons Convention (BWC) and the Mutual and Balanced Force Reduction (MBFR) talks covering conventional weapons in Europe.

As the United States and the Soviet Union faced one another as military, political, and ideological rivals, the conduct of bilateral negotiations became very formal. Agreements took years to reach. Every possible implication for the strategic balance was scrutinized, while increasingly complex provisions for verification became part of the process to guard against cheating. Even when a treaty was concluded, the benefits and pitfalls of arms control were hotly debated among the national security elites. SALT II was never ratified by the U.S. Senate, even after its signing in 1979 following seven years of painfully slow negotiations. The pros and cons of the Antiballistic Missile (ABM) Treaty became a perennial issue after Pres. Ronald Reagan renewed the U.S. quest for strategic defenses. Soviet (and later, Russian) nationalists argued that too many concessions had been made to the United

States during the START process and the agreements undermined their own security.

Arms Control and the Close of the Cold War

The dissolution of the Soviet Union and of the Warsaw Pact has transformed the content and perceived importance of arms control in just a few short years. As the Iron Curtain fell and the former republics of the Soviet Union declared independence, the ideological and military threats to the United States from the East dissipated. The imperative to manage the strategic nuclear balance between the superpowers faded. The place of arms control on the national security agenda began to drop. By the early 1990s, commentators began to question whether the lengthy, formalistic negotiations and highly structured forums established for arms control during the Cold War were not slowing the pace of defense reductions but were rather causing nations to wait for a treaty before undertaking actions already planned. The utility of past arms control agreements has been debated in light of the changed strategic situation in Europe.[3] Others have questioned whether arms control remains a useful tool for national security at all.[4]

Meanwhile, the Gulf War brought a new set of issues into the limelight. Iraqi pursuit of a range of advanced arms—including nuclear weaponry, ballistic missiles, and super-long-range artillery—affected the conduct of the war, as well as leaving most of the industrialized members of the UN coalition chastised for helping to build the Iraqi war machine, however unwittingly. Iraq's progress toward a nuclear weapons capability while remaining a member of the nuclear NPT regime and subject to International Atomic Energy Agency (IAEA) inspections frightened many observers. At the same time, the dissolution of the Soviet military machine has created opportunities for weapons, military technologies, and know-how to flow to other states and even nonstate actors: Su-27 fighters and surface-to-air missiles have been sold to China;[5] Russia transferred cryogenic engine technology to the Indian space program;[6] smugglers have been caught in Germany with small quantities of (presumably) Russian plutonium.[7] Proliferation has risen quickly to the top of the security agenda of the United States and other Western nations.

The Gulf War led the way in pointing to other new security concerns. The breakdown of the bipolar international system coincided with a rise in regional instability. Conflict has begun to break out around the globe. Domestic conflicts are spilling over the borders of crumbling, multiethnic states. Vicious, even genocidal, fighting in Africa, in Yugoslavia, and within the confines of the former Soviet Union make some observers long for the relative calm of the latter stages of the Cold War. Tensions are high in other areas, such as the Korean peninsula. Humanitarian and moral imperatives have led to UN and U.S. intervention in many of these situations.

Yet the early 1990s also saw the refocusing of public attention within the United States on problems at home. Revitalizing the economy and improving U.S. economic competitiveness became central focuses of the 1992 presidential race. Other countries in the developed and developing worlds confront similar challenges. Japan has faced political scandals and numerous changes in government. Germany has the daunting task of integrating a formerly communist-ruled region suffering from decay of work incentives, an outdated industrial base, and massive environmental problems. Defense needs compete with other crucial priorities in an era of shrinking federal budgets and economic competition from abroad.[8] Environmental issues have also pushed their way onto the security agenda. The defense establishment increasingly must concern itself with the need to limit and clean up the impact of its activities. Others see transnational problems such as pollution and global warming as new sources of potential conflict.[9] The post–Cold War nature of national security and the role of military forces have yet to be clearly defined.

Arms Control in the Post–Cold War Era

As the Cold War ended, the conception and execution of what was referred to as arms control began to change, first with an increase in the number and types of bilateral arrangements between the superpowers, starting with the Intermediate-Range Nuclear Forces (INF) Treaty signed in December 1987. After the precedent set by the INF Treaty, negotiations on nuclear arms control began to pick up pace, resulting in the START I agreement in July 1991. This treaty was expanded to include Ukraine, Belarus, and Kazakhstan through the Lisbon Protocol signed in May 1992. START II mandated even deeper cuts in strategic forces and was agreed to in January 1993. Additionally, numerous unilateral declarations and reductions have been made by both sides regarding their nuclear forces. Increasingly, the United States and Russia have moved away from a competitive approach to security based on deterrence to a cooperative approach based on reassurance.[10]

As rapprochement between the superpowers deepened, the forums and scope for other negotiations began to broaden. Under the auspices of the Conference on Security and Cooperation in Europe (CSCE), multilateral agreements were reached in Europe, beginning with confidence- and security-building measures (CSBMs). CSBMs were first included in the Helsinki Final Act in 1975. Interest in these measures picked up momentum during the 1980s, leading to the 1986 Stockholm and 1992 Vienna Documents, which laid out extensive sets of CSBMs. Negotiations on conventional forces culminated in the Conventional Forces in Europe (CFE) Treaty in December 1990 and the CFE 1A Agreement in July 1992; these two agreements dramatically limited the size and structure of conventional forces.

Regions beyond Europe also began to turn to arms control as a means to build security. The Middle East peace talks under the direction of the United States and Russia after the Gulf War had a very significant security component. In May 1991, the Bush administration proposed the Middle East Arms Control Initiative, calling on the five permanent members of the UN Security Council to "establish guidelines for restraints on destabilizing transfers of conventional arms" to the region.[11]

Numerous regional nuclear confidence-building agreements have been pursued, with varying degrees of success. Despite ongoing tensions, India and Pakistan have managed to reach a series of agreements since 1985, including pacts not to attack each other's nuclear facilities and notification of military exercises. In Latin America, Brazil and Argentina signed an agreement with the IAEA renouncing the pursuit of nuclear weapons and allowing for the inspection of facilities. This agreement renewed progress toward full compliance with the Latin American nuclear-free zone established by the Treaty of Tlatelolco in 1967. In 1992, the two Koreas signed a Joint Declaration on the Denuclearization of the Korean Peninsula, although further progress toward cooperation proved difficult.

Significant progress was made on global regimes as well. The UN Conference on Disarmament negotiated a Chemical Weapons Convention (CWC), which was opened for signature on 1 January 1993. In December 1991, a UN General Assembly resolution also established a Register on Arms Transfers providing for the voluntary provision of information on arms exports and imports. Over 80 states provided reports during the first year of operation, and the register may become an increasingly important tool in tracking conventional arms around the world. After the September 1991 Third Review Conference of the 1972 Biological and Toxin Weapons Convention (BWC), the Secretary-General established a group of government experts to analyze the possibility of strengthening the convention through the creation of verification procedures.

New Approaches to Arms Control

Other aspects of arms control are changing to accommodate the new arms control agenda. The very formal, structured approach to reaching agreement has been broadened to include more informal modes of cooperation. In particular, the use of unilateral and reciprocal declarations such as those made by the superpowers regarding tactical nuclear weapons and the cancellation of new strategic systems between September 1991 and January 1992 resulted in dramatic steps outside formally established negotiating procedures.[12] Numerous similar types of commitments—such as unilateral declarations by states such as Israel, South Africa, Russia, and China to abide by the provisions of the Missile Technology Control Regime (MTCR)—may presage a major change in how states approach arms control.

Security negotiations between states have also developed an increasingly operational focus; they no longer simply pursue agreements to limit types and numbers of weapons. The growing interest in transparency is highlighted by the increasingly strict verification provisions written into treaties pioneered by the on-site inspection portions of the INF Treaty, as well as new agreements to share data—such as in the CFE Treaty and through the UN Register of Conventional Arms. As mentioned earlier, since 1975 the CSCE accords have included ever-broadening CSBMs to include advance notification, limits on size and number, and observation of military exercises. The Open Skies Treaty allows at least 25 countries to conduct, and be obligated to receive, observation flights by unarmed aircraft carrying optical and video cameras as well as infrared sensors and side-looking radar.[13] Efforts to deal with growing concerns about the leakage of nuclear materials to potential proliferants are likely to be dealt with through CSBMs rather than formal treaties.

New international organizations have evolved to implement agreements. UN Security Council Resolution 687 created a UN Special Commission in 1991 to monitor and eliminate Iraq's ballistic missile and weapons of mass destruction capability. CWC provisions include the creation of the Organization for the Prohibition of Chemical Weapons (OPCW) based in The Hague to monitor and enforce the treaty. Other international institutions with an arms control role, particularly the IAEA, have received renewed attention as proliferation concerns became prominent in light of new information on Iraq's activities prior to the Gulf War. Similarly, the MTCR has assumed an increasingly important role in efforts to limit technological diffusion in the missile area.

Certainly, as of the writing of this text the news is not all good. Proliferation concerns remain prominent in dealing with almost all the former Soviet republics. Ukraine demonstrated great intransigence in ratifying START and accepting the NPT regime. Russia complains of difficulty implementing chemical weapons agreements because of a lack of resources. The Middle East Arms Control Initiative died after China pulled out to protest U.S. F-16 sales to Taiwan.[14] The United States has accused both Russia and China of violating their pledges to adhere to MTCR restrictions. The future of the CWC in the Middle East is very uncertain because some Arab states intend to withhold ratification based on Israel's suspected possession of nuclear weapons. North Korea has stalled IAEA inspections numerous times, has threatened withdrawal from the NPT, and has raised tensions on the peninsula. The U.S. Senate keeps a close eye on these situations in deciding whether to ratify agreements. This causes delays in the entry into force and implementation of agreements. Arms control has resolved some, but certainly not all, of the diverse security challenges that face today's states.

However, no one can deny that a great deal of progress has been made through activities usually labeled "arms control." Arms control has a place in dealing with the new concerns of advanced weapons proliferation, regional instability, and economic and environmental security. The new and old arms control approaches will coexist while important dimensions of the exercise are redefined. The future of arms control as a means of achieving security needs rigorous examination.

What Is Arms Control?

This book lays out a framework that identifies the underlying principles of arms control and then analyzes their continued relevance to the pursuit of national security at the end of this century. This introduction provides a definition of arms control as a point of departure.

The Security Dilemma and Arms Races

In a system of sovereign states with the capability to build and maintain sizable armed forces, a situation known as a security dilemma exists. States cannot ensure that rival states will not attempt to achieve undue influence through the pursuit and maintenance of military superiority. Trust often does not exist. States, therefore, interpret incoming information on the military capabilities of rival states in the worst light. Evidence of a new military program or spending by one state "requires" other states to respond in a similar fashion to avoid the other side achieving superiority whether through larger forces or technological breakthroughs. An upward spiral, or arms race, can ensue, even at the cost of a state neglecting its domestic needs; for example, many experts view huge defense expenditures as a primary contributing cause of the collapse of the Soviet Union. Additionally, an arms race increases political tension between states, raising the probability and severity of crises and possibly causing war. Arms control tries to address the negative effects of the security dilemma.[15]

Early arms control theorists defined arms control in the broadest sense to refer to all forms of military cooperation between potential enemies in the interest of reducing the likelihood of war, the political and economic costs of preparing for war,[16] and the scope and violence of war if it were to occur. Yet, until recently, our political leaders and media seem to have had a more limited definition. They generally confined arms control to a limited set of activities dealing with specific steps to control a class or related classes of weapons systems, codified in formal agreements or treaties.

The impetus for controlling arms is not limited solely to constraining arms competitions or proliferation. Another common motive is to disarm perceived aggressors—as was done with Germany after World War I, Germany and Japan after World War II, and Iraq after the Gulf War. Quite possibly, states and international organizations may attempt to accomplish such punitive arms control in the post–Cold War era. However, this type of action falls outside the focus of the definition that we outline for this text and therefore is not a major topic of discussion.

For the purposes of this text we will define arms control as *a process involving specific, declared steps by a state to enhance security through cooperation with other states.* These steps can be unilateral, bilateral, or multilateral. Cooperation can be implicit as well as explicit. As we consider what steps states might take to achieve their security objectives, we should keep this broad definition in mind, not limiting ourselves to thinking of arms control as dealing only with numbers and types of weapons.

Arms Control Versus Disarmament

There is a difference between conceiving of arms control as a means to achieving a larger goal and seeing arms control as an end unto itself. As defined earlier, the arms control process is intended to serve as a means of enhancing a state's national security. Arms control is one of a number of approaches a nation has available for achieving this goal. Arms control could even lead states to agree to increases in certain categories of armaments if such increases would contribute to crisis stability and thereby reduce the chance of war. This concept of arms control should be distinguished from that of general and complete disarmament. Proponents of disarmament as an end in itself see the goal of arms control as more simply reducing the size of military forces, budgets, explosive power, and other aggregate measures.

One way of illustrating the difference between complete disarmament and arms control is to examine the prospects for eliminating all nuclear weapons. To proponents of general disarmament, the prospect of a world free of nuclear weapons seems very desirable. The world's political leaders apparently support such a goal. Former Soviet president Mikhail Gorbachev pledged to work toward the elimination of all nuclear weapons by the year 2000. The goals of the U.S. Arms Control and Disarmament Agency (ACDA) include achieving general and complete disarmament. Substantial progress toward reducing the number of nuclear weapons has been made recently (although most of the actual reductions will not be complete until after the turn of the century).

Yet many worry about the consequences of ever achieving a nuclear-free world. Nagging questions exist. If all nations pledged to give up their weapons, would the United States take them at their word or would it require some means of ensuring their commitment had been carried out? Could the United States verify such a pledge? Does the technology currently exist to accomplish such verification? Even if the international community could verify at some point in the future that no nuclear weapons existed, would humankind be forever free from nuclear destruction? Could we ever eradicate the technical knowledge required to construct such weapons? In a conflict involving national survival, might nations again attempt to build and use such weapons? Would not great incentives exist to use newly constructed nuclear weapons to maintain a nuclear monopoly if rival states were also trying to build these weapons? Could we ensure that nonstate actors never developed and used such weapons? The goal of complete disarmament, nuclear and otherwise, may appear desirable at first glance. However, the apparent barriers to achieving such a goal and its possible consequences require us to examine less radical, though still important, steps to improving our national security through arms control.

Of course, advocacy of disarmament as part of a state's arms control policy can also be part of a "means to an end" approach. For example, the United States and other countries have negotiated global conventions that endeavor to rid the world of chemical and biological weapons. The United States unilaterally decided that neither chemical nor biological weapons would enhance its security, even if they were possessed by other states. Efforts to rid the world of such weapons generally are perceived to enhance the security of all states. Similarly, in recent years, the United States and the Soviet Union (now Russia) have managed to agree to eliminate certain classes of strategic arms. The important distinction centers on what arms control is intended to achieve—lower numbers of weapons or improved security for the parties involved.

Overview of the Book

The remainder of this book wrestles with the central issue of the continuing relevance of arms control. Advocates of arms control are challenged now by a broader range of issues. New areas of negotiation include operational issues of transparency and confidence building, as well as the older structural issues of strategic stability and reduction of the arms overhang remaining from the Cold War. Arms control discussions will also be less formal, yet more dynamic and complex, as demands for stringent verification and information sharing compete with other needs, including national sovereignty, commercial competitiveness and shrinking budgets.

The central theme of this book is that *while the negotiating methods, regions of concern, and weapons involved may be changing, the underlying principles and objectives of arms control remain relevant in the post–Cold War world.* Because of the broadening scope and complexity of negotiations and agreements, arms control could affect national security more deeply than in the past. Although less in the media limelight, arms control may emerge as a practical, usable tool for managing security rather than a political barometer of superpower relations and a football for partisan politics. At a minimum, the national security establishments of many nations must implement and live with the accords already in place.

Part 1: Underlying Principles

Part 1 establishes the underlying concepts and principles that guide the conduct of arms control. Kerry Kartchner begins the book with an analysis of the objectives of arms control, as outlined by the seminal thinkers in the late 1950s and early 1960s. He then analyzes how these objectives were applied during the Cold War. Arms control must, first and foremost, be a means to the end of greater national security, rather than an end in itself. According to Kartchner, the traditional goals of arms control are still relevant; these objectives transcend the changes to the international system witnessed since the late 1980s. The chapter concludes with observations on the proper prioritization of arms control objectives after the Cold War.

Trevor Taylor tackles the interplay between the international system and arms control in Chapter 2. He pays particular attention to how existing political relationships between states provide the basis for analyzing how arms control can improve security, as well as the likely limits to progress on cooperation. He characterizes the types of arms control negotiations in the course of his discussion. Taylor also describes three types of arms control that the West has pursued: arms control for ourselves, such as the nuclear Non-Proliferation Treaty; arms control for others, such as the Treaty of Tlatelolco; and arms control for everyone, such as global efforts like the Chemical Weapons Convention.

In Chapter 3 Jennifer Sims refocuses the reader's attention by looking within the state to examine how domestic factors have affected the pursuit of arms control in the United States. She begins by analyzing the significance and influence of strategic culture. She reviews the arms control process and key actors involved in the United States, with particular attention to each organization's role and agenda. In her conclusion she reviews the importance of the domestic interactions and compromises that occur as a state pursues its arms control objectives.

Joseph Pilat's chapter on verification and transparency concludes the first section. Beginning with a historical overview of verification, he analyzes the crucial impact that verification had on defining the boundaries of what was possible during Cold War arms control. Verification and trust are critical to the successful conclusion of an arms control treaty and to its full implementation. Pilat also looks at the inherently political nature of arms control verification and the way patterns of verification are adapting to a changed international environment. He concludes with an examination of the growing significance of transparency and confidence-building measures. He describes the utility of these measures as means for building trust in new areas where more stringent verification would be difficult, if not impossible.

Part 2: The Legacy of the Cold War

Part 2 of the book focuses on the efforts by the superpowers and their allies to use arms control during the Cold War to enhance security, as well as the legacy of these efforts on the post–Cold War environment. Forrest Waller tackles the lengthy record of superpower progress on strategic offensive arms control. Arms control attempted to develop and maintain a balance of terror between the two states, which relied on mutual deterrence through the promise of mutual assured destruction should something go wrong. To preclude anything going wrong, arms control measures attempted to stabilize the situation between the two countries. Waller starts with an analysis of factors influencing the superpowers' pursuit of arms control during different periods of the Cold War. He outlines the contemporary nature of strategic offensive arms control, highlighting recent changes in approach and the relationship to our current nuclear strategy. He finishes with a look at possible future paths in this area.

In Chapter 6 Sidney Graybeal and Patricia McFate look at the flip side of the Cold War strategic dynamic—strategic defensive arms control. The central focus is on the nature of the ABM Treaty and its impact on overall U.S. security objectives. The treaty's origins, provisions, and compliance record are outlined. The authors examine the relationship between the possible pursuit of both tactical and national ballistic missile defenses and the treaty. According to the authors, the treaty still has a valuable role to play in the U.S.-Russian strategic relationship and remains in the national interest of the United States—although it must be updated and clarified if it is to allow new theater missile defense systems. The technology and source of ballistic missile threats has changed since 1972, and the treaty must be modified to reflect those changes.

Jeffrey McCausland changes the focus from nuclear to conventional arms control as he examines efforts to manage the conventional balance in Europe. He reviews the evolution of the forum and the subject of these negotiations, highlighting the crucial role of the Organization for Security and Cooperation in Europe. The final negotiation and provisions of the Conventional Forces in Europe Treaty are outlined. In analyzing the future, he examines the challenges presented by a rapidly changing political environment in Europe. The successful implementation of the CFE accord is a key element in any future European security structure and could become a model for similar agreements elsewhere in the world.

James Wirtz concludes this section by providing both an evaluation of arms control during the Cold War and a look at how the new era may differ. Based on the objectives laid out in Chapter 1, he analyzes the historical record before describing the challenges facing arms control in the changed international system at the dawn of a new century. Did arms control work in the Cold War? Is arms control succeeding today? Wirtz answers in the affirmative, albeit with reservations about arms control's future prospects.

Part 3: Preventing the Spread of Arms

Part 3 analyzes the prospects for progress and the problems facing global arms control efforts in the next decade, focusing particularly on the problems of weapons proliferation. Chapter 9, by Virginia Foran, deals with the highly visible topic of nuclear proliferation and efforts to limit this problem. She outlines the international community's efforts to deal with the advent of nuclear weapons and the evolution of the Non-Proliferation Treaty and the International Atomic Energy Agency. The nature of responsibilities and obligations under the nuclear nonproliferation regime are outlined. Foran analyzes four phases of nuclear nonproliferation that have occurred since 1945, with the dissolution of the Soviet Union ushering in a fifth phase—one whose character and dimensions are not yet fully developed. The chapter concludes with an analysis of the 1995 NPT Review and Extension Conference and a look at its possible impact on future efforts in this realm.

Amy Smithson and Marie Chevrier address the related but distinct problems of chemical and biological weapon nonproliferation efforts. With regard to chemical weapons, Smithson outlines the groundbreaking nature of the recently concluded Chemical Weapons Convention. She believes that ratifying the CWC remains in the best interests of the United States. Chevrier examines the unique features of biological weapons and also provides an overview of the existing Biological Weapons Convention. She concludes that maintaining and expanding the BWC remains in the security interests of the United States. Both authors thoroughly cover the critical concerns regarding verification that accompany these conventions, and both examine the future prospects for international cooperation in these efforts.

Jo Husbands covers a range of topics as she outlines efforts to limit the spread of conventional weapons and means of delivery. She addresses several subjects, including the fundamentals of the global arms trade, Cold War legacies affecting international efforts to constrain the spread of arms, and the variety of international and unilateral efforts to combat conventional weapons proliferation (such as the UN Register, the Missile Technology Control Regime, and bans on inhumane weapons such as land mines). Her review of the illicit and legal conventional weapons trade helps put the problems in perspective. She highlights the underlying dilemmas of such restraints: economic trade-offs, perceived discrimination on the part of developing states, and difficulties in verification. Transparency measures such as the UN Register of Arms may help, as would unilateral arms transfer restraint by suppliers. Nevertheless, such efforts are feeble attempts to change a long-standing and lucrative business. She is pessimistic about the ability of arms control to succeed in this arena in the near term.

Part 4: Regional Issues

In Part 4 three short case studies are presented to outline different regional arms control efforts, highlighting the importance of avoiding ethnocentrism. Specific regional factors are discussed, such as geography, history, and strategic culture. Christopher Carr begins by analyzing the past failure and future prospects of limiting conventional arms transfers to the Middle East under the guise of a Middle East Arms Control Initiative (MEACI). Carr holds out some hope for the future of the MEACI, given the Israeli-Palestinian Accord of 1994 and the financial constraints of the Gulf Arab states. Cynthia Watson examines the factors underlying successful efforts to free Latin America of nuclear weapons by focusing on how Argentina and Brazil resolved their nuclear rivalry. She highlights the critical importance of domestic factors such as regime type and the debt crisis. Peter Lavoy presents a less sanguine appraisal of the situation in South Asia. India and Pakistan, while making some limited progress through arms control measures, remain adversaries reserving the nuclear weapons option.

Part 5: Conclusion

Jeffrey Larsen concludes the book with a review and appraisal of the themes that run through the chapters. We list here the major themes that can be found throughout the book, as identified by Larsen.

- The U.S.-Russian strategic balance is no longer the preeminent arms control concern.
- The validity of Cold War agreements is, in some cases, in question.
- The legacy of the Cold War lives on in the emphasis placed on the control and dismantlement of the strategic arsenals of the formerly antagonistic superpowers.
- Bilateral negotiations will be supplanted by multilateral/global discussions or unilateral announcements.
- Without showing some reciprocal efforts at disarmament, the major powers will no longer be able to dictate to the rest of the world their preferred version of an international system or to achieve consensus on nonproliferation regimes.

- There is growing value and acceptance of the need for effective verification, including intrusive measures.
- There is growing difficulty in confirming compliance with arms control accords.
- The nature and scope of arms control has grown as a result of the end of the Cold War. Areas of primary concern include proliferation of weapons of mass destruction and regional conflicts.
- Arms control faces challenges from public perceptions that it is no longer needed.
- Nevertheless, the arms control enterprise in and of itself is no longer controversial; it has been "domesticated."
- Disarmament may be returning to the realm of legitimate arms control goals.

Notes

1. Christopher J. Lamb, *How to Think About Arms Control, Disarmament and Defense* (Englewood Cliffs, N.J.: Prentice Hall, 1988), p. 11.

2. Richard D. Burns, ed., *The Encyclopedia of Arms Control and Disarmament* (New York: Charles Scribner's Sons, 1993), p. 568.

3. See Richard K. Betts, "Systems for Peace or Causes of War? Collective Security, Arms Control and the New Europe," *International Security* (Summer 1992), pp. 5–43, and the ensuing debate between Betts and Michael J. Mazarr in "Correspondence: A Farewell to Arms Control?" *International Security* (Winter 1992–1993), pp. 188–200.

4. See Colin S. Gray, *House of Cards: Why Arms Control Must Fail* (Ithaca, N.Y.: Cornell University Press, 1992), and *Weapons Don't Make War: Policy, Strategy and Military Technology* (Lawrence: University of Kansas Press, 1993).

5. Steven Erlanger, "Russia Sells War Machine to Pay the Cost of Peace," *New York Times*, 3 February 1993, p. 1, and "Su-27 Fighter Aircraft Sold to China," FBIS-SOV-92-242, 16 December 1992, p. 16.

6. *Arms Control Reporter* (Cambridge, Mass.: Institute for Defense and Disarmament Studies), p. 706.A.3.

7. Numerous press reports have detailed four incidents that occurred between May and August 1994. For example, see "Officials Say Contraband Not a Threat," *Washington Post*, 28 August 1994, pp. A1, A20, and "Nuclear Smugglers Spark Worries Over Russian Safeguards," *Arms Control Today* (September 1994), p. 25.

8. See Peter G. Peterson, "The Primacy of the Domestic Agenda," in *Rethinking America's Security: Beyond the Cold War to New World Order* (New York: W. W. Norton, 1992), pp. 57–93. More specifically, two major works address the impact of disproportionately high defense expenditures: Paul Kennedy, *The Rise and Fall of Great Powers: Economic Change and Military Conflict 1500–2000* (New York: Random House, 1987), and David Calleo, *Beyond American Hegemony* (New York: Basic Books, 1987).

9. See W. Harriet Critchley and Terry Teriff's chapter "Environment and Security" in *Security Studies for the 1990s* (Washington, D.C.: Brassey's, 1993), pp. 327–345, for a discussion of this evolving area of national security studies.

10. Various experts have commented on this evolution. In particular, see Ivo Daalder, "The Future of Arms Control," *Survival* (Spring 1992).

11. Malcom Chambers, Owen Greene, Edward J. Laurance, and Herbert Wulf, eds., *Developing the UN Register of Conventional Arms* (United Kingdom: University of Branford Press, 1994), p. 3.

12. The possibilities for implicit agreement and unilateral initiatives were discussed in the seminal work of Thomas C. Schelling and Morton H. Halperin, *Strategy and Arms Control* (Washington, D.C.: Pergamon-Brassey's, 1985), originally published in 1961. Schelling reinforces this point with an article entitled "What Went Wrong with Arms Control" in *Foreign Affairs* (Winter 1985–1986), pp. 219–233.

13. Science Applications International Corporation, "Open Skies," *Profile Summaries of Arms Control Treaties* (McLean, Va.: Science Applications International Corporation, 1994), p. 1.

14. Chambers et al., *Developing the UN Register*, p. 3.

15. Two classics dealing with arms races are Samuel P. Huntington, "Arms Races Prerequisites and Results," *Public Policy: Yearbook of the Graduate School of Public Administration* (Cambridge: Harvard University Press, 1958), and Colin Gray, "The Arms Race Phenomenon," *World Politics* (October 1971).

16. Schelling and Halperin, *Strategy and Arms Control*, p. 3.

PART 1

Why Arms Control? Underlying Principles

1

The Objectives of Arms Control

Kerry M. Kartchner

Because arms control is an instrument of national security strategy, its objectives are integrally linked to those of a nation's overall defense priorities. For planning purposes, defense priorities are developed and applied on at least two levels: the grand strategy level, representing general security aspirations, and the operational level, where the broadly stated objectives of grand strategy are translated into more specific goals to guide actual military operations. The same is true for arms control, where objectives have been articulated at the grand strategy and operational levels as well.[1]

The basic grand strategic objectives of arms control as an instrument of national security remain virtually unchanged, at least in general terms. U.S. national security interests at the highest level of abstraction are essentially the same as during the Cold War: to protect and preserve the fundamental freedoms and institutions of the United States by deterring or preventing attack on U.S. national interests at home and abroad. New threats, nonetheless, have necessitated reordering the priorities among traditional U.S. national security objectives. Deterring nuclear attack is now less urgent than preventing or countering proliferation of weapons of mass destruction, for example.

However, the conceptual problems now facing defense planners and arms control policy makers at the operational level are fundamentally different from those that confronted the founders of traditional arms control theory in the late 1950s and early 1960s. During that time, the strategic planners' task was to manage an escalating nuclear arms competition between two superpowers locked in an ideological and geopolitical rivalry on a global scale. The stakes were unambiguous and absolute because the survival of the United States itself was at risk and the adversary was clearly identifiable. Every military and diplomatic maneuver of that era was animated and overshadowed by the prospect of a shockingly swift surprise nuclear attack with the potential for unthinkably devastating consequences. The paramount task of political and military policymakers was, therefore, to reduce, deter, or eliminate the prospect of mutual and instantaneous annihilation by surprise nuclear attack. Classical (or, traditional) arms control theory was developed in direct response to the "surprise attack imperative"—the urgent need to find and institutionalize whatever means possible to mitigate the threat of a surprise nuclear attack.[2]

The surprise attack imperative has receded into history and has lost the urgency it once commanded. The superpower rivalry has all but disappeared with the disintegration of the former Soviet empire, and mutual nuclear deterrence no longer seems so urgent or relevant. Indeed, new and emerging sources of danger do not appear susceptible to traditional deterrence. There is no global arms race to speak of, only a myriad of regional arms competitions. The near-term survival of the United States itself is not at risk. The stakes in terms of U.S. national interests are now fraught with ambiguity and uncertainty. Most important, the threat of a surprise nuclear attack, which was the touchstone of traditional arms control theory, can no longer be considered even a viable planning scenario.[3]

These considerations raise some obvious questions. If arms control was initially the product of the surprise attack imperative, and that imperative is now obsolete, are the original objectives of arms control still relevant? Are the assumptions and conceptual framework developed by the founders of traditional arms control now inapplicable? If not, must these assumptions and objectives be reprioritized and adapted to meet the immediate and pressing security dilemmas facing today's defense and foreign policy decisionmakers?

This chapter reviews the basic objectives of arms control as originally espoused in traditional arms control theory and explains how the theory was developed to support overall U.S. national security goals during the Cold War. It also proposes a reprioritization of objectives at the grand strategy level, as well as new objectives at the operational level, in light of U.S. defense and security priorities on the eve of the twenty-first century.[4]

Arms Control and National Security

The founding premise of traditional arms control theory—that arms control can be an important adjunct to national security strategy—has not always been obvious nor consistently observed in practice because arms control is inherently a counterintuitive approach to enhancing security. Consider the following: arms control makes national security dependent to some degree on the cooperation of prospective adversaries. It often involves setting lower levels of arms than would otherwise appear prudent based on a strict threat assessment. It mandates establishing a more or less interactive relationship with putative opponents and, in the case of mutual intrusive verification and data exchanges, exposing sensitive national security information and facilities to scrutiny by foreign powers. It requires seeking and institutionalizing areas of common ground where the potential for conflicts of interest seemingly far outweigh objectives in common. Arms control is fundamentally a high-stakes gamble, mortgaging national survival against little more than the collateral of trust and anticipated reciprocal restraint, often in a geopolitical context fraught with political hostility and tension. It is, in fact, a voluntary (and not always reversible) delimitation of national sovereignty. Viewed from this perspective, arms control is not obviously better than its alternative—unilaterally providing for one's own security.

What compels the United States and other nations, then, to structure so much of their national security posture on an approach that seemingly contradicts a country's natural instincts toward self-sufficiency and self-preservation? The answer to this apparent paradox is that the theory of arms control as developed in the late 1950s and early 1960s—if conceptually valid and faithfully implemented—allows us to anticipate that an otherwise equivalent degree of security may be established by negotiation at weapons levels lower than would be the case if these levels were determined unilaterally.

The Development of Arms Control Theory

The phrase *traditional arms control theory* refers to the assumptions and premises of those strategic analysts who first developed the objectives and possibilities of arms control as an adjunct to national security during 1958–1962.[5] Traditional arms control theory was the product of a unique confluence of factors, and it reflected the assumptions, analyses, and policy priorities of defense analysts and policy makers of the late 1950s and early 1960s. Of course, seeking negotiated solutions to national security dilemmas was not new, but the rethinking of arms control in this period was part of a general reevaluation of U.S. defense and foreign policy that was precipitated, first of all, by considerable dissatisfaction with the postwar diplomatic and arms control stalemate. The United States had sought to establish through diplomatic means a variety of disarmament arrangements since 1945 (e.g., the Baruch Plan, the Open Skies Treaty), but long negotiations and multiple proposals had yielded no tangible results, primarily because of Soviet objections to those verification regimes deemed essential by the Western allies. In the mid-1950s, policymakers began to rethink an approach that had emphasized general and complete disarmament and to consider instead limited, partial measures that would gradually enhance confidence in cooperative security arrangements. Thus, more modest goals, under the rubric of "arms control," came to replace the propaganda-laden disarmament efforts of the late 1940s and early 1950s.

Additionally, each major war seems to precipitate the rise, 10 to 15 years later, of a new generation of military leaders and strategic theorists who are free of traditional biases and who promulgate a revisionist outlook on strategy, tactics, and technology. In this case, the development of traditional arms control theory benefited from the emergence of leaders who were predisposed to favor arms control as a cooperative approach to enhancing security, who were under political pressure to seek diplomatic solutions and reduce defense budgets, and who recognized the public's growing fear of nuclear weapons.

Finally, by far the most important factors leading to the development of traditional arms control theory were the Soviet launching of Sputnik in 1957 and the reverberations this event had for U.S. thinking about defense and security in the nuclear age. This stunning technological achievement on the part of the Soviet Union stripped the U.S. psyche of its traditional sense of insular security and profoundly affected everything from U.S. educational priorities to U.S. defense and foreign policy. More specifically, it caused considerable anxiety regarding the long-term viability of nuclear deterrence and sensitized U.S. defense intellectuals to the danger of technological threats to strategic stability. Beginning with this event, U.S. political and military leaders collectively turned their attention to thwarting the new danger of a surprise nuclear attack. In fact, the very first modern arms control effort, incorporating the basic assumptions of emerging arms control theory, was the 1958 Surprise Attack Conference, held in the immediate aftermath of Sputnik.[6]

Basic Tenets of Traditional Arms Control Theory

The period that began with the Surprise Attack Conference and ended with the publication in 1962 of the proceedings of the 1960 Woods Hole Summer Study produced the basic canons of modern arms control theory.[7] From the literature of this golden era of arms control thinking emerged a virtual consensus on several key assumptions, which may be considered the basic tenets of traditional arms control theory.

First, arms control was conceived as an instrument whose purpose was to enhance national security. As Hedley Bull, one of the founders of traditional arms control theory, succinctly explained: "Arms control or disarmament was not an end in itself but a means to an end and that end was first and foremost the enhancement of security, especially security against nuclear war."[8] And as Thomas Schelling and Morton Halperin state near the end of their book: "The aims of arms control and the aims of a national military strategy should be substantially the same."[9] This principle established as the dominant goal of arms control the enhancement of national security, not the reduction of arms per se. In fact, it was understood that not all reductions were necessarily useful. There was an explicit recognition that arms control could be harmful if not properly guided by overall national security strategy: "It is not to be assumed that the level of forces and weapons most favorable to international security is the lowest one."[10] This meant that arms control policies should be developed with national security strategy clearly in mind.

Second, the superpowers shared a common interest in avoiding nuclear war; this common interest could and should be the basis for effective arms control agreements. According to Bull, "The fact that the United States and the Soviet Union were locked in a political and ideological conflict, one moreover that sometimes took a military form, did not mean that they could not recognize common interests in avoiding a ruinous nuclear war, or cooperate to advance these common interests."[11] This assumption was one of the most important (and controversial) conceptual departures from past thinking promulgated by the new arms control theory. Previously, it was assumed that relaxation of political tensions had to precede achieving substantive arms control agreements. The founders of traditional arms control theory, on the other hand, believed that the threat of global nuclear annihilation was so paramount that it transcended political and ideological differences. If true, this meant that it was not necessary to fully resolve political conflicts before proceeding to negotiate arms control agreements—solutions to both could be advanced simultaneously. Nevertheless, original arms control theorists also recognized that where too much political tension existed, arms control would be impossible, and where there was little tension between countries, arms control would be superfluous: "Only the existence of international tension ... makes arms control relevant. It is relevant when tension is at a certain point, above which it is impossible and beneath which it is unnecessary.... When the relations between nations are marked by sympathy and amity, arms control appears to be irrelevant."[12] Moreover, certain political conditions were essential. According to Bull, "Unless the powers concerned want a system of arms control; unless there is a measure of political détente among them sufficient to allow of such a system; unless they are prepared to accept the military situation among them which the arms control system legitimizes and preserves, and can agree and remain agreed about what this situation will be, there can be little place for arms control."[13]

Third, arms control and military strategy should be used together to promote national security. The unity of strategy and arms control was a central tenet of traditional arms control theory. Such unity was essential if arms control theorists and defense policy strategists were to avoid working at cross-purposes. For example, if the implementation of U.S. defense strategy required deploying certain types of weapons that were restricted by arms control agreements, this could defeat the overall purpose of U.S. national security posture and erode the legitimacy of both the arms control process and U.S. defense policy. The founders of traditional arms control theory asserted that arms control negotiators and defense policy makers should strive toward the same goals and operate on the basis of the same general assumptions regarding which weapons were desirable and which were destabilizing.

Finally, arms control regimes need not be limited to formal agreements but could also include informal, unilateral, and verbal agreements. To cite Bull again: "If arms control was cooperation in military policy between antagonistic states to advance interests that they perceived to be common ones, then this included not only the attempt to negotiate formal agreements to limit the character, deployment, or use of their arms, but also informal agreements to restrain arms competition and indeed to restrain military conflicts themselves, and also unilateral actions that advanced perceived common interests and were not merely directed toward the advantage of one side."[14]

The Original Objectives of
Traditional Arms Control Theory

For arms control to be an effective instrument of national security, its objectives must be determined by, and be in close harmony with, the broader objectives of overall national security strategy.[15] At the most basic level of abstraction, three grand conceptual dilemmas dominated strategic thinking and the formulation of U.S. national security objectives during the Cold War: (1) What deters? (2) How much is enough? (3) What if deterrence fails? These dilemmas involve (1) determining how best to deter whom from doing what, (2) assessing and establishing the adequacy of weapons and resources committed to deterrence, and (3) grappling with the unthinkable consequences should deterrence fail and a (nuclear) war actually occur.[16]

The founders of traditional arms control theory realized that if arms control were to be an adjunct of national security it should address these same grand conceptual dilemmas, and they believed that negotiated solutions could effectively contribute to resolving them. Traditional arms control theory was based on the premise that the superpowers inherently shared an area of common ground (i.e., avoiding nuclear war) and that this "element of mutual interest" could serve as the basis for limited, cooperative arrangements involving reciprocal restraint in the acquisition of weapons of mass destruction. In defining the scope and application of arms control, theorists set forth three general objectives for arms control that directly corresponded with the three grand conceptual dilemmas of the Cold War:

> We believe that arms control is a promising, but still only dimly perceived, enlargement of the scope of our military strategy. It rests essentially on the recognition that our military relation with potential enemies is not one of

pure conflict and opposition, but involves strong elements of mutual interest in *the avoidance of a war that neither side wants*, in *minimizing the
costs and risks of the arms competition*, and in *curtailing the scope and violence of war in the event it occurs*.[17] (emphasis added)

Clearly, establishing the requirements of deterrence must precede and
form the basis for the creation of policies for reducing the risk of nuclear
war, the goal of reducing defense spending must be informed by some notion of what constitutes sufficient levels of weapons, and any scheme for
limiting damage should war occur must presuppose at least some thought
as to the nature of warfare and the way forces are to be employed in combat.
Thus, the primary objectives of traditional arms control theory—reducing
the risk of war, reducing the costs of preparing for war, and reducing the
damage should war occur—are necessarily determined by the three major
dilemmas of military policy.

The First Objective: Reducing the Risk of War

In practice, U.S. defense strategy sought to reduce the risk of nuclear war
through some form of deterrence. It followed logically that arms control
should therefore promote deterrence as the principal means of reducing the
risk of war. The task for arms control negotiators became, then, to establish
means and methods for enhancing and institutionalizing mutual nuclear
deterrence and to restrict to the extent possible any threat to the preservation or stability of that deterrence.

Defining the essence of deterrence for purposes of arms control was
relatively straightforward. Given the state of technology at the time and the
lack of suitable means for limiting damage from, or defending against, nuclear
attack, this necessarily meant codifying a condition of mutual assured destruction. However, restricting to the extent possible threats to the preservation (or stability) of deterrence was more complicated. One possible threat
to strategic stability involved uncontrolled arms races, which could result in
the development of unilateral military advantages for one side or the other.
Arms control was seen as a prime means for setting limits on and restraining strategic arms race behavior. Thus, arms race stability became a component objective of traditional arms control theory at the operational level.

Moreover, for early arms control theorists, restraining certain types of
technology was practically synonymous with reducing the risk of war and
enhancing deterrence: "A main determinant of the likelihood of war is the
nature of present military technology and present military expectations."[18]
Again, the underlying premise was that war is most likely to begin with a
surprise nuclear attack made possible by modern developments in ballistic
missile, guidance and control, and nuclear weapons technology. Therefore,
those weapon systems employing technologies that in theory most contrib-

uted to the ability to execute a surprise nuclear attack against the nuclear retaliatory forces of the other side, or that undermined the ability of either side to hold deterrent targets at risk, became principal candidates for arms limitation agreements.

The Second Objective: Reducing the Costs of Preparing for War

The assumptions underlying the second objective proceeded logically from the basic theory of arms control. This objective presumed that arms control "releases economic resources: that armaments, or armaments races, are economically ruinous or profligate, and that disarmament or arms control would make possible the diversion of resources now squandered in armaments into other and worthier channels."[19] If arms control succeeded in providing the same degree of security at lower levels of weapons than would otherwise be the case, it could lead to the necessity of fielding fewer weapons and thus lower overall defense spending. Further, if certain types of technology were mutually outlawed, there would be fewer costs associated with defense research and development, weapons production, force deployment, operations, and maintenance. The savings thus realized would be diverted to domestic economic priorities and would promote overall prosperity.

The Third Objective: Reducing the Damage Should War Occur

The theoretical postulations behind the third objective likewise seem self-evident, but they present something of a conundrum. If fewer weapons were fielded as a result of arms limitation agreements, should war nevertheless occur, overall damage would be less than it would otherwise have been. But fielding fewer weapons is not the only way to reduce damage in the event of war. Damage could be limited by also developing certain types of strategies and technologies, such as ballistic missile defense, which is designed to limit damage from ballistic missile attack. Therefore, arms control agreements that permitted, even encouraged, ballistic missile defenses would seem compatible with the goal of reducing damage should war occur.

However, there was an inherent contradiction between this arms control objective and the operationalization of the first objective. The first objective was translated in practice into promoting mutual assured destruction (or, in other words, mutual societal vulnerability), which derives its deterrent value from the threat of inflicting massive damage. By definition, this contradicts the goal of limiting damage. Furthermore, the option of reducing or limiting damage through active defenses was discarded by arms control and defense policy makers alike because of the presumed technological infeasibility and strategic provocativeness of missile defenses. Consequently, the objective of reducing damage should deterrence fail and war occur fell by the wayside of arms control practice. Reducing damage should war occur nevertheless remained an important goal of arms control negotiations.

Prioritizing Arms Control's Objectives

In practice, the first of the three main objectives proposed by traditional arms control theory came to eclipse and overshadow the other two. Achieving the first objective would indirectly satisfy or render mute the other two. Stabilizing mutual nuclear deterrence at lower levels of forces than would otherwise be the case would necessarily result in reduced defense costs, with fewer weapons to field and maintain. And, it was implied, avoiding a nuclear war altogether would obviate the necessity of limiting damage should a war occur (but still begs the question of what to do if, for whatever reason, deterrence fails). Again, the Cold War focus on strategic arms control generally left untouched the issue of reducing damage during conventional conflicts. Thus, reducing the risk of war, or the risk of war through surprise nuclear attack, became the paramount objective of traditional arms control thinking.

Rethinking the Objectives of
Traditional Arms Control Theory

The objectives established by traditional arms control theory transcend any given historical era. These objectives apply equally to weapons of mass destruction and conventional weapons systems and scenarios. They must, however, be adapted at the operational level to the prevailing circumstances if arms control is to remain a viable instrument of national security strategy.

As noted earlier, the three principal objectives of arms control as they were interpreted operationally were closely linked to the three main conceptual dilemmas of strategic thinking in the nuclear age: What deters? How much is enough? What if deterrence fails? However, the answers to these three questions have changed dramatically since the end of the Cold War. Therefore, to evaluate the current relevance of the basic objectives we must fundamentally reexamine the traditional answers to these dilemmas.

What Deters? Or, Reducing the Risk of War

The implementation of traditional arms control theory came to embrace an assured destruction approach to deterrence and strategic stability that relied exclusively on the offensive threat of punitive retaliation. Traditional arms control theorists assumed defense was neither a technologically feasible nor strategically viable option. Both of these assumptions are now subject to reconsideration for several reasons.

First, the technologies may now exist to create militarily effective ballistic missile defenses at sustainable cost.[20] However, suggesting that technology is no longer the obstacle it once was is not to say that it is strategically or politically prudent to proceed with deploying ballistic missile defenses at the present time. Myriad difficult and complicated issues need further clarification before making such a decision, including the likely impact of such deployments on current and prospective nuclear arms reduction agreements. Nevertheless, great strides in interceptor and target acquisition technology have convinced political leaders to pursue full-scale development of theater ballistic missile defenses while deferring the question of strategic missile defenses to a later date.

Second, given the deteriorated and exhausted state of the Russian economy, the real progress to date in U.S.-Russian relations, and the domestic preoccupations of the Russian leadership, it is difficult to take seriously the danger of a renewed strategic nuclear arms race between East and West. In other words, the action-reaction dynamic is no longer operative, and consequently deployment of a U.S. ballistic missile defense system is unlikely to trigger a massive Russian offensive force buildup.[21] Thus, the two major objections to reducing the risk of war through damage limitation strategies and capabilities—technological infeasibility and strategic instability—are less supportable than they might have been during an earlier era.

Most important, the assured destruction approach may not be effective in deterring the principal regional threat scenarios faced by the United States and its allies in the post–Cold War era. In the future, the United States is increasingly likely to face regional crisis situations where local animosities are intense, risk-taking propensities are high, the willingness to absorb casualties is great, a rogue power faces imminent defeat or other powerful incentives to resort to using nuclear or other weapons of mass destruction, and the stakes involved are infinitely greater for the regional players than for the United States, whose interests will be relatively limited. In such circumstances, how viable is U.S. possession of nuclear weapons as a deterrent without overt threats to use them? Furthermore, the United States is unlikely to make such threats for fear of legitimizing the pursuit of weapons of mass destruction on the part of regional hegemonies, undermining international normative constraints against all types of proliferation, and squandering the moral high ground in world politics. Bear in mind that U.S. nuclear weapons, with an overwhelming capability to completely obliterate Iraq many times over, did not deter Saddam Hussein from invading Kuwait. Nuclear use in this situation was simply not a credible threat.

Finally, since surprise attack is no longer the dominant threat scenario, the United States no longer needs an emphasis on punitive retaliation as a deterrent. The danger of surprise nuclear attack was deemed amenable only to the threat of punitive retaliatory strikes that would inflict unacceptable damage. With this requirement now greatly diminished, the United States can consider shifting the emphasis of its security policy to developing those capabilities necessary to deter attacks and to reducing the risk of war by limiting, rather than inflicting, wholesale damage.

How Much Is Enough? Or, Reducing the Cost of Preparing for War

The second major objective of traditional arms control theory has been to reduce the burden of maintaining a large defense establishment. This objective is traditionally interpreted at the operational level in economic terms, but it is inseparable from considerations of force sizing, or strategic adequacy, since maintaining the size, composition, and posture of deployed forces largely contributes to the cost of our defense establishment.

It is generally accepted that arms control as practiced during the Cold War never fulfilled the aspiration of reducing defense budgets. However, this objective of arms control remains quintessentially relevant in the aftermath of the Cold War and is perhaps even more achievable than ever before.

The collapse of the Soviet threat is dramatically altering our calculations of defense sufficiency, with profound implications for arms control. These calculations have recently been addressed in Department of Defense reports in both the "Nuclear Posture Review" of strategic force requirements and the "Bottom Up Review" of conventional force requirements. In all likelihood, these assessments are only the beginning of an ongoing process that will result in even further downsizing and restructuring of U.S. forces. The matter of military sufficiency will, therefore, be of continuing relevance for the foreseeable future.

The "Bottom Up Review" outlined the U.S. need for the capability to fight two near-simultaneous major regional contingencies anywhere in the world. The planning baseline for these contingencies was a Gulf War scenario. Along with maintaining preparedness for these contingencies, U.S. forces have become heavily involved in supporting peacekeeping, peacemaking, and humanitarian operations with varying degrees of success. Finally, major technological changes—such as the evolution of stealth techniques, the development of precision-guided weapons, and the growing importance of information on the battlefield—are prompting serious consideration of how we will conduct warfare in the future. These considerations must be reflected in assessing strategic sufficiency for arms control purposes.

Whatever the final outcome of deliberations over nuclear or conventional sufficiency in terms of long-range policies, clearly the United States in the near future will dramatically reduce its overall level of strategic weapons and its degree of reliance on nuclear deterrence as an instrument of national security. Arms control can codify and multilateralize such considerations to help deter any reversal in the process of global denuclearization and demilitarization now under way.

What If Deterrence Fails? Or, Reducing Damage Should War Occur

As noted earlier, the objective of actively limiting damage (a form of war fighting) was categorically rejected by the arms control community during the Cold War, due partly to a belief that the notion of deterrence failing was unthinkable, to technical obstacles facing ballistic missile defense, and to fear of aggravating the nuclear arms race. Any contribution of past arms control efforts to the objective of reducing damage should war occur, then, was necessarily an indirect by-product of actually reducing weapons.

In the aftermath of the Cold War, limiting damage should be the paramount objective (at least at the strategic level) of both arms control efforts and military strategy. The prospect of regional powers, who are undeterred by threats of punitive retaliation, acquiring their own weapons of mass destruction or advanced conventional weapons argues for developing the means to limit the damage that could be inflicted by such rogue states. Since it cannot always be anticipated where or when such threats will emerge, nor can it always be known what threats such regional powers will find credible or persuasive, the United States can never be totally confident of successfully deterring every eventual threat to its territory or that of its allies. The United States must recognize that deterrence could fail—and should deterrence fail, it must be prepared to limit damage to itself and its allies and interests abroad.

Conclusion

As noted at the outset, the problems and dilemmas confronting defense planners and arms control policy makers today are in many ways different from those that faced the original founders of traditional arms control theory in the late 1950s and early 1960s. These theorists were principally concerned with the danger of a civilization-threatening surprise nuclear attack; they developed arms control as one mechanism for suppressing and confining that danger, which has receded with the passing of the Cold War. Nevertheless, the general objectives of traditional arms control theory at the grand strategy level remain applicable to the full range of contemporary arms control efforts, including arms control aimed at regional stabilization and the regulation of conventional, chemical, and biological weapons. After all, we still want to reduce the likelihood of war; only the probable location, nature, and participants in future wars have changed, meaning that how we deter or prevent these future wars must change as well. Minimizing the burden of security and defense will always be a high priority in democratic societies that consider warfare to be a deviation from normal international relations. And reducing the damage and violence should war occur also continues to be a desirable objective. Ultimately, the success or failure of arms control must be evaluated in terms of its contribution to these three objectives.

Reducing the risk of war remains an important objective of U.S. national security strategy, but the sources and causes of war are now so diffuse and complex that no single strategy can address all of them. Moreover, deterrence is no longer a viable threat-reduction strategy, at least in many of the regional situations of greatest concern, since many of the new and emerging sources of danger cannot be deterred by traditional assured-destruction-type blandishments (i.e., punitive threats of massive attacks against populations). Because the United States is faced with the prospects of not always being able to prevent regional conflicts from erupting and not always being able to deter emerging threats to the U.S. homeland from proliferating weapons of mass destruction and long-range delivery systems, future U.S. defense strategy must emphasize the ability to limit damage to U.S. territory, to protect U.S. forces deployed abroad, and to safeguard the vital interests of U.S. allies. If arms control is to effectively fulfill its preordained mission of enhancing national security and to remain a viable instrument of broader national defense strategy, it must be adapted to promote the objective of limiting damage during conflicts. This mandate raises one of the traditional arms control objectives, previously forsaken by arms control policy makers of the Cold War era, to a new position of preeminence as a hedge against deterrence failure in an unstable and unpredictable world.

Concluding that there is a need to limit damage means that ways must be found to surmount the traditional incompatibilities between the requirements of verifiable arms control (i.e., open and observable forces) and the requirements of an operational damage limitation strategy (which necessarily requires protected and survivable forces). As a preliminary answer, arms control may contribute to the new requirement for limiting damage to U.S. interests and assets in the following ways: by avoiding unnecessary restrictions aimed at U.S. defensive capabilities; by encouraging the deployment of residual nuclear or conventional forces (i.e., those that remain after implementing arms reduction agreements) in survivable basing modes; by facilitating the conversion of defense industries in the newly independent states of Eastern Europe and the former Soviet Union; and by fostering cooperative regimes aimed at controlling the spread of weapons of mass destruction and other destabilizing technologies.

To remain a vital and sustainable component of U.S. national security, arms control must expand its charter into the arenas of democratization, demilitarization, defense conversion, regional stabilization, and countering proliferation. In short, arms control must be, in form and substance, responsive to U.S. national security priorities on the eve of the twenty-first century.

Suggested Reading

Blacker, Coit D., and Gloria Duffy, eds. *International Arms Control: Issues and Agreements.* Stanford, Calif.: Stanford University Press, 1984.

Brennan, Donald G. "Setting and Goals of Arms Control," in Donald G. Brennan, ed., *Arms Control, Disarmament, and National Security.* New York: George Braziller, 1961, pp. 19–42.

Brodie, Bernard. "On the Objectives of Arms Control," in Robert J. Art and Kenneth N. Waltz, eds., *The Use of Force,* 2d ed. Lanham, Md.: University Press of America, 1983, pp. 420–438.

Bull, Hedley. *The Control of the Arms Race.* New York: Praeger Press, 1961.

———. "The Classical Approach to Arms Control Twenty Years After," in Uwe Nerlich, ed., *Soviet Power and Western Negotiating Policies,* vol. 2. Cambridge: Ballinger, 1983, pp. 21–30.

———. *Hedley Bull on Arms Control.* Selected and introduced by Robert O'Neill and David N. Schwartz. New York: St. Martin's Press, 1987.

Freedman, Lawrence. *The Evolution of Nuclear Strategy,* 2d ed. New York: St Martin's Press, 1989.

Glynn, Patrick. "The Sarajevo Fallacy: The Historical and Intellectual Origins of Arms Control Theology." *National Interest,* Fall 1987, pp. 3–32.

Gray, Colin S. *Strategic Studies and Public Policy.* Lexington: University Press of Kentucky, 1982. Chap. 6: "Arms Control and Central War," pp. 72–85.

Schelling, Thomas C. *Arms and Influence.* New Haven: Yale University Press, 1966.

Schelling, Thomas C., and Morton H. Halperin. *Strategy and Arms Control.* Reissued with a new Preface. Washington, D.C.: Pergamon-Brassey's, 1985.

Sheehan, Michael J. *Arms Control: Theory and Practice.* Oxford: Basil Blackwell, 1988.

Van Cleave, William R. "The Arms Control Record: Successes and Failures," in Richard F. Staar, ed., *Arms Control: Myth Versus Reality.* Stanford: Hoover Institution Press, 1984, pp. 1–23.

U.S. Arms Control and Disarmament Agency. *Arms Control and Disarmament Agreements: Texts and Histories of the Negotiations.* Washington, D.C.: Government Printing Office, 1990. Updated aperiodically.

Notes

1. Military writings often refer to a third level of abstraction, the tactical level. In arms control terms, tactical objectives would be those applied in the context of specific negotiations or treaties. They are not discussed here because many of the following chapters deal with such tactical perspectives.

2. Note the emphasis given to arms control as a response to the danger of surprise attack in Thomas C. Schelling and Morton H. Halperin, *Strategy and Arms Control* (New York: Twentieth Century Fund, 1961), pp. 10–14. See also the chapter on surprise nuclear attack in Hedley Bull, *The Control of the Arms Race* (New York: Praeger Press, 1961), pp. 158–174. These two books are part of the original canon of classical arms control theory.

3. Although Russia retains (and will retain for the foreseeable future) a nuclear arsenal sufficiently large to physically threaten the utter destruction of the United States, many strategic planners are convinced that a Russian surprise attack against the United States is an extremely remote possibility at this time, given improving U.S.–Russian relations, the internal preoccupations of Russian policymakers, and the scarcity of resources in a devastated and exhausted economy.

4. For a thorough and insightful survey of the history of nuclear arms control during the Cold War period that also traces the myriad revisions and adaptations in the theory of arms control as applied in practice, see the chapter titled "Strategic Arms Control" by Joseph DeSutter in Shuyler Foerster and Edward Wright, eds., *American Defense Policy*, 6th ed. (Baltimore: Johns Hopkins University Press, 1990), pp. 349–381.

5. One of the key founders of traditional arms control theory uses the term "classical" when referring to the assumptions and premises: see Hedley Bull, "The Classical Approach to Arms Control Twenty Years After," in Uwe Nerlich, ed., *Soviet Power and Western Negotiating Policies*, vol. 2 (Cambridge: Ballinger, 1983), pp. 21–30.

6. A thorough history of the Surprise Attack Conference and its relationship to contemporary arms control endeavors can be found in Johan J. Holst, "Strategic Arms Control and Stability: A Retrospective Look," in Johan J. Holst and William Schneider, Jr., eds., *Why ABM? Policy Issues in the Missile Defense Controversy* (New York: Pergamon Press, 1969), pp. 245–284.

7. The three basic canons of traditional arms control theory were published in 1961: Schelling and Halperin, *Strategy and Arms Control*; Bull, *The Control of the Arms Race*; and Donald G. Brennan, ed., *Arms Control, Disarmament, and National Security* (New York: George Braziller, 1961); earlier published as a special issue of *Daedalus: Proceedings of the American Academy of Arts and Sciences* (Fall 1960).

8. Bull, "The Traditional Approach to Arms Control Twenty Years After," p. 21.

9. Schelling and Halperin, p. 142.

10. Bull, *The Control of the Arms Race*, p. 37.

11. Bull, "The Traditional Approach to Arms Control Twenty Years After," p. 22.

12. Bull, *The Control of the Arms Race*, p. 75.

13. Ibid., p. 10.

14. Bull, "The Traditional Approach to Arms Control Twenty Years After," p. 24.

15. In the introduction to their seminal book, Schelling and Halperin state: "There is hardly an objective of arms control to be described in this study that is not equally a continuing urgent objective of national military strategy—of our unilateral military plans and policies" (p. 3).

16. Throughout much of the Cold War, these three dilemmas were elaborated mostly in nuclear terms (e.g., What deters nuclear war? How many nuclear weapons are enough? What if nuclear deterrence fails?), but they are equally applicable to the full range of defense scenarios, including policies and threats involving conventional, chemical, biological, and other types of weapons.

17. Schelling and Halperin, p. 1.

18. Ibid., p. 3.

19. Bull, *The Control of the Arms Race*, p. 3.

20. Few would dispute the fact that the advances over the past few years in ballistic missile defense technologies have been remarkable. For example, coatings have been developed that make mirrors for space-based lasers so reflective that they

need no cooling, thus reducing their weight. See William J. Broad, "From Fantasy to Fact: Space-Based Laser Nearly Ready to Fly," *New York Times,* 6 December 1994, p. B5. Of all the prospective ballistic missile defense options, space-based lasers are the most technologically demanding. For a broader treatment of the development and maturation of ballistic missile defense technologies, including computers, optical sensors, interceptors, kinetic kill vehicles, and directed energy weapons, see Donald R. Baucom, *The Origins of SDI, 1944–1983* (Lawrence: University of Kansas Press, 1992), especially pp. 97–106.

21. Nevertheless, the Russians are not eager for the United States to proceed in this direction without mutual consultations, so deploying such a system could exacerbate or undermine recent progress in the U.S.-Russian relationship and jeopardize implementation of START and ratification of START II. A decision to initiate such a deployment would have to involve a careful weighing of these considerations.

2

The Arms Control Process: The International Context

Trevor Taylor

The Concept of Arms Control and an Approach to Its Relationship with Politics

Despite the periodic appearances through history of unilateral and multilateral restrictions on weapons and their transfer, arms control was not recognized as a specific process in international relations until well into the Cold War period. Texts on international politics published before the 1960s show virtually no reference to arms control, although disarmament and the reduction of armament were common focuses of concern.[1] Indeed, the idea of arms control emerged in international relations only at the end of the 1950s.[2] At that time, superpower efforts to achieve extensive disarmament were clearly unsuccessful, as was the 1958 Surprise Attack Conference. However, there was recognition that nuclear weapons and the means for their rapid delivery posed new problems, and progress was made in some aspects of military cooperation.

Most notably, agreement was reached in 1959 on the permanent demilitarization of the Antarctic, and in the late 1950s the United States and the Soviet Union unilaterally stopped testing nuclear weapons in the atmosphere. Although the Soviet Union initiated the breaking of the moratorium after the Berlin crisis of 1959 and the U-2 incident in 1960, the Cuban missile crisis in 1962 led to an improvement in East-West relations. Reflecting this, the Partial Test Ban Treaty was signed in 1963 and the Hot Line Agreement followed soon after. Thus the concept of arms control emerged as a means of making sense of a growing cluster of intergovernmental agreements and of directing future cooperative state behavior on military matters. However, arms control for a long time generated more academic attention than political success, leading Thomas Schelling to observe in 1976 that "the volume of literature on arms control contrasts sharply with the dearth of results in actual armaments limitation or control."[3]

During the Cold War the adversarial relationship of the superpowers had an enormous impact on arms control. The most prominent negotiations of the détente period, the Strategic Arms Limitation Talks (SALT I and II), held between 1969 and 1979, were concerned with putting high ceilings on superpower strategic arms delivery systems and introducing a degree of strategic dialogue between Washington and Moscow. Other agreements, such as the Incidents at Sea in 1972,[4] were focused on the avoidance of accidental war and the control of conflict. In addition, however, the hostile, competitive relationship among the United States, the Soviet Union, and their respective allies had an impact on many regions and colored what was possible in arms control anywhere. When the United States and the Soviet Union were competing vigorously for influence in the Middle East after 1955, the prospects for arms export restraint deteriorated. The 1950 Tripartite Declaration among Britain, France, and the United States, which had restricted arms supplies to the region, collapsed. Only as the Cold War ended did efforts succeed in introducing real cuts in nuclear arsenals through the Intermediate-Range Nuclear Forces (INF) Treaty of 1987 and the first Strategic Arms Reduction Treaty (START I) of 1991. The START II Treaty was signed in 1993. It planned the reduction of strategic warhead arsenals to around 3,000–3,500 on each side, around a quarter of their peak during the Cold War.

After the Cold War, in an international system featuring conflicts and rivalries but where aspirations for international cooperation are on the increase among, for instance, the North Atlantic Treaty Organization (NATO) and former Warsaw Treaty states, Israel and its neighbors, and the Association of Southeast Asian Nations (ASEAN) countries, the opportunities for arms control to play a significant role should be growing. The global arms control picture of the future might not be dominated by Washington and Moscow. In view of the proliferation of weapons of mass destruction and conventional arms, the relevance of arms control needs to be explored in a wide range of international political relationships. The following discussion seeks to illuminate the arms control arrangements appropriate in different regions and political environments.

The analysis here is not completely atheoretical (indeed, there are periodic references to particular areas of theory), but it is not built on any single theoretical basis. In stressing the overt characteristics of relationships, I somewhat neglect the driving forces that generated those relationships and that could change them in the future. In international relations, the driving forces are often poorly understood and contested, and the theory directed at explaining interstate relationships is intellectually stimulating but quite diverse.[5]

A Typology of Interstate Relations

Individual interstate relationships can be considered as falling somewhere along a friendship–hostility range marked by three extremes and two internal divisions—a conceptualization that presents five categories of relationship (see Figure 2.1).

The forked end of the range has two rather different sorts of relationship. At the end of one fork are relationships between countries whose ties are so positive, extensive, and cooperative that the threat and use of force plays no part in them. Such countries form what Karl Deutsch termed pluralistic security communities (he focused his attention on the whole North Atlantic area).[6] Although what causes the creation of a security community is not clear, in the North Atlantic region a combination of factors seems to have played a part, including an extreme experience with modern war, a deliberate increase in economic and social integration, and the widespread presence of liberal democratic political systems. Some argue that relations between all liberal democratic states are inherently peaceful; they anticipate that the growth in number and strength of such states would increase the number of interstate relationships not marred by the threat and use of force.[7]

At the other end of the fork are remote relationships, in which cases one party's existence and policies are viewed as having few direct security implications for the other. As in a security community, the threat and use of force does not really have a part in relations among such states, but that is because those relations are remote rather than good. The Philippines, Chile, and Egypt have mutual relations that fall into this category, which also often involves a reflection of geographic distance. Clearly, if a system of true global collective security were ever successfully introduced, the significance of geographic distance would largely disappear, since it would involve, for instance, Latin American states facing the possibility of being required to act against aggression in Southeast Asia.

At the opposite end of the spectrum, away from the fork, are interstate relations in which the governments have such serious real conflicts and clashing ambitions that the use of force appears to them justified and its threat is constant. In such relations, at least one party is actively seeking to change the status quo in a significant way (by force, if necessary) and the other is determined to resist. The relationship during the 1950s between Syria and Egypt on the one hand and Israel on the other could be said to have fallen into this category. Hostility of this extreme is generated by one government actively pursuing an aim such as the overthrow and replacement of the other government or the seizure of some or all of the other state's territory. For example, the beginning of the Cold War showed the Soviet Union seemingly bent on the takeover of all Berlin and the West refusing to accept the division of Europe. Disputes are most intense when neither side can be charac-

Figure 2.1   A Typology of Interstate Relations

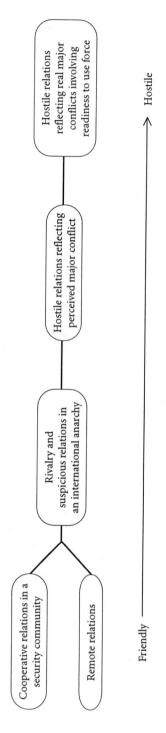

terized as a status quo power and both are bent on radical change. Such relationships in modern international life are relatively rare.

An initial intermediate category comprises state relationships where important conflicts of interest are perceived but are not real—that is, where there is a degree of mutual misunderstanding as to objectives. A government can misperceive the aim that another government is actively pursuing and react accordingly, thus causing alarm in the other capital. Arguably, the relationship between the Soviet Union and the United States in Europe after 1961 fell into this category, with the United States believing that the Soviet Union was actively seeking the political and military domination of all Europe and Moscow fearing that the United States was seeking to "roll back the Iron Curtain" and to overthrow communism by force if necessary. Indeed, each saw the other as ready to use force if the chance arose. Yet by building the Berlin Wall the Soviet Union had signaled its acceptance of the Western presence in that city, and NATO had long made clear its character as a purely defensive alliance. This category thus is made up of governments with an exaggerated sense of the extent to which they are in conflict.

A second intermediate position occurs when two states have no significant, defined dispute and may enjoy "normal" diplomatic and economic relations, but they nonetheless remain wary of the capabilities of the other and are keen not to allow any opportunity for successful intimidation or the use of force. Each sees the other as a rival if not an enemy. These are the kind of relations that political realists, stressing the security dilemma of sovereign states operating in an international anarchy, see as typical of international relations. Should a settlement be forthcoming among Israel, the Palestinians, and the neighboring Arab states, relations between Israel and its neighbors will fall into this category. The Arab states will remain wary of Israel's capabilities and Israel will continue to want to offset its neighbors' military strength. As another example, Brazil and Argentina often present themselves as rivals but not adversaries.[8]

There are four initial qualifications about this framework. First, obviously two states' relations are not fixed for all time at one point in the range. They can move backward or forward; indeed, the transformation in Western European relations since 1944 has been dramatic. However, further change could occur, and some writers (notably John Mearsheimer) feel that the Western European security community may well not survive the end of the Cold War.[9]

Second, arms control agreements can least controversially be anticipated when they are obviously compatible with the existing relationship of states at a particular point in the range. An example is the Hot Line Agreement, which reduced the risk of inadvertent superpower war between countries that perceived each other as major threats.

Third, a more demanding expectation of arms control is that it can promote the movement of relations to a new, more cooperative, less adversarial point in the range. Such an asserted role for arms control defines it not just as a series of isolated agreements but as a process in which the way negotiations are conducted may be as influential as the details of the linked agreements that might emerge. A wider arms control process arguably helped strengthen the overall cooperative relationship between Russia and the United States after 1990, as the Conventional Forces in Europe (CFE) and the START I and II agreements were concluded, as the two countries discussed the future of the Antiballistic Missile (ABM) Treaty, and as they worked together to get the Chemical Weapons Convention (CWC) finalized and the UN Conventional Arms Register into operation. Arms control can be seen not just as a means of reflecting trust but also as a way of building it. This is particularly true of confidence-building measures, which do not normally involve restrictions on equipment, numbers, or quality but provide increased transparency about military activities or place limits on deployments so that effective surprise attack becomes more difficult. In recent years U.S.-Russian relations have become more friendly, and even Egyptian-Israeli relations have become less hostile, in part because of the reassurance that arms control and confidence-building measures between them have encouraged.

Fourth, relations among states may deteriorate, as they did in Europe in the 1930s with the rise of right-wing regimes in Germany and Italy. Under major political stress, arms control cannot prevent a deterioration of interstate relations. In the Middle East, for example, if Israel insists on expanding settlements on the West Bank and maintaining control there, thus preventing the emergence of an effective Palestinian authority, its peaceful relations with Egypt may not survive.

This conception of the possible types of interstate relationship highlights three central questions relating to arms control: What sorts of arms control activities are compatible with the different categories of relationships? How can arms control activities help move interstate relationships away from the hostility end of the spectrum? And how should arms control address the possibility of deteriorating political relations?

Types of Arms Control Negotiations

Although a range of specific ends can be associated with arms control, including the political target of improved relations (as Chapter 1 explains), arms control agreements have long been recognized as serving one or more of three basic military-strategic purposes: to make war less likely between states by stabilizing deterrence and reducing the opportunity for the successful use of force; to reduce the costs of defense; and to reduce the horror of war should it occur.[10]

However, arms control commitments can also be classified according to the type of process by which they emerge. Some come from unilateral measures, anticipating reciprocal action from the other party, rather than from negotiated deals. In 1992, Pres. Boris Yeltsin and Pres. George Bush separately committed their governments to end the deployment of all tactical nuclear weapons (except air-launched systems) and nuclear weapons on ships except submarine-launched ballistic missiles (SLBMs). Britain and France then made similar commitments. Advantages of this approach in this instance were that no party felt it was making a great sacrifice (because the need for such weapons had declined with the withdrawal of Soviet forces from Central Europe), change could be introduced quickly, treaty ratification processes were avoided, and the issue of verification, which would have been enormously difficult in the case of tactical nuclear weapons, was skirted. An apparent disadvantage of unilateral measures is that they may prove fragile when the political environment changes. As noted, the implicit test ban practiced through U.S. and Soviet restraint at the end of the 1950s was ended by the Berlin and U-2 crises.

Most arms control agreements come from formal negotiations. These can be bilateral, such as the strategic weapons talks that produced the SALT and START Treaties and the talks that produced the INF Treaty. They can also be multilateral, such as the CFE Treaty, which was negotiated by all the members of NATO and the Warsaw Treaty Organization. Finally, they can be virtually global, as when all the members of the UN had a voice in generating the UN Register of Conventional Arms agreed to in 1991.

In general, a negotiation has the best chance of reaching a meaningful agreement if it includes all the states that need to be involved but as few countries as are needed. To date, only the United States and the former Soviet Union have needed to be involved in strategic arms control because their arsenals dwarf those of the other states (China, France, and the United Kingdom) that deploy strategic weapons. If and when Russian-U.S. strategic arms control moves toward minimum deterrent forces of perhaps 1,000 warheads each, the smaller nuclear arsenal states will probably have to take part in talks. Global negotiations, such as those that produced the CWC and the UN Register of Conventional Arms, usually involve the establishment of a working or steering group of a smaller number of states. Such a group brings together a wide range of expertise on technical issues (such as verification problems and opportunities), as well as reflecting the interests of different governments. Its task is to agree on a draft that can be submitted later to a plenary group for approval. Reflecting the problems of a negotiating forum of 180 participants, the UN has established in Geneva a Committee on Disarmament (CD), which has tended to grow over the years but which still comprises less than a quarter of the UN membership. This forum tackles global matters and works for consensus. With agreement within the CD achieved, it is reasonably expected that most of the rest of the UN's membership can then be persuaded to fall into line.

Once engaged in a negotiation, governments seek the best arms control deal possible for their country; extensive, complex, and sometimes futile bargaining has often been involved. During the Cold War, arms control was often stressed in the United States as an aspect of national strategy—a means of securing a national advantage. The Reagan administration, which perhaps felt pushed into strategic arms control talks by domestic and allied opinion in the early 1980s, felt confident of the long-term capacity of the United States to prevail in an arms race. The administration was therefore willing only to contemplate favorable deals for the United States. This strategy would limit strategic offensive systems and minimize the restrictions of the ABM Treaty so that strategic defense work could proceed.

Arms control negotiations and even agreements can serve to damage rather than improve relations among participants. Governments that have real or perceived conflicting aims might enter into arms control talks not to stabilize their relationship but solely to gain a unilateral advantage. They can hope to pressure their adversary into concluding an agreement in which the benefits are very unequally allocated.

In practice, however, suggestions for asymmetrical benefits are likely to be identified by the opponent. During the Cold War, periodic Soviet proposals for both sides to abandon their foreign bases would have hurt the United States most. Similarly, the United States stressed the need to cut accurate, land-based intercontinental ballistic missiles (ICBMs) rather than the less precise SLBMs with which the United States was well supplied. These types of proposals were quickly analyzed by the other side as conferring asymmetrical benefits and were dismissed accordingly. The tabling of proposals whose implementation would give a significant advantage to the proposer indicates that there is no real interest in cooperation and thus can contribute to worsened relations.

A rather traditional and simplistic observation is that extensive arms control negotiations can succeed only in relationships where they do not matter and are doomed in the hostile relationships where they appear most needed. This is the view favored by Colin Gray, among others.[11] He stressed in 1993 that armaments in and of themselves do not affect states' relations but rather reflect the motives and concerns of states:

> States do not threaten war, or go to war, because they are armed. Rather states arm, and counterarm competitively, because they anticipate the possibility of war. ... Because weapons are only instruments of political forces

and desires, arms control can never withstand the traffic of heavy political antagonism, and must always fail to meet reasonable expectations.[12]

He goes further to assert, in the face of much thinking about deterrence, that "there are and can be no aggressive, offensive or destabilizing weapons. Weapons do not make war; national leaders do" and that "there has been no notable correlation between great crisis instability (in military terms) and the outbreak of war, or between arms race instabilities and the outbreak of fighting."[13]

While respecting the importance of politics and recognizing that the record of arms control is far from glorious, I reject the view that armaments and arms levels can be treated simply as dependents of political processes. Armaments and armed forces should be seen as an element within political processes, because government A's perception of government B will be affected by the arms with which government B has equipped itself. I present arms control as much affected by the political objectives of states but assert that armed force preparations, and arms control negotiations and agreements, can have an influence on how perceptions and political relationships evolve. It is clear, for instance, that arms control must have a central and multidimensional role in any settlement of the Arab-Israeli dispute,[14] as a means of reassurance for Israel and its Arab neighbors.

The integration of arms control in wider political relationships is reinforced by the consideration that even during the Cold War the adversaries were concerned with three categories of arms control. These categories are still of some relevance. They may be summarized, perhaps rather crudely, as "arms control for us," "arms control for everyone," "and arms control for them."

"Arms control for us" concerns the measures taken to formalize and consolidate the cooperative military dimensions of relationships between, principally, the members of NATO and the former Warsaw Treaty Organization. Agreements in this area, like the START I Treaty and the CFE Treaty, bind only the players in the two alliances at the center of the Cold War. In these agreements, states signaled that their intentions were not aggressive by restricting, to a greater or lesser degree, their capabilities.

"Arms control for everyone" involves measures that the former adversaries of the Cold War hope to see endorsed by more or less all the members of the UN. The Biological and Chemical Weapons Conventions are examples of restraints intended for all states. Even during the Cold War, the Cold War protagonists cooperated to promote the global application of such measures.

"Arms control for them" is politically the most sensitive area because it relates to restraints that "we," the former Cold War adversaries, wish upon others but not ourselves. The relevant others may be located in particular regions, such as the Middle East, Southeast Asia, or the wider world. Broadly speaking, "we" are content to see nuclear weapons and long-range ballistic missiles play a central role in our security, but "we" hope, through nonproliferation regimes, to induce (persuade and/or pressure) other states to rely on conventional forces. Similarly vulnerable to charges of discrimination are proposals that the international trade in arms should be further restricted while developed states are left free to produce what they want for themselves.

With this background, the place of arms control in different sorts of interstate relationship can be analyzed. The starting point is that arms control appears to be of varying degrees of practicability and relevance at different points in the political spectrum.

Arms Control and Political Relationships

Arms Control in Security Communities and Among Remote States

Arms control should be of comparatively little relevance in a security community, where interstate relations are not affected by the threat and use of force. However, as European experience reflects, this does not mean that arms control is not of interest to the members of a security community in their bilateral and multilateral relations with each other. Certainly, Franco-German reconciliation after 1945 was assisted by the restrictions that Germany accepted on its rearmament programs, restrictions that were formally monitored by the Western European Union (WEU). Certain rearmament moves could kindle new fears. One reason why the Western Europeans are keen that the U.S. commitment to European defense should remain in place is that, without a U.S. nuclear guarantee, Germany might feel that it needed its own nuclear weapons. Such a move by Germany would place great strain on several German bilateral relationships, not least that with France.

A less alarming reason for security community interest in arms control is that some or all of the members of a security community may feel affected by the impact of one of them on the wider world. Thus Germany and other European Union (EU) members are concerned by the stances that Britain and France take on a Comprehensive Test Ban Treaty given that such a treaty could restrict and discourage horizontal nuclear proliferation. In the late 1980s, Britain and France, along with others, were worried about the flaws in German export controls, which meant that Libya could build a chemical weapons plant at Rabta with German help. Within a security community, states are often reluctant to criticize publicly the arms acquisition, export, and control policies of their friends and neighbors, but they clearly have interest in them. After the Maastricht Treaty, two of the four areas where the EU states expressed an aspiration to develop common policy concerned arms control: nuclear proliferation and the export of arms and dual-use technology. However, the capacity of the EU states to agree on a common arms export policy has been limited to date. Prior to 1990, for instance, France was an exporter of arms to Iraq, whereas other EU states were much more reluctant to become deeply involved.

Similar reasoning applies to arms control linking states whose relations are marked by remoteness. Egypt, Chile, and South Korea have a mutual concern with nonproliferation because it could affect each of them. In significant ways security has an indivisible as well as a regional character. It is widely believed that if North Korea or Iraq succeeded in defying the nuclear nonproliferation regime, that regime would be weakened globally as well as in the Asia Pacific area or the Middle East.

Clearly, the arms control measures of mutual interest to remote states are those, like the nuclear Non-Proliferation Treaty (NPT), that have a global rather than a local or regional scope. However, this generalization must be qualified, since a state in one region may be interested in exploring the applicability of an arms control measure designed for another region. As an illustration, if comprehensive long-term peace agreements are made between Israel and its neighbors, arms control and confidence-building measures will be involved. Undoubtedly, there will be an attempt to adapt some of the approaches developed in Europe to a Middle East context. Restrictions on deployment of the major conventional weapons useful for large-scale surprise attack, which were set out in the 1990 CFE Treaty, are of interest in the Middle East, as are Conference on Security and Cooperation in Europe (CSCE) confidence-building measures restricting the scale of exercises. Another example of a region's experience being of interest elsewhere is the Treaty of Tlatelolco to establish a nuclear-free zone in Latin America. All countries interested in nuclear-free zones want to know about that treaty and its operation. Thus even remote states may be interested in their respective arms control activities.

Arms Control in Relationships of Hostility

At the opposite end of the spectrum, where interstate relations are marked by deep hostility and a readiness at least on one side to change the status quo by force if necessary, arms control would appear to have very limited scope. When a bilateral relationship is conceived as close to a zero-sum game, there is very limited scope for cooperation between the parties. But arms control remains of some relevance, for at least four reasons.

First, regardless of the condition of their relationship, states do not want to get involved in war by accident and may be ready to enter into some cooperation to avoid this. The Hot Line Agreement and its subsequent strengthening constitutes an example of such reasoning.

A second consideration is that even hostile states may find it valuable at least to enter into some forms of arms control negotiations for strategic or public relations reasons. As observed earlier, a government may enter an arms control negotiation in the hope of gaining disproportionately from an adversary's unwise concession. Even in hostile relationships neither side may want to appear opposed in principle to cooperation and may judge that arms control negotiations at least offer an opportunity to portray an opponent in a poor light. In such cases, negotiations are likely to prove sterile. However, domestic and international audiences observing a hostile relationship may conclude that continuing arms control talks indicate that neither side has written off the possibility of cooperation. Domestic factors in favor of arms control should prove most influential when few real restrictions on military activity are envisaged (see Chapter 3 for a full discussion of domestic political considerations in arms control). Arguably, a major role of nuclear arms control before 1987 was to make Western publics believe that cooperative restraints on the arms race were in place, while leaving the Soviet and U.S. defense ministries free to execute their plans in tacit cooperation.[15]

Third, the parties in a dispute may be ready to contemplate the use of force but they may wish to avoid its worst manifestations. Thus they may accept that some weapons are too horrific to threaten or to use. The conventions on inhumane weapons, environmental modification, chemical weapons, and biological weapons all reflect efforts to build a global consensus that some weapons should be outlawed as too terrible to be used in any circumstances. Clearly, such agreements should in principle be feasible between intense adversaries.

However, the global nuclear weapons issue would appear to complicate efforts to specify any other weapons as too awful to threaten or use. The potential damage involved with nuclear war is massive and unpredictable. The long-term planetary changes associated with the use on a significant scale of nuclear warheads cannot be calculated with confidence, although there is serious scientific evidence that nuclear winter affecting the entire planet could follow significant nuclear exchanges. It is hard to conceive of a more horrific weapon than the thermonuclear weapon. Yet because of its deterrent value there is no global consensus that it is too awful to be threatened.

The awkward question of why nuclear weapons cannot be globally outlawed, or at least delegitimized, because of their effects (when chemical and biological weapons can be) has been avoided in an East-West framework, where Russia, the United States, and the Western European states have access to nuclear guarantees. But in the Middle East, where only Israel is widely perceived to have a nuclear capability, there has been a reluctance by several states to accept the CWC and the NPT because of the asymmetry of the parties. Most of the UN membership has taken the view that the fewer the states that possess nuclear weapons the better, and the NPT presses the great majority of states to renounce nuclear weapons. But the logic is unclear as to why a few states should be able to deploy nuclear weapons forever.

A fourth consideration putting arms control on the agenda of even hostile states is that, although the individual relations between adversaries are a central consideration in arms control, external players can have an impact. In particular, the great power backers of adversary states can press them to accept arms control measures. As noted, the former Cold War adversaries are interested in arms control for others as well as themselves. In the Middle East, the United States and others have worked hard to promote signatures to the CWC, and Israel completed a return to the UN Register of Conventional Arms in 1993 only because of U.S. insistence. States outside a conflict can obviously supply arms to adversaries, but they can also press for arms control between them.

Clearly, arms control agreements concluded in such circumstances are liable to collapse under pressure. A government in a hostile relationship and under pressure from an outside backer may be ready publicly and privately to forgo the use of a weapon of mass destruction in any offensive activities but will be tempted to change its position if it is facing imminent defeat and invasion. The formal arms control agreement between Iran and Iraq outlawing the use of chemical weapons was violated once Iraq became desperate to avoid defeat and end the protracted war. Arguably, the end of the Cold War will hinder the imposition of arms restraint on others by the major powers. Moscow and Washington have become less interested in influencing behavior in the wider world. Consequently, many of their former clients may feel less protected and more inclined to rely on their own capabilities. Also, with reduced major power involvement, the possibility of a local war escalating into an East-West conflict has been reduced. This could well make major states more relaxed about the outbreak of war in many parts of the international system. Of course, the end of the Cold War has also strengthened the potential for arms control cooperation between the United States and Russia, for instance on ballistic missile exports.

Arms Control in Relationships of
Perceived Conflict, Rivalry, and Suspicion

A most complex area for arms control is among states without a real major grievance that could justify the use of force but whose relations are marked by perceived conflict or at least suspicions and a persistent sense of rivalry. This represents a broad range of relations encompassing the intermediate categories in Figure 2.1. For the political realist, most relations among neighboring states can be expected to have a character within this range.

States can come to this position as a result of real conflict because one or more of the parties change their objectives and ambitions. At least one motive for abandoning an ambition to change the status quo can be that the pursuit has become too expensive and damaging in economic and other terms. For example, after 1973 Egypt clearly abandoned any ambitions it may have had with regard to the destruction of Israel, feeling that it had sacrificed enough blood and treasure for the Arab cause. In another case, once President Gorbachev came to power, the Soviet Union gave up its ambitions to compete against the United States on the global stage and be able to overrun Western Europe in a short period.

In such circumstances arms control agreements can be used to stabilize previously highly competitive relationships if they can reduce the options for the possible successful use of force. In areas where nuclear or other weapons of mass destruction do not have a place, the burden of deterrence must rest upon conventional forces. While in some ways conventional deterrence might be seen as inherently less stable than one based on nuclear forces, there is the telling argument that states will not deliberately initiate large-scale conventional war unless they expect a quick victory. Such a victory normally relies on a degree of surprise being attained. Arms control measures that reduce the capacity for a successful surprise attack should reinforce deterrence. This was the logic behind the CFE agreement, which cut inventories of those systems most useful in a surprise attack. It was also the basis for the arms control/confidence-building agreements between Israel and Egypt, which provided for the virtual demilitarization of the Sinai and the presence of the UN multilateral force in the desert to monitor compliance.

However, even when the political circumstances for arms control appear favorable, its achievement may be difficult because of geopolitical considerations. Building a stable Arab-Israeli military balance has always been difficult because Israel has to mobilize such a high proportion of its population to fight effectively against its more populous neighbors. Israel has thus been able to contemplate short wars only—longer struggle would bring its economy to a standstill. Israel also has limited territory to concede in the event of invasion. Thus, in its arms acquisitions and defense preparations it has always sought the capacity to defeat its enemies quickly, even if they attacked simultaneously. Its neighbors, on the other hand, have wanted the individual capacity to hold off an Israeli offensive and have been worried that they might be left alone to fight Israel. The challenge for the Syrian-Israeli bilateral negotiations and for the related multilateral arms control talks will be to come up with some way of reconciling these asymmetries through the use of demilitarized zones, zones of very limited deployment, transparency measures, and, perhaps, peacekeeping forces.

Once states abandon objectives that seriously conflict with those of others, arms control can help to stabilize the situation. But how can arms control processes contribute to the further easing of suspicions and rivalries and the movement toward yet more cooperative security relationships?

Relative gains.   Political realists have argued that, in an international system marked by a contest for power, whether a form of cooperation will occur will depend on more than whether all parties would benefit. Of crucial significance is whether the relative gains for all the parties are compatible with existing power relationships, since a state is not expected to cooperate in a way that would make it relatively less powerful.

Arms control can promote the transformation of relationships when states are willing to accept an asymmetrical distribution of benefits in a particular military agreement in the hope that this will lead in turn to wider cooperation and more gains. This sort of thinking is quite compatible with idealist thinking, which stresses that governments are capable of identifying their long-term, enlightened self-interest and then pursuing it; it can also be accommodated within the political realist model, which stresses the acquisition of power. However, this latter approach struggles to account for sustained cooperative behavior among states.

By way of illustration, in the SALT I and II agreements deterrence was somewhat stabilized, but the agreements had no great influence on the overall nature of U.S. and Soviet relations. Indeed, SALT II was never ratified in the United States, in part because of an extraneous political development: the invasion of Afghanistan by the Soviet Union. From 1987, however, the Soviet Union sent serious signals about its long-term cooperative intent when it accepted some clearly asymmetrical deals. It agreed to destroy all its 300-plus deployed SS-20 missiles in the 1987 INF Treaty, while in return the United States agreed to destroy a much smaller number of Pershing 2 and cruise missiles. In December 1988 President Gorbachev announced significant unilateral cuts in tank and armed force personnel numbers, which paved the way for the CFE negotiations and treaty. This treaty required the Soviet Union to destroy much greater volumes of equipment than the West.

The arms control arrangements reached with Moscow have not just taken advantage of improved relations but have also promoted further cooperative security. This is because, by accepting asymmetrical cuts in armed forces, Moscow has clearly signaled that it would like to see improved relations in other important areas such as trade, aid, and technology transfer. On the Western side, the unilateral limitations that Germany accepted on its forces as part of the "two plus four" agreement endorsing German unification clearly sent a reassuring signal to Germany's neighbors, especially Moscow.

Integration theory.   Just how much arms control alone can achieve in promoting cooperative international security relationships is a matter for theory-based reasoning. Integration theorists stress that security communities, where the threat and use of force has no part to play in an international relationship, require a network of social, economic, and political contact between the societies involved, so that war becomes both impractical and unthinkable in view of the interdependencies of the societies and the mutual empathy that the peoples have for each other. They place no emphasis on arms control. As noted, democratic peace theorists assert the importance of the political regimes in power—relations among liberal democratic governments are expected to be peaceful.

However, two arguments suggest that the long-term significance of arms control need not be marginal. The first asserts that the climate of increasing confidence in harmonious relations and cooperative behavior that arms control can generate is very supportive of the development of the economic, social, and other links between societies, which integration theorists appreciate. Within contemporary Europe, the CFE Treaty and other arms control measures have discouraged growth of mistrust and rivalry among Central and Eastern European states freed from Soviet control. This in turn has facilitated their movement toward integration with Western organizations such as NATO, the EU, and the WEU.

The second argument says that in regions such as the Middle East and the Asia Pacific area, arms control could be a relatively more important element in cooperative relations given that liberal democratic regimes are rare and economic and social integration seems likely to remain limited among many dyads of states for many years. Arms control could therefore be a particularly important stabilizing element in areas where other sources of intrinsically peaceful relations are lacking.

Purposes of arms control.   The central relevant purposes of arms control in areas of rivalry and suspicion but not real conflict are likely to be to reduce the horror of and risks of war (by reinforcing deterrence and making accidental war less likely). The widespread desire even among nonnuclear states to restrict nuclear proliferation and to outlaw other weapons of mass destruction reflects an interest in restricting the horror of war (as well as pressure from the larger powers).

Historically, arms control measures meant mainly to reduce the cost of preparing defenses have been rare. This seems likely to continue in the future. Implicit in the earlier analysis is that it is difficult to conceive of political relationships in which arms control primarily designed to limit the costs of defense and deterrence is appealing. Arms control measures inspired by this logic should appeal only to one side in a relationship—that which feels less able to afford the ongoing or rising costs of defense. Arms control primarily designed to limit spending would appear to have a chance only when all parties overestimate the capability of their rivals to sustain the cost of an uncontrolled situation. Rival states are unlikely to be able to agree on holding down the cost of their arms competition, especially if one of the parties perceives itself as better able to live economically with the arms competition.

However, this is not to say that economic pressures may not lead states to take the drastic course noted at the beginning of this section: to reconsider their objectives and ambitions and thus revise their interstate relationships. If radical objectives (such as the destruction of Israel or Iran's presumed aim of overthrowing the Saudi monarchy) are abandoned, real conflicts can disappear and the opportunities for arms control grow accordingly. President Gorbachev, seeing the damage that the defense effort was doing to the Soviet economy, was not moved to look for arms control measures that would directly enable some money to be saved but that would leave U.S.-Soviet global rivalry intact. Instead he sought to transform the nature of the relationship between the two states. Economic pressures certainly had a role in pushing Egypt toward peace and arms control with Israel; Yahya Sadowski has recently argued that general arms control prospects in the Middle East are improving because of the unacceptable cost of the arms race in that region.[16]

Finally, consider the perspective stressed by Gray of what happens to arms control when the political ambitions of at least one of the parties are changing and relations deteriorate. Gray's argument is that arms control can then discourage appropriate countermeasures by states that favor the status quo.[17] In the interwar years, the Washington Naval Treaty acted as a hindrance to rearmament by the states opposed to Germany. This implies that an arms control agreement should never be seen by governments as an isolated and self-contained event but as part of wider political and military processes that involve, inter alia, regular discussions about the continued implementation and interpretation of an agreement, any appropriate adjustments, the need for further supportive agreements, and the way the wider political context is evolving. To stay healthy, arms control agreements should be constantly monitored and subjected to regular review.

Conclusion

This chapter has offered a framework in which the political environment of arms control can be discussed. Emerging from it are the following propositions:

- Individual interstate relationships can be located somewhere along a range, with pluralistic security communities and remote relationships at one end and very hostile relationships based on conflicting objectives at the other.
- Even remote states and states within security communities will have disagreements and some arms control topics to discuss.
- In terms of the three widely acknowledged purposes of arms control, states in very hostile relationships are likely to be interested in arms control mainly for its capacity to reduce the possibilities of accidental war and to rule out the possibility of some particularly horrific weapons being used. Seeking change in the status quo, they will not be

interested in arms agreements that stabilize deterrence by reducing the possibilities for the effective use of force. Hostile states may, however, enter arms control talks in the hope of strategic advantage, and/or appreciate the public relations value of participation in arms control negotiations, and/or may have arms control pressed upon them by external great powers.

- Arms control in relationships of perceived conflict or rivalry is feasible insofar as it can stabilize military relationships by reinforcing deterrence or reducing the horror of war. The extent to which arms control can go further than simply reflecting existing political relationships and promoting warmer relations will depend on the readiness of governments to accept asymmetrical military gains in arms control agreements for the sake of their wider political impact.
- Arms control agreements that are not aimed at changing the basic nature of relations but that allow existing relationships of rivalry to continue at a lower cost appear to have limited feasibility. Economic considerations do, however, appear as important factors leading states to sometimes reconsider their basic objectives and so move a relationship away from the hostile end of the range.
- An assessment of the significance of arms control and its potential to change the political environment as well as to be affected by that environment will depend on the theoretical positions adopted about the fundamentals of interstate behavior.
- In the region from the Atlantic to the Urals, the potential and significance of arms control has been transformed in the past decade, and East and West have taken great advantage. The challenges for arms control negotiators in the next few years will be to support the peace process in the Middle East, to take advantage of the desire of many governments in the Asia Pacific area to introduce more cooperative security to their region and to rely less on the U.S. oversight and presence, and to discourage the spread of weapons of mass destruction whose effects are widely regarded as unacceptable. The states that act on a global scale (whose possibilities for cooperation have been enhanced by the end of the Cold War) need to cooperate so that in relationships of real and perceived conflict, deterrence is reinforced and the opportunities for the successful use of force are minimized. States should impose stabilizing arms control measures wherever they can.

Suggested Reading

George, A. L., P. J. Farley, and A. Dallin. *US-Soviet Security Cooperation.* Oxford: Oxford University Press, 1988. This is a series of case studies of the diplomacy associated with a range of arms control negotiations during the Cold War. They can be used to illustrate the links between arms control and the political environment in specific instances.

Gray, Colin. "Arms Control Does Not Control Arms." *Orbis,* Summer 1993, pp. 333–348. This is a clearly articulated attack on the potential and significance of arms control in international politics, stressing that major arms limitations are possible when they are not needed.

"Restraints," in Andrew Pierre, *The Global Politics of Arms Sales.* Princeton, N.J.: Princeton University Press, 1982. This is a classic analysis of the arms trade and the hindrances on efforts to control it.

Stanford Arms Control Group. "Arms Control: The Political, Legal, and Ethical Context" and "Towards an Evaluation of Arms Control," in C. D. Blacker and G. Duffy, eds., *International Arms Control: Issues and Agreement,* 2d ed. Stanford, Calif.: Stanford University Press, 1984, pp. 11–32, 335–344. These chapters, part of a broad survey of arms control produced during the Cold War, address the hopeful beliefs of the contributors about arms control's achievements and potential.

Walker, Jenonne. *Security and Arms Control in Post-Confrontation Europe.* Oxford: Oxford University Press for Stockholm International Peace Research Institute, 1994. This is an assertion of the continued relevance of arms control in the political environment of post–Cold War Europe.

Notes

1. General international relations texts of the 1950s paid comparatively little attention even to disarmament, which is not surprising given the state of East-West relations. *Regulation of armaments* was a phrase used more often than *arms control.*

2. See M. J. Sheehan, *Arms Control: Theory and Practice* (Oxford: Oxford University Press, 1988), Chap. 1.

3. "On the Objectives of Arms Control," originally published in *International Security* (Summer 1976), reproduced in R. J. Art and K. N. Waltz, *The Use of Force,* 3d ed. (New York: Lanham, 1988), p. 618.

4. This agreement, formally titled the Agreement on the Prevention of Incidents On and Over the High Seas, produced a code of conduct for the two countries' navies.

5. As useful guides on international relations theory, see J. E. Dlugherty and R. L. Pfaltzgraff, *Contending Theories of International Relations: A Comprehensive Survey,* 3d ed. (New York: Harper and Row, 1990); A. J. R. Groom and Margot Light, *Contemporary International Relations: A Guide to Theory* (London and New York: Pinter, 1994); T. L. Knutsen, *A History of International Relations Theory* (Manchester and New York: Manchester University Press, 1992); R. Little and M. Smith, *Perspectives on World Politics,* 2d ed. (London: Routledge, 1992); and P. R. Viotti and M. V. Kauppi, *International Relations Theory: Realism, Pluralism, Globalism* (New York: Macmillan, 1987).

6. Karl Deutsch, *Political Community and the North Atlantic Area* (Princeton, N.J.: Princeton University Press, 1957).

7. For a stimulating summary of the debate on this issue and some contrasting findings, see the first three articles in the Fall 1994 issue of *International Security* and also Bruce Russett, *Grasping the Democratic Peace* (Princeton, N.J.: Princeton University Press, 1993).

8. For an analysis of how the states of Latin America, despite a primary concern with counterinsurgency and internal security, nevertheless tended in the 1960s to monitor and match their rivals' arms acquisitions, see John Stanley and Maurice Pearton, *The International Trade in Arms* (London: Chatto & Windus, 1972), pp. 210–221.

9. "Back to the Future: Instability in Europe After the Cold War," *International Security* (Summer 1990), pp. 5–56.

10. See Hedley Bull, *The Control of the Arms Race* (London: Weindenfeld and Nicholson, 1961), Chap. 1. Bull referred to reducing the horror of war as the moral dimension of arms control. Jozef Goldblat, *Arms Control: A Guide to Negotiations and Agreements* (London: Sage, 1994), lists nine functions of arms control, all of which can be encompassed within the three used here.

11. See Colin Gray, *House of Cards: Why Arms Control Must Fail* (Ithaca and London: Cornell University Press, 1993), and also his "Arms Control Does Not Control Arms," *Orbis* (Summer 1993), pp. 333–348.

12. Gray, "Arms Control Does Not Control Arms," p. 335.

13. Ibid., p. 347.

14. See Ahmed S. Khalidi, "Security in a Final Middle East Settlement: Some Components of Palestinian National Security," *International Affairs* (January 1995), pp. 1–18, for a thoughtful assertion of Palestinian needs, including a regional Arab-Israeli settlement.

15. See A. Myrdal, *The Game of Disarmament: How the United States and Russia Run the Arms Race* (New York: Random House, 1976).

16. Yahya M. Sadowski, *Scuds or Butter: The Political Economy of Arms Control in the Middle East* (Washington: Brookings, 1993).

17. A feature of Gray's argument is that it is fundamentally applicable to any international treaty or law that a group of states accepts. Any such agreement can be put under stress by changing political circumstances, and Gray's onslaught against arms control can be seen as an attack on international law in general.

3

The Arms Control Process: The U.S. Domestic Context

Jennifer E. Sims

Governments have practiced regulated war and weapons restraint for centuries. Yet arms control has never had as bold, vigorous, or enduring a champion as the United States after World War II. Since the defeat of Japan and Germany, the United States has persistently advocated negotiated restraints. Arms control theory has permeated the literature on national security and has been tested repeatedly by policymakers. U.S. policymakers have sustained an arms control process that has become an integral part of U.S. national security policy, despite the opposition of a public that remained skeptical of its value until at least the 1980s.

The intensity of the U.S. fascination with arms control is explained in part by the public's fear of nuclear war. But this observation begs troubling questions. In a polity gripped with nuclear fear, what kind of fascination permitted decades of arms control accompanied by exponential growth, diversification, and proliferation of weapons arsenals? How have domestic forces shaped a process that most people find morally compelling and yet unpersuasive, if not opaque in its outcomes? How has the United States practiced arms control, and why for so long?

The Domestic Context for U.S. Arms Control

In the United States, as in most democracies, arms control outcomes are shaped by four domestic factors: the ideas of key elites; the political and legal processes for exploring, negotiating, and conducting arms control; the role and involvement of key interest groups (e.g., weapons builders, the military, politicians, and pacifists); and public opinion. Although considerable attention has been paid to the formal processes for negotiating and implementing arms control agreements, these processes constitute just one vehicle by which compromises are reached. Formal processes or institutional arrangements limit options and define brokers for any accord. But the engines of U.S. arms control have always been public opinion, policy advocates, and the ideas around which they rally.

Strategic Culture

The politics of U.S. arms control turns on U.S. strategic culture—"that national soup of ideals, interests and propensities upon which decision-makers have been nourished as professionals and as citizens."[1] Strategic culture helps to explain why particular arms control solutions win, why they sometimes fail to be accepted abroad, and why, even when discredited, they may nevertheless regularly reappear.

The keys to unlocking any country's strategic culture are the ideas, myths, and national beliefs that are regularly recorded in academic literature, the speeches of politicians, and the press releases of policy advocates. The dominance of the national security agenda throughout the Cold War has left a particularly rich record of arms control ideas. Understanding the most influential of these ideas, and the political orientations from which they spring, aids in unlocking arms control's past as well as its future.

The tradition of unilateralism.   U.S. strategic culture rests on a mix of scientific rationalism, political realism, and unilateralist preferences—albeit often tied to concepts of U.S.-led internationalism. Interest in preserving the country's "freedom of action," well understood since George Washington's farewell address, has biased U.S. citizens against locked embraces, including binding agreements, with foreign powers. As Pres. Woodrow Wilson discovered when he sought popular support for U.S. entry into the League of Nations after World War I, even liberals and progressives of an internationalist bent could blanch at the prospect of tying U.S. fortunes to those of other nations.[2]

It should thus not be surprising that, to the extent that it has involved binding U.S. defense policies to agreed and verifiable limits, arms control has often been a hard sell. U.S. citizens have easily endorsed moral examples (such as the 1925 Geneva Convention against the use of chemical weapons) but have not easily ratified treaties. Indeed, the golden age of arms control, from the late 1950s to the early 1960s, built on an approach that denigrated formal agreements: tacit agreements and the signaling of defensive intentions became the focus of arms control policy, while its objective, stability, required the maintenance of a bipolar equilibrium of power. Arms control became absorbed with maintaining each side's ability to obliterate the other with nuclear weapons and with preserving sufficient conventional capabilities so that lesser interests could be litigated without resort to nuclear war.[3]

Formal, ratified agreements were advocated as much for the military options they preserved as for those they foreclosed. The Limited Test Ban Treaty (LTBT), for example, reduced environmental contamination but, in driving testing underground, hardly slowed warhead development. The 1968 Non-Proliferation Treaty (NPT) slowed nuclear proliferation without significant enforceable constraints on the United States or other nuclear weapon state signatories. The Strategic Arms Limitation Treaty (SALT) contained the bipolar strategic competition within certain stabilizing parameters but permitted both sides to retain the technological option of pursuing multiple independently targetable reentry vehicles (MIRVs), the technology Washington believed would redress a strategic balance tilting dangerously in the Soviets' favor. Until the Strategic Arms Reduction Talks (START) of the late 1980s, only the Antiballistic Missile (ABM) Treaty arguably eliminated an option that the United States might have later chosen if it had been free to do so.

U.S. exceptionalism. Closely tied to the U.S. preference for unilateralism has been a deep belief in U.S. exceptionalism. This belief, based on faith in the advantages of free enterprise and the U.S. work ethic, has translated into expectations that U.S. technological development would guide the technological choices of others and, left unconstrained, would naturally prove superior. Such beliefs help explain the U.S. notion that the Soviets could be taught what a stabilizing force structure might look like and could be made to accept it by force of example as well as reason. This notion of U.S. prowess and force of example lay behind the strengthening through arms control of mutual assured destruction (MAD)—the force sizing that built on the pressured stability of bipolar "second strike" capabilities. Three assumptions were key to MAD's broad-based support: that the United States would retain its technological edge; that the concept of a second strike guarantee combined with limited resources would convince the Soviets not to seek superiority or even "equality" in offensive technologies; and that the Soviets would accept the U.S. logic that in an age of mutual deterrence, defensive technologies were destabilizing and should be eschewed by both sides.

The belief of the United States in its own technological superiority was, however, repeatedly challenged throughout the Cold War. The first Soviet nuclear test in 1949, Soviet acquisition of thermonuclear weapons in 1953, and the Sputnik I launch of 1957 fed a national paranoia that the Soviets must be stealing U.S. secrets (which history has demonstrated they often did). Later the Soviet challenge to U.S. scientific prowess inspired not only technological competition but also a certain respect for the adversary. The U.S. public went from regarding the Soviet system as crude and unsophisticated in the late 1940s to regarding it as almost invulnerable as it teetered on the verge of collapse in the 1980s.

National leaders who have framed national security programs compatible with the major elements of U.S. strategic culture—particularly the notion of U.S. exceptionalism—have found the public a powerful ally. For example, few modern arms control or defense proposals have more quickly captured the U.S. public's imagination as did Pres. Ronald Reagan's 1983 proposal known as the Strategic Defense Initiative (SDI).[4]

If Europeans viewed the defensive nature of the initiative as an unwelcome reminder of the flip side of the U.S. unilateralist impulse—isolationism—they also recognized the ingenuity of it. Washington was welding the nation's moral drive to a new technological challenge for which the United States was uniquely suited and around which military services, weapons builders, advanced civilian industries, and politicians could rally. Few nations would be able to compete in an effort fueled by so much domestic support.

SDI appealed to the U.S. public people for another reason: it seemed to champion a new scientific frontier as a reasoned response to the latest strategic challenge.

Scientific rationalism.   Political theorists have observed that people in the United States have historically held reason and science in high regard; World War II accentuated this trend as nuclear triumph brought the influence of scientists to a peak. Since then, the scientific community has had considerable influence on national security arms control policy, but its role has not been monolithic nor its impact uniform. After World War II the U.S. scientific ethic, which incorporates principles of universalism and openness, became infused with a potent internationalism. Émigré scientists who had fled excessively authoritarian regimes in Europe held deep suspicions of the state system. After Hiroshima, some of these scientists, articulating an ever-deepening distrust of government's use of science for augmenting national power, warned that the United States ought not to trust its political or technological ingenuity to preserve nuclear peace. To these scientists, the nuclear era meant the end of exceptional states and the arrival of the imperative of world government and global disarmament.

Yet, for others, the postwar stature of science brought new faith in scientific and social engineering. Many respected scientists joined an increasing number of their behavioralist colleagues in the social sciences in applying scientific principles to the art of changing international society and managing—not abolishing—the nuclear weapons establishment. These scientists believed the state system ought not be ignored or abolished but reorganized instead. Arms control would be the instrument of such reform. David Lilienthal, chairman of the Tennessee Valley Authority in the 1940s and a chief architect of the first U.S. effort to control the atom after World War II, advocated a scientific methodology and functionalist approach to controls. His disarmament plan, based on rigorous study of scientific "facts," was later endorsed by Bernard Baruch when the latter pressed his revision of the Acheson-Lilienthal plan on the international community.[5]

By the mid-1960s, social and "hard" scientists had coalesced in arms control advocacy and study groups under the auspices of organizations such as the American Academy of Arts and Sciences (AAAS) and Pugwash. Scientists' influence on arms control literature throughout the postwar period was profound; a volume produced by the AAAS that captured much of this influence has often been referred to as the bible of U.S. arms control thought.[6]

Although the special stature accorded scientific expertise was temporarily lost during the period of virulent anticommunism known as the McCarthy era, it reemerged in the late Eisenhower administration with the establishment of the Presidential Science Advisory Committee and has endured ever since. Such deference to "experts" has been so strong and long-lived that it may have contributed to public complacency as arms control became increasingly formulaic and opaque to the general public during the 1970s and 1980s. By the time SALT II was negotiated and Reagan was elected president, the arcane business of planning stabilizing strategic limitations had become politically rootless. Indeed, the public's rapid endorsement of the Reagan administration's simpler proposals for strategic arms reductions, and of its extraordinary plan for strategic defense, was arguably a reflection of the nation's faith in scientific expertise under a new guise.

The U.S. Realist School and Arms Control Thought

The influence of science on politics following World War II triggered an intellectual revolt from the U.S. realist school that has become a persistent theme in postwar arms control debates. Realist theorists objected both to scientific rationalism's excessive influence in Western political culture and to the notion of exceptionalism so deeply ingrained in the U.S. strategic psyche.

In the 1940s Reinhold Niebuhr, an eminent theologian and foreign policy critic, decried the U.S. "civil religion" of scientific rationalism. He believed a preoccupation with international reform and institution building after World War II had deflected policymakers from ensuring peace through a balance of power.

Similarly, Hans J. Morgenthau, a political scientist at the University of Chicago, cautioned against U.S. visions of sustainable superiority at the start of the Cold War. He noted that "nations have a natural propensity to underrate their enemy or to overrate themselves. These distortions are the weeds in the garden of patriotism and national pride." Writing in his influential book *Scientific Man Versus Power Politics,* Morgenthau went on to criticize any excessive faith "in the power of science to solve all problems and, more particularly, all political problems which confront man in the modern age."[7]

Morgenthau believed that scientism's universalistic, liberal bias had come to dominate Western political thought since the eighteenth century and had led to its decline. Indicative of this trend had been the rise of legalistic, ahistorically optimistic solutions to world order problems as epitomized by Wilson's League of Nations and evolving notions of "scientific disarmament."[8]

As postwar efforts to achieve internationalist solutions to the arms race collapsed in the late 1950s, it was the joining of realist balance of power principles with rationalist methodologies that created the most powerful and cohesive arms control school of modern times. This theoretical approach, termed elsewhere the Cambridge approach to arms control,[9] dominated arms control and general strategic thought in the United States for over two decades. Its basic tenets, outlined in the first chapter of this volume, not only became well-accepted principles of arms control in this country but constituted what became almost universally accepted as the dominant school internationally.

Knowledge of the intellectual backdrop to U.S. arms control helps explain the texture of the defense policy and arms control debates of the post–World War II period. However, texture cannot necessarily describe or predict outcomes. Ideas are the tools wielded by advocates; political processes determine who will have the opportunities to influence arms control outcomes.

The Arms Control Policy Process and the Role of Advocacy Groups

Arms control involves two parallel political processes: negotiations with one or more adversaries and internal negotiations between competing domestic interest groups and bureaucracies. Outcomes may be affected as much by the latter as by the former. During the interwar period, U.S. presidents successfully negotiated agreements with foreign governments only to be foiled in getting them ratified at home. Even initially popular treaties foundered in the absence of conscious efforts to rally domestic interest groups and, most important, the support of key members of Congress. Thus Wilson lost in his effort to secure U.S. participation in the League of Nations, and Calvin Coolidge failed to win ratification of the 1925 Geneva Protocol against chemical and bacteriological warfare, a U.S. initiative that 30 nations had already signed.

During the Cold War, as arms control became an institutionalized element of national security policy, intragovernmental negotiations over the formulation and ratification of arms control agreements became routinized. These bureaucratic interactions had a decisive impact on the shape of treaties and agreements and the evolution of the defense establishment more generally. To understand the modern process of formulating arms control and its impact on U.S. security policy, a brief review of the formal process of negotiation ratification and implementation is in order. This will be supplemented with a discussion of how the system actually works in practice. Domestic interests have a substantial effect on arms control outcomes, which in turn shape future efforts—sometimes in unanticipated ways.

The Constitutional Framework: How It Works in Practice

The U.S. Constitution provides several instruments for concluding international arms control agreements: treaties, congressional-executive agreements, and presidential agreements. Of these, the first and second are of greatest weight because they are legally interchangeable and, once concluded, constitute the law of the land.[10]

The Presidency

The Constitution provides, in Article II, Section 2, that the president "shall have the power, by and with the advice and consent of the Senate, to make treaties, provided two-thirds of the Senators present concur."[11] The president's constitutional power to negotiate allows the country all the flexibility, secrecy, speed, and surprise that that office can provide and that is so often necessary for the conclusion of agreements favorable to U.S. interests.

The president sets the overall pace and tone of an administration's arms control policy. Yet the manner in which he organizes his administration can affect the success of his program. Because negotiators must have leverage to win favorable terms in any draft accord, arms control policy makers rely heavily on good access to the president and strong bureaucratic staff work. The president generally has delegated authority to negotiate treaties to the secretary of state, who in turn has delegated these powers to specially appointed ambassadors, under-secretaries, or assistant secretaries. However, the president has also exercised his option to appoint special negotiators. This has at times caused tension in the arms control community. Perhaps the most famous case from the post–World War II period involved the Eisenhower administration.

From 1946 to March 1958 disarmament was managed out of the State Department. In 1955 Pres. Dwight Eisenhower named Harold Stassen as special assistant to the president for disarmament and provided him cabinet rank, direct access to the White House, and an independent budget. Later that year Eisenhower established the interdepartmental Special Committee on Disarmament Problems and named Stassen as chairman. Stassen's growing power miffed Secretary of State John Foster Dulles. In 1957, after considerable pressure from Dulles, the president dissolved Stassen's office and transferred its functions to State. Later that year Dulles caught Stassen in a misstep in negotiations and forced his resignation.

The Stassen incident illustrates that bureaucratic stature and access alone provide no guaranteed success for an arms control negotiator. Because national security policy involves a broad range of departments, successful policymaking requires consensus building. Presidential guidance and bureaucratic power also matter. In the later years of the Eisenhower administration, a cabinet-level committee advised the president on arms control policy. However, the president's insistence on consensus decisions meant that policymaking became paralyzed whenever disagreements ran deep. Such divisions and paralysis partly explain the failure to develop a consistent policy on negotiating a test ban in the late 1950s.

The Arms Control and Disarmament Agency

By the end of the Eisenhower administration the weakness of arms control policy making was widely acknowledged. Congress created the Arms Control and Disarmament Agency (ACDA) in 1961 by passing in amended form legislation submitted by Pres. John F. Kennedy to fix the flaws that were perceived in the institutional infrastructure. ACDA was to be a quasi independent agency attached to the State Department but with direct access to the president. The intent was to lend bureaucratic weight to arms control interests within the executive branch and to provide Congress better access to information on policy developments.[12] While other departments, including State, originally concurred in this development, official opinion was deeply divided.[13]

Although the bureaucratic influence of ACDA and its director waxed and waned over subsequent decades, the tension created by its awkward position both within and outside the Department of State continued through the SALT, START, and post–Cold War periods. ACDA's substantive bureaus (as of 1995) overlap with those of State and deal with most aspects of arms control: Multilateral Affairs; Strategic and Eurasian Affairs; Intelligence, Verification and Information Support; and Nonproliferation and Regional Arms Control. These bureaus support ACDA's significant responsibilities for implementing arms control agreements. However, without an authoritative voice on broader foreign policy questions or possession of an independent intelligence component (the Bureau of Intelligence, Verification and Information Support is not part of the intelligence community), ACDA has tended to be eclipsed by State on matters outside the confines of highly structured negotiations.

In 1993 the Department of State initiated a direct challenge to the existence of ACDA when the under-secretary for science and technology sought to subsume responsibility for arms control policy in a new bureau under her control. Congress regarded this, correctly, as a direct challenge to the integrity of ACDA and quickly blocked the move. However, the incident demonstrated that ACDA remains vulnerable; direct access to the president does not make up for the handicap of having to operate on a day-to-day basis at subcabinet level or being excluded from the deliberations of the National Security Council, as has occurred at times. ACDA's longevity may in fact reflect the ease with which any president can effectively include or exclude it from inner policy circles, as has been ACDA's fate on and off since its creation.

The Intelligence Community

The intelligence community plays a critical role at all stages of the arms control process. Apart from testifying before congressional committees on the government's ability to monitor compliance with any given accord, the community also must maintain adequate capabilities to support existing agreements, laws, and negotiations. The intelligence community funds research, technological development, and deployment of collection capabilities for desired or anticipated arms control measures to maximize the prospects of successfully negotiating and ratifying them. Those who advocate arms control sometimes forget that the effectiveness of the agreements and laws they advocate depends on the intelligence community's ability to monitor them. Legislating new sanctions, controls, or regulations is meaningless without intelligence to trigger them.

The critical support role the intelligence community plays can, however, cause considerable friction with arms control policy makers. First, the intelligence community's assessments of monitoring capabilities with regard to a proposed treaty can undermine prospects for ratification. U.S. intelligence, which is often credited with embodying objectivity and balanced consideration of facts, has wielded a powerful voice during the course of rationalistic U.S. debates on national security policy. It is precisely when significant national security issues arise, such as the ratification of an arms control treaty, that the intelligence community is asked to assess its ability to monitor the accord and the risks that others will cheat. To guard against unforeseen monitoring issues arising at the treaty ratification stage, modern presidents have usually required that intelligence officers work closely with delegations negotiating accords. But conflicts can develop as policymakers, anxious to build a policy consensus on negotiating strategy, discover contrary intelligence community views. Charges of politicization have thus arisen from both supporters and opponents of arms control.[14]

Second, particularly in eras of budget downsizing, the intelligence community can make financial or budgetary decisions that affect prospects for

an accord by underfunding research, development, or procurement of intelligence collection capabilities critical to monitoring it. Neither ACDA nor
the Department of State has a direct role in the intelligence programming
and budgetary process at the working levels where cuts by separate, low-
level programmers may make independent sense but collectively destroy a
crucial monitoring capability. When negotiations get under way or Congress holds hearings on the subject, policymakers can be either blindsided
or accused by Congress of being disingenuous. ACDA or State officials may
also suspect that an accord opposed by Defense has been deliberately if quietly sabotaged in this budgetary manner.

Third, the intelligence community can, in its efforts to fulfill its statutory obligations to protect sources and methods, object to or delay the use
of intelligence to diplomatically maneuver a foreign government suspected
of being in violation of a law or treaty or to share intelligence with international organizations dedicated to implementing safeguards or monitoring a
control regime.

Fourth, since the establishment of the congressional intelligence oversight committees, the intelligence community has tended to regard Congress as a legitimate consumer of its products. Executive branch officials
have often chafed at the willingness of intelligence officials to provide products and tailored briefings to individual members intent on building cases
against administration arms control policies or appointments. Sometimes
the better and more tailored the intelligence product, the greater the risks
attending disclosures on the Hill: any opponent of policy can leak intelligence out of context to disrupt negotiations.

Despite these sources of friction, the policy community has generally
developed a close, complex, and healthy relationship with the U.S. intelligence establishment. If problems occasionally arise, they are more than overshadowed by the strength of the mutual support and mutual dependence
that characterizes both communities' day-to-day business.

The Military

The Department of Defense (DOD) has been a key player in the U.S. arms
control process ever since arms control was distinguished from disarmament and accepted as a legitimate and integral aspect of national security
policy. This change in thinking about arms control began in the early 1950s
under Secretary of State Dean Acheson but did not become institutionalized until the Kennedy administration. By that time, arms control thought
had progressed to the point where substantial weapons restraint was believed possible through manipulation of force deployment and doctrine
alone. Under Robert McNamara, the Department of Defense began using
its annual statements on doctrine and budgets to signal the government's

interest in stabilizing deployments and force sizing concepts. Even though DOD's approach to self-restraint was later largely abandoned, the office of the secretary of defense has remained heavily involved in arms control policy.

The reasons behind DOD's involvement are several. In the first place, arms control strategy and policy can significantly affect force sizing, deployment, and doctrine. Negotiating strategies can drive defense policies and spending priorities by accelerating or decelerating weapons building programs to create or deny bargaining chips.[15] Second, arms control, regulatory, export, or security assistance policies can jeopardize the health of key industries in defense or high-technology commercial sectors. DOD has often weighed in strongly on Capitol Hill and in the executive branch to ensure that policymakers are aware when arms control policies may jeopardize technological capabilities in civilian or defense-related areas. DOD is often at its strongest when allied with firms that have active, engaged, and well-positioned representatives on Capitol Hill. Yet, to the extent that arms control infuses budgetary life into systems or technologies that are unnecessary or obsolete, such congressional-industry relations work against DOD interests.

DOD also manages a substantial part of the arms control monitoring infrastructure, including the On-Site Inspection Agency and its associated overseas gateways, and the logistical infrastructure for providing access to foreign inspectors coming to the United States.[16] Therefore any increase in monitoring activities will have a direct impact on DOD budgets and personnel allocations.

The Joint Chiefs of Staff (JCS) testify separately on treaties and are expected to give an unvarnished view of their military impact. The JCS has, on occasion, opposed administration policies—almost always severely damaging the administration position. For example, until 1993, the JCS consistently opposed a nuclear test ban in the belief that reduced reliability of warheads would be destabilizing. Military opposition, which has plagued the pursuit of a testing ban for years, has a powerful impact on public opinion. This is particularly true when the nation's top military officials appear before Congress to testify.

Congress

Congress participates in the arms control process by shaping public opinion, ratifying treaties, regulating commerce (export controls and sanctions), appropriating funds, and legislating changes in the organization of executive branch departments or their statutory authorities.

Congress has obviously had an impact on the organization of the executive branch for the negotiation and implementation of arms control policy *'local' interest*

through its statutory powers to create agencies and appropriate money for them. The role of Congress in these regards is not always altruistic; committees (and individual senators or representatives) have been known to redirect monies and programs from one agency to another more in the interest of wresting legislative power from other weaker committees than in the interest of a broader national purpose.[17]

Yet Congress's arguably greater powers lie in its role in amending and ratifying treaties and passing executive agreements. The Senate can also add unilateral statements, such as reservations or declarations, which modify the legal effect of the treaty for the United States. However, such steps can threaten to destroy the agreement if other parties to the treaty object. Unilateral declarations may clarify an understanding or interpretation that is shared among the parties. Once concluded, most legal opinion holds that treaties can be terminated only by the president or the president and Senate acting together.

Although the Constitution specifies no particular role for the House of Representatives in the treatymaking process, the implementation of treaties often requires the passage of domestic laws or appropriations of funds that require the involvement of the House.[18] In practice, the Senate and House work closely together as the relevant committees consider the terms of treaties.

The Chemical Weapons Convention (CWC), signed in 1993 and before the Senate for ratification in 1994 and 1995, is an excellent example of a treaty demanding coordinated consideration. While it is an arms control treaty that technically requires only concurrence of the Senate, implementing legislation necessarily involved multiple committees on both sides of the Hill. Senators and congresspersons must consider the impact of the CWC's arrangements for international "demand inspections" of suspect facilities (which may include private firms or households) on constitutionally protected privacy rights. Moreover, appropriations for funding the large bureaucracy necessary for handling the convention's national reporting requirements, which will involve U.S. firms creating or using chemicals for civilian and military purposes, and for creating the international secretariat to administer the convention required House approval.

Both houses of Congress are also involved in the regulation of commerce and the provision of military assistance and foreign aid. Congressionally authorized and funded security assistance programs and annual authorization and appropriations acts have proven to be particularly attractive tools for legislating the sanctioning of states that fail to abide by arms control norms.[19] The Arms Export Control Act, which authorizes the president to control the export of defense-related equipment and services, prohibits firms from marketing destabilizing or dangerous technologies and provides for punishment of those who do.

When Congress acts on any of its authorities, it almost always uses formal hearings or briefings to establish a historical and legal record. Given the opportunities that hearings provide for shaping subsequent votes on the floors of the House or Senate, presidents have been wise to co-opt key senators, congresspersons, or even congressional staff in positions to influence the hearing process. The executive may offer concessions on political appointments, give in on legislative matters, or, perhaps most effective, offer senators participation on delegations to the arms control talks. In return, senators may make public speeches of support. However, of equal import may be their efforts to exert quiet influence through the process of selecting witnesses, timing hearings to the administration's advantage, or meeting with fence-sitting colleagues to trade favors or votes. Of course, a president who ignores Congress may have all these subtle efforts turned against him, resulting in a congressional momentum powerful enough to sink treaties once considered publicly popular.

Treaty ratification involves the Senate Foreign Relations Committee (SFRC), Senate Armed Services Committee (SASC), and Senate Select Committee on Intelligence (SSCI). The last two committees submit reports to the first, which in turn reports to the full Senate. One of the more significant developments in the domestic politics of modern arms control has been the weight and significance attached to the intelligence hearings and the SSCI's detailed analysis of the prospects for monitoring and verifying any proposed accord.

The Private Sector

The formal and informal arms control policy process offers rich opportunities for citizens to engage. Since U.S. citizens do not vote on arms control programs or agreements per se, however, their impact on particular arms control issues is primarily made by activists and interest groups, many of whom have informal ties to the government.

As mentioned earlier, the arcane nature of modern weapons-related issues has meant that the most influential private sector opinion leaders on arms control have generally been well-known scientific or technical experts. The better the ties these individuals have had within the government, the more influential their views. During the late 1970s, Paul Nitze, a well-known strategic theorist and arms control expert, created the Committee on the Present Danger to publicize the jeopardy that conservatives felt attended the Carter administration's approach to SALT negotiations. His influence on the negotiations was substantial because of his close, cultivated connections with members of the delegation, Congress, and the press—all of which made him a force to contend with during the ratification process.

The number of private research organizations such as the Committee on the Present Danger increased dramatically during the Cold War, helping to frame often arcane and technical debates in laypeople's terms. The impetus for their creation came from concerned citizenry (who formed groups such as Ground Zero and the Federation of American Scientists), military services interested in linking strategic concepts to force planning (via studies done at research centers such as the RAND Corporation), and former bureaucrats turned policy advocates, waiting for turnovers of the executive branch.

Some of these institutes were created specifically to support or level focused opposition against the arms control process. These issue-based advocates blanket the Hill with leaflets and briefings designed to oppose particular accords. Other institutes have acted in quiet ways to prevent presidents from either intentionally or unintentionally killing treaties with neglect. For example, the prospects for timely ratification of the CWC were substantially improved by the role Washington's Stimson Center and other institutes played in informing congressional staff and thus keeping the convention alive during the transition between the Bush and Clinton administrations. The center also provided a repository of expertise on the CWC, which was lost when the Democrats in the new administration cleaned house after 12 years of Republican rule.

Industry

Industry has also been an active lobbyist on arms control issues. Most major private sector firms have Washington-area offices. These offices focus on courting key congressional members and staff on defense- and arms control–related committees. They also keep in close contact with representatives from the districts or states that host any of their facilities. These senators and members of Congress often weigh in with the executive branch if arms control policies threaten to hurt their companies or constituents. The best industrial lobbying efforts equip politicians to shape decisions early and quietly. Arms control efforts are politically difficult to oppose or alter for parochial reasons once they come before the Congress as matters of national security policy. Chemical manufacturers blocked the ratification of the 1925 Geneva Protocol on toxic gases by starting early to prepare; they understood that the public mood some years earlier had favored such a ban and feared the anticipated losses. Such lobbying techniques are often successful when used to shape the terms and timing of arms transfers, such as the 1991 sale of F-15s to Saudi Arabia. McDonnell Douglas, which faced a shutdown of its production line if the sale were successfully opposed, effectively lobbied Congress and the executive branch by assembling data on the geographic distribution of the new jobs that the contract would directly or indirectly create. Senators' offices provided the forum for discussions with the Israeli lobby about technical aspects of the sale in hopes that strong objections could be neutralized.

Of course, arms control has its industrial lobbyists too. Monitoring technologies often involve some of the most important U.S. high-tech firms in major, multimillion-dollar projects. Many of the firms that gain from weapons sales also gain from an expanded need for monitoring equipment and technology.

The evolving role of industry in arms control has had some interesting domestic effects and dynamics. Sometimes arms control negotiations have pitted firms against each other. For example, major chemical manufacturers, recognizing the impact the CWC would have on their industry, were able to devote resources and personnel toward helping to design the terms of the accord. Part of their plan was to secure an international agreement that would obviate the need for many of the burdensome licensing and export restrictions that had been applied over the years by Congress and the executive branch. But, in helping to shape the accord, these large manufacturers expressed a willingness to accept reporting requirements and inspection arrangements that smaller manufacturers believed might put them out of business. Their involvement, rather than helping the administration, threatened to backfire on it.

The general public is often unaware of the potential power of the industrial lobby because the extent of arms control's domestic economic impact is little appreciated. The CWC would affect not just the entire chemical industry but all firms that use chemicals either in processing or in final products, increasing their administrative costs. The comprehensive test ban has long been opposed by those who fear that without tests to perform, the U.S. infrastructure for weapons research and development would weaken as scientists looked for jobs elsewhere. Such economic fallout has been used as an argument for rejecting agreements with those adversaries who have a command economy; little can be done by the government in a capitalist country to bolster or even insulate an industry affected by an arms control agreement so that it is positioned to deter or respond to cheating by the adversary. In contrast, command economies can ensure that industries and their associated cadres of experts are kept intact even if costs skyrocket and markets collapse because of controls or prohibitions placed on their products. Of course, such command economies pay in other ways for their subjugation to national security priorities.

The Press and Public Opinion

The primary facilitator—and sometimes key initiator—of intragovernmental negotiations on arms control is the press. The press in turn owes much of its power to its other role as educator of the people.

In its formal role the press reports on developments in negotiations, characterizes the issues at stake, reports on the outcome of hearings, and publishes leaks. Informally, the press helps power brokers make contact with one another, doing favors and pocketing returns. Strobe Talbott recounts instances when members of the press brought players in the SALT negotiations together for a back-channel reconciliation and joining of the issues, some of which led to resolutions.[20]

The press also shapes public attitudes to treaties. Although the U.S. public is sympathetic to arms control purposes, it can strongly oppose particular treaties if they can be characterized as sacrificing a U.S. strategic advantage or are concluded by an administration that appears weak or untrustworthy on other grounds. The public's ambivalence on arms control allows politicians to use particular treaties to position themselves favorably at election time. Strong presidents interested in highlighting their roles as peacemakers often seek to push through arms control agreements before elections. Senators who have voted against defense spending or in favor of concessions on other national security matters under negotiation have sought to bolster their standing on national security by announcing their opposition to treaties they would have otherwise supported. Sen. Frank Church, a consistent supporter of arms control, opposed SALT II during his tough 1980 reelection campaign against a conservative Republican. Despite private hopes for passage of the agreement, Sen. Howard Baker opposed SALT II as well; he had supported Pres. Jimmy Carter on the Panama Canal Treaties and could not afford another "weak" position on a matter of national security policy.

While strategic culture explains some of the U.S. public's ambivalence to arms control and the ease with which politicians have shifted their allegiances, politicians have also used the economics of arms control to rally support or opposition to particular treaties or the arms control process more generally. On the one hand, and despite some of the economic advantages industries may gain from any particular agreement, arms control is still associated in the public mind with disarmament and economic recession. This is the legacy of public opposition to the military-industrial complex and the notion that government and industry have provoked wars and weapons building to raise the country out of recession at the turn of the century and intermittently thereafter. Thus, should presidents announce massive savings from arms control, opponents could dredge up latent fears of economic decline. In truth, however, arms control has rarely brought savings, and presidents have rarely, since World War II, argued that it would.

Conclusion

Although international politics helps to explain why states conclude arms control agreements, the particulars, including the content and timing of negotiations, turn on domestic politics and processes. In democracies, great ideas do matter—particularly if they resonate with the popular political culture. The art of leadership in the national security domain involves no little salesmanship.

Yet bureaucratic politics can also overwhelm salesmanship. In the interest of limiting intragovernmental bargaining and driving negotiations forward, access to policy has at times been limited and the chances for domestic consensus thus ruined. On the other hand, efforts to ensure access and regularize policy formulation, including the creation of ACDA, have led critics to charge that the arms control establishment has become more interested in sustaining the integrity of the process than in achieving meaningful agreements.

Such tensions inhere in any democracy; they need not be crippling. Indeed, the serious strategic threat that has provided the backdrop for all post–World War II U.S. arms control debates has contained them and made them manageable.

With the end of the Cold War, the collective sense of purpose that has provided arms control its domestic support and consistency may be weakening. Several trends that may lower domestic support for arms control are worth noting in this context: weakening of the arms control imperative, arms control's economic impact, government downsizing, and the potential decline of the intelligence budget.

Possible weakening of the arms control imperative.   The United States became involved in the arms control business largely because of the nuclear threat following World War II. As the bipolar balance of power became locked into place, arms control became a principal mechanism for ensuring that the tension inherent in the strategic relationship did not slide the United States into nuclear war. The prospect was so grim that U.S. citizens were willing to pay the high cost of an arms control establishment in order to avoid war. This may no longer be the case. With the collapse of the Soviet Union and the diminished threat of strategic nuclear war, the U.S. preference for economy, unilateralism, and freedom of action may move its policy away from negotiated arms control regimes and binding agreements. A return to old impulses does not mean that past agreements, such as the NPT, will not be supported or extended—only that new multilateral accords or complicated priority and inspection regimes are unlikely to be sought. That limits the military capabilities of all parties. The United States will readily support the disarmament of others, confidence building, and hortatory measures, but the era of pursuing "managed stability" through classic arms control negotiations and agreements may have passed.

Although the proliferation of weapons of mass destruction is competing for top billing among significant security threats, a domestic campaign to seek new or stronger agreements in this area has not materialized and seems unlikely to do so. The mood instead seems to have swung toward counterproliferation, the policy of developing technologies to fight and win battles involving nuclear, biological, and chemical weapons or unilaterally obstructing other states' efforts to acquire them. The alternative models for post–Cold War nonproliferation policy have been forcible disarmament (as practiced in postwar Iraq) and security battering (as described in the North Korean framework agreement).

The latter represents the first U.S.-promoted accord in which a disarmament objective is sought not through mutual restraint but through trade. The United States is buying out the North Korean nuclear weapons program with the assistance of donor states that stand to gain enhanced security once the North Korean program is dismantled. Monitoring exists, but it is one-way; weapons restraint is involved, but it is unilateral. Security battering may be the ideal U.S. approach to a post–Cold War environment in which the threats are acknowledged and security must be assured, but accords must bring evident gain, such as opened markets, at minimal costs or with minimal constraints on U.S. freedom of action. In this connection it is interesting to note that although the International Atomic Energy Agency's role was critical to the development of the framework negotiations, the public U.S. debate on the framework's merits was laced with criticisms of the IAEA and the NPT regime. The North Korean crisis was viewed by some in the Washington security establishment as an object lesson in the inadequacy of multilateral efforts at arms control—a judgment that was more widely, publicly, and fairly reached in retrospect on the Iraqi program, which was nurtured by a government in good standing as party to the NPT. Unfortunately, the reawakening of the U.S. unilateralist impulse could delay or undermine new multilateral initiatives or regimes that could provide real security benefits. Indeed, in the chemical weapons area, the CWC languished for almost three years as legislators seriously weighed the arms control gains against the domestic economic costs of a broad but nonaggressive multilateral accord.

The rising importance of arms control's economic impact.   The U.S. commitment to arms control has, until recently, fit neatly with the country's political culture. Negotiations on the strategic nuclear balance with the Soviet Union certainly highlighted U.S. rationalism and technological prowess; and while the costs of the arms race were high, they had more to do with building sophisticated defenses than with monitoring accords. In any case, the expense could be blamed on Moscow.

However, arms control designed to impose multilateral controls on technology or to raise others' confidence may soon get more expensive than the United States believes warranted by the threat. Recent chemical attacks in Japan and the 1995 Oklahoma City bombing suggest that multilateral regimes may be irrelevant in a world where individual terrorists are the culprits and their access to weapons is through illicit markets over which governments have little control. While the CWC will contribute to deterring state actors, it will also require the establishment and funding of a major new international organization, for which the United States will pay the greatest share, and which will levy information requirements on individual firms in each participating country. Intrusive inspections may bring foreign inspectors to all corners of the United States to probe the operations of U.S. plants. Any interruption in operations to accommodate the government could be expensive—either for the company or for the taxpayer. To the extent that facilitating CWC inspections involves compromises on principles such as the prohibition on warrantless searches, the nonmonetary costs will seem even higher. While action on the CWC was expected in 1995, the vetting of the agreement by Capitol Hill staff has already exposed the contentiousness of the agreement in conservative quarters. Selling the treaty will require advocates to persuade the U.S. public that the terrorist threat has not eliminated the threat from adversarial states and that the gains are worth the costs. This argument seems clearly to be getting tougher, despite the long-term value of the accord.

Government downsizing.   The budgetary consciousness of the post–Cold War U.S. public is also having an impact on the existing U.S. arms control establishment. The debate over the merits of retaining ACDA is likely to persist; in fact, political momentum seems to be building for abolishing the institution. Though this change, should it occur, may not have a significant effect on the practice of arms control, it would silence independent advocacy of arms control interests at the highest government levels and would likely fold the development and execution of arms control policy back into the Department of State. This would return the process to its form in the early 1950s, when the secretary of state largely determined the pace and salience of the arms control agenda.

The potential decline of the intelligence budget.   Perhaps least appreciated of the trends likely to significantly affect arms control over the next 10 years is the expected decline in the intelligence budget. As the budget is squeezed, intelligence for the war fighter is likely to make first claim on resources. Since budget planning and programming rests largely with the director of central intelligence and the secretary of defense, intelligence capabilities for new or anticipated arms control negotiations may decline, or at least become less robust. Such decline will influence what can be negotiated as well as the prospects for Senate ratification of any agreement that has been reached. Given the length required to develop and deploy intelligence assets, even a desirable agreement may not be salvageable if inadequate monitoring capabilities are determined to exist.

It is difficult to discern at this point which set of themes is correct. After all, the United States has been motivated both by its ideals and its self-interest in all aspects of foreign and national security policy. The indicators are, nonetheless, that U.S. preferences for unilateralism will dominate the post–Cold War arms control environment and that financial factors will become weightier considerations in U.S. endorsement of arms control measures than they have in the recent past. Whichever trends become dominant, domestic consensus—or lack thereof—will be a major determinant of what the United States can accomplish in arms control at the turn of the century.

Suggested Reading

Adler, Emmanuel. "Arms Control, Disarmament and National Security: A Thirty-Year Retrospective and a New Set of Anticipations." *Daedelus, Journal of the American Academy of Arts and Sciences,* vol. 120, no. 1, winter 1991. The author explores the relationship between U.S. strategic culture, politics, and the nuclear arms control process after World War II. Other articles in the volume are also of interest.

Asgood, Robert. *Ideals and Self Interest in America's Foreign Relations.* Chicago: University of Chicago Press, 1953. The classic work on U.S. strategic culture and national security policy.

Kissinger, Henry A. *American Foreign Policy.* New York: W. W. Norton and Co., Inc., 1969. Includes somewhat difficult but enlightening exposition of the role domestic factors play in foreign and national security policy by a significant player in Cold War arms control policy who is often charged with having overlooked them.

Moore, John Norton, Frederick S. Tyson, and Robert F. Turner. *National Security Law.* Durham, N.C.: Carolina Academic Press, 1990. This volume is an excellent comprehensive resource for those wishing to understand the legal and culture foundations for U.S. national security policy. Although all chapters are relevant, those on constitutional processes, security doctrine, nuclear weapons, and arms control are worth special study.

Sheehan, Michael J. *Arms Control Theory and Practice.* New York: B. Blackwell, 1988. The author discusses the origin and nature of U.S. arms control theory and practice, distinguishing them from disarmament. Sheehan also covers domestic aspects of the process often overlooked in other texts: economic implications, the politics of domestic bargaining on arms control, and technological change. Sheehan focuses on why superior strategic arms control achieved so little during the Cold War.

Talbott, Strobe. *The Master of the Game.* New York: Vintage Books, 1989. A very readable account of the career of Paul Nitze, a key figure in the history of post–World War II arms control and national security policy. An excellent text for exploring the ways in which U.S. strategic culture affects the outlook and actions of individuals making arms control policy.

Notes

1. Jennifer E. Sims, *Icarus Restrained: An Intellectual History of Nuclear Arms Control, 1945–1960* (Boulder, Colo.: Westview Press, 1990), p. 4.

2. William C. Widenor, writing about the politics of Wilson's lost peace, notes that the Progressive Party was split on the issues of the treaty and the league. See Widenor, "The League of Nations Component of the Versailles Treaty," in Michael Krepon and Dan Caldwell, eds., *The Politics of Arms Control Treaty Ratification* (New York: St. Martin's Press, 1991).

3. The guidelines for the U.S. strategic building program designed to ensure U.S. deterrence at reasonable cost became, when projected onto a bipolar map, arms control's formula for strategic stability: mutual assured destruction.

4. For more on SDI, see Chapter 6.

5. See Chapter 5 for further discussion of the Baruch Plan.

6. See Chapter 1.

7. Hans J. Morgenthau, *Scientific Man Versus Power Politics* (Chicago: University of Chicago Press, 1946), p. vi.

8. Sims, *Icarus Restrained*, p. 61. See also Hans J. Morgenthau, "The H-Bomb and After," *Bulletin of Atomic Scientists* (March 1950), pp. 76–79.

9. Sims, *Icarus Revisited*, esp. pp. 19–45. This approach is also summarized in Jennifer Sims, "Arms Control: Thirty Years On," in *Daedalus* (American Academy of Arts and Sciences: Winter 1991), pp. 251–272.

10. Unlike treaties, congressional-executive agreements may be ratified by majorities of both houses of Congress. The Supreme Court has found such agreements to have the same domestic legal authority as treaties; presidential agreements, which are based on powers that inhere only in the executive, do not.

11. For excellent legal background on the treatymaking process and other matters of law related to arms control, see John Norton Moore, Frederick S. Tipson, and Robert E. Turner, *National Security Law* (Durham, N.C.: Carolina Academic Press, 1990).

12. The White House, citing executive privilege, had often denied Congress important information while the Departments of State and Defense had tended to relegate arms control to a second-order priority.

13. Former secretary of defense Robert Lovett announced that the agency would be "a Mecca for a wide variety of screwballs"; the Joint Chiefs of Staff worried that the director's access to the president might undermine defense interests and national security policy; Sen. Barry Goldwater opined that the United States was "developing a new mother-love type of agency." Duncan L. Clarke, *Politics of Arms Control: The Role and Effectiveness of the U.S. Arms Control and Disarmament Agency* (New York: Free Press, 1979), pp. 22–23.

14. Such charges were evident during the debate over whether to sanction Pakistan under the Symington Amendment for having developed a nuclear explosive device. The intelligence community repeatedly stressed then, and on other occasions, that its job is to expose what is known but not to pass judgment on whether any given set of facts is sufficient for triggering sanctions.

15. Bargaining chips are assets brought to the negotiating table primarily to be used as items for trade during discussions with one's competitor.

16. FBI and DOD counterintelligence is also engaged in protecting U.S. military and industrial secrets from foreign spies who might be participating in such inspections.

17. Often such raids on a committee's power are done with the collusion of the raiding committee's client department in the executive branch. In 1993 the Senate Armed Services Committee raided a weak Senate Foreign Relations Committee (SFRC) by authorizing significant new activities and funds to the DOD for conducting counterproliferation policy. The SFRC and the State Department were both

caught by surprise, but their protests brought only minimal changes in the new authorities.

18. While legal opinions have varied on the subject, it is generally agreed that the House may not refuse to pass laws or appropriate funds for treaties signed by the president and ratified by the Senate. However, in practice, the senators' close consultations with House colleagues have meant that controversial funding or legal provisions have been dealt with collegially and as part of the ratification process to avoid congressional division or abrogation of obligations. (*National Security Law,* pp. 792–796.)

19. The term *security assistance* generally refers to programs associated with the Arms Export Control Act and Part II of the Foreign Assistance Act (22 U.S.C. SS 2751-276c, 1982, and SS 2301-2349aa-b 1982). These programs have changed in scope, character, and geographic orientation since World War II. While their scope has grown overall, grants have given way to sales on credit, and assistance has spread from Europe to East Asia and the Middle East. Michael John Matheson, "Arms Sales and Economic Assistance," *National Security Law,* pp. 1111–1125.

20. Strobe Talbott, *Masters of the Game: Paul Nitze and the Nuclear Peace* (New York: Vintage Books, 1988), pp. 151, 353.

4

Arms Control, Verification, and Transparency

Joseph F. Pilat

As outlined in Chapter 1, arms control agreements have traditionally been assessed on the basis of their ability to meet three objectives—to reduce the risks of war, to reduce defense costs, and to limit damage should war occur. Whether these objectives have the same importance in the future as they did during the Cold War, the ability to meet them in a treaty or agreement depends ultimately on whether the parties are in compliance. Indeed, the entire arms control enterprise has often been judged on compliance grounds. So it should not be surprising that the acceptability of proposals to limit or eliminate nuclear and other arms since 1945 has been largely perceived not only on the basis of the proposals' potential impact on global power relations and domestic politics but also on their provisions for verification.

For the United States during this period, the capability to ensure that an accord on arms was being implemented by the other party or parties has been a critical, albeit not the only, criterion for entering into an arms control agreement. As a consequence, arms negotiations were limited in scope and number during the Cold War. Even before the fall of the Berlin Wall and the end of the Cold War, verification was becoming more and more important and intrusive, as attitudes in the Soviet Union changed, as the challenges of arms control became increasingly more complex, and as monitoring and verification technologies improved. Though these changes allowed certain achievements, the growing complexity of negotiations and the increasing requirements for intrusive verification suggested that for the duration of the Cold War arms control efforts would be limited.

The future may, however, be unlike the past. The end of the Cold War and the collapse of the Soviet Union may have fostered arms control, but the movement began before these landmark events. Since the mid-1980s arms control has flourished, with the conclusion of agreements on the elimination of intermediate- and shorter-range nuclear forces, the reduction of strategic nuclear forces, the limitation of conventional armed forces in Europe, the elimination of chemical weapons, and a host of lesser agreements regulating arms and promoting confidence primarily in U.S.-Soviet and European arenas. Not all of these agreements are in force, but together they appear to represent a golden age of arms control. Will it mark the end of an era? Will arms control as we have known it during the Cold War have only a limited role in the post–Cold War era? Will the future of arms control be less dependent on verification? What will be the fate of the extensive verification regimes provided for in agreements that were negotiated during the Cold War? Will openness, transparency, and confidence-building measures be used in arenas once reserved for formal verification measures?

Arms Control and Verification: Historical Overview

The earliest U.S. arms control initiatives after World War II, including the Baruch Plan and Pres. Dwight Eisenhower's Atoms for Peace proposal, envisaged stringent on-site verification measures. The Soviet Union, on the other hand, favored vague, unverifiable proposals that sought to capture the high moral ground and, irrespective of whether agreement was reached, offered political advantages.

During the Cold War, the U.S. position on the importance of verification remained largely unchanged, and the Soviets also gradually came to accept the need for verification. Soviet moves toward the U.S. position over the last decades were possible not only because U.S.-Soviet relations improved but also because new technologies for remote detection and monitoring lessened the need for physically intrusive verification measures and thereby reduced Soviet fears of possible U.S. intelligence benefits derived from treaties and agreements.

During the 1950s the United States could not adequately monitor Soviet nuclear weapon testing and production sites. Nor could the United States monitor Soviet missile launch sites. U.S. initiatives to make Soviet weapons activities more transparent were consistently rejected by the Soviet Union. These included overflights by aircraft, envisioned in President Eisenhower's 1955 Open Skies proposal, along with on-site inspection proposals. Until the early 1960s, disagreements over the necessity of verification and mutually acceptable verification provisions were significant factors in the failure of U.S.-Soviet efforts to conclude arms control agreements. Aside from political and military considerations, these disagreements arose because the technologies available necessitated intrusive measures for detecting and monitoring areas that might be covered by the terms of a treaty or an agreement. During this period, on-site inspection provisions (although not on the territory of the United States or the Soviet Union) were contained in the agreement on limiting arms in Antarctica (1959) and in the safeguards administered by the International Atomic Energy Agency (IAEA), which was established in 1957.

Only after the launch of Sputnik in 1957 did a remotely sensing, mutually acceptable means of verification present itself. Space-based observation and sensing devices made possible many of the arms control achievements between the United States and the Soviet Union in the 1960s and 1970s. The importance of space-based verification capabilities is evident in the areas of testing and strategic arms limitations. The 1963 Treaty Banning Nuclear Weapon Tests in the Atmosphere, in Outer Space, and Under Water (also known as the Limited Test Ban Treaty [LTBT]) was made possible because of the development of verification technologies, notably the Vela program.[1] And the strategic arms limitation treaties (SALT I and II) of the 1970s were made possible by the availability of space-based surveillance technologies that allowed each side to monitor the missile launch sites of the other.

Multilateral agreements concluded during this period—including the Outer Space Treaty (1967), the Seabed Treaty (1972), and the Biological and Toxin Weapons Convention (1972)—frequently had no verification provisions and were largely unverifiable except to the extent that national technical means (NTM—technical intelligence collection capabilities, such as remote sensing satellites) could play a role in assessing the activities of the states. A notable multilateral exception was the 1968 nuclear Non-Proliferation Treaty (NPT). The treaty was acceptable not because of NTM, which in any event were insufficient for the task, but primarily because of the development of technologies for on-site inspection utilized in IAEA safeguards. This development made possible some assurances that materials in civil use were not being diverted to proscribed military uses. Of course, the NPT did not provide for mandatory on-site inspection of the nuclear facilities of the nuclear weapon states party to the treaty but only of the nonnuclear weapon states party to the treaty.[2]

With respect to the testing restraints envisioned at this time, there have been suggestions that a comprehensive test ban was within reach in the early 1960s.[3] However, the United States simply did not have the means to verify compliance with a ban on underground testing at the time. Technologies for verifying underground nuclear testing have since been developed, allowing U.S. and Soviet negotiators to conclude the Threshold Test Ban Treaty (TTBT) of 1974 and the Peaceful Nuclear Explosions Treaty (PNET) of 1976 and to enter into negotiations during 1977–1980 on a comprehensive test ban treaty. However, seismic methods envisaged and available for these earlier efforts were limited. Due to U.S. concerns about verification, the TTBT and PNET were not ratified until those specific concerns were remedied by protocols that allowed on-site inspections to limit the ambiguities of teleseismic detection and monitoring. The recent reopening of comprehensive test ban negotiations hinges on improved teleseismic methods, changes in the political climate after the Cold War, and the belief that pursuing a comprehensive test ban would enhance the extension prospects of the NPT.

In the nuclear arena, the reduced size and greater mobility of new armaments, as well as moves to actually reduce rather than merely limit arms, have vastly complicated the verification problems experienced during the strategic arms negotiations of the late 1960s and 1970s. However, the Soviet Union (now Russia) has been willing to accept intrusive on-site inspection provisions that allowed the completion of the Intermediate-Range Nuclear Forces (INF) Treaty in 1987 and the Strategic Arms Reduction Treaties (START I and II) of the early 1990s. The INF Treaty contained unprecedented verification measures, including on-site inspections of the elimination of intermediate-range nuclear forces at special installations and missile sites, as well as of declared and formerly declared missile operating bases and missile support facilities; continuous on-site monitoring of the portals of designated missile production facilities; noninterference with NTM; and other cooperative measures. START verification measures are even more stringent than those of the INF Treaty. These include data exchanges, baseline inspections to verify the accuracy of the data, on-site observation of the elimination of systems to achieve treaty limits, continuous on-site monitoring of the perimeters and portals of certain production and support facilities, short-notice on-site inspections of declared and formerly declared facilities and suspect sites, noninterference with NTM, and cooperative measures.

The problems of verification in the chemical, biological, and conventional areas are even more difficult, although fundamental shifts in the political landscape have made agreements here possible as well. Accords aimed at building confidence on conventional arms, like the Stockholm Agreement (1986) and the more recent confidence- and security-building measures agreements of the early 1990s, are limited and in many ways peripheral to arms reductions. They are verifiable, to the extent required, by national technical means and on-site inspection provisions. But verification of the ambitious Conventional Forces in Europe (CFE) Treaty (1990), which involves significant arms reductions and geographic restraints on deployments, requires extensive data exchange, NTM, on-site inspections, and cooperative measures.

Verification, Intelligence, and Compliance: Issues and Assessments

Verification and Intelligence

In principle and practice, verification involves monitoring treaty-limited items and activities and assessing compliance on the basis of that monitoring and other relevant information. Aside from this declared purpose of verification, a common goal of verification provisions is to deter the parties from violations. This objective already presumes a reasonable level of effectiveness for the measures. But it is a difficult standard for verification, because like broader deterrence policies, it is difficult to know what deters and under what conditions deterrence operates. What risks is a party to a treaty willing to take? What is its sense of the benefits of cheating? What is its expectation of a significant response?

Setting Verification Standards

Some level of trust and some expectation of good faith on the part of the participants in arms control agreements are probably prerequisites of their being negotiated, but the stakes are usually too high to rely on such considerations alone. One could also presume compliance with arms control and disarmament treaties and other agreements based on clearly defined mutual interests, but even this has not been deemed sufficient in most cases. The Outer Space Treaty, the Seabed Treaty, and the Biological Weapons Convention (BWC) are notable exceptions to these rules. While these treaties do not have verification provisions, there is new interest in establishing a verification protocol for the BWC. Most agreements have some verification provisions, which provide a means of monitoring compliance.

The debate over verification has not focused on the need to verify compliance—for this requirement of arms control and disarmament is widely if not universally accepted—but rather on the degree to which the verification measures can be effective in ensuring compliance. While this issue of effectiveness is important in itself, the debate has often masked a larger debate about the value of arms control in general or of the specific treaty or agreement being considered. The advocates of stringent verification measures have been charged with trying to scuttle arms control, while those willing to accept less intrusive or comprehensive measures appeared to their critics as advocating empty agreements for their own sake, agreements that could only provide a false sense of confidence. These positions are difficult to assess in a vacuum; what is clear is that there are no means to ensure compliance at anything near 100 percent. Yet the inability to do so has not been seen as damning to the arms control endeavor. Indeed, ensuring the practicability of agreements as well as their political acceptability has frequently meant forgoing the most intrusive means possible.

Measuring Verification Effectiveness

The measure for verification effectiveness must in the end be national security. As Pres. Dwight Eisenhower recognized, all arms control involves some level of risk to national security, but that risk must be balanced against the benefits. The manner in which that risk has been discussed involves the military significance of noncompliance or cheating. If an agreement involves a significant security risk from cheating, the verification standards must be higher; if it does not, they can in practice be relaxed. The agreement's verification provisions must be able to provide early warning of militarily significant noncompliance, with sufficient time to allow the appropriate military or other response. In assessing verification requirements, such factors as the probability of cheating and the prospects of detecting noncompliance must be taken into account.

Progress in technologies, especially those deployed on satellites, has allowed these concerns to be addressed and has helped make possible far-reaching arms control agreements. Technologies have in essence made it possible to obtain good information without being physically intrusive or requiring a large contingent of human inspections on the territory of the other parties to an agreement. National technical means, including photo reconnaissance, radar and electronic surveillance, and seismic and acoustic sensing, are critical to the monitoring on which verification depends. Technologies are also important to on-site inspections, which have become more important in the post-INF environment.

Treaties and agreements have historically provided for enhanced verification measures such as noninterference with NTM, on-site inspections, data exchanges, cooperative measures, and bodies to address disputes. Whatever the specific verification provisions of treaties and agreements, however, all the knowledge a party has about the other party or parties comes into play in the verification process. Intelligence is thus closely related to verification, and intelligence can guide verification by providing an alarm or triggering mechanism for, say, challenge inspections (prompt adversarial inspections called for by a party or parties to an agreement to prove or disprove a suspected treaty violation by another party or parties). This means that verification is facilitated by open societies. The activities of closed totalitarian systems are difficult to verify. To the extent that we are witnessing a global democratic revolution, formal verification standards may be eased and will certainly become less significant. Verification, by providing information related to forces or activities, can provide political benefits to a state's intelligence apparatus, whether or not related to the verified accord. For this reason alone states without strong intelligence capabilities might pursue more intrusive verification during treaty negotiations. On the other hand, states with intelligence assets may not have to rely on agreed verification provisions as much as others.[4]

Assessing and Responding to Noncompliance

A key question confronting the verification process is how to determine compliance and noncompliance. Ultimately this must be a matter of judgment.

Because verification often involves sensitive intelligence, charges of noncompliance are difficult to address and assess publicly. Indeed, the consequences of revealing intelligence sources may inhibit the use of available intelligence. This difficulty is compounded by the fact that arms control agreements may be hundreds of pages long and have ambiguous or arcane language, leading to loopholes that one or the other side may exploit without technically being in violation of the agreement. Moreover, judgments may not be based on clear information but may themselves be ambiguous. Such violations as the discovery of the construction of the Krasnoyarsk radar, which was clearly prohibited by the Antiballistic Missile (ABM) Treaty, are one matter. But disputes over the alleged violations by the Soviet Union of the TTBT and SALT II have been far more difficult to assess.[5]

One of the problems when encountering noncompliance is how to respond, because international organizations, including the UN, have not been able to act effectively, especially if permanent members of the Security Council (with a veto) are involved. UN or other collective action, as provided for by treaties and agreements, can be more effective if the violator is a pariah state or a small power or has been defeated in war. However, even in these cases the results of collective action are by no means certain.

If a violation is clear or probable, diplomacy will certainly be attempted to rectify the problem, but its effects are uncertain. In the U.S.-Soviet context during the Cold War, diplomacy had some utility but was often slow and ultimately unsatisfying. Embargoes, sanctions, and the threat or use of military force in response to violations could be significant in themselves if diplomatic solutions fail, and they may even have a deterrent effect. The problem is getting a consensus on action, which is very difficult. Responses are in the hands of the party or parties that are affected by the cheating, a situation that may not provide the aggrieved party many good options, especially if it is a small or weak state. Of course, violations may be ignored by the parties, depending on the way they assess their response options and on the political and security context. A response may be equivalent to abrogating the agreement. Even publicly airing violations has dangers, as it may undermine the agreement, particularly if no action is taken against the violator or violators.

Violations cannot and should not be ignored, but dealing with them is by no means easy. Even if a violation is not significant, it may indicate a pattern of behavior or be a test of a party's resolve. If it is not responded to, the violating party might feel it has carte blanche to violate the agreement further, thereby undermining the legal regime established by the agreement. It may even lead to repudiation of the treaty or agreement. Violations brought before the public can bring the domestic political forces and the international community into the picture and indicate to a violator the costs of its actions. Or, as suggested above, such publicity could undermine the agreement.

Changing Patterns of Verification

Verification efforts will for the foreseeable future be defined by recent agreements—agreements on which negotiations began during the Cold War. These agreements, especially the CFE and the START treaties, have elaborate verification systems that reflect Cold War concerns. Given post–Cold War uncertainties about Russia and the former Eastern bloc, intrusive verification provisions remain important to the United States and the West. But already these agreements and their verification provisions seem marginal to what are now seen as higher-priority concerns: the fate of the old Soviet nuclear arsenal and special nuclear material stockpiles, conflict in the former Yugoslavia, and the like. These new concerns can at best be only marginally affected by existing arms accords and are being dealt with through ad hoc measures such as the Cooperative Threat Reduction Program. As a consequence, we will see the verification mechanisms of these agreements being carried out, and they will be particularly important if Russia continues to veer to the right. Otherwise, they can be expected to decline in significance over time and are not likely to be duplicated in future efforts to restrain or reduce arms.

The Drive Toward Multilateralism

Unlike the situation during the Cold War, in recent years the interest in and debate over verification appear to be moving from a bilateral and Europe-centered matter to a global issue, which raises questions about verification and its future role. The general sense of expectations is well reflected in a recent UN report. UN Secretary-General Boutros Boutros-Ghali stated the following in a report on post–Cold War arms regulation and disarmament in 1992:

> What has happened in the relationship between the two major military powers, the Russian Federation and the United States of America, is remarkable. ... [It] has permitted each to undertake unilaterally profound nuclear disarmament measures—notably in the field of tactical nuclear weapons—which augurs well for the institution of confidence-building as an important element of the evolving international security system. Such steps should not be confined to the exclusive domain of these two nations. We must strive to create conditions in other regions of the world which would enable more States to undertake similar commitments.... The goal is to extend disarmament efforts to include not only bilateral agreements but also multilateral arrangements in a world-wide process involving all States.[6]

The reasons behind these views are many. First, some of the most striking successes in arms control have been in the area of verification, where provisions calling for unprecedented intrusiveness have allowed the completion of agreements previously held to be impracticable. While there have been limits on intrusiveness, it is the progress in breaking down old barriers that has most captured attention. There is, as a consequence, a desire to emulate in multilateral forums the successes in the bilateral arena, either out of a genuine commitment to internationalism or from a fear of becoming irrelevant to the dynamics of a changing world.

Second, there is a perceived need to move rapidly in some areas of great interest that, in the view of virtually all states, can be effectively considered only on an international or regional level. With this new reality come assertions of the rights of all states to play a role in prospective verification regimes. This interest has been accompanied in some important cases by a strong distrust of the role of international organizations, whether embedded in the UN or in technical organizations like the IAEA.

Third, even when the scope of the arms control effort does not require or even makes unlikely the participation of other states, as in strategic nuclear arms control, other states have frequently sought a role in verification. Fearing ignorance, or dependence on information and on assessments of the situation by the United States or the former Soviet Union in areas that are seen to affect their security, these states have proposed international verification schemes such as France's proposal for an International Satellite Monitoring Agency (ISMA) and Canada's PAXSAT, or "peace satellite" verification initiative.[7] In a related manner, European support for the Open Skies Treaty was, at least in part, based upon the efforts of both Eastern and Western European states to carve out a more active role in monitoring arms and arms control activities in a rapidly changing post–Cold War European security environment.

In addition to such political motives for promoting international and multilateral verification regimes, there are technological forces at work as well. The technologies essential for verification, especially the remote surveillance technologies used in the national technical means of the United States and the former Soviet Union, are, like other military technologies, being driven by developments in the commercial sector. Technologies once the preserve of the superpowers alone are becoming more widespread—for example, France's SPOT satellites, which sell high-resolution imagery on the open market. With that technological spread have come schemes for multilateral technical means, or for international cooperation in the development of enabling technologies. These and related concepts are being put forward along with the actual use of commercial capabilities to provide military and arms control monitoring capabilities. In this vein, Russia also has offered to sell high-quality, high-resolution imagery from satellites for a variety of uses, including verification. With the disintegration of the Soviet Union, these capabilities (and more) can be expected to be for sale on the open market.

The spread of these technologies, then, appears inevitable. It will not occur without disruptions to the status quo of current surveillance capabilities and related fields. Whether these technologies will truly revolutionize international and multilateral arms control, however, is still uncertain. A series of practical impediments, not the least of which is cost, could limit the application of these technologies by the great majority of states and, perhaps as a consequence, limit their role in broader arms control efforts.

Despite some real practical limitations, such factors have led to a resurgence of interest in old, grandiose schemes for a UN verification organization and international satellite monitoring agency, among others. Yet, it is unlikely that this interest will bear fruit in the foreseeable future, except in isolated cases. In the chemical arena, for example, the Chemical Weapons Convention (CWC)'s verification regime is being developed, in part, on the basis of IAEA experience. Continuing regional arms control activities can be expected to be promoted for political ends as a more expansive Europe seeks an appropriate security structure.

The Future of Multilateral Verification: Problems and Prospects

The grounds for pessimism in this assessment are numerous. First, neither the United States nor Russia, nor indeed any other Soviet successor state engaged in inherited arms control efforts, permits international or neutral third-party verification of bilateral or otherwise limited accords now and is unlikely to do so in the future. In this regard, the IAEA efforts to get involved in the verification of bilateral nuclear accords have been singularly unsuccessful for over a decade. Interest in pursuing this matter again exists within the agency. Some support existed within the Clinton administration for using the agency, for example, to monitor "excess" plutonium and highly enriched uranium from dismantled nuclear weapons and other defense programs. Such involvement would not only have been highly inappropriate during the Cold War, but by placing the agency at the center of possible U.S.-Soviet disputes and by drawing scarce IAEA resources it could have threatened the performance of the agency in implementing its primary mission, which is safeguarding civil nuclear facilities to prevent diversions to illicit military purposes. Besides, the old bilateral verification process had in the waning years of the Cold War already resulted in a level of intrusiveness that the IAEA continues to seek to emulate.

For these and other reasons, in the foreseeable future international or third-party verification is highly unlikely to become the rule. The reason for this assessment is simple—verification is not politically neutral. When intrusive verification has been successful, from IAEA to INF inspections, it has generally involved some degree of reciprocity. Reciprocity also is germane when one considers the possible transfer of both proprietary information and weapons technology through inspections—after all, there are facilities or activities that the United States could allow Russians to inspect, with the expectation that such inspections would not be furthering Russian nuclear weapons programs. Similar inspections, however, would be unacceptable if performed by a non-NPT party.

Second, beyond the CWC, which was concluded in 1993, and a prospective chemical test ban, there do not appear to be many prospects for an international accord requiring international verification measures. While these agreements will require, if fully realized and implemented, extensive international verification activity, proponents of a greater international role have expected more. Nevertheless, nonproliferation verification is unlikely to expand dramatically.

To be sure, the experience in Iraq after the Gulf War and in North Korea in the mid-1990s demonstrated the limits of the international nuclear nonproliferation regime. Other areas of nonproliferation (e.g., missile technology and fissile material controls) are less mature, so no grand new international regimes are likely. Efforts to improve the nonproliferation regimes will more likely occur through ad hoc, incremental initiatives. To date, only chemical weapons, proliferation, and the negotiations on a comprehensive test ban have spurred a consensus in the international community on an urgent need for action. There is, however, considerable interest in the UN and the Conference on Disarmament (CD) in pursuing outer space arms control, a radiological weapons convention, and other international initiatives. A possible additional regime may exist in the area of a verification protocol to the BWC.

Beyond Europe, there are currently few prospects for regional accords that would not be verified primarily on a national basis rather than multilaterally, unless one is dealing, as in the case of Iraq, with a defeated power. Even in the case of Iraq, multilateral verification required intense cooperation. Such cooperation is difficult to achieve where it is most essential, as in the Middle East or South Asia, which is not to say that partial efforts are useless. But only if other regions move in Europe's direction, beginning slowly with such initiatives as modest confidence-building measures, will the prospects for regional arms control verification regimes rise. In that event, they may have more a political than a security coloring.

Even with cooperative efforts, there are difficulties in establishing and maintaining international verification bodies, as the long history of efforts to establish a viable Agency for the Prohibition of Nuclear Weapons in Latin America (OPANAL) under the Treaty of Tlatelolco suggests. Bringing appropriate technological capabilities to their efforts is equally difficult. Removed from national intelligence means, such capabilities are less useful and the organization wielding them is weakened. Amendments to the Treaty of Tlatelolco in the early 1990s formally brought to a close verification responsibilities that were not used.[8]

Another concern about developing and sharing the required technological capabilities in an international verification organization is their intrinsic dual-use capability—the same systems that allow a state to survey an adversary's military capabilities allow, in principle, that state to understand and target those capabilities.

Without a legal framework, verification capabilities are ultimately very limited in their utility. Even if organizations and capabilities exist or could be created that could serve the goal of international or multilateral verification, they are likely to be irrelevant if not applied specifically to problems of compliance arising out of the terms of some legal instrument, whether it be a full-blown arms accord or some other instrument.

In addition to such concerns, some arms activities are intrinsically unverifiable. We are moving toward incorporating into accords limits on systems that are more numerous, smaller, and more mobile, along with items limited by treaties or agreements that are by nature dual-purpose. To the extent that such activities can be monitored at all, it depends on sharing knowledge of technologies and operations that can make systems vulnerable to countermeasures or, possibly, preemptive attacks. But systems that are not sufficient to adequately monitor items limited or eliminated by arms accords may be effectively used to monitor a country's natural resources, from oil to gold. This is extremely sensitive, albeit presumably not as sensitive as national security matters. While the long-term presence of NTM capabilities in the United States and the former Soviet Union has reduced bilateral sensitivities in these areas in terms of space surveillance, the Open Skies negotiations revealed that air surveillance was, for the former Soviet Union, far more sensitive and controversial.

Coercive Verification?

New technological developments, along with the collapse of the Soviet Union, have furthered the old bilateral arms control process, but they have not yet had an impact on multilateral arms control efforts. As we have seen, there are formidable problems in concluding and implementing multilateral and international arms control agreements, especially in the sensitive area of verification. Changes in verification technologies will certainly change the way we look at these problems, but they may not be sufficient to resolve them. At the same time, we should not forget that fundamental changes in weapons-related technologies will require a watchful eye and a continuing updating of verification regimes. The security and arms control environments will continue to be dynamic.

The inspections in Iraq after the Gulf War offer one vision of the shape of things to come, showing both the limits of and the prospects for short-notice, suspect-site inspections. Despite the number of intrusive nuclear inspections conducted there in which (after some initial difficulties) the inspectors had carte blanche to do what they wanted, we may never know exactly what level the Iraqi program achieved. Further inspections as well as continuous monitoring are required for reasonable assurances about Iraq's "denuclearization." On the other hand, what was seen during the second inspection, despite Iraq's interference with the inspectors' access, led ultimately to Iraq's admissions about its uranium enrichment programs. This experience confirms what we have long known about the value and limits of on-site inspections and can help increase public awareness of the opportunities and risks associated with this type of verification measure. In this vein, the disclosures of Iraq's nuclear program should offer opportunities to strengthen the IAEA's safeguards agreements to undertake special inspections, which began to emerge even before the extent of the Iraqi nuclear program was realized.[9]

The Iraqi experience could also help to promote certain technologies, techniques, and procedures, such as aerial inspection, thereby establishing a strong rationale for their place in the new arms control panoply. Yet neither the inspections nor the continuous monitoring regime applied to Iraq is likely to have a place per se in future bilateral, regional, or international accords. Parties are not likely to accept instruments that treat them as defeated powers in terms of access. The United States could not accept such an approach either constitutionally or as a matter of U.S. security policy.

Verification, Openness, Transparency, and Confidence Building

Some of the problems surrounding verification derived from the fact that this requirement of arms control and disarmament emerged and developed its current meaning and significance during the Cold War. In particular, dealing with a closed Soviet Union drove verification requirements for the United States and the West in the bilateral sphere, whereas other agreements were deemed either so unimportant or so clearly to embody mutual interests that they did not require verification provisions. But the world is changing, and verification requirements are changing with it. Coercive verification, as we have seen, may be a very limited instrument.

On the other hand, openness, transparency, and confidence-building measures, which also came into their own during the Cold War, may have broader future application. Because the Soviet Union was so secretive, it was (with few exceptions) unwilling to move seriously in this area until the mid-1980s. Consequently, measures that have been in the background of arms control are becoming more significant.

The UN Secretary-General stated in 1992 that he was encouraged by the steady progress being made toward the goal of increased transparency in armaments. To be sure, transparency is no substitute for reductions in arms, but when properly applied it can be conducive to confidence building among states and helpful in alerting the global community to excessive accumulations of armaments. Thus it could serve as another useful tool in facilitating nonproliferation efforts.[10] Boutros-Ghali elaborated on the role of openness and transparency, noting that misinterpretation is a key cause of problems in international affairs. He stated:

> Openness and transparency are crucially important as part of the process of building confidence. Their significance must be emphasized, particularly at regional and subregional levels, in order to make military behavior more predictable and to reassure concerned states of the nonthreatening intentions of potential rivals. Openness and transparency can also be useful early-warning instruments in the process of preventive diplomacy.[11]

In the Secretary-General's assessment, openness and transparency are clearly ideas whose time has come. The development of openness and transparency measures, or confidence-building measures, has long been held as desirable. These efforts are designed to make military behavior more open and predictable, to build confidence and to reassure states, and to provide early warning of dangerous activities and of the proliferation of arms. Successes in the more distant past, including the Hot Line and the Incidents at Sea Agreements, were important but rare. They were designed to solve specific problems of mutual interest, when it was believed conflict could otherwise result and it was clear that broader agreements were not feasible.

Openness and Transparency: Goals and Limits

The agreements of the past decade are more widespread than their predecessors and have broader goals:

- To foster more formal arms control by breaking down barriers and obstacles
- To avoid more formal arms control measures and verification procedures
- To encourage and reinforce improved political relationships
- To lessen tensions and build confidence
- To reduce costs, difficulties, and intrusiveness of monitoring compliance
- To obtain information about military activities and deployments of other countries

- To obtain insights into other countries' defense planning, thinking, and decisionmaking
- To allow more predictability in planning defense requirements.[12]

These objectives are more attractive at present because of the new strategic environment, in which the certainties and stabilities of the Cold War are eroding. But there are prospects for greater cooperation with Russia. Formal negotiated arms control as it was practiced during the Cold War is giving way to less formal negotiated and nonnegotiated measures that are probably not verifiable with traditional tools (e.g., registries of nuclear weapons, warhead special nuclear material disposition, and the like) because of the rising importance of regional conflict and the proliferation of weapons of mass destruction, which have not been amenable to formal arms control measures.

Openness and transparency also have risks and limits, including the prospect that classified, sensitive, or proprietary information will be compromised or released, the possibility of information channels being used for misinformation from the other parties, and the creation of a false sense of confidence, the questionable value of information obtained compared with intrusive verification, and the like. But opportunities exist and must be balanced with the risks. In this context, can openness and transparency make a genuine contribution? Can these measures make a difference?

The line between verification and openness, transparency, and confidence building is not clear. Verification can serve the latter objectives, particularly confidence building, by demonstrating compliance and thus reassuring the other parties. Some parties may wish explicitly to show their good faith through effective verification measures. In other words, they wish their activities to be transparent to the other parties. For example, IAEA safeguards have for years allowed states an opportunity to show that their civil nuclear programs are not being misused for military ends.

Finally, good verification can demonstrate the good faith of the parties to the broader international community, which may have an interest in whether the parties are complying with their treaties or agreements even if the community at large is not directly involved.

Toward Greater Transparency

Despite the extensive formal nuclear agreements between the United States and Russia, there is a growing sense that they do not get to the heart of today's most pressing nuclear dangers. Accordingly, there is considerable interest in expanding openness and transparency measures. Such measures would supplement the already extensive provisions contained in the START agreements but would also cover areas of interest not addressed by formal agreements.

Two areas of special interest, which have been outside of nuclear arms control historically, are nuclear warheads (as opposed to delivery vehicles) and weapon materials. While both are virtually impossible to verify in any meaningful and practicable way, declarations on stocks, visits to storage areas, and other such measures could be important in promoting openness and transparency. One specific area would be exchanges on the safety, security, and dismantlement of nuclear weapons. Such initiatives could greatly contribute to reassuring each other and the world that the dangers of the nuclear forces developed during the Cold War are diminishing. In addition, broader exchanges on defense budgets, planning, and decisionmaking, on defense R&D, and on nonstrategic forces could promote predictability, mutual confidence, and other desired objectives.

In the post-CFE security environment in Europe there is considerable scope for information exchanges, technical assistance, and the like regarding military budgets, doctrines, and force structure. This is especially the case for actions with little or no budgetary impact. To the extent that such modest actions promote openness and transparency and thereby reduce tensions and insecurities, they could actually address the heart of current problems. They are by their very nature, however, limited and useful only insofar as the positive trends of the present time continue. If the goal is security and stability in Europe, promoting openness and transparency through multiple endeavors rather than further quantitative or qualitative limitations on conventional forces appears to deserve the highest priority by policymakers.

Neither subregional issues, such as of Cyprus, or extraregional issues of special concern in Europe, including the Middle East and North Africa, appear susceptible to any but the most modest confidence-building measures for the foreseeable future, although even modest measures could be useful. Such issues remain divisive in European and Atlantic councils and have long been a bane to achieving formal arms control agreements, but these issues do not yet appear ripe for resolution.

A host of confidence-building measures and unilateral actions (reciprocal and coordinated)—from mere dialogue on unresolvable issues to unilateral deep cuts in some areas of conventional forces in Europe—is possible and would seem to be the best approach to the outstanding issues confronting European security. However, the implementation of the rather ambitious Open Skies Treaty in the new climate will be difficult. This, however, does not reflect a rejection of the goal of openness and transparency. Rather it is a demonstration of what is now possible because of budgetary and other constraints. In any case, this openness and transparency regime will exist and has the possibility of developing over time. What is critical is the political imperative for transparency that led to the Open Skies Treaty, even if it will be largely symbolic for the foreseeable future.

A key question is whether these trends will hold for other, more conflict-prone regions. Much attention has recently been devoted to adapting measures developed in Europe and in the old bilateral relationship to the situations in the Middle East, South Asia, and elsewhere. Exchanges among the civilian and military officials of adversaries, declarations about military force levels, exercises, and the like are promising. There have been discussions of expanding Open Skies, or at least the concept, to regional settings, but this idea may not be practicable. While such measures might break impasses and lead to more formal and comprehensive measures, they may be ill-suited to tense regions because of fears that they may be misused for the advantage of one of the participants.

Conclusion

Verification's importance has changed dramatically over time, although it always has been in the forefront of arms control. The goals and measures of verification and the criteria for success have also changed with the times, reflecting such factors as the centrality of the prospective agreement to East-West relations during the Cold War, the state of relations between the United States and the Soviet Union, and the technologies available for monitoring.

Although national technical means, and especially overhead surveillance, were sufficient for verification of the LTBT and SALT agreements, further testing restraints, along with recent agreements in the areas of nuclear, conventional, and chemical weapons, have posed different challenges and have required additional verification measures. While changes in the political environment, along with existing and developing verification technologies, have made the conclusion of agreements in these areas possible, they require highly intrusive verification. These agreements will have to rely heavily on cooperative measures that are possible, and probably acceptable, in a climate of improving East-West relations, but they might leave us with hollow verification regimes if relations deteriorate.

Current and future verification challenges are, then, quite formidable. Monitoring capabilities have grown considerably, but further improvements are necessary. There are technologies derived from the U.S. nuclear weapon program and nuclear arms control verification experience that have been adapted to enhance verification in nonnuclear areas. Adapting current technologies to new problems will be necessary. So will exploring new technologies specifically designed for areas in which arms control activity is now occurring and has captured the world's attention. But the limits and costs of verification raise serious questions about such an endeavor.

The effectiveness and cost of verification were hotly debated during the Cold War, especially from the late 1970s to the mid-1980s, but we have seen that these concerns may be less important in the future. Verification regimes are extraordinarily expensive, and increasingly they are contributing only marginally to intelligence in the monitoring of agreements. This trend can be expected to continue to the extent that arms control agreements deal with items that are either difficult or impossible to monitor—that is, as it moves into areas that are essentially unverifiable. Of course, on the basis of future budgetary decisions, verification may become far less important, and perhaps absent from some agreements. If societies become more open, this will not pose a problem. Moreover, it may be expected that arms control negotiations and agreements will be given less attention by presidents, parliaments, and publics than will, say, global environmental monitoring. This will raise anew the question of the value of verification. There may be battles over whether to target NTM on verification of treaty compliance or to use it for environmental monitoring. The stage is now being set for an expansion of intelligence collection to nontraditional intelligence users, like the Environmental Protection Agency, where anticipated intelligence requirements in the decade ahead are greater.

The prospects for the declining role of verification will be, first and foremost, affected by the high costs of traditional arms control, especially those associated with requirements for verification. Moreover, the growing interest in informal, or nonnegotiated, arms control does not allow for verification provisions by the very nature of these arrangements. Multilateral agreements are also becoming more prominent and argue against highly intrusive verification measures, in part because of fears of promoting proliferation by opening sensitive facilities to inspectors from potential proliferant states.

As a result, it is likely that openness, transparency, and confidence-building measures will achieve greater prominence, both as supplements to and substitutes for traditional verification. Such measures are not panaceas and do not offer all that we came to expect from verification during the Cold War, but they may be the best possible means to deal with current problems of arms reduction and restraint at acceptable levels of expenditure.

Suggested Reading

Potter, William C., ed. *Verification and SALT: The Challenge of Strategic Deception.* Boulder, Colo.: Westview Press, 1980.

———, ed. *Verification in Arms Control.* Cambridge, Mass.: Ballinger, 1985.

Tsipis, Kosta, David W. Hafemeister, and Penny Janeway, eds. *Arms Control Verification: The Technologies that Make It Possible.* Washington, D.C.: Pergamon-Brassey's International Defense Publishers, 1986.

Notes

1. The Vela program, begun in 1960, was a systematic program designed to provide space-based detection of nuclear explosions. For further information, see Jeffrey Richelson, *The U.S. Intelligence Community* (Cambridge, Mass.: Ballinger, 1985), pp. 157–159.

2. Nuclear weapon states are defined in Article IX.3 of the treaty as states that had "manufactured and exploded a nuclear weapon or other nuclear explosive device prior to January 1, 1967." All nuclear weapon states now voluntarily allow IAEA inspectors at certain civil nuclear facilities.

3. See, for example, Glenn T. Seaborg with the assistance of Benjamin S. Loeb, *Kennedy, Krushchev, and the Test Ban* (Berkeley: University of California Press, 1981).

4. Additional sources of information may come into play when formal agreements or verification provisions cannot be agreed upon: openness and transparency measures and confidence-building measures. In practice, such measures may facilitate meeting all the goals of more traditional arms control.

5. For the disputes over alleged Soviet violations of the Threshold Test Ban Treaty, see Warren Heckrotte, "Verification of Test Ban Treaties," in William C. Potter, ed., *Verification and Arms Control* (Lexington, Mass.: Lexington Books, 1985), pp. 70–71. For possible Soviet violations of the ABM Treaty and the SALT II Treaty, see ibid., p. 246.

6. Boutros Boutros-Ghali, *New Dimensions of Arms Regulation and Disarmament in the Post–Cold War Era,* Report of the Secretary-General, United Nations A/C 1/47/7, 27 October 1992, p. 9.

7. For a fuller discussion of ISMA and PAXSAT, see UN Institute for Disarmament Research, *Prevention of an Arms Race in Outer Space: A Guide to Discussions in the Conference on Disarmament* (New York: UN, 1991), pp. 118–128 and 154–159.

8. See John R. Redick, "Latin America's Emerging Non-Proliferation Consensus," *Arms Control Today* (March 1994), p. 8.

9. At the time of their origin, IAEA safeguards were an unprecedented on-site inspection measure. These same procedures subsequently were used to verify provisions of the NPT, as well as the Treaties of Tlatelolco and Rarotonga (which established nuclear-weapon-free zones in Latin America and the South Pacific, respectively). The IAEA is no longer at the forefront of on-site inspections; U.S.-Soviet agreements as well as the Stockholm Document, the CFE Treaty, and confidence- and security-building measures now surpass its intrusiveness. The IAEA is studying the lessons of other arms control agreements with a view to assessing possible improvements of safeguards; in this vein, it is also seeking to develop procedures for special inspections, interest in which has grown as a result of disclosures about Iraq's nuclear program.

10. Boutros-Ghali, *New Dimensions,* p. 18.

11. Ibid., pp. 18–19.

12. See, for example, Lewis A. Dunn and Patricia McFate, *Transparency: Aspects, Prospects, and Implications,* briefing at Lawrence Livermore National Laboratory, Livermore, Calif., 24 September 1992.

PART 2

The Legacy of the Cold War

5

Strategic Offensive Arms Control

Forrest Waller

On 29 July 1991, two exhausted arms control delegations and a large contingent of the international press met at the Soviet Mission in Geneva to observe the final plenary session of the Strategic Arms Reduction Talks and to witness the formal completion of the START Treaty. A double irony was at work during the plenary. The first came at the expense of the press and the millions of viewers who watched the ceremony on television. The START Treaty was so long that it could not be printed on its special treaty paper in time for the meeting. So, the public watched the U.S. and Soviet ambassadors initial 600-page "treaties" composed almost entirely of blank pages.

The second irony came at the expense of the arms control negotiators who had brought the nine-year-long START negotiations to a close. In less than six months, the Soviet Union would dissolve, and the START Treaty's entry into force would be delayed nearly four years. Never again would U.S. and Soviet delegations meet, as they had done routinely for almost half a century, to negotiate limitations on strategic offensive weapons.

The passing of the Cold War arms control era is not something to look back upon with nostalgia or regret. Cold War arms control began boldly and badly, but it finished well. Mistrust, posturing, and advantage-seeking characterized strategic offensive arms control efforts for many years. Then, in the late 1980s, strategic arms control policy became one of the most successful policy arenas in which the governments of the United States and Soviet Union cooperated. The dissolution of the Soviet Union in 1992 brought the era to a close.

This chapter is about the future of strategic offensive arms control, but it is not about prediction. The stunning changes that have occurred since the late 1980s—the peaceful reunification of Germany, the peaceful dissolution of the Warsaw Pact, the collapse of the Soviet Union, and the rise of democratic reform in former Soviet republics—should teach humility to those who predict the future. They also should caution us against placing arbitrary limits on the amount of change we perceive possible. This chapter attempts to identify the trends and developments that have the most potential to influence the future course of strategic arms control policy, and it characterizes the range of possibilities for that policy.

This examination of the future of nuclear arms control develops in four sections. The first section surveys the evolution of U.S. strategic arms control policy in U.S. national security affairs. The objectives are to provide historical background and to show how the role of U.S. strategic arms control developed over the last 50 years. The second section discusses contemporary strategic offensive arms control. The Cold War period of strategic arms control has ended, and a post–Cold War successor has not yet appeared to take its place. The contemporary period appears to be one of transition. This section identifies the characteristics of this transitional period and their implications for strategic offensive arms control. The third section discusses the changing role of U.S. nuclear weapons, a critical issue because the future of strategic offensive arms control in the United States will depend in large measure on whether Washington continues to perceive "utility" in possessing nuclear arms. The final section addresses the range of possible futures for strategic arms control policy. This section categorizes and describes the ideas of forward-thinking individuals and organizations who turned their attention to the future of strategic arms control.

The Evolution of U.S. Strategic Arms Control Policy

The development of U.S. strategic offensive arms control policy from 1945 to the present can be divided into four periods. During each period, the United States struggled to balance its vital interest in controlling nuclear weapons with its vital interest in relying on nuclear weapons to deter war. Balancing the two interests was difficult. International crises and Cold War competition exacerbated the difficulty, but the progress of U.S. arms control policy demonstrates substantial growth, change, and success.

Period 1: Disarmament Solutions (1945–1955)

Before dawn on 7 July 1945, the United States detonated the world's first nuclear explosive device at the Trinity test site near Alamogordo, New Mexico. By 9 August the United States had dropped nuclear bombs on two Japanese cities and brought World War II to a conclusion. Well before the Trinity test and the destruction of Hiroshima and Nagasaki, U.S. nuclear armaments specialists had raised concern about U.S. national security in an age of nuclear weapons. They understood that the United States could not base its security permanently on its nuclear monopoly. Eventually, other states would develop nuclear weapons and pose a threat to the survival of the United States.

In September 1945, Secretary of War Henry L. Stimson proposed to Pres. Harry Truman that the United States discuss the control and limitation of atomic weapons with the Soviets. Truman presented Stimson's proposal to his cabinet and discovered his closest advisers deeply divided over the issue. Nonetheless, in March 1946 an interagency group met at Dumbarton Oaks in Washington, D.C., to develop the first U.S. nuclear arms control proposal. It was a proposal for comprehensive nuclear disarmament.

The alternative to arms control was a new defense strategy—nuclear deterrence. Deterrence emerged early as a strategic concept for U.S. national security in the nuclear age, but the concept did not inspire confidence. In late 1944, the Jeffries Committee of the Manhattan Project identified the threat of devastating nuclear retaliation as the basis for an uneasy truce between nuclear-armed rivals, but the committee doubted whether deterrence could be stable or result in lasting peace.[1] Others, however, forcefully defended deterrence. In November 1945, Gen. Henry H. Arnold provided Stimson with his assessment of the atom bomb's impact on postwar national security:

> This country ... must recognize that real security ... in the visible future will rest on our ability to take immediate offensive action with overwhelming force. It must be apparent to a potential aggressor that an attack on the United States would be followed by an immensely devastating [nuclear] air attack on him.[2]

When confronted with the stark choice between nuclear disarmament and nuclear deterrence, Truman adopted an approach that served as a precedent for subsequent presidential administrations: he selected both alternatives. In 1946 he approved the proposal fashioned at Dumbarton Oaks, and in early 1947 he expressed shock when told how few atom bombs the United States actually had (fewer than 15, and none was an assembled weapon).[3] Truman subsequently ordered the most significant nuclear weapon modernization programs of any U.S. president.

The Baruch Plan.   On 14 June 1946 at the first session of the UN Atomic Energy Commission, U.S. ambassador Barnard Baruch introduced the U.S. proposal for nuclear disarmament. The Dumbarton Oaks Plan (thereafter known as the Baruch Plan) called for the complete transfer of all U.S. atomic weapons, atomic power facilities, and atomic know-how to international control. The plan called for the creation of an international organization to be responsible for all aspects of the development and use of atomic energy. (Details of the plan are provided by Virginia Foran in Chapter 9.)

The Baruch Plan was more restrictive than any of the other great powers was willing to accept. The Soviets rejected the U.S. proposal immediately, calling it a transparent effort to monopolize nuclear weaponry to the disadvantage of all other states. The Soviets counterproposed that the United States disassemble its nuclear weapon production infrastructure and destroy its nuclear arsenal completely as the first step in the process of general disarmament. Also, U.S. allies in Western Europe were unwilling to support the Baruch Plan. Both the United Kingdom and France also had nuclear programs under way. For the next 10 years, the U.N. Disarmament Commission negotiated one disarmament proposal after another without success.

Arms control's subordination.   While arms control efforts languished, U.S. defense policy changed rapidly in response to international tension with the Soviet Union. The threat of conflict with the Soviet Union was real in the late 1940s and early 1950s, and the United States was unprepared for conventional war. The U.S. response to the threat of war was to integrate atomic weapons into U.S. war plans, develop tactical nuclear weapons, and produce the hydrogen bomb. From 1945 to 1955, U.S. arms control policy was subordinate to a U.S. defense policy whose objective was nuclear supremacy. U.S. political leaders recognized arms control's advantages, but they were either unwilling or unable to rely on it. Political leaders in major capitals around the world regarded nuclear weapons as a major source of political clout and military leverage.[4] Eventually, Moscow, London, Paris, and Beijing would develop nuclear weapons. The perceived political-military utility of nuclear weapons weighed heavily against arms control's success.

Period 2: Initial Progress, Limited Results (1958–1966)

Following the failure of U.S. efforts to negotiate a disarmament agreement, the United States changed its approach. Instead of comprehensive disarmament solutions, the country tried to negotiate agreements on discrete arms control problems about which there appeared to be little controversy or risk of failure. These negotiations were based on the premise that it was easier to exclude nuclear armaments from areas where they had not yet appeared than it was to control or eliminate them once they had arrived.[5] It also helped the negotiations' probability of success that the contemplated restrictions prohibited nothing the United States or Soviet Union would have considered remotely desirable. The treaties prohibited nuclear weapon deployment in areas that were extremely inhospitable to begin with, would have caused program costs to soar, and would have raised nearly insurmountable problems for nuclear weapon maintenance, retrieval, and safety. Such treaties included the Antarctic Treaty in 1959, the Outer Space Treaty (finished in 1967), and the Seabed Treaty (finished in 1971). They were negotiating successes, but they made insignificant contributions to national security.

The 1963 Limited Test Ban Treaty (LTBT) (also known as the Partial Test Ban Treaty [PTBT]) was atypical. The LTBT permits nuclear testing only underground and on conditions prohibiting the spread of radioactive debris across international borders (see Appendix 2). The LTBT negotiations attracted and sustained considerable international political interest because of the health hazard aboveground nuclear testing posed to the public. The LTBT shared at least one thing in common with the other three agreements reached during this period. Ending the negative impact of aboveground testing was uncontroversial. Neither the United States nor the Soviet Union wanted to poison the environment with their nuclear tests, and both, along with other nations, were willing to stop atmospheric tests as soon as viable alternatives were available and acceptable conditions for negotiation were obtainable. The Cuban missile crisis provided the catalyst to reach this agreement and achieve ratification.

Arms control institutionalized.   During this period, arms control considerations became institutionalized in the U.S. national security policy arena. When John F. Kennedy ran for the presidency in 1960, he campaigned for an independent agency to take the lead on U.S. arms control and disarmament matters. Kennedy was concerned that a large, institutionalized bureaucracy existed to promote U.S. defense programs without being balanced by an agency devoted exclusively to arms control. In 1961, Congress and the president created the Arms Control and Disarmament Agency (ACDA).[6] Even in the Kennedy administration, however, nuclear arms control was subordinate to U.S. defense policy. However, a useful environmental change had taken place with the creation of an institutional voice to speak out for arms control. The change set the stage for more ambitious arms control efforts.

Period 3: Strategic Arms Limitation (1967–1980)

Negotiations to limit strategic offensive arms eventually became a permanent feature of U.S.-Soviet relations. As a matter of law, they became obligatory; as a matter of national security policy, they were a necessity. Arms control negotiations became permanent largely for two reasons: the negotiation of the nuclear Non-Proliferation Treaty (NPT) and the loss of U.S. nuclear supremacy.

Nonproliferation.   Neither the United States nor the Soviet Union wanted to see other states deploy nuclear weapons. Deterring one nuclear adversary was difficult enough. Multiple nuclear adversaries potentially added an unacceptable degree of complexity and unpredictability to defense strategy. Thus, the superpowers cooperated with other states in the pursuit of a nonproliferation agreement. (This agreement is covered in depth in Chapter 9.)

Loss of U.S. nuclear supremacy.   By the late 1960s, the United States had lost its strategic supremacy over the Soviet Union. This development was not un-expected. Advisers to U.S. presidents had predicted nuclear stalemate for nearly 20 years.[7] However, some in the United States began to wonder whether ad-visers to Soviet presidents had given the same advice. Soviet strategic mod-ernization programs appeared ready to advance well beyond the quantitative requirements of nuclear equality and created concern about the survivability of U.S. retaliatory forces and the stability of the nuclear balance.

Pres. Richard Nixon came into office hoping to restore U.S. nuclear su-periority, but defense policy's tools—building new weapon systems and changing the doctrines for their employment—could only assure the United States of nuclear parity. U.S. nuclear force structure had been frozen for eight years when Nixon entered office, and there was little hope of enlarging it in ways that the Soviets could not match. Nuclear weapon employment policies could change, and did, but these changes did not alter the strategic nuclear balance. Defense policy's tools were unable to provide a long-term remedy to the perceived vulnerability of U.S. strategic forces.

Nixon turned to arms control for help. The administration defined its se-curity requirements in terms that facilitated arms control. Weapon system re-quirements and arms control planning were closely integrated.[8] The objective of U.S. strategic arms control policy was to ensure strategic stability through mutual societal vulnerability. This approach to nuclear stability was the foun-dation of a nuclear doctrine called mutual assured destruction (MAD).

Strategic arms limitation.   The United States and the Soviet Union negotiated two major agreements limiting strategic offensive arms.[9] The forum for the ne-gotiations was called the Strategic Arms Limitation Talks (SALT). The first agree-ment, SALT I,[10] was a temporary accord restraining the growth of U.S. and So-viet strategic forces while a more elaborate treaty was negotiated. The second agreement, which was not completed until the Carter administration, was the SALT II Treaty (see Appendix 2 for descriptions of the SALT Treaties).[11] It set limits on the number of deployed strategic systems the sides could possess and required minor reductions in Soviet ballistic missile launchers. SALT I put ceil-ings on each side's strategic programs, placing the United States at a numerical disadvantage in deployed strategic systems. As the quality of Soviet forces im-proved, U.S. strategic forces came to be at a numerical disadvantage in deployed ballistic missile warheads. Eventually, the vulnerability of U.S. land-based stra-tegic nuclear forces became an urgent national security concern.

The SALT II Treaty was supposed to ameliorate the U.S. vulnerability problem. On the right side of the political spectrum, however, critics pointed out that the treaty did nothing to improve the survivability of U.S. retalia-tory forces, and they complained that SALT II even made matters worse by granting the Soviets a unilateral advantage in heavy intercontinental ballis-tic missiles (ICBMs).[12] On the left, critics pointed out that SALT II did not limit deployed warheads. They predicted that U.S. and Soviet nuclear weapons would grow in number and destructive power as modern multiple-warhead systems replaced older systems with only one warhead.

The critique of SALT II and U.S. arms control policy was bitter medicine, but the treaty probably would have been ratified anyway. The Joint Chiefs of Staff testified in favor of the treaty, provided that the U.S. strategic modernization went forward. Congress appeared willing to approve both the treaty and a strategic modernization program. However, in December 1979 the Soviets invaded Afghanistan on the pretext that Moscow had been invited to defend the Afghan government against subversion. Understanding that the Senate would not ratify the SALT II Treaty because of the invasion, the Carter administration withdrew the treaty from consideration and embarked on a major military modernization program. Nonetheless, the United States announced that it would not undercut the SALT II Treaty with U.S. modernization programs, provided that the Soviets did the same.[13]

Equal partnership. The strategic arms limitation period was important institutionally because U.S. arms control policy became an equal partner with U.S. defense policy. The partnership was not always harmonious, and people honestly disagreed about the value of the partnership's achievements, but the process created to blend arms control and defense policies worked. Bureaucratic practice adapted to incorporate arms control considerations in the development of defense strategy, and arms control initiatives adapted to accommodate vital national security programs.

Period 4: Strategic Arms Reduction (1981–1991)

The critique of SALT II resonated with California governor Ronald Reagan. When he became president in 1981, he refused to resubmit the SALT II Treaty to the Senate for ratification, ended the U.S. policy of remaining within treaty numerical limits, and won congressional funding for strategic defense programs that would have replaced the mutual assured destruction doctrine. Reagan proposed entirely new negotiations to reduce U.S. and Soviet strategic offensive arms. The flagship of the U.S. arms control effort was START, the objective of which was to negotiate an effectively verifiable agreement calling for deep reductions of strategic offensive arms to equal numerical levels. The administration emphasized stabilizing reductions—that is, reductions in the types of strategic weapons that were most threatening to U.S. strategic nuclear forces (Soviet ICBMs). The administration also wanted to constrain nondeployed missiles and "break out" potential.[14] It proposed to ban mobile ICBMs, cut the Soviet heavy ICBM force by one-half, and cut deployed warheads by 50 percent. Additionally, the United States wanted to achieve parity in long-range theater nuclear systems in Europe. These objectives placed a disproportionate burden of reduction on the Soviet Union, and the Soviets were not pleased. But the United States would not budge from the goal of negotiating "equal" treaties that contributed to stability as defined by the administration.

The 1980s initially saw the START negotiations go through a series of starts and stops related to Reagan's Strategic Defense Initiative (SDI) as well as accusations back and forth regarding violations of other agreements and general lack of good faith. However, the growing economic difficulties within the Soviet Union and the rise of Mikhail Gorbachev to power created new imperatives for the Soviets to engage in serious strategic offensive arms control discussions. At the same time, the strength of the nuclear freeze movement and declining public support for high defense spending combined to exert pressure on the Reagan administration to show progress in arms control.

The grand finale.   The late 1980s and early 1990s saw U.S. strategic arms control policy achieve spectacular results. The Intermediate-Range Nuclear Forces (INF) Treaty eliminated an entire class of nuclear offensive arms and established an intrusive on-site inspection regime. START I limited U.S. and Soviet strategic offensive forces to no more than 1,600 deployed systems, 6,000 accountable deployed warheads, 4,900 warheads on deployed ballistic missiles, and 1,100 warheads on deployed mobile ICBM systems. In addition, START built upon the INF precedents in verification, establishing a complex regime for data exchange, access to telemetry, and on-site inspection. START II went further, limiting each side to 3,000–3,500 total deployed warheads, eliminating land-based multiple independently targetable reentry vehicle (MIRV)ed ballistic missiles, and stepping up the pace of reductions. (See Appendix 2.)

The START I and START II agreements are particularly important because they are, respectively, the last nuclear arms control agreement of the Cold War and the first agreement of the post–Cold War period. In combination, they create an arms control environment that is highly advantageous to the United States and Russia. The advantages to Russia are largely economic. The reductions called for in the treaties save funds that Moscow cannot afford to spend. The advantages to the United States are both economic and strategic. The treaties undo Russian strategic advantages that the United States could never have eliminated in any other way. By the end of the nuclear arms reduction period (and the Cold War), arms control policy was making the continuous contribution to U.S. national security that Pres. John F. Kennedy had hoped for when he institutionalized arms control in the national security policy process.

Contemporary Strategic Offensive Arms Control

The dissolution of the Soviet Union in December 1991 changed the context in which strategic offensive arms control takes place and the content of strategic offensive arms control negotiations. In the post–Cold War period, economic considerations have assumed major importance in setting U.S. nuclear arms control policy. In mid-1991, just as the START Treaty was being prepared for signature, the Department of Defense prepared for the White House a list of operational practices, nuclear systems, and nuclear modernization programs it could no longer afford given projected cuts in the U.S. defense budget. Along with the list, the Department of Defense recommended that the United States attempt to secure parallel cuts in Soviet nuclear programs. This recommendation resulted in the presidential nuclear initiatives of 1991–1992.[15] In September 1991 and January 1992, President Bush announced several unilateral steps the United States was taking to further reduce nuclear tension and invited Moscow to match them (see Appendix 3). Soviet president Gorbachev and later Russian president Boris Yeltsin responded with unilateral initiatives of their own.[16] As a result of these initiatives, both sides withdrew substantial numbers of tactical nuclear weapons from forward deployment sites, canceled a variety of nuclear force modernization programs, initiated efforts to implement START I early, and relaxed the alert posture of their respective strategic offensive forces.

START II Treaty

As economic conditions in the former Soviet Union deteriorated in 1992, the United States recognized that Moscow could not deploy a strategic offensive force structure as large as the one permitted under the START Treaty. Sensing an opportunity to reduce simultaneously the threat posed by Russia's nuclear arsenal and lessen the expense of U.S. strategic forces, the United States proposed a START II Treaty with lower deployed warhead ceilings and other provisions designed to increase the survivability of retaliatory forces. In June 1992 Presidents Bush and Yeltsin accepted a framework agreement for the START II Treaty, which they signed in January 1993. The entire START II negotiating process took only one year.

START II builds on the procedural rules of the START I Treaty, but START II caps deployed warheads at 3,500, limits deployed SLBM warheads at 1,750, and bans MIRVed ICBMs.[17] START II's obligations require Moscow to eliminate much of the high-quality nuclear combat potential the Soviets created during 1970–1990. In many ways, the agreement is a lopsided one favoring the United States. A combination of factors may explain why the Russians accepted the agreement. In early 1992 President Yeltsin faced the prospect of serious political upheaval and economic distress. He needed U.S. and Western political and economic support. START II offered a way to reinforce the impression that the Russian Federation was not only a new Russian government but also a new form of government with which the West could deal confidently. In addition, the Soviet government was in such disrepute domestically that it was probably easy to ignore the concerns of former Soviet national security specialists who may have argued against the agreement. Finally, it would be a mistake to forget the impact of the new atmosphere that accompanied the end of the Cold War. Decisionmakers on both sides undoubtedly saw opportunities to reduce the Cold War threat and lessen the expense of defense programs. They seized the moment, but the U.S. negotiators got the better deal.

The Future of Strategic Arms Control

Since the signing of the START II Treaty, the focus of strategic arms control has begun to change in important ways. Formerly, strategic offensive arms agreements concentrated on military systems. They limited articles of equipment and monitored compliance by counting treaty-limited items (military hardware). Today, strategic arms control focuses increasingly on industrial processes associated with the production or dismantlement of weapons and the disposition of critical weapon materials. Greater attention is paid today to providing U.S. expertise and assistance to our treaty partners on weapon safety and security matters. This focus has created new challenges for verification and has drawn upon expertise new to the arena of strategic arms control negotiation.[18]

Early implementation arrangements for new strategic arms control treaties are increasingly common. These arrangements usually are not spelled out in detail. They depend almost entirely on unilateral interpretation of implementation requirements. The implementation of such arrangements is frequently unverifiable. However, ensuring strict verification procedures does not have the urgency today that it had during the Cold War. Arms control policy makers are concerned about the rising implementation costs associated with verification provisions and are slow to accept requirements that impose additional financial burdens. Moreover, the end of the Cold War has changed the perception of U.S. leaders about the risk of conflict with Moscow. They genuinely perceive Moscow to be less threatening today than during the Cold War. Thus, arms control verification does not claim the priority it once did.

Strategic offensive arms control is an evolving concept. The distinction between tactical and strategic nuclear weapons has become virtually meaningless. Strategic offensive arms control has begun to lose its "compartmentalization" and recognize its thematic connections with, and interest in, other arms control issues, including the prohibition of fissile materials production, the prohibition of nuclear testing, limitations on strategic defenses, and nonproliferation. In short, strategic offensive arms control is a more comprehensive concept today than it has been at any time since the period of comprehensive nuclear disarmament.

The implications of this evolution are that strategic offensive arms control is likely to be more technical in nature and involve less "high politics" than it formerly did. Highly technical negotiations lend themselves to small expert working groups, not large delegations of national security policy specialists. As bilateral negotiations between the United States and Russia grow more complex technically, the more difficult it may be to persuade other nuclear weapon states to join the process. Technical negotiations delve deeply into matters that are sensitive. The other nuclear weapon states may be uncomfortable with that complexity and the openness it requires. Finally, strategic offensive arms control will be more sensitive to the costs of implementing and verifying any new agreements. None of the nuclear weapons states will find it easy to consent to proposals that come with a high price tag.

The Future Role of U.S. Nuclear Weapons

In 1994 the Department of Defense completed a year-long review of U.S. nuclear posture. The review was the first of its kind in 15 years and the first to take place since the dissolution of the Soviet Union. The Nuclear Posture Review (NPR) recognized that Western security had improved dramatically as a result of the dissolution of the Warsaw Pact and reform in the former Soviet Union. The NPR also recognized that U.S. defense budget constraints[19] had contributed to the termination or truncation of 11 nuclear programs and the retirement (without replacement) of seven others. The Department of Defense also faced the task of implementing two strategic offensive arms reduction agreements. Much of the implementation task was on an accelerated schedule. These factors contributed to the need for a careful review of the role of U.S. nuclear forces. With nuclear weapon dismantlement taking place at a rate of 2,000 weapons per year, nuclear weapons were beginning to "play a smaller role in our security strategy than at any time since their inception."[20]

The full dimensions of the role change for U.S. nuclear weapons can be appreciated when one understands the following:

- Today, no U.S. nuclear systems are targeted on Russia or any other country; U.S. heavy bombers are no longer on alert.
- A smaller portion of U.S. ballistic missile submarines is on alert than ever before.
- U.S. airborne command posts operate on a significantly reduced operations tempo.
- No new U.S. nuclear warhead designs are under consideration.
- No nuclear weapons remain in the custody of U.S. ground forces.
- The U.S. Navy no longer deploys tactical nuclear weapons at sea.

- The total active U.S. nuclear stockpile has been reduced by 59 percent (compared with 1988).
- The active stockpile of U.S. tactical nuclear weapons has been reduced by 90 percent.[21]

The Nuclear Posture Review determined that U.S. nuclear weapons retain a role in deterring attack on the United States and its allies and in hedging against the failure of reform in Russia. It rebalanced U.S. strategic offensive force structure to be consistent with the START II ceiling of 3,500 deployed strategic warheads, and it rejected a "no first use" pledge.[22] It recommended keeping U.S. nuclear weapons in Europe. The review concluded that U.S. nuclear posture should help shape the future of the international security environment by creating conditions in which the role of nuclear weapons shrinks even further. In concert with the public announcement of the NPR's conclusions, the Department of Defense announced a new, derivative nuclear doctrine, mutual assured safety (MAS).[23] According to Secretary of Defense William Perry, MAS marks the Department of Defense's abandonment of the mutual assured destruction doctrine.[24]

The Nuclear Posture Review makes the long-term role of U.S. strategic offensive arms uncertain as a matter of policy. Three other factors contribute to this uncertainty. First, the role of U.S. military power in general is less clear today than formerly. The current National Security Strategy of the United States has enlarged the arena of U.S. national security concerns to include international pollution, drug trafficking, migration, and ethnic conflict. Military power appears to have little relevance to most of these problems, and U.S. nuclear weapons have no relevance to them.

Second, the United States has declared a moratorium on nuclear testing and supports a comprehensive nuclear test ban treaty. A test ban treaty is an element of the broad U.S. strategy for preventing nuclear proliferation and makes up part of the nuclear posture of the United States. The Nuclear Posture Review calls for responsible stewardship over nuclear weapons, meaning that the United States must figure out how to maintain the reliability and safety of its nuclear stockpile without nuclear testing. However, in the long run, a moratorium (or a nuclear test ban) could undermine public confidence in the stockpile. The United States is not a proliferator that can be satisfied with a clandestine program's high risks to life and property. If the U.S. public begins to question nuclear weapon safety and reliability, the contribution of nuclear weapons to U.S. security will be reappraised, and the outcome of that reappraisal cannot be predicted.

Third, the United States has no plans to introduce a new ICBM, SLBM, heavy bomber, or nuclear cruise missile for the foreseeable future. It has no plan for introducing a "new type" of strategic offensive arm.[25] Eventually, more than one strategic modernization program will be needed if the United

States intends to maintain a triad or dyad of nuclear forces.[26] The defense budget through the year 2000 could not sustain a new strategic program at current or anticipated levels of spending. Indeed, modernization program cancellations, curtailments, and delays are much more likely over the next five years than modernization program starts.

These factors suggest an inevitable decline in U.S. reliance on strategic offensive arms for security and a corresponding increase in emphasis on strategic offensive arms control and other defense programs as a way to reduce U.S. requirements for nuclear testing and strategic modernization.[27] What are the directions that strategic arms control policy might take?

Alternative Directions in Strategic Arms Control Policy

Since the collapse of the Soviet Union, more than a dozen proposals have been presented on the direction that U.S. strategic arms control policy should take. These proposals share many of the same perspectives on strategic arms control, but there are degrees of difference in emphasis and outlook that allow them to be categorized differently. In the first category are analysts who view the implementation of existing arms reduction agreements as arms control policy's paramount concern. The second category includes analysts who value additional deep reductions. In the third category are analysts who believe the post–Cold War period affords an extraordinary opportunity to deconstruct the nuclear threat. Finally, a fourth category, nuclear disarmament, exists, but it has few proponents.

Implementation First

The implementation of the START Treaties is an objective that all supporters of strategic arms control share. The START agreements result in roughly a two-thirds reduction in U.S. and Soviet strategic offensive arms deployed in 1991. Without effective implementation of these treaties, the entire process of U.S.-Russian strategic offensive arms reduction would come to a halt, and the cooperative atmosphere of U.S.-Russian relations would undoubtedly cool. The slow progress of formal treaty implementation (START I) and treaty ratification (START II) has increased the concerns of some that the START Treaties' contributions to nuclear stability may be lost because of delayed implementation. Moreover, the United States is committed to several other high-priority arms control efforts that will consume U.S. policymakers' attention for years to come. These efforts include the 1995 extension of the Non-Proliferation Treaty, conclusion of the Comprehensive Test Ban Treaty, and an agreement banning the production of fissile materials. In short, the negotiating agenda for U.S. arms control is ample already without the addition of another round of strategic arms reduction negotiations. For many in official circles, the period until the year 2003 should emphasize START implementation or operational restrictions, not deeper reductions.[28]

This emphasis on implementation receives the support of conservative realists who recognize that the threat to the United States may grow over the next decade. The spread of weapons of mass destruction or the failure of reform in the former Soviet Union could require the United States to reconstitute nuclear capability. The spread of nuclear weapons to additional countries could increase the U.S. requirement for nuclear forces to deter aggression or the threatened use of force. Similarly, if Washington finds itself facing another hostile government in Moscow, the United States could require more nuclear weapons for deterrence. This group is uncomfortable with talk of deep reductions of U.S. strategic offensive arms below START II levels.[29]

Deep Reduction

At the June 1990 Washington summit, Presidents Bush and Gorbachev agreed to follow-on negotiations once the START Treaty was completed. Many proponents of arms control began to consider how far START's momentum could carry strategic offensive arms reductions. The common feature among these studies was their confidence in the ability of the arms control process to set ceilings as low as 1,000 accountable warheads on each side.[30] Reductions of this magnitude would have major implications for U.S. and Russian force structure.

Advocates of deep reductions disagree on the effect such reductions would have on strategic force structure. Many are open to the possibility that a triad of strategic forces could be preserved, because they believe a triad contributes to nuclear stability.[31] However, others believe that elements of a triad may be destabilizing and undesirable. For example, vulnerable systems present lucrative targets and may contribute to the failure of deterrence during extreme crisis. Systems with high war fighting potential pose a similar problem for stability. The force structures established by the United States and the Soviet Union during the Cold War had considerable war fighting capability, but arms control agreements have reduced that combat potential considerably. The weight of stability considerations would tend toward force structure diversity.

Supporters of deep reductions also disagree about the effect that reductions would have on the role of U.S. nuclear weapons. Many accept the traditional roles that nuclear weapons have played in U.S. security, although a few believe that extended deterrence would lack credibility with only 1,000 warheads. A few argue for a U.S. no first use pledge, even though the pledge would undermine extended deterrence and jeopardize important alliance relationships. Many advocates of deep reductions believe that nuclear targeting becomes a key issue at lower levels of deployed warheads. Some doubt that the United States would be able to support damage-limiting counterforce options with so few warheads. They call for a return to mutual assured destruction's emphasis on socioeconomic targets. Others emphasize targeting general-purpose forces exclusively or a mix of military facilities.

In short, deep reduction raises many important issues about U.S. nuclear policy, but the common ground among its advocates is very narrow. The lack of common ground potentially makes deep reductions a difficult option for the arms control community to adopt.

Threat Deconstruction

One of the boldest proposals for strategic offensive arms control has come from those who see in the new international security environment an opportunity to deconstruct nearly the entire Cold War nuclear threat. Supporters of threat deconstruction call for reductions to the level of a few hundred accountable warheads on each side.[32] Although they disagree on issues of process and timing, supporters agree that the role of nuclear weapons is to deter nuclear attack on the United States and its close allies. They also support a no first use pledge. However, neither of these ideas is new. The most interesting contribution from the deconstruction camp has been in the realm of nuclear sufficiency.

Nuclear sufficiency is the judgment that one's nuclear forces are sufficient in number and capability to carry out the political-military objectives set for them. Nuclear sufficiency repeatedly has been an issue in the United States since the late 1960s.[33] Threat deconstruction raises these issues again at a time when arms control agreements (START II) appear to have set them in the background for the foreseeable future. To their credit, threat deconstructionists address the issue squarely.

For the United States and Russia to reduce their strategic offensive arms to a few hundred deployed warheads, threat deconstruction advocates recommend that the following conditions be met:[34]

- Continuation of a cooperative security environment between the United States and Russia
- Continued progress toward reform and stability in Russia
- Establishment of an effective nonproliferation regime
- Agreement to reassess force reductions if a rogue state violates the nonproliferation norm
- Agreement by all five nuclear weapon states and the "threshold" states to limit their stockpiles to 200 warheads each

- Adoption of a nuclear weapon employment policy based on defensive last resort
- Acceptance of a verification regime based on the START model

These conditions are very close to a list of potential proposals for a multilateral arms control negotiation involving the five acknowledged nuclear weapon states. They build upon and broaden existing strategic arms control agreements. As such, threat deconstruction is a paradigm for significant evolution in the traditional, bilateral approach to strategic offensive arms control. The only approach that is more ambitious than nuclear deconstruction is total nuclear disarmament.

Nuclear Disarmament

Eventually, the end of the Cold War may return us to the origin of U.S. strategic arms control policy, nuclear disarmament. There is less discussion of nuclear disarmament today in the United States than there was 50 years ago, which may be because there is less confidence in international institutions. Unlike nuclear arms reduction, nuclear disarmament implies treaty supervision and enforcement by an international organization powerful enough to command respect and obedience. In the United States, there is long-standing suspicion about powerful supranational institutions and long-standing concern about the cost, bureaucracy, and timidity of international organizations whose purpose is the implementation of arms control agreements. It would be a major irony if the most serious obstacle to nuclear disarmament was U.S. hostility to the development of international organizations. A detailed plan to develop an international organization to enforce a worldwide nuclear disarmament agreement already exists; it is a U.S. plan. The plan failed to gain acceptance when first announced because the fundamental political conditions for its success did not exist. Today, conditions have changed, and the Baruch Plan provides a model for fresh consideration and innovation.

Conclusion

In surveying the progress of strategic offensive arms control over the past 50 years, two trends stand out. The first is strategic arms control policy's maturation as a tool of U.S. national security. Strategic arms control has developed from a subordinate tool to a full partner with defense policy. In the process, strategic offensive arms control has produced a series of breakthrough agreements that are exciting not only for their content but for their variety of form. There is genuine momentum in strategic arms control, as advocates of deep reduction suggest. There is a level of confidence today in the arms control process that makes threat deconstruction conceivable.

The second trend is the growth of uncertainty about the role of nuclear weapons. Over the last half-century, nuclear weapons have played a crucial role in U.S. national security affairs. Today, however, that role appears to be shrinking, and a stated objective of U.S. policy is to make the role of nuclear weapons shrink even more. Paradoxically, the improvement in U.S. national security in the post–Cold War period also has blunted the urgency of aggressive new arms control efforts. Implementing the important agreements in hand appears to have taken priority.

Deep reduction, threat deconstruction, and nuclear disarmament are approaches with great promise for achieving the broad, traditional objectives of arms control policy. Each approach holds potential for further reductions in the risk of war, savings in defense expenditure, and reduction of war's destructiveness. Threat deconstruction and nuclear disarmament support the possibility of expanded participation in the arms control process by other nuclear weapon states. However, if the last 50 years reveal anything, it is that strategic arms control is neither inevitable nor linear. Strategic offensive arms control is part of a national security process. Arms control has never dominated the process, and it never should. Governments see utility in possessing nuclear weapons even when they dread the prospect of using them; hence the desire in official circles of the U.S. government to concentrate, at least for a time, on arms control treaty implementation. If the United States is to reshape the future of the international security environment and reduce the role of nuclear weapons in human affairs, then it must be prepared to deal with the underlying conditions that contribute to international conflict and make strategic offensive arms useful.

Suggested Reading

Bull, Hedley. *The Control of the Arms Race: Disarmament and Arms Control in the Missile Age.* New York: Praeger, 1965.

Bundy, McGeorge, et al. "Reducing Nuclear Danger." *Foreign Affairs,* Spring 1993.

Daalder, Ivo. *Stepping Down the Nuclear Ladder: How Low Can We Go?* Paper No. 5, Project on Rethinking Arms Control. Center for International Security Studies, University of Maryland, June 1993.

Dunn, Lewis. "Rethinking the Nuclear Equation." *Washington Quarterly,* Winter 1994.

Glaser, Charles. "Nuclear Policy Without an Adversary: US Planning for the Post-Soviet Era." *International Affairs,* Spring 1992.

Goodpaster, Andrew J. *Further Reins on Nuclear Arms: Next Steps of the Major Powers.* Washington, D.C.: Atlantic Council, 1993.

National Academy of Sciences. *The Future of the US-Soviet Nuclear Relationship.* Washington, D.C.: National Academy of Sciences, 1991.

Newhouse, John. *Cold Dawn: The Story of SALT.* New York: Holt, Rinehart and Winston, 1973.

Talbott, Strobe. *Endgame: The Inside Story of SALT II.* New York: Harper and Row, 1979.

U.S. Department of Defense. *Nuclear Posture Review.* Washington, D.C., 1994.

Notes

1. The Jeffries Committee considered a variety of policy issues associated with the development of nuclear weapons. One of the major contributions of the committee was its report on the impact of nuclear weapons on postwar international security.

2. *Final Report to the Secretary of War,* November 1945.

3. Michael O. Wheeler, *Nuclear Weapons and the Korean War,* Lessons from Nuclear History Project, Center for National Security Negotiations, November 1994, p. 54.

4. In December 1946, Baruch tried to get the UN Security Council to put the U.S. disarmament plan to a vote. Only two states, China and the United States, voted to put the Baruch Plan to a vote. Four of the five permanent members of the council had nuclear weapons development programs in 1946.

5. *Arms Control and Disarmament Agreements: Texts and Histories of the Negotiations* (Washington, D.C.: Arms Control and Disarmament Agency, 1990), p. 20.

6. The purpose of ACDA is to formulate, coordinate, and carry out arms control policies; conduct and coordinate arms control related research; prepare and manage U.S. participation in arms control negotiations; and disseminate public information about arms control.

7. National Security Council Memorandum-162/2, Basic National Security Policy, was the analysis on which massive retaliation doctrine was based, and it predicted the loss of U.S. nuclear superiority.

8. Jerome H. Kahan, *Security in the Nuclear Age* (Washington, D.C.: Brookings Institution, 1975), p. 171.

9. The SALT process also produced the Antiballistic Missile Treaty and established the relationship between strategic offensive and defensive forces that has existed ever since. The SALT negotiations also established mutual assured destruction as the basis of U.S. nuclear strategy.

10. *The Interim Agreement Between the United States of America and the Union of Soviet Socialist Republics on Certain Measures with Respect to the Limitation of Strategic Offensive Arms,* 1972.

11. *Treaty Between the United States of America and the Union of Soviet Socialist Republics on the Limitation of Strategic Offensive Arms,* 1979.

12. Soviet heavy ICBMs were the SS-9 and SS-18.

13. The treaty involved the issue of multiple independently targetable reentry vehicles (MIRVs). The major limits of the treaty were 1,320 MIRVed strategic launchers (MIRVed ICBMs, submarine-launched ballistic missiles [SLBMs], and air-launched cruise missle [ALCM]-carrying heavy bombers), 1,200 MIRVed strategic ballistic missiles, and 820 MIRVed ICBMs for each party to the agreement. (See Appendix 2 for a more complete listing of treaty provisions.)

14. *Break out* refers to the capacity of a nuclear weapon state to expand its number of deployed systems, deployed warheads, or both in a relatively short period of time.

15. In September 1991 and January 1992, the United States unilaterally promised to remove from alert status all ICBMs scheduled for deactivation under START, accelerate the elimination of such systems once START was ratified, terminate the mobile Peacekeeper program, cease production of Peacekeeper ICBMs, terminate the Small ICBM program, cease production of new warheads (W-88) for sea-based ballistic missiles, remove all U.S. strategic bombers from alert, cancel the short-range attack missile (SRAM II) program, and halt purchase of the advanced cruise missile.

16. Soviet/Russian unilateral initiatives included removal of 503 ICBMs from alert, restrictions on rail-mobile ICBM production/operation/deployment, termination of a small mobile ICBM, elimination of 130 ICBM silos, retirement of three SSBNs (nuclear-powered ballistic missile submarines) and dismantlement of six others, reduction of SSBNs on patrol by 50 percent, removal of heavy bombers from alert, termination of a short-range nuclear missile, cessation of production of two heavy bomber types, limitation of heavy bomber exercises to include no more than 30 aircraft, and cessation of production of existing types of long-range ALCMs.

17. START II allows MIRVed ICBMs with as many as six warheads to be kept in the inventory provided that they are downloaded to a single warhead system. Downloading is subject to other numerical constraints.

18. At one time, technical advisers to strategic arms control negotiations were experts on strategic arms control policy, force structure, and strategic force operations. Today, technical advisers are likely to be experts in industrial processes, safety procedures, and security practices.

19. The NPR predicted that the budget for strategic nuclear weapons in 2003 would fall by roughly two-thirds (constant fiscal year 1995 dollars) compared with the same budget in 1989. *Nuclear Posture Review Presentation,* press/public version, Department of Defense, 1994.

20. Remarks by the Honorable John D. Holum, U.S. Arms Control and Disarmament Agency at the Ministry of External Affairs, New Delhi, India, 1 November 1994. Official text. ACDA Public Affairs.

21. *Nuclear Posture Review Presentation,* press/public version, Department of Defense, September 1994. The NPR is not a classical government report. It is a DOD presentation that has classified and unclassified versions.

22. No first use is a formal pledge by a nuclear weapon state not to use nuclear weapons first in conflict.

23. "New US Nuclear Strategy Called Mutual Assured Safety," *Washington Times,* 23 September 1994.

24. This is the third time a U.S. secretary of defense has abandoned MAD. Secretary of Defense James Schlesinger did it in 1974 with the announcement of the Schlesinger Doctrine. Secretary of Defense Caspar Weinberger did it in the early 1980s when he implemented NSDD-13 and created the Strategic Defense Initiative Organization.

25. *New type* is a term from the START I Treaty. It refers to strategic offensive arms that are not ICBMs, SLBMs, or heavy bombers. When the United States protected new types in START, it did so with a particular new type in mind, hypersonic boost-glide vehicles.

26. The terms *triad* and *dyad* refer to two distinct force structures for strategic offensive forces. A triad of nuclear forces has three elements: ICBMs, SLBMs, and heavy bombers. A dyad consists of two elements.

27. Two nonnuclear programs have the potential to take up some of the burden now placed on U.S. strategic offensive arms. These are precision conventional munitions and ballistic missile defenses.

28. Remarks by Mr. Thomas E. McNamara, assistant secretary of state for political-military affairs, Fifth Annual Arms Control and Verification Conference, November 1994, Southern Methodist University, Dallas, Tex.

29. T. C. Reed and M. O. Wheeler, *The Role of Nuclear Weapons in the New World Order (The Reed Report)*. P. Nitze testimony to the Senate Foreign Relations Committee on the START Treaty, 25 February 1992.

30. *The Future of the U.S.-Soviet Nuclear Relationship (National Academy of Sciences Report)*, National Academy of Sciences, September 1991; S. Drell testimony to the Senate Foreign Relations Committee on the START Treaty, 3 March 1992. J. Dean testimony to the Senate Foreign Relations Committee on the START Treaty, 5 March 1992; C. L. Glaser, "Nuclear Policy Without an Adversary: U.S. Planning for the Post-Soviet Era," *International Security* (Spring 1992), pp. 34–78; P. Warnke, "Missionless Missile," *Bulletin of the Atomic Scientists* (May 1992), pp. 36–38; M. Bundy, W. Crowe, and S. Drell, "Reducing Nuclear Danger," *Foreign Affairs* (Spring 1993), pp. 140–155.

31. Force structures composed of ICBMs, SLBMs, and heavy bombers are said to contribute to stability because they increase the operational complexity of a successful preemptive strike.

32. A. J. Goodpaster, *Further Reins on Nuclear Arms: Next Steps for the Major Nuclear Powers* (Washington, D.C.: Atlantic Council, August 1993); and I. Daalder, *Stepping Down the Thermonuclear Ladder: How Low Can We Go?* (Baltimore: University of Maryland Center for International and Security Studies, 1993).

33. In the late 1960s, the United States lost its nuclear superiority over the Soviet Union. See any *Annual Report of the Secretary of Defense* published in the 1970s.

34. A. J. Goodpaster, *Further Reins on Nuclear Arms.*

6

Strategic Defensive Arms Control

Sidney N. Graybeal and Patricia A. McFate

Strategic defense in the nuclear age has focused on ballistic missile defense (BMD), particularly since the Soviet Union launched its Sputnik satellite in 1957. There are, of course, other delivery means for nuclear warheads and other weapons of mass destruction; it follows that there are other means of defending against these threats besides BMD. For example, high- and low-altitude air-breathing threats, whether manned or unmanned (e.g., airplanes and cruise missiles), can be met by strategic air defenses (early warning systems, ground-based missiles, and interceptor aircraft carrying a myriad of weaponry). Strategic nuclear missile submarines can be countered by antisubmarine warfare techniques and systems (e.g., SOSUS listening devices, attack submarines), as well as by antiballistic missiles. Enemy satellites can be attacked by antisatellite (ASAT) weapons. Yet none of these threats has carried the same emotional charge as the fear of attack by ballistic missiles on U.S. forces and civilians. This explains the U.S. preoccupation with strategic ballistic missiles and strategic BMD. Strategic defensive arms control has been similarly focused on BMD systems.

This chapter will, accordingly, emphasize strategic defensive arms control as it relates to ballistic missile defenses, in particular the 1972 Antiballistic Missile (ABM) Treaty.

The Historical Development of Strategic Defense Systems

After the Soviet Union's detonation of a nuclear device in August 1949, the United States, taking into account the intelligence community's projections of Soviet long-range bomber capabilities, embarked on the development of a strong air defense capability. The North American Air Defense Command (NORAD) was established in 1957, and around the same time, the United

119

States deployed Nike air defense missile units and its long-range surveillance radar systems became operational. As the U.S. air defense capability
was beginning to mature, two events took place that were considered additional indications of the emerging Soviet threat: a successful Soviet intercontinental ballistic missile (ICBM) test in August 1957 and the launching
of Sputnik in October of that year.

In both the United States and the Soviet Union, ABM defense concepts
and programs were being developed concurrently with ICBMs. Soviet development of ABM systems, which began by the 1950s, was concentrated at
the Sary Shagan test range in Kazakhstan. Construction of a primitive ABM
system near Leningrad was begun in 1961, but it was soon abandoned. In
1963, construction of the Tallinn system began. While this system was designed as a long-range, high-altitude air-defense system with little ABM capability, there was a major debate within the U.S. government on whether
the system could be upgraded for an ABM role. This "SAM-upgrade" question was a serious concern throughout the ABM Treaty negotiations, and it
remains an issue related to theater missile defenses.

It was clear by the early 1960s that a large-scale Soviet ABM program was
under way, a conclusion reinforced by General Secretary Nikita Khrushchev's
claim, in 1962, that the Soviet Union could "hit a fly in outer space." In 1962–
1963, construction began on a large ABM system at Moscow, utilizing a nuclear-
armed ABM interceptor. Originally, the Soviet Union appeared to be planning
eight ABM complexes at Moscow, each armed with 16 interceptor launchers.
However, in 1968, construction of the Moscow system slowed, and only four of
the complexes, with a total of 64 launchers, were ever completed.

With the emergence of Soviet ICBM and SLBM (submarine-launched
ballistic missile) capabilities, U.S. priorities shifted in the 1960s from air
defense to ballistic missile defense, resulting in the construction of the Ballistic Missile Early Warning System (BMEWS). At the same time, the U.S.
government assigned the highest priority to the development and testing of
the Nike Zeus BMD system.[1]

In the Kennedy and Johnson administrations, Secretary of Defense Robert McNamara's view of strategic deterrence was embodied in the concept of
mutual assured destruction (see Chapter 5). Arms control was considered
consistent with this strategy; BMD was not. McNamara was not convinced
that a BMD system was technically feasible and capable of defending the
U.S. population against the Soviet threat. By the mid-1960s, China had initiated testing of nuclear weapons, and it was developing strategic ballistic
missiles. In late 1967, McNamara announced deployment of the Sentinel
BMD system, which was intended to defend against a projected modest Chinese ballistic missile threat rather than the larger, more sophisticated Soviet
threat. This deployment decision was the first official shift away from the
original BMD mission of protecting the U.S. population and its cities and

industries from a Soviet ICBM and SLBM threat. By early 1969, Secretary of Defense Melvin Laird, after evaluation of the technological capabilities of the U.S. BMD program and the arguments associated with the ongoing debate within the scientific community about BMD, determined that the primary mission of the BMD program, the Safeguard system, was defense of Minuteman ICBMs.

Origin and Rationale of the ABM Treaty

During the Glassboro, N.J., summit meeting between Pres. Lyndon Johnson and Premier Aleksei Kosygin in June 1967, Secretary McNamara argued that there was a direct relationship between ABMs and strategic ballistic missiles that affected both crisis and strategic stability. When the United States raised the desirability of limiting ABM systems on the grounds of this link between strategic offensive and strategic defensive arms, Kosygin reportedly responded, "Why do you want to limit ABMs? They don't kill people; they protect them." A few months earlier, according to *Pravda*, Kosygin had stated: "I think that a defensive system which prevents attack is not a cause of the arms race. ... Perhaps an antimissile system is more expensive than an offensive system; but its purpose is not to kill people but to save human lives." McNamara pointed out the potential destabilizing effects of nationwide ABM defenses: with deployed effective nationwide BMD systems on both sides, there could be a temptation to shoot first in a time of crisis inasmuch as the initiator's offensive forces would be able to penetrate the other side's defenses and its own defenses would be able to defend against the reduced, ragged retaliatory attack. McNamara also pointed out the likelihood of such defenses contributing to an arms race in which both sides attempted to acquire more and better strategic offensive forces.

While Premier Kosygin had not been convinced of the desirability of limiting ABM systems at Glassboro, Soviet agreement to bilateral negotiations on limiting strategic offensive and defensive arms was announced by President Johnson on 1 July 1968, the day of the signing of the Non-Proliferation Treaty (NPT). The Soviet occupation of Czechoslovakia in August forced Johnson to postpone the negotiations, leaving the issues for Pres. Richard Nixon's administration to settle. In October 1969, Nixon announced that he had agreed with the Soviet leaders to begin talks on strategic arms. The negotiations, known as the first round of the Strategic Arms Limitation Talks (SALT I), began in Helsinki, Finland, on 17 November 1969.

During the early rounds of SALT, it became clear that the Soviets were prepared to limit ABM systems. It is not clear whether this change in previous Soviet views was based upon a recognition of the logic of McNamara's strategic stability arguments or a desire to curtail U.S. ABM systems. Both sides proposed strict limits on ABM systems, but serious differences over offensive limitations emerged. These disagreements reflected major dispari- ties in the makeup of the two sides' strategic forces, especially the Soviets' reliance on large land-based ICBMs and their desire to include in the accord the strategic forces held by U.S. allies and U.S. forward-based weapons on aircraft carriers and foreign bases.

Faced with the prospect of delays in progress due to disagreements over offensive limitations, the Soviet Union proposed that the sides agree on an ABM Treaty while leaving offensive forces to a subsequent negotiation. How- ever, the United States insisted on a dual agreement, hoping to use its ongo- ing ABM deployment program to gain Soviet concessions on offensive arms. In a back channel negotiation, Henry Kissinger, Nixon's national security adviser, and Anatoly Dobrynin, the Soviet ambassador to the United States, reached agreement in May 1971 that a comprehensive ABM accord would be accompanied by a more limited agreement on offensive arms, leaving more comprehensive offensive limitations to SALT II.

One year later, on 26 May 1972, President Nixon and Soviet leader Le- onid Brezhnev signed the SALT I agreements, including both the ABM Treaty and the Interim Agreement on Limiting Strategic Offensive Arms (see Ap- pendix 2). The ABM Treaty banned nationwide ABM systems, while allow- ing each side to maintain the ABM site it then possessed and, for the sake of symmetry, to build one of the type then being built by the other side. The interim agreement froze each side's missile launchers at the level then op- erational or under construction for five years, but it did not place any limits on multiple independently targetable reentry vehicles (MIRVs), bomber forces, or forward-based systems.

The U.S. Senate gave its advice and consent to ratification of the ABM Treaty on 3 August by a vote of 88 to 2, and both houses of Congress gave similarly overwhelming approval to the interim agreement. The accords entered into force on 3 October 1972.

The Scope of the ABM Treaty

The basic purpose of the treaty is contained in Article I, which prohibits deployment of an ABM system for "the defense of the territory" or provi- sion of a "base for such a defense." The former prohibition refers to a na- tionwide defense; the latter encompasses items that could be the long-lead- time supporting elements for a deployed land-based ABM system (e.g., large phased-array radars [LPARs]). All other treaty articles and agreed statements are designed to support Article I.

The 1974 protocol to the ABM Treaty limits each side to one ABM de- ployment site. The authorized deployment area, with a radius of 150 kilometers, must be centered either on the national capital area or on an ICBM field. All deployed ABM components must be located within the designated deployment area, and they must be fixed land-based components. Further limitations in Article III include a ceiling of 100 ABM launchers and 100 ABM missiles "at launch sites" in the ABM deployment area. Article V (2) prohibits certain capabilities of fixed land-based components, such as automatic, semiautomatic, or rapid reload ABM launchers and launchers that could launch more than one ABM interceptor missile at a time. Agreed Statement E extends these prohibitions to ABM interceptors with more than one independently guided warhead. No other prohibitions are placed on the ABM interceptors. The prohibition against a "defense of the territory" is achieved by the aforementioned limits and not by any limits on the range or velocity of the ABM interceptors themselves.

Verification of the ABM Treaty

Provisions of the treaty are to be verified solely by national technical means (NTM).[2] A unique aspect of the ABM Treaty verification regime was that it prohibited each party from interfering with the NTM of the other party, and it prohibited the use of deliberate concealment measures that would impede verification by NTM.

Verification is not tied to specific performance limitations on ABM interceptors or on "tests in an ABM mode." Such quantitative limitations were not negotiated for three main reasons: the United States wanted to maintain flexibility in its ABM interceptor designs and testing; it wanted to be able to challenge possible upgrading of any of the Soviet surface-to-air missile (SAM) systems; and it recognized the difficulty of monitoring specific quantitative limitations by NTM alone.

Implementation of the Treaty

Early in the SALT negotiations, both sides recognized the need for an implementing body. There were no serious problems in negotiating Article XIII of the treaty, which calls for the prompt establishment of a Standing Consultative Commission (SCC) to promote the objectives and implement the provisions of the treaty. The charter of the SCC is contained in a memorandum of understanding signed in Geneva on 21 December 1972; a protocol with regulations for the SCC was signed on 30 May 1973.[3] The SCC meets at least two times a year; additional sessions may be requested by either commissioner. The proceedings of the SCC are conducted in private; they may not be made public without the express consent of both commissioners.

During its 22 years of operation, the SCC has successfully negotiated the dismantling or destruction procedures called for in the ABM Treaty and in the interim agreement, has dealt effectively with ambiguities and compliance issues, and has negotiated legally binding clarifications to the treaty.

Article XIV calls for a review of the treaty at five-year intervals. To date, four reviews have been conducted. The first and second reviews, in 1977 and 1982, essentially affirmed the parties' adherence to the goals and provisions of the treaty. The third review, which was postponed at the request of the United States, took place in August 1988 during the Nuclear and Space Talks rather than in the SCC. This review resulted in separate statements by the two parties: the Soviet statement was directed at preservation and observance of the treaty; the U.S. statement focused on the right of the United States to continue those activities associated with the 1983 Strategic Defense Initiative (SDI) program that it had tabled in the Defense and Space Talks. The most recent review took place in the SCC in the fall of 1993. The participating states agreed on the following concluding statement: "Commitment to the ABM Treaty was reaffirmed and it was agreed that maintaining the viability of the Treaty in view of political and technological changes remains important. The delegations at the Review advocated continued efforts to strengthen the ABM Treaty."

The ABM Treaty and National Missile Defense

As noted earlier, the basic purpose of the treaty is to prohibit a defense of the territory of both parties, thereby reducing the dangers of a first strike in times of crisis and avoiding an arms race in strategic offensive weapons. Although some consideration was given to zero ABMs during the SALT I negotiations, it was clear that both sides, for different reasons, wanted to maintain the options for research and development and limited deployments. In the U.S. case, the Defense Department and the Joint Chiefs of Staff (JCS) recognized that obtaining funds from Congress for R&D with no ability to deploy would be difficult; in addition, the JCS argued for limited deployment to gain operational experience with ABM systems. In the Soviet case, the Soviets were deploying ABM systems around Moscow, and they did not wish to abandon this defensive capability of their capital. As a result, the parties agreed to two ABM deployment sites for each side (later reduced to one site by the 1974 protocol to the treaty).

The Soviets, and now the Russians, have continued an active missile defense research and development program since the treaty was signed, including traditional ABM components and new technologies, such as lasers. In addition, the single permitted ABM system at Moscow has been retained and upgraded. After treaty signature, the United States continued work at its Grand Forks site and terminated work at its Malmstrom site. The Grand Forks site achieved initial operational capability in April 1975 and full operational capability in October 1975; however, its limited defensive capability against projected Soviet ballistic missiles and its high operational costs led to a congressional decision to terminate all Safeguard operations except those associated with the perimeter acquisition radar (PAR) in February 1976. The PAR was transferred to the air force and continues to operate as an early warning radar. Grand Forks was deactivated, not dismantled or destroyed; thus, should the U.S. government decide to deploy national missile defense (NMD), extensive dismantling or destruction of the missile site radar (MSR) and the Spartan and Sprint launchers would be required to meet the procedures agreed to in the SCC.

U.S. NMD took a dramatic turn with the "Star Wars" speech of Pres. Ronald Reagan on 23 March 1983. In the speech, the president announced a proposal to develop an antimissile defense system so comprehensive that it would render "nuclear weapons impotent and obsolete." Reactions to the proposal ranged widely: some condemned it as impossible and destabilizing, while others saw it as the potential savior of the nation. While senior officials supported the proposal, in large part because it represented a personal commitment on the part of the commander in chief, Richard DeLauer, Pentagon chief of research and development stated, "There's no way an enemy can't overwhelm your defenses if he wants to badly enough."[4]

In January 1984, the Strategic Defense Initiative Organization (SDIO) was created to undertake a program to develop technologies associated with ballistic missile defense. The first SDI budget and program was submitted to Congress in February 1984.

The U.S.-Soviet Nuclear and Space Talks (NST), which commenced on 12 March 1985, incorporated discussions of strategic offensive and strategic defensive systems and their relationship. There were major areas of substantive disagreement in the Defense and Space (D&S) forum of the NST. The Soviets contended that an agreement concerning compliance with the ABM Treaty was a condition of a reduction in strategic offensive arms; the United States opposed linkage. The United States tabled a draft treaty in 1988 calling for research, development, and testing of advanced defenses based on the "broad interpretation" of the treaty; the Soviets rejected the interpretation. The United States called for its rights to withdraw from the treaty after a specified period of time; the Soviets argued that Article XV of the treaty did not permit withdrawal simply in view of the successful development of an effective strategic defensive program. While the United States proposed making a transition from deterrence based on the threat of nuclear retaliation (mutual assured destruction) toward increased reliance on defenses against ballistic missiles (mutual assured survival), the Soviets sought a comprehensive ban on research, development, testing, and deployment of "space-strike arms."[5]

On 11 October 1985, President Reagan announced his determination that a broader interpretation of the ABM Treaty was fully justified. Under the broad interpretation, or the so-called reinterpretation of the treaty, ABM systems that are based on "other physical principles" (i.e., other than ABM interceptor missiles, ABM launchers, and ABM radars known in 1972) and including components capable of substituting for ABM interceptor missiles, ABM launchers, or ABM radars may be developed and tested but not deployed, regardless of their basing mode. Under the narrower, traditional interpretation, development and testing of ABM systems based on other physical principles are allowed only for fixed land-based systems and components. Immediately after the announcement, Secretary of State George Shultz explained that while the new interpretation reflected U.S. legal rights, the United States would not change its policy of conducting the SDI program according to the narrow interpretation of the treaty.

The most effective opponent of the reinterpretation was Congress, in particular the Senate. The lead role of challenging, and eventually defeating, the reinterpretation was undertaken by Sen. Sam Nunn, then chairman of the Senate Armed Services Committee. Senator Nunn's review of the ratification record found that the Nixon administration presented the Senate with the historic interpretation of the treaty's limits on space-based and other mobile types of exotic systems, and the Senate clearly understood this interpretation when it gave its advice and consent to the ratification of the treaty. The immediate result of congressional review was to block the administration's switch to the broad interpretation. In the defense authorization acts of fiscal years 1988 and 1989, Congress enacted provisions requiring that SDI funds be spent only on activities consistent with the narrow interpretation. By this time, even Nixon, who had signed the ABM Treaty in 1972, had stated publicly his unequivocal support for the historic interpretation.[6]

The Reykjavík summit meeting on 11–12 October 1986 between President Reagan and General Secretary Gorbachev came close to an agreement on significant reductions in U.S. and Soviet strategic offensive ballistic missiles. The Soviets proposed that the United States provide a 10-year commitment not to withdraw from the ABM Treaty; the United States offered to accept the commitment through 1996, provided research, development, and testing in accordance with the broad interpretation could continue. The Soviet response, which was unacceptable to Reagan, was a proposal to ban testing of space-based elements of a missile defense system outside of laboratories. Thus, the summit failed to make progress on either reduction of strategic offensive arms or ABM Treaty clarifications.

The ultimate goal of the SDI program was complete U.S. homeland protection from a massive Soviet nuclear attack. But the plan was to be developed incrementally. The initial step, Phase One, was designed to blunt, not completely stop, a massive attack. One of the key elements in the defensive system was the use of space-based interceptors and sensors. At first, SDIO considered individual space-based interceptors but found their cost prohibitive. Then came the idea to place up to 10 space-based interceptors into "space garages" that would cut costs but provided an attractive target. The next step was called Brilliant Pebbles, envisioned as a system of low-cost, mass-produced, highly autonomous, and individually deployed space-based interceptors. However, the Brilliant Pebbles program never lived up to the promises of its advocates, and Congress had deep concerns about weapons in space and a program that was clearly noncompliant with the ABM Treaty.

As time passed, the initial enthusiastic endorsements for the SDI diluted as the scientific and technological community weighed in with their skeptical responses. A report of the American Physical Society in April 1987 estimated that "even in the best of circumstances, a decade or more of intensive research would be required to provide the technical knowledge needed for an informed decision about the potential effectiveness and survivability of directed energy weapon systems."[7] Similar questions were raised by the Congressional Office of Technology Assessment in a report dated June 1988. The report warned that because of the difficulty of testing the elaborate SDI computer systems under realistic conditions, there would be "a significant probability that the first (and presumably only) time the BMD system were used in real war, it would suffer a catastrophic failure."[8]

In January 1988, Senator Nunn proposed that near-term SDI research be redirected toward exploring the feasibility of an Accidental Launch Protection System (ALPS), a very limited treaty-compliant system designed to defend against a few missiles launched by accident or without authorization. Nunn's proposal touched off a wide-ranging discussion of whether accidental or unauthorized attacks represented a significant threat and of the pros and cons of the ALPS approach to dealing with them.

SDIO announced the Global Protection Against Limited Strikes (GPALS) plan in 1991. Its goal was to completely protect the United States from an unauthorized, accidental, or Third World nuclear attack of up to 200 warheads; the maximum number of warheads represented a boatload of submarine-launched ballistic missiles or the missiles controlled by a single commander of a ground-based ICBM deployment in the former Soviet Union. The initial plan also envisioned improved theater defense deployed in the mid-1990s. The completed system was to have an overlay of about 1,000 Brilliant Pebble interceptors that would aid both a U.S. homeland defense (of about 750 ground-based interceptors) and advanced theater defenses.

In the Missile Defense Act of 1991, Congress went on record as supporting deployment of a U.S. missile defense. The act endorsed the concept of a limited defense "designed to protect the United States against limited ballistic missile threats, including accidental or unauthorized launches or Third World attacks." One of the key provisions was a mandate to develop an NMD by 1996 or as soon as the technology was ready. The single U.S.

defensive site was to contain 100 ground-based interceptors and be fully compliant with the ABM Treaty. This approach was completely consistent with Senator Nunn's ALPS proposal of 1988.

On 17 June 1992, Presidents Bush and Yeltsin signed a joint statement in which they agreed to cooperate in the development of a concept for a Global Protection System (GPS). The Russians used the term Global Defense System; they believed that this system could be accomplished outside of but consistent with the ABM Treaty. At the Washington summit, Bush and Yeltsin agreed to "explore on a priority basis" potential opportunities for sharing data in a ballistic missile early warning system, for cooperating in ballistic missile defense capabilities and technologies, and for developing a legal basis for the implementation of GPS, including the possible negotiation of new treaties.

Although U.S. theater missile defense (TMD) systems are receiving the highest priority, the Department of Defense is also developing for deployment a ground-based, treaty-compliant NMD system as a hedge against the possibility that new strategic ballistic missile threats may emerge after the turn of the century. The threat of an intercontinental ballistic missile attack on the United States has markedly changed. The Cold War threat—an all-out, high-level attack from the Soviet Union—has disappeared. Limited ballistic missile threats to the continental United States from accidental or unauthorized Chinese or Russian launches are unlikely in the foreseeable future. However, some Third World countries could acquire long-range ballistic missile capabilities within the next 10 years. As former director of central intelligence James Woolsey has noted, "After the turn of the century, some countries that are hostile to the United States might be able to acquire ballistic missiles that could threaten the Continental United States … over the next ten years we are likely to see several Third World countries at least establish the infrastructure and develop the technical knowledge that is necessary to undertake ICBM and space launch vehicle development."[9]

While a defense of the continental United States against these possible small threats could be provided by a single treaty-compliant site at Grand Forks, this NMD system would not provide any protection for Alaska or Hawaii. Thus, if the United States decides to deploy an NMD system, the ABM Treaty would need to be amended to allow for defense of all U.S. states. Deployments of such defensive systems would not be inconsistent with the basic purpose of the treaty and are probably negotiable.

ABM Treaty Compliance Issues

Article XIII of the ABM Treaty charges the SCC to, inter alia, "consider questions concerning compliance with the obligations assumed and related situations which may be considered ambiguous." Numerous compliance questions and ambiguities have been raised and clarified in the SCC. However, with the discovery of the LPAR near Krasnoyarsk in 1983, the Reagan administration charged the Soviet Union with "a continuing pattern" of violation of arms control agreements, including the ABM Treaty. The Bush administration claimed that the "totality of Soviet ABM and ABM-related activities" suggested that the Soviet Union might have been preparing a defense of its national territory.

The Krasnoyarsk radar was a clear violation of the treaty, even though it was not considered a militarily significant violation—the radar was not located along the country's periphery or oriented outward, as required by Article VI(b). In 1989, Soviet foreign minister Eduard Shevardnadze admitted that the Krasnoyarsk radar was, "to put it bluntly, a violation of the ABM Treaty. At last we resolved this issue and announced we would dismantle the station." Subsequently, the United States agreed that Russia could convert the radar installation to a furniture factory; to date, there is no evidence that this conversion has taken place.

In SCC sessions, the Soviets have mentioned a number of U.S. activities that could cause concern in regard to treaty compliance. Most of these issues were clarified, and none was considered to be a clear violation by the United States. When the United States raised the compliance issue associated with the Krasnoyarsk radar, the Soviet Union raised questions regarding the U.S. radars at Thule, Greenland, and Fylingdales Moor, United Kingdom. These radars, the Soviets contended, were inconsistent with Agreed Statement F, which prohibits LPAR deployments except as provided for in Articles III (ABM deployments) and IV (test ranges). The United States has steadfastly maintained that these radars existed at the time the treaty was negotiated and that the treaty permits their modernization and replacement; thus, they are not a violation of the treaty.

The ABM Treaty and Theater Missile Defense

On 13 May 1993, Secretary of Defense Les Aspin renamed the Strategic Defense Initiative Organization the Ballistic Missile Defense Organization (BMDO). BMDO, which reports to the under-secretary of defense for acquisition, encompasses programs on theater missile defense, national missile defense, and follow-on research on more advanced BMD technologies. The TMD initiative was given the highest priority by the Clinton administration. Its mission is to protect U.S. forces, U.S. allies, and other important countries, including areas of vital interest to the United States, from theater missile attacks. The mission includes protection of population centers, fixed civilian and military assets, and mobile military units.

Though it is impossible to provide exact numbers of countries that have, or are developing, weapons of mass destruction (WMD), official U.S. intelligence estimates suggest that at least 25 countries may be developing such weapons and delivery systems for their use. Informed estimates suggest that 24 countries have chemical weapons programs in various stages of development, about 10 countries have biological weapons programs in various stages of development, and at least 10 countries reportedly are interested in nuclear weapons development.

Coupled with WMD proliferation is the expansion of the number of countries that have acquired, or are seeking to acquire, theater ballistic missiles. At least 12 developing countries now have basic Soviet SCUD-class or better missiles. Of particular concern are those missile programs in Iran, Syria, Libya, and especially North Korea. The most prevalent missiles among these proliferant countries are the SCUD-B, with an approximate range of 300 kilometers, and some longer-range derivatives. More worrisome, however, is the development of new, longer-range ballistic missiles.

New suppliers, primarily China and North Korea, are introducing missiles that are longer in range and more effective than the SCUD-B, including the Chinese M-9 and the North Korean Nodong-1. North Korea is also known to be developing the Taepo Dong-1 and Taepo Dong-2 ballistic missiles, which, according to the CIA, could eventually threaten all of Japan, China, Australia, New Zealand, and Southeast Asia. These ballistic missiles will be capable of delivering conventional high explosive, chemical, biological, or nuclear warheads. Some of the missiles could also incorporate submunitions containing high explosive, chemical, or biological agents. Releasing submunitions in the early stages of a missile's flight would pose serious problems for achieving effective TMD systems because it would be an effective countermeasure. Unless the missiles can be intercepted prior to their release, it would be difficult, if not impossible, to intercept each submunition.

Proliferation poses both direct and indirect threats, each of which could be severe. The near-term direct threat to U.S. and allied military forces and to urban centers overseas is the most obvious. Unless the proliferation of WMD and delivery means is countered, U.S. and allied expeditionary forces will confront opponents capable of striking rapidly at cities, seaports, airports, forward bases, and troop concentrations. Proliferation of WMD and advanced delivery means could also undermine the capacity of the United States to form coalitions and to mount power projection operations at an acceptable level of risk. The indirect threat involves the effect that the possibility of WMD strikes would likely have on decisionmaking concerning regional crises. Military operations that have been considered reasonable options, such as U.S. leadership in Desert Shield and Desert Storm, could become too dangerous to be considered politically acceptable. Effective TMD can prove an important element in countering the proliferation threat and facilitating the formation of coalitions.

In the time that it will take to field an effective defense against these real and emerging threats—five to eight years—more-capable delivery systems could further proliferate. These ballistic missiles will not disappear regardless of the many international nonproliferation and counterproliferation efforts and proposals, such as a global intermediate-range nuclear forces agreement (built upon the 1987 bilateral U.S.-Soviet INF Treaty, which eliminated ballistic missiles with ranges between 500 and 5,500 kilometers). The United States and Russia recognize the need to provide effective TMD systems for protection against these real and emerging ballistic missile threats.

The Clinton administration is seeking an agreed clarification of the ABM Treaty in the SCC to facilitate the acquisition of effective TMD systems to meet the emerging threat consistent with the purpose and intent of the treaty. Antitactical ballistic missile (ATBM) systems, the systems for TMD, are not limited per se by the treaty. However, Article VI(a) states that the parties must not give non-ABM components the "capabilities to counter strategic ballistic missiles or their elements in flight trajectory" and they must not be tested "in an ABM mode."

Implementing Article VI(a) in the new international security environment requires an agreed clarification of the current differences between strategic and tactical/theater ballistic missiles. In 1972, strategic ballistic missiles, in the context of the ABM Treaty, were those limited by the interim agreement; these missiles included the SS-N-6, a 3,000-kilometer-range missile with maximum velocity close to 5 kilometers per second. The few remaining SS-N-6 missiles will probably be removed from Russian strategic forces in the mid-1990s. The emerging theater ballistic missile threat includes missiles with ranges on the order of 3,000–3,500 kilometers and maximum velocities of about 5 kilometers per second. Most current modern strategic ballistic missiles have ranges over 9,000 kilometers and maximum velocities over 7 kilometers per second. Permitting ATBM testing against ballistic missiles with velocities up to 5 kilometers per second, as proposed by the Clinton administration in the SCC, would facilitate achieving effective TMD systems without violating the ABM Treaty. The buffer of 2 kilometers per second between theater and strategic ballistic missiles would be verifiable by NTM, the only verification means for the treaty.

The Clinton administration adopted the "demonstrated" criterion for judging capabilities of ballistic missile defense systems. Although simulations or computer projections, which include "footprint" or likely warhead coverage calculations, are very useful for design engineers and program managers, the capabilities derived through use of these simulations cannot be verified by NTM. Thus, utilizing simulations or computer projections to determine whether system capabilities violate ABM Treaty limits would result in a dual standard: the United States would tie its hands without the ability to access and evaluate Russian computer simulations of capabilities. The only verifiable means for determining the capabilities of a ballistic missile defense component or system is by demonstrated activities, such as testing in an ABM mode. No military commander will accept for operational use a system whose capabilities have not been demonstrated by actual flight testing.

Adoption of the demonstrated approach, perhaps buttressed by confidence-building measures, is completely consistent with the intent of the treaty and its verification. The Senate has adopted a congressional finding (Sec. 234 [a][7] of P.L. 103-160) that states that the treaty does not apply to TMD systems unless such systems are "tested against or have demonstrated capabilities to counter modern strategic ballistic missiles."

A treaty compliance issue involving the Theater High Altitude Air Defense (THAAD) system came to light with the publication of the Senate fiscal-year 1995 DOD Authorization Bill. The report language reads, in part: "Based on U.S. computer simulations, the Administration has determined that the THAAD system could possess a 'significant' intercept probability against some strategic reentry vehicles, but only after the full UOES [User Operational Evaluation System] system is in place, including battle management software to receive cueing information from external sensor sources." This statement clearly indicates that the U.S. judgment on the compliance of the THAAD system with the treaty was based on computer simulations. Unfortunately, the administration appears to have adopted a dual standard for determining compliance with the treaty, to the detriment of its achieving timely, effective TMD systems needed to meet the real and emerging theater ballistic missile threats and without the ability to impose and verify the same standard on Russia. Verification of the ABM Treaty is by NTM alone; this verification regime does not permit access to computer simulations.

Space-Based Sensors and the ABM Treaty

The issue of the compliance of space-based sensors continues to be raised, both within the government and in the arms control community outside the government. Congress clearly stated its belief that space-based sensors are not prohibited by the treaty in the Missile Defense Act of 1991, as modified by the fiscal-year 1993 DOD Authorization Act, when it indicated that there should be "optimum utilization of space-based sensors, including sensors capable of cueing ground-based antiballistic missile interceptors and providing initial targeting vectors, and other sensor systems that are not prohibited by the ABM Treaty."

While there are limits on ABM radars in the treaty, the only constraints on non-ABM radars or other sensors are placed on the deployment of early warning LPARs; they must be located along the periphery of the country and oriented outward. There are no limits on the amount and quality of data that may be transmitted to a battle management center, and there are no treaty limits on battle management. Thus, data from early warning radars can be transmitted to NORAD, just as data from LPARs can be transmitted to Moscow.

This position regarding LPAR data and its use was confirmed in the Bush administration Compliance Report to Congress dated 19 January 1993. The report stated that the U.S. government

> now judges that the support of ABM systems by early warning radars providing precise handover data will not constitute use of the early warning radars as ABM radars in violation of the ABM Treaty. Specifically, [the U.S. government] will not consider as prohibited the handover of precise target state vectors by properly located and oriented early warning radars to ABM systems or ABM components.[10]

The report concludes that "handover by an early warning radar to an ABM system or ABM component would not constitute 'testing in an ABM mode,' nor giving of 'capability to counter strategic ballistic missiles,'" which are the limits provided in Article VI(a) of the treaty. This position was accepted by the Clinton administration.

The foregoing conclusions on ground-based sensors should also apply to data from space-based sensors, as well as sea-based and air-based sensors. All these external sensors can transmit data to battle management centers, which can then be used to enhance the capabilities of either an ABM or ATBM system completely consistent with the treaty.

Verification by NTM alone was a key consideration during the treaty negotiations. The United States could not monitor transmissions over land lines from LPARs to the Moscow ABM battle management center; however, there were opportunities to monitor transmissions directly to ABM interceptors in flight. The only way these external sensors would violate the treaty would be if they became ABM components (e.g., if they substituted for an ABM radar by transmitting data directly to an ABM interceptor in flight). Such transmissions would be subject to detection by NTM. It is recognized that the transmission of these data via a battle management center to an interceptor requires only a few seconds; it was also recognized and accepted in 1972 in regard to data from LPARs. Neither space-, air-, sea-, or land-based sensors, nor the quantity or quality of the data they transmit, are limited by the treaty unless the data are transmitted directly to an ABM interceptor while in flight.

Multilateralization of the Treaty

Although the ABM Treaty has survived efforts to diminish its authority, to rewrite its provisions, or to destroy it totally, it now faces an issue that could not possibly have been envisioned when it was negotiated: the question of which country or countries should be considered the successor to the Soviet

Union for purposes of continued treaty implementation. On 9 October 1992, the heads of state of all but one of the republics of the former Soviet Union that belong to the Commonwealth of Independent States (CIS) signed what is known as the Bishkek Agreement. The agreement says that the signatory states are the successor states to the former Soviet Union and that they will implement the terms of the treaty.

The successor state question is a key issue for Russia because, as indicated in Map 6.1, some LPARs and ABM test ranges are located outside its borders. Delegations from Belarus, Kazakhstan, Russia, and Ukraine are participating in the ongoing SCC negotiations. The successor issue needs to be resolved for political and tactical reasons and because some of the badly needed clarifications or modifications to the treaty could be affected by the outcome. Also, future adjustments to the treaty could become more complex and difficult as more parties are included in the negotiations.

Recent Negotiations on Clarifying the Treaty

In December 1993, the Clinton administration announced its goal to seek a clear, negotiated demarcation between ABM and non-ABM systems to clarify the ABM Treaty provisions. SCC sessions since then have involved proposals to provide for multilateral succession to the treaty and to clarify the demarcation between ABM systems limited by the treaty and non-ABM systems.

To resolve the demarcation between strategic and theater ballistic missiles utilizing the demonstrated standard for determining capabilities, the Clinton administration proposed permitting TMD tests against theater ballistic missiles with ranges up to 3,500 kilometers and maximum velocities of 5 kilometers per second. It has been widely reported that Russia has proposed additional technical constraints. Resolution of the demarcation issue is necessary for the United States to achieve fully effective TMD systems. During the May 1995 Moscow summit, Pres. Bill Clinton and President Yeltsin reached agreement on a joint statement, which committed both countries to the ABM Treaty, "a cornerstone of strategic stability," and established basic principles to guide further negotiations on the demarcation issues.

Conclusion

The preamble of the ABM Treaty contains its basic premise: "Effective measures to limit anti-ballistic-missile systems would be a substantial factor in curbing the race in strategic offensive arms and would lead to a decrease in the risk of outbreak of war involving nuclear weapons." This premise remains valid at least through the implementation of the START agreements,

Map 6.1 ABM Facilities in the Former Soviet Union

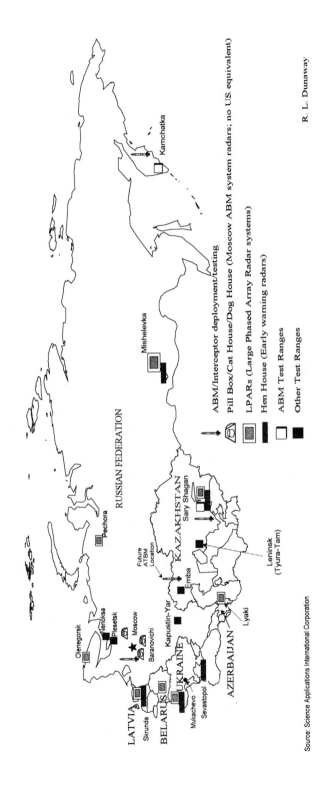

ABM/Interceptor deployment/testing

Pill Box/Cat House/Dog House (Moscow ABM system radars; no US equivalent)

LPARs (Large Phased Array Radar systems)

Hen House (Early warning radars)

ABM Test Ranges

Other Test Ranges

RUSSIAN FEDERATION

Kamchatka

Mishelevka

KAZAKHSTAN

Sary Shagan

Leninsk
(Tyura-Tam)

Emba

Future
ATBM
Location

Pechora

Olenegorsk

Venöksa

Plesetsk

Moscow

Baranovichi

Kapustin-Yar

LATVIA

Skrunda

BELARUS

Mukachevo

UKRAINE

Sevastopol

AZERBAIJAN

Lyaki

Source: Science Applications International Corporation

R. L. Dunaway

when substantially lower levels of strategic forces should lessen the risk of war, as well. The offense–defense link and concerns about strategic stability will continue into the next century; indeed, Russia has specifically linked START limitations to maintaining the treaty.

In 1972, the year in which the ABM Treaty entered into force, the United States possessed approximately 4,000 warheads on some 1,700 strategic ballistic missiles; the Soviet Union had approximately 2,050 warheads on about the same number of strategic ballistic missiles. Even when the START II limits are reached in 2003,[11] each side will still be able to retain 3,000–3,500 strategic warheads, a significant number of which will remain on strategic ballistic missiles. In September 1994, Secretary of Defense William Perry noted that the United States must hedge against a reversal of reform in Russia involving an authoritative military regime hostile to the United States and armed with nuclear weapons. Thus, the ABM Treaty still has a useful role to play in the U.S.-Russian strategic relationship.

While the treaty remains in the national security interest of the United States, it must be updated and clarified to facilitate achieving effective TMD systems. Since 1972, ballistic missile threats have changed. Advanced technologies are available for development of both theater ballistic missiles and BMD systems. The ABM Treaty was intended to be a living document, to be clarified and modified, taking into account emerging threats and advancing technologies.

The importance of the current treaty negotiations is stressed in a White House document: "The on-going negotiations initiated by the United States to clarify the ABM Treaty by establishing an agreed demarcation between strategic and theater ballistic missiles and update the Treaty to reflect the break-up of the Soviet Union reflects the Administration's commitment to maintaining the integrity and effectiveness of crucial arms control agreements."[12] The ABM Treaty is of indefinite duration. As the international security environment changes, further clarifications and modifications will undoubtedly be required to maintain its viability.

The United States and Russia are exploring opportunities for sharing ballistic missile early warning data. If bilateral relations continue to improve, the two nations could begin sharing data and cooperating in BMD exercises, capabilities, and technologies. To meet the future proliferation of advanced cruise missiles, this cooperation could also extend to advanced defenses against aerodynamic vehicles.

Suggested Reading

Bunn, Matthew. *Foundation for the Future: The ABM Treaty and National Security.* Washington, D.C.: Arms Control Association, 1990.

Chayes, Antonia H., and Paul Doty, eds. *Defending Deterrence: Managing the ABM Treaty Regime into the 21st Century.* Washington, D.C.: Pergamon-Brassey's, 1989.

Graybeal, Sidney N., and Patricia A. McFate. *The ABM Treaty and Ballistic Missile Defense: Can the Circle Be Squared?* American Association for the Advancement of Science Publication No. 93-26S, 1993.

Newhouse, John. *Cold Dawn: The Story of SALT.* Austin, Tex.: Holt, Rinehart and Winston, 1973.

Nitze, Paul H. *From Hiroshima to Glasnost.* New York: Grove Weidenfeld, 1989.

Smith, Gerard. *Doubletalk: The Story of SALT I.* New York: Doubleday, 1980.

Willrich, Mason, and John B. Rhinelander, eds. *SALT: The Moscow Agreements and Beyond.* New York: Free Press, 1974.

Notes

1. Ballistic missile defense consists of programs and technologies designed to counter ballistic missile threats. National missile defense provides defenses for the U.S. homeland against limited long-range (strategic) ballistic missile threats. Theater missile defense provides defenses against shorter-range theater ballistic missiles.

2. National technical means include reconnaissance satellite systems using a variety of sensors, ground- and sea-based radars, seismographs, communications collection stations, and underwater acoustic systems.

3. A coauthor of this chapter, Sidney N. Graybeal, who negotiated Article XIII and the SCC charter and regulations, was appointed by President Nixon to serve as the first U.S. commissioner for the SCC in June 1973 and served in this capacity through 1976.

4. Arms Control Association, *Star Wars Quotes* (July 1986), p. 34.

5. Discussion of the U.S. negotiating position is based on the Arms Control and Disarmament Agency's *Annual Report to Congress, 1988.* Discussion of the Soviet position is based on a translation of the article "Scientific Fact Must Back Political View of Disarmament," by Aleksey Georgiyevich Arbatov in *Mirovaya Ekonomika* (April 1988), pp. 10–22.

6. Matthew Bunn, "Nixon Supports Nunn on ABM Treaty," *Arms Control Today* (May 1988), p. 21.

7. American Physical Society Study Group, *Science and Technology of Directed Energy Weapons* (April 1987), p. 2.

8. Office of Technology Assessment, *SDI Technology Survivability and Software* (May 1988), pp. 4–5.

9. Testimony before the Senate Governmental Affairs Committee on 24 February 1993.

10. "Adherence to and Compliance with Arms Control Agreements and the President's Report to Congress on Soviet Noncompliance with Arms Control Agreement," U.S. Arms Control and Disarmament Agency, transmitted to the U.S. Congress by Pres. George Bush on 19 January 1993, p. 11.

11. The date may be earlier than 2003. An agreement between Presidents Clinton and Yeltsin signed on 28 September 1994 calls for an expedited deactivation process once START II is ratified.

12. *A National Security Strategy of Engagement and Enlargement* (U.S. White House, February 1995).

7

Conventional Arms Control

Jeffrey D. McCausland

Arms control is not a product of the nuclear age. For centuries states have used arms control as a policy tool to improve their security, save money, or reduce the damage associated with conflicts. This chapter will examine the conventional arms control efforts in the post–World War II period. It will focus on U.S. arms control policy and its place in overall U.S. national security strategy. The most comprehensive agreement during this period is the Conventional Armed Forces in Europe (CFE) Treaty, signed in 1990. It will be reviewed here in some detail. Its successful implementation is a key element in a new European security structure and could establish a basis for further agreements in Europe and elsewhere. The chapter will also examine the nature of conventional arms control after the Cold War and prospects for future negotiations.

Most conventional arms control efforts in the last century sought reductions or at least limitations on forces, although some did seek to restrain advances in technology. In 1899, for example, 108 delegates from 26 countries met at The Hague to discuss three areas—armament, the laws of war, and conflict arbitration. At this conference the Russian empire proposed a five-year moratorium on armament production, largely because of domestic economic difficulties. The conference also considered banning the use of balloons as platforms from which to launch projectiles or to drop bombs, outlawing the dum-dum bullet, and eliminating chemical weapons. During these discussions the United States firmly opposed efforts to restrict the size of naval forces because of its geostrategic position and growing fleet. Subsequent meetings were held in 1907 and included 256 delegates from 44 nations. Nothing was accomplished in the area of arms control or disarmament, although some agreement was reached on basic laws for the conduct of warfare.

Following World War I, early proponents of the League of Nations advocated the nationalization of arms production and the elimination of standing armies. Supporters of this approach believed that World War I had occurred, at least in part, because of the power of private arms producers. These so-called merchants of death had stimulated the massive arms racing that had taken place in the two decades before the war. The transformation of Europe into an "armed camp" had in turn contributed to the outbreak of war and its horrendous consequences in terms of death and destruction. These believers in the idealist precepts of international relations theory were disappointed in their efforts. The international system remained state oriented, and national self-interest retained its predominant role in the formulation of foreign policy.

In November 1921 the Washington Naval Conference (officially known as the International Conference on Naval Limitation) opened. The meeting included representatives of Belgium, China, France, Great Britain, Italy, Japan, the Netherlands, Portugal, and the United States. The conference was held to promote better relations among the nations having potentially conflicting interests in the Pacific Ocean and Far East. It concluded on 6 February 1922 with a treaty signed by the five major naval powers that limited the total tonnage of capital ships (ships of more than 10,000 tons displacement) to a ratio of 5:5:3:1.7:1.7 for the United States, Great Britain, Japan, France, and Italy, respectively. The agreement also stipulated that the status quo with respect to fortifications in the Pacific would be maintained.

This agreement is interesting for several reasons. First, it was asymmetrical in character, as it allowed Japan smaller forces than those of the United States and Great Britain; Japan could have only 60 percent of the capital ships allowed the other powers. Second, the motivation of most participants to accept the treaty was based primarily on economic concerns and the huge cost of World War I. Third, the military in Japan strongly opposed the agreement as contradictory to Japanese national security. As a result, it eventually forced the imperial government to exceed its restrictions.[1]

The Washington Naval Conference reflected aspects of both realism and idealism, as well as the technological difficulties associated with conventional arms control. The associated Four-Power Treaty among the United States, Great Britain, France, and Japan required the countries to respect each others' possessions in the Pacific, which reflected the realistic emphasis on balance of power. The treaty did not, however, include any verification procedures, but rather idealistically assumed states would naturally respect their obligations. Lastly, many would argue that the agreement was inevitably flawed by its omission of submarines and the advent of aircraft carriers.

These early efforts differed from initiatives that have occurred since World War II. They reflected idealistic theory to a degree and focused solely on reducing weaponry. Still, they suggest several conclusions that are pertinent today. First, self-interest and security are stronger motivations for states to seek arms control than are altruism and a desire for peace. Second, criteria that establish parity in armaments are essential to any negotiations and represent a central quandary that must be reconciled. Third, conventional arms control will normally be conducted in a multilateral forum. Consequently, consensus is difficult to achieve because the various players calculate their security requirements and threats differently. Also, multilateral negotiations involve participants' political and economic institutions (besides their respective militaries). The results must satisfy domestic constituencies, improve the general security, and be consistent with agreed alliance strategy.[2] Lastly, the military resources at issue in a conventional negotiation are complex components of a nation's complete military capability, and no two nations' armed forces are structured in a sufficiently similar fashion in terms of weapons or organization. Consequently, these asymmetries in formations and hardware complicate the problem of establishing parity of forces.[3] These factors suggest that conventional arms negotiations are more difficult and less likely to result in success than is nuclear arms control.

In formulating conventional arms control proposals, states have consistently shown that arms control serves as only a part of any nation's national security strategy. As such, it is a method to be used in seeking the objective of improved security—it is not an objective in itself. Though the focus of any negotiation is on the details of the prospective agreement, the arms control process must always be consistent with the direction of national (or alliance) security strategy. Consequently, arms control is a political process and cannot be divorced from other aspects of a nation's security or foreign policy. It is affected by domestic events, other issues between states, and the bureaucratic process of the participating parties. In this regard, progress in one arms control forum may be influenced (positively or negatively) by the success or failure of other negotiations, previous agreements, and the general state of the political relationship between negotiating parties.

The recent history of these efforts further suggests that arms control differs significantly from disarmament. Arms control, as previously mentioned, is a policy method by which states seek through negotiation to improve their security. It cannot change ideologies and may not reduce hostilities. Normally, the objectives are to reduce the number of weapons, to improve predictability, to diminish the possibility of miscalculation (particularly in a crisis), and to reduce confrontation. Disarmament, however, has been either unilateral or imposed on states by the victors in war. Modern examples are Germany and Japan after World War II and Iraq (to some degree) following the Gulf War.

The CSCE and MBFR Negotiations

In 1973, after roughly 25 years of Cold War confrontation, the United States and the Soviet Union initiated the Conference on Security and Cooperation in Europe (CSCE) and the Mutual and Balanced Force Reduction (MBFR) talks. The road to these negotiations and the subsequent agreements under CSCE reflect an evolution in the two nations' relationship and respective strategies. U.S. and Soviet leaders compromised on several contentious issues for reasons of alliance unity and in response to domestic pressures. The Soviet Union initially proposed a Europewide security conference in the late 1950s. Moscow's strategy was to entice the Western Europeans to a negotiation that included all its Eastern European satellites but excluded the United States.[4] The Soviet Union also wished to confirm the borders established by World War II and its hegemony over Eastern Europe. The West rightfully rejected this idea as contrary to the alliance's best interests.

By the late 1960s, attitudes had changed. Beginning in 1966 Sen. Mike Mansfield began his call for unilateral reductions in U.S. forces deployed to Europe. He brought this proposal to the floor of the U.S. Senate in January 1967 with the support of 42 other senators. In many ways this served as a catalyst to negotiations. Both the United States and the Soviet Union feared the impact that a large-scale unilateral reduction in U.S. forces might have on their security. The Nixon administration feared what it might do to Western defenses and the viability of NATO. The Soviets feared that it could lead to the British and French sharing their nuclear secrets with the Germans, as well as a large-scale increase in the Bundeswehr to compensate for the departed U.S. forces.[5]

NATO presented the results of a study group formed to examine future tasks of the alliance later that same year. This group was motivated by the spirit of the era of détente. The Harmel Report had the concomitant purpose of refocusing the strong currents that were running against traditional alliance security policy. The report stated that the alliance had two primary tasks: to maintain sufficient political unity and military readiness to deter an attack by the Warsaw Pact and to seek a more stable relationship with the East that would allow underlying issues to be resolved.[6]

Negotiations did not, however, commence for five years because of conflicts in other areas of the East-West relationship. In 1968 the Soviet Union and its Warsaw Pact allies invaded Czechoslovakia and crushed the so-called Prague Spring. This caused a dramatic increase in tension between East and West. It also forestalled any possibility of beginning negotiations. But the Warsaw Pact invasion temporarily dampened pressure to remove U.S. troops unilaterally. In the spring of 1972, success in the Strategic Arms Limitation Talks (SALT) signaled that the political climate had warmed sufficiently to move forward in conventional discussions.

Mutual and Balanced Force Reduction Talks

The MBFR talks began in October 1973. The initial Western proposal emphasized asymmetrical reductions to a level of parity in troop strength. This was due to the Warsaw Pact's overwhelming superiority in manpower and ability to reinforce the theater rapidly. In the first phase the Soviet Union would remove a tank army of roughly 69,000 troops from Eastern Europe; the United States would withdraw 29,000 soldiers. Western analysis suggested that to reach an eventual common ceiling of 700,000 troops would require a 3:1 reduction of Warsaw Pact to NATO forces.[7] The Soviets rejected this proposal and the concept of unequal reductions. It was clear from the onset of these negotiations that the Soviet Union wished to preserve the political status quo. While acceptance of this initiative would have reduced the possibility of a surprise attack for either side, it also would have reduced Soviet control over Eastern Europe.

In response, the West added a nuclear package to its proposal in 1976. This was known as Option III, and it consisted of a one-time reduction of U.S. short- and intermediate-range nuclear systems in return for a reduction in Soviet manpower.[8] This responded to Soviet insistence that any proposal focusing solely on troops (the Warsaw Pact advantage) was unfair without an associated reduction in Western nuclear systems (NATO's advantage). Option III was unsuccessful in breaking the impasse in the negotiations and was withdrawn in 1979.

Largely because of the unwillingness of the Soviet Union to accept significantly higher reductions in its forces and to agree that the other members of the Warsaw Pact achieve parity, the MBFR talks stalemated. Over the years several important precedents were established, however, that were essential to the next reduction forum—the CFE negotiations. The East eventually accepted the notion of a reduction in forces to a common ceiling, unlike their initial position that clearly sought maintenance of Warsaw Pact superiority. They further agreed that the Western data on NATO forces was valid.

Still, MBFR probably will be best remembered for what prevented an agreement. First, the Soviets never accepted the West's data on Warsaw Pact forces as correct and continually presented figures that characterized Eastern and Western forces as equal.[9] This was in part disingenuous, and it underscored the difficulty of using manpower as an effective item to limit in any agreement. Even if a definition of *manpower* could be found that was acceptable to all participants, the verification of any agreement that used personnel as an item to be limited would be very difficult. Furthermore, U.S. and Soviet forward deployed forces had an important deterrent value that exceeded simple numerical comparisons. Second, the MBFR talks did not include all NATO and Warsaw Pact members but focused on so-called Central Europe. This included, for the West, the Federal Republic of Germany, the Netherlands, Belgium, and Luxembourg, and for the East, the German Democratic Republic, Poland, and Czechoslovakia. Nations with territory or forces in this region were included as direct participants, and countries bordering the region of reduction were indirect participants.[10] The possibility of the direct involvement of Hungary was left undecided, and France refused to participate in the discussions. Lastly, both sides used the negotiations to secure long-sought foreign policy objectives. The Soviet Union wished to weaken NATO and to reduce the U.S. presence as a means to intimidate the Western Europeans. The Soviet Union also sought to limit the size of West German armed forces. Conversely, the United States used the negotiations to forestall congressional efforts to reduce forward deployed forces unilaterally while seeking to reduce Soviet influence in Eastern Europe.

Conference on Security and Cooperation in Europe

The CSCE also convened in 1973. This negotiation was in some ways a Western concession to the Soviet Union in return for its agreement to participate in MBFR, as it closely approximated the earlier Eastern suggestion for a Europewide security conference. It also embodied the idea of détente, which had been enunciated in the Harmel Report.

The concluding document of the conference (the Helsinki Final Act) was signed by the 35 participants (the United States, Canada, and all European countries except Albania) on 1 August 1975. The repetitive language on territorial integrity that appears in 5 of the 10 principles of the Final Act emphatically underscores the participants' intent to recognize the borders established after World War II.[11] The Helsinki Final Act launched the so-called CSCE process that called for balanced progress in three areas—security; cooperation in science, economics, technology, and the environment; and human rights (often called Baskets One, Two, and Three, respectively).

Basket One eventually resulted in modest agreements on confidence- and security-building measures (CSBMs) (see Appendix 3). CSBMs were designed to reduce the "dangers of armed conflict and of misunderstanding or miscalculation of military activities which could give rise to apprehension."[12] The first of these was a commitment to provide 21 days' advance notification to all signatories of any military exercise involving more than 25,000 troops. It also encouraged voluntary notification of smaller military training events, major military movements, and the invitation of observers to maneuvers. CSBMs represented a significant shift from technical arms control focusing on reductions to emphasis on transparency in military operations; consequently, they emphasized intentions as opposed to military capabilities. The successful conclusion of this agreement was in many ways a compromise by the Soviet Union, which had long insisted that restrictions on military activities could not be agreed upon until reductions had first taken place. The Western position had always been to seek such CSBMs before reductions.

As part of the CSCE process the Stockholm Conference on Disarmament in Europe (CDE) was established in 1984 to deal with other Basket One initiatives. In 1986 CDE members agreed to additional CSBMs that required notification of exercises involving 13,000 troops, mandatory invitation of observers from other participating countries to attend military activities above a certain threshold, exchange of annual forecasts for all notifiable military activities, and on-site inspection from air or ground to verify compliance (see Appendix 3). This was further amended in the 1991 Vienna Document in the following manner: the number of troops involved in an exercise requiring advance notification was lowered; more participation of observers was allowed; the number of exercises that a state can conduct was restricted; and the CSCE members agreed to an annual exchange of military data on the location, strength, and composition of ground and air force units, as well as an annual exchange of military budgets.[13]

These agreements were obviously consistent with the objective of reducing the possibility of war in Central Europe. In addition, the level of transparency and confidence established provided a basis for actual force reductions. Agreements in other areas, such as intermediate-range nuclear forces (INF), also suggested a vastly improved political climate that increased the likelihood of future agreements. Curiously, however, the CSCE may have made its most memorable contribution in Basket Three (human rights), which was, in fact, almost an afterthought to the initial Helsinki agreement. This gave the West an important policy tool that played a key role in the demise of the entire communist political system and the eventual end to the threat of an East-West military conflict.

Conventional Armed Forces in Europe Treaty

On 19 November 1990 the Conventional Armed Forces in Europe Treaty was signed in Paris following the successful completion of 20 months of negotiations between the members of NATO and the Warsaw Treaty Organization (WTO). The rapid pace of the CFE negotiations, the ability of participating states to deal with extraordinary change, and the steady progress toward full implementation illustrate many of the primary aspects of arms control in general and conventional arms control specifically.

At the treaty's completion, Pres. George Bush hailed the agreement as ending the "military confrontation that has cursed Europe for decades."[14] Despite the dramatic nature of this document, the large-scale reduction required, and the complex inspection regime it established, the completion of the treaty was overshadowed by the ongoing deterioration of the Warsaw Pact, the fall of the Berlin Wall, and impending conflict in the Persian Gulf. Even these events paled in comparison with the dissolution of the Soviet

Union roughly one year later. As a result, many observers announced the imminent demise of the CFE Treaty. The *London Times,* for example, sounded a particularly distressing note when it claimed that "Europe's most ambitious arms control treaty risks becoming unworkable because of the Soviet Union's disintegration."[15]

Almost paradoxically, the CFE Treaty survived the early reports. This is perhaps testimony to its value and the relative importance that participating states attach to it. Ongoing changes did slow its entry into force, as the treaty was not provisionally applied until 17 July 1992. It became legally binding on all parties 10 days after the last country deposited its instruments of ratification on 9 November 1992.[16]

The CFE Treaty has over 100 pages encompassing 23 articles, several protocols, two annexes, plus several legally binding statements and political documents (for details of the treaty, see Appendix 2).[17] It limits five categories of weapons—tanks, artillery, armored combat vehicles, combat helicopters, and attack aircraft—on the European territory of the members of NATO and the former Warsaw Pact. This area is frequently called "the Atlantic to the Urals" and is further subdivided into five subregions. Each of these areas has associated alliance limits for each type of weaponry. The treaty only defines totals for each alliance (e.g., each is allowed a total of 20,000 tanks). Using these totals, NATO and the WTO negotiated national limits for each of their respective members. Following the dissolution of the Soviet Union in 1991, the successor states also negotiated national limits based on the Soviet Union's allocation.

Because of the problems in defining constraints for military strength, limitations on personnel were removed from CFE and transferred to a separate negotiation—CFE 1A. The CFE 1A discussions began in November 1990, shortly after the signing of the CFE Treaty. Despite the initial problems resulting from the dissolution of the Soviet Union, an agreement was achieved by July 1992. The concluding document is not a treaty but rather a political agreement called the Concluding Act of the Negotiation on Personnel Strength of Conventional Armed Forces in Europe (see Appendix 2). Under this accord the participating states commit themselves after March 1996 (the end of the implementation period for CFE) not to exceed the number of air, ground, and naval personnel they have declared for the CFE area of application.[18] For example, the declared limit for the United States is 250,000 and the actual count of U.S. forces after 1994 was slightly over 100,000.

Although the amount of equipment, geographic limitations, and number of personnel are important, they are still only a technical reflection of the strategic goals that both sides had when the negotiations commenced. The mandate for the CFE Treaty described its goals more clearly. They included strengthening stability and security in Europe through the creation of balanced conventional forces; establishing lower levels for conventional armaments and equipment; eliminating disparities prejudicial to stability and security; and, as a priority, precluding the capability for launching surprise attacks or large-scale offensive operations.[19] The treaty and its mandate illustrate the traditional arms control efforts to reduce the risk of war, to limit damage if war occurs, and to lower the costs associated with military forces. The mandate is also an appropriate mechanism to evaluate the value of accord in the post–Cold War environment.

The members of NATO still agree that the treaty should be fully implemented and established as a key component in a general European security framework despite the tremendous changes since 1990. Most U.S. experts are also convinced that it fosters the objectives outlined and remains in the best interests of the United States for several reasons. First, the stabilizing limits established prevent any participating signatory from exceeding the aggregate limits in any category of forces or increasing its CFE-limited arsenal without both the concurrence of the other members in its group and corresponding reductions by one or more states in the group. Consequently, it serves as a restraint to arms races throughout the continent. While this may be most important in troubled areas in the Commonwealth of Independent States, it also provides Hungary the means to prohibit the expansion of the Rumanian military and Turkey a mechanism to limit Greece.[20]

Second, the treaty enhances conventional deterrence by expanding the transparency that states have with each other's military forces and reducing the possibility of accidental conflict. Deterrence is further enhanced by the asymmetrical nature of reductions that requires NATO (in the aggregate) to reduce only a fraction of the amount required of the former members of the Warsaw Pact. The result is balanced forces between NATO and the Warsaw Pact, referred to as the two "groups of states parties" in the treaty.

Third, the treaty requires notification of any change in the size and character of the military forces of the participants and an annual exchange of information. Fourth, the strict inspection and verification regime ensures compliance. This, coupled with the annual information exchange, provides all members a great deal of predictability in forecasting the military forces of their neighbors. Lastly, while requiring all sides to live up to stringent requirements, the treaty also establishes a clear momentum in the process that may bear fruit in other areas.

In attempting to calculate the value of CFE for the United States, it is also important to remember that the United States successfully protected certain operational objectives during the negotiations. These included the maintenance of alliance unity, exclusion of nuclear weapons or naval forces from the discussions, preservation of U.S. rights to store prepositioned matériel in Europe, avoidance of the mandatory disbandment of withdrawn U.S. forces, or any permanent limitations on the overall size of U.S. forces. These advantages have not been compromised by events since and may be even more important today. In summary, the treaty appeals to the enlightened self-interest of the United States as well as of its alliance partners. U.S. national security is more effectively enhanced by its final implementation than by its abrogation.

Implementation of the treaty has proceeded surprisingly well. The verification regime established targets for states to achieve during the 40 months outlined for implementation (see Appendix 2). The lengthy period of implementation was due to the overwhelming complexity of the treaty and the monumental task of destroying a vast array of equipment—roughly 35,000 pieces of treaty-limited equipment (TLE) for the Warsaw Pact and 17,000 for NATO. The initial target (September 1993) required participants to meet 25 percent of their total reduction. Goals of 60 percent by September 1994 and 100 percent by November 1995 were also established. Four months were then allocated to verify residual force levels. When this is accomplished a review conference of all signatories will be convened (in May 1996) to discuss difficulties, possible changes to the treaty, and potential future agreements.

It is perhaps axiomatic for successful arms control agreements that they receive their most intense public scrutiny during the negotiations and little attention is paid to the implementation process. CFE is no exception and has proceeded forward quietly. All participants (except Armenia and Azerbaijan, because of the ongoing conflict in Nagorno-Karabakh) reached their reduction goals in September 1993 and 1994. As of early 1995 roughly 24,000 pieces of treaty-limited equipment had been destroyed in the former Warsaw Pact countries. The Russian Federation alone disposed of over 6,000 items. None of the inspections of this process revealed discrepancies of a significance to suggest circumvention or violation of treaty provisions.

The process of implementation has also changed to meet the evolving international conditions in Europe, and this has presented NATO with opportunities as well as difficulties. The preamble of the treaty includes a clause that commits the participants to strive "to replace military confrontation with a new pattern of security relations based on peaceful cooperation."[21] Though the agreement is very specific in its technical content, it does not provide any description about how these new patterns are to be created. The North Atlantic Cooperation Council (NACC), which includes all the former members of the Warsaw Pact as well as NATO, was created in some measure to adjust the security environment in light of the end of the Warsaw Pact. This has resulted in an increase in the flow of information and ideas on the conduct of implementation between East and West, including seminars on verification run by NATO for the other NACC members, attendance by Eastern European officers at the NATO arms control inspection course, and access to NATO's verification data base.[22] In addition, the creation of NATO's Partnership for Peace may expand these possibilities into such things as the participation of non-NATO observers on Western inspections as part of the partnership.

Despite this overall progress, serious difficulties exist that may imperil final implementation of CFE. The final subregion (the so-called flank zone) limits the number of forces that the Russian Federation can position in the northern Caucasus and Leningrad military districts (see Appendix 2). This limitation went into effect at the end of the implementation period (November 1995). Since early 1993, Russian leaders repeatedly complained that these internal restrictions were discriminatory and permitted them insufficient forces to meet new security requirements. Consequently, they formally requested that Article V of the treaty (covering the flank limits) be suspended. Russian leaders maintain that the northern Caucasus area is a region of both internal instability and external threats that requires forces beyond those allowed under CFE. These fears are exemplified by the war between Armenia and Azerbaijan, civil war in Georgia, problems in Moldova, and fighting in Chechnya. Russian officials have also argued that they need the bases located in the flank area to house forces returning from Eastern Europe.[23]

The flank limits also place internal limits on Ukraine, and it has also voiced concerns. Ukrainian defense experts argue that the new environment created by the end of the Cold War and the dissolution of the Soviet Union demands that their forces be more evenly deployed across their territory. This is also an economic problem for Ukraine. Compliance with the flank limits would force the abandonment of infrastructure in the southeastern portion of the country. Because of the serious economic difficulties Ukraine is suffering, it cannot afford the costs associated with meeting this requirement.[24]

The United States and its NATO allies have refused to accept the suspension of Article V. They argue that to allow significant alterations to the treaty would encourage other states to ask for additional changes and endanger the agreement entirely. Furthermore, they have suggested that Russia has neither made a sufficient case for increased forces in the flank area nor explained why it cannot achieve its goals within the framework of the accord. At the September 1994 summit with Pres. Bill Clinton, Russian president Boris Yeltsin announced that Russia would seek a solution within current treaty guidelines.[25]

While this is encouraging, the invasion of Chechnya (which is in the flank zone) in late December 1994 and subsequent heavy fighting indicate that the Russian Federation will keep a large force in the area to quell this disturbance and discourage other regions from flaunting Moscow's authority. It will be difficult for Russia to do this and meet its requirements under CFE. The war in Chechnya also could adversely affect the overall East-West relationship. Many Western experts have begun to question the intentions of the Russian Federation and whether it is willing to live up to international agreements such as CFE. They point out that the invasion of Chechnya was a violation of CSCE agreements that require prior notification of the movement of large military formations and of the Code of Conduct for Military

Forces that was signed in Budapest in early December 1994. Some have also suggested that it could be contrary to CSCE human rights accords.

Where Do We Go Now?

The CFE Treaty is designed to continue with no time limit. Still, if solutions are found to the difficulties discussed and the treaty is implemented, several issues will be of immediate interest in subsequent negotiations. First, Russia and Ukraine will press for the removal of Article V covering flank limits. Second, several Eastern European states will insist that the bloc-to-bloc character of the treaty be removed since one of the groups of states parties is gone. This may be inevitable, but its implications must be thoroughly considered. For example, if the treaty evolves into a multilateral accord, NATO will lose the flexibility to shift forces or entitlements between members of the alliance. This also would have important implications for the verification regime and the allocation and conduct of inspections. Third, destruction procedures and costs must be reviewed. Several states have complained that the precise procedures for destruction make implementation very expensive. Furthermore, the treaty is mute on the procedures states may use to maintain numerical limitations once residual levels have been verified in the spring of 1996.[26] Some participants have already questioned whether the destruction of TLE below authorized levels must be done along the strict guidelines established in the treaty.

There is, however, little interest in extending the agreement to other pieces of equipment or in negotiating lower levels of TLE for the participating states—though there has been some suggestion in Russian publications of including naval forces or placing limits on naval activities.[27] While the treaty may never be extended to other categories of equipment, the procedures established to update the Protocol on Existing Types of Conventional Armaments and Equipment are important and must be strictly adhered to in order to categorize new TLE models as they are brought into service.

Harmonization and the OSCE

Article XVIII of the treaty does say that states "shall continue the negotiations on conventional armed forces with the same mandate and with the goal of building on this Treaty."[28] Therefore, many experts argue that the agreements reached in the Forum for Security Cooperation (FSC) in Europe have created a requirement to seek harmonization between CFE limitations among its 30 signatories and the CSBMs of the 52 members of the CSCE—referred to as the Organization for Security and Cooperation in Europe (OSCE) following the Budapest Conference in December 1994. The

Czech Republic, Hungary, Poland, and Slovakia initially proposed harmonization in October 1992. France also supports harmonization as part of its proposal for a Pan-European Security Treaty. They recommended the creation of national force levels for non-CFE states (primarily the former neutral and nonaligned states—Switzerland, Sweden, Finland, Austria, and states of the former Yugoslavia) that might be simply a declaration of current levels (with no need for reductions). These limitations would be coupled with adherence to the verification and inspection regime, the process to categorize new equipment, and an annual exchange of information.[29] Obviously, states currently participating in the CFE accord would be required to notify non-CFE states of the details of their residual force levels.

As previously suggested, arms control is a means to reduce tensions between states. It has little possibility of success when states are engaged in warfare and may have little meaning or momentum when they enjoy good relations. Consequently, there has been little interest by states that are not currently signatories to the CFE Treaty. The Swiss, for example, have openly questioned the value of an agreement, and the feasibility of including Serbia in such an accord is extremely unlikely before the resolution of current hostilities. Efforts to include these countries in a harmonized agreement are further complicated by the nature of their militaries and their views on deterrence. Many depend heavily on reserve forces and militias for their defense. A verification regime that included a transfer of information on mobilization procedures, depot locations, restrictions on the activities of these forces, and so on would be construed by experts in these countries as harmful to their national security.

Proponents of harmonization argue that it confronts the changed European environment in which there is no longer threat of attack by the Warsaw Pact but rather there are regional conflicts. At a fundamental level, however, there are serious implications for the United States beyond arms control that must be considered. At its ultimate extreme, harmonization suggests the transformation of the OSCE into a regional organization that coordinates security activities on the European continent and would logically place NATO in a subordinate role. This may be desirable and is supported by various European governments. French experts, for example, support this approach to "establish the structures and procedures that are required to allow Europeans to act autonomously if necessary."[30] Foreign Minister Andrei Kozyrev from the Russian Federation has also proposed the conversion of the OSCE into a full-fledged international organization with "a genuine division of labor between the CIS [Commonwealth of Independent States], NATO, European Union, NACC, and WEU [Western European Union] with the OSCE playing a coordinating role."[31] Such a result would, however, reduce the role of the United States in European security and could become a means for the Russian Federation to legitimize the CIS as a regional organization while undermining NATO. This could be dangerous to U.S. interests and inconsistent with the overall direction of U.S. national security policy.

There have also been suggestions to create so-called regional tables that could either build on previous agreements or use the concepts applied in CFE or CSBMs to reduce tensions. In Europe the suggestion has been applied to the former Yugoslavia (in an initiative led by Hungary).[32] Others have recommended it for the Baltic states (Estonia, Latvia, and Lithuania) because of their concerns over Russian forces stationed in the Leningrad military district and Kaliningrad that border their territory. Some scholars have even speculated that regional tables, agreements similar to CFE, or CSBMs may be applicable in Korea or the Middle East.[33] While these approaches would be consistent with the regional focus of U.S. strategy, it must be recognized that the prospects for immediate success appear slight. Enormous problems—such as defining the region of interest, the mandate, and the role of the great powers—would have to be solved. Furthermore, the past accomplishments in CFE and the CSCE process suggest that improved political relationships are the basis for success in conventional arms control, and confidence-building measures are the first step. The key, therefore, may be to develop an arms control dialogue in tandem with a more formal peace process. Neither is likely to achieve decisive results by itself, but together they may create the critical mass necessary for a final settlement.[34]

Proposals for the Future

In preparing for the future, European conventional arms control policies must remain consistent with evolving NATO strategy if they are to achieve consensus in the alliance. Conventional arms control in Europe has now shifted from challenging the status quo to locking it in place. Corresponding deterrence strategies are less focused on deterring a specific adversary and more concerned with deterring a "condition." This could cause conventional arms control to stagnate as a policy tool, particularly in Europe.

New proposals must conform to the emerging environment that is focused on subregional conflict. Problems in conventional arms control will require not only new and innovative ideas but also the development of a more comprehensive conceptualization of security. This conceptualization must reflect the new environment as well as the relationship among diplomacy, defense policy, international institutions, and collective security.

With this in mind, one area of conventional arms control may deserve renewed attention. The character of arms control is moving toward qualitative aspects and conflict prevention. Though Europe and the United States have reduced the level of their national armaments, they remain the primary arms producers and exporters. As a result, those in the United States and Europe (including the former members of the Warsaw Pact) bear a heavy responsibility for fueling conventional arms races and conflicts around the globe (discussed in detail in Chapter 11).[35] As the CFE Treaty enters its sustainment period, there will be increased pressure in many states to expand exports to maintain industries and employment. Consequently, it seems prudent to consider the use of the Vienna Center for Conflict Prevention (established by the OSCE),[36] a more comprehensive approach to the UN Arms Trade Registry, or other forums to consider national conventional arms export policies. Such an effort should seek to limit arms sales to regions experiencing turmoil and create international incentives to encourage the conversion of excess defense industrial capacity.[37]

Conclusion

As we consider what role conventional arms control should have in future U.S. national security strategy, it is essential to remember that it remains a means to an end. It is also important to maintain both short- and longer-term perspectives. For the near term, the final implementation of CFE is not assured, and it will not occur without concerted action by the United States. The failure of this agreement would adversely affect European security and reduce the prospects for conventional arms control elsewhere.

We must remember that our arms control policies have tremendous resonance in broader areas having to do with the evolution of the U.S.-European relationship. As a result, answers to wider questions may well serve as a guide to arms control policies. Does the United States wish to continue its role as the leader of NATO? Will the alliance continue to be the premier security organization on the continent? What is the strategic vision for the U.S.-European relationship? These are questions of tremendous complexity, and today's tactical choices in CFE may define their ultimate answers.

Conventional arms control can still be an effective policy tool. As we approach the next millennium, however, we must be aware that the demands placed on this instrument have expanded beyond improving security, saving money, and reducing damage in war. Some experts believe it can assist in the settlement of traditional quarrels as well as ethnic struggles that have reappeared since the end of the Cold War. We also should recognize that the international system, with its emphasis on self-interest as the primary motivation for national policy, remains relatively intact. Consequently, although much can be learned from past efforts, future success depends on incorporating a revised view of arms control with new comprehensive strategies.

Suggested Reading

Daalder, Ivo. *Cooperative Arms Control: A New Agenda for the Post–Cold War Era.* College Park, Md.: Center for International Security Studies, 1992.

Dean, Jonathan. *Ending Europe's Wars.* New York: Twentieth Century Fund Press, 1994.
Falkenrath, Richard. *Shaping Europe's Military Order.* Cambridge, Mass.: MIT Press, 1994.
Freedman, Lawrence, Catherine Kelleher, and Jane Sharp, eds. *The Political Context of Conventional Arms Control in Europe.* Hamburg, Germany: Nomos Publishing, forthcoming 1996.
Keliher, John G. *The Negotiations on Mutual and Balanced Force Reductions.* New York: Pergamon Press, 1980.

Notes

1. Sadao Asada, "The Revolt Against the Washington Treaty—The Imperial Japanese Navy and Naval Limitation, 1921–1927," *Naval War College Review* (Spring 1993), pp. 82–95.
2. Ralph A. Hallenbeck and David E. Shaver, *On Disarmament: The Role of Conventional Arms Control in National Security Strategy* (Carlisle Barracks, Penn.: Strategic Studies Institute, 1990), pp. 17–18.
3. Amos A. Jordan and William J. Taylor, Jr., *American National Security—Policy and Process* (Baltimore: Johns Hopkins University Press, 1990), p. 543.
4. Richard Schifter, "The Conference on Security and Cooperation in Europe: Ancient History or New Opportunities?" *Washington Quarterly* (Autumn 1993), pp. 121–123.
5. John G. Keliher, *The Negotiations on Mutual and Balanced Force Reductions* (New York: Pergamon Press, 1980), pp. 144–145.
6. *The North Atlantic Treaty Organization 1949–1989* (Brussels: NATO Information Service, 1989), p. 31.
7. James R. Golden and Asa A. Clark, eds., *Conventional Deterrence* (Lexington, Mass.: D. C. Heath and Company, 1984), pp. 30–36.
8. Keliher, *Negotiations,* p. 146.
9. Ibid., p. 148.
10. North Atlantic Treaty Organization, *NATO Handbook* (Brussels: NATO Information Service, 1992), p. 234.
11. Schifter, "Conference," p. 123.
12. U.S. Arms Control and Disarmament Agency, *Arms Control and Disarmament Agreements—Texts and Histories of the Negotiations* (Washington, D.C.: U.S. Government Printing Office, 1990), pp. 319–320.
13. Lynn E. Davis, *An Arms Control Strategy for the New Europe* (Santa Monica, Calif.: RAND Corporation, 1992), p. 14.
14. Lee Feinstein, "CFE: Off the Endangered List?" *Arms Control Today* (October 1993), p. 3.
15. Ibid., pp. 2–3.
16. NATO Office of Information and Press, "Basic Fact Sheet—Chronology of Key Arms Control Treaties and Agreements (1963–1994)" (Brussels: NATO Information Service, April 1994), pp. 3–5.
17. U.S. Department of State, *Treaty on Conventional Armed Forces in Europe (CFE),* Treaty Document 102-8 (Washington, D.C.: U.S. Government Printing Office, 1991).
18. Jonathan Dean, *Ending Europe's Wars* (New York: Twentieth Century Fund, 1994), pp. 300–301.

19. *CFE Treaty,* pp. 2, 223.

20. Feinstein, "CFE," p. 3.

21. *CFE Treaty,* p. 223.

22. Necil Nedimoglu, "NATO and Partner Countries Cooperate in Implementing CFE Treaty," *NATO Review* (June 1994), pp. 18–20.

23. Col. Gen. Mikhail Kolesnikov, chief of general staff of the Russian Federation, "Problems of the Flanks and Future of Treaty on Conventional Armed Forces," *Kraznay Zvezda (Red Star),* 19 April 1994, pp. 1, 3. For a thorough discussion of the flank issue, see Richard A. Falkenrath, *Shaping Europe's Military Order* (Cambridge, Mass.: MIT Press, 1994), pp. 231–239.

24. Lt. Gen. Gennadiy Gurin, first deputy chief of the general staff of the armed forces of Ukraine, "Statement to the Joint Consultative Group CFE Treaty," 27 September 1994, p. 2.

25. "Flank Limits Issue Unlikely to Mar December CFE Meeting," *Arms Control Today* (December 1994), p. 23.

26. *CFE Treaty,* p. 33.

27. Charles Dick, *The Military Doctrine of the Russian Federation* (Camberley, England: Conflict Studies Research Center, 1994), pp. 6–7, 14–15.

28. *CFE Treaty,* p. 242.

29. John Borawski and Bruce George, "The CSCE Forum for Security Cooperation," *Arms Control Today* (October 1993), pp. 13–14.

30. Phillipe H. Mallard and Bruno Tertrais, "France's European Priority," *Joint Forces Quarterly* 5 (Summer 1994), pp. 19–21.

31. A. Kozyrev, "Document 433: Letter of the Minister for Foreign Affairs of the Russian Federation to the Chairman of the CSCE," presented at the CSCE Parliamentary Conference, Vienna, Austria, 30 June 1994.

32. Borawski and George, "CSCE Forum," p. 14.

33. Gerald M. Steinberg, "Middle East Arms Control and Regional Security," *Survival* (Spring 1994), pp. 126–141.

34. Ivo Daalder, "The Future of Arms Control," *Survival* (Spring 1992), p. 160.

35. Dick, *Military Doctrine,* p. 20.

36. Gregory F. Treverton, ed., *The Shape of the New Europe* (New York: Council on Foreign Relations, 1991), p. 210.

37. Lee H. Hamilton, "The United States Needs a Conventional Arms Policy," *Christian Science Monitor,* 13 September 1994, p. 18.

8

Is Arms Control Succeeding?

James J. Wirtz

"Is arms control succeeding?" The answer to this question must appear obvious to today's students of national security. After all, the Soviet Union collapsed with a whimper, not a bang. It would thus seem logical to conclude that the arms control agreements that were signed with increasing frequency during the second half of the Cold War played some role in putting the Soviet monster safely out of its misery. But it was not so long ago that policymakers and academics hotly debated the merits and risks of arms control; indeed, the concept of arms control discussed in this volume was revolutionary when it was first introduced in the early 1960s.[1] So this question, like so much of Cold War history, will provide plenty of grist for future historians and social scientists.

Another obstacle to providing a concise response to this question is that the answer is highly dependent on one's perspective and the exact treaties in question. Within the U.S. government, for instance, opinions about the purpose and success of a treaty are likely to reflect bureaucratic affiliations and interests. In other words, it would be unlikely that officials in the Arms Control and Disarmament Agency, members of Congress, or officers serving on the Joint Staff would evaluate the objectives and success of any given treaty the same way. Additionally, what constitutes successful arms control is often debated. For example, is the Non-Proliferation Treaty succeeding because it helps make transparent the efforts of some states to acquire nuclear weapons, or is it failing because it did not stop these efforts to build nuclear weapons in the first place? If one takes into account various political and ideological agendas, to say nothing of dozens of other national perspectives on the subject, then the effort to develop anything short of a book-length answer to this question is bound to leave most readers dissatisfied. Nevertheless, let us try.

Keeping these important qualifications in mind, I will venture a short, if not so simple, evaluation of the Cold War arms control record. So far, arms control is succeeding. Russia, the United States, and literally dozens of other nations for the most part continue to abide by Cold War arms control agreements. Major initiatives to limit the spread of chemical, biological, and nuclear weapons are currently under way. So it makes sense to think about arms control as an ongoing enterprise. Maybe the heyday of arms control occurred during the height of the Cold War, but the concept of arms control, let alone the arms control agreements signed by the United States and the Soviet Union, did not end with the demise of the Soviet Union. Recent critics of arms control would even suggest that the real test of Cold War agreements lies in the future.

The remainder of this essay is devoted to explaining why the author believes that arms control succeeded during the Cold War and to describing the hurdles that the arms control enterprise must overcome if it is to contribute to future U.S. security.

Arms Control During the Cold War

Although specialists in foreign affairs have taken some heat recently about their failure to predict the demise of the Soviet Union, those involved in arms control have generally done a reasonable job at projecting current trends approximately one decade into the future.[2] Thus, scholarly debates about arms control policy usually anticipate the actual events—often having to do with weapons development and procurement—that make changes in policy necessary. Seen in this manner, classical arms control could be viewed as a 1950s response to problems coming down the road in the not too distant future. So what did the phrase "if current trends continue" imply for scholars as they looked across the 1960s? What were the problems and opportunities that they expected to encounter by the early 1970s?

Thomas Schelling recently stated that in the late 1950s the intellectual founders of classical arms control were motivated by a desire to "hold off disaster."[3] Looking back, it is clear that they had much to worry about. By the mid-1950s, reasonable people might have concluded that nuclear threats were becoming a permanent fixture in diplomatic discourse. During the Suez crisis (1956), the Soviet Union made some veiled nuclear threats against Britain and France to encourage them to pull their forces out of Egypt.[4] The Eisenhower administration also made nuclear threats against the People's Republic of China during the Offshore Islands crises (1955 and 1958).[5] Additionally, the Bomber Gap (1955) and the Missile Gap (1957) raised concerns that the United States was falling behind the Soviets in bomber and missile production, while the launch of Sputnik provoked widespread fears that U.S. science and education were not up to the Cold War competition with the Soviets.[6] Nikita Khrushchev's efforts at "Sputnik diplomacy," publicly exaggerating the size and delivery capabilities of the Soviet nuclear arsenal, succeeded in scaring the United States, but they also spurred a U.S. nuclear buildup that would give it a decisive military advantage by the early 1960s.[7] Defense intellectuals were becoming concerned that a reciprocal fear of surprise attack, which arose following the development of intercontinental ballistic missiles, might provoke one or both of the superpowers to unleash their nuclear arsenals in a crisis that might otherwise be solved peacefully. Indeed, in policy circles, Albert Wohlstetter's analysis of the vulnerability of forward-based U.S. bombers raised the notion of crisis instability: the U.S. Air Force, instead of serving as a deterrent, was actually just providing the Soviets with a tempting target.[8] U.S. citizens were jittery, and the signs of strain were showing domestically; McCarthyism and a pervasive fear of nuclear war were not distant memories in the late 1950s.[9]

These trends indicated that both Soviet and U.S. forces would continue to increase in capability; there was nothing to stop the growth, regardless of how one measured it, in nuclear arsenals.[10] Eventually, this expansion in the superpowers' arsenals would culminate in what is now known as mutual assured destruction (MAD). Defined as a situation in which two actors have the capability to deliver a catastrophic retaliatory strike after suffering the worst that their opponent has to offer, MAD can exist at a variety of force levels. In a military sense, the only significant difference between a nuclear balance in which both sides are armed with 10,000 versus 100,000 nuclear warheads is in the resources expended to create the larger arsenal. Here is an instance when logic and politics coincide; the Soviet Union and the United States both had an interest in maintaining the nuclear standoff at "reasonable" force levels. Resources not spent on a nuclear arsenal could always be used for something else.

In the late 1950s, however, there was reason to believe that the nuclear arms race would terminate in war, not stalemate. Three general concerns had surfaced about the nuclear future. First, one side might discover that some technological or quantitative breakthrough had rendered its nuclear arsenal obsolete or hopelessly outclassed. Alternatively, one side might obtain weapons that yielded great benefits if fired early in a crisis. These developments would lead to crisis instability, a situation in which states involved in a dispute could derive political or militarily significant advantages by being first to use nuclear weapons.[11] The 1962 Cuban missile crisis—prompted by the Soviet gamble in Cuba to correct quickly a strategic nuclear imbalance—generally validated this scholarly concern over crisis stability.[12] Even though the United States, and to a lesser extent the Soviet Union, resisted pressures to launch a preemptive attack during the showdown, both risked war to reduce the other side's incentive to preempt in a future crisis.[13]

Second, there was concern that a sort of technological determinism, possibly driven by worst-case planning, would override common sense, leading to the creation of weapons that best remained figments of some engineer's imagination.[14] For example, the possibility that the Soviets would put nuclear weapons in orbit remained a real concern until October 1963, when both superpowers jointly resolved not to place nuclear weapons in outer space.[15] Indeed, given the principle that what goes up must come down, would people anywhere feel more secure with nuclear weapons "permanently" orbiting overhead? Why not head off a race to deploy nuclear weapons in space before it began?

Third, analysts were worried about the possibility of "accidental" nuclear war.[16] Scholars were concerned about events that were truly accidental (e.g., the unauthorized and unintentional launching or detonation of weapons brought about by human or mechanical error).[17] They also were worried about what is often described as inadvertent escalation, a process in which the close interaction of opposing conventional forces during a crisis or conventional hostilities unintentionally leads to escalation to a strategic nuclear war.[18] In hindsight, it appears that concerns about both varieties of accidental nuclear war were well founded, even though the superpowers managed to avoid a nuclear exchange. The United States, for instance, has experienced dozens of nuclear accidents, one of the most severe being the 1968 crash of a B-52 near Thule, Greenland.[19] And, as one watches film of Soviet and U.S. tanks maneuvering at point-blank range while Soviet border guards erect the Wall during the 1961 Berlin crisis, the prospect of inadvertent escalation takes on a tangible quality. Even in hindsight, the peaceful conclusion of the Cold War was not inevitable.

Viewed in this light, arms control was extraordinarily successful because it helped to reduce the risk of war and cut the number of casualties suffered in a superpower nuclear war to zero. Arms control contributed to U.S. and Soviet security because it helped to manage the transition from a world in which it was possible to fight and win a nuclear war to a world in which both sides recognized, albeit never welcomed, MAD.[20] This was no small accomplishment. The notion that it would be counterproductive to eliminate societal vulnerability to nuclear attack was a difficult idea to swallow.[21] For example, Soviet prime minister Aleksei Kosygin reacted in horror at the 1967 Glassboro summit when Secretary of Defense Robert McNamara attempted to explain why efforts to construct an antiballistic missile system would be crisis destabilizing. Kosygin found it incredible (as Sidney Graybeal and Patricia McFate note in Chapter 6) that anyone would believe that defending one's homeland was a bad thing.[22] Ironically, by the 1980s, Soviet prime minister Mikhail Gorbachev would lecture the United States about how the Strategic Defense Initiative (SDI) would threaten crisis stability.[23] By providing a forum for the exchange of these kinds of ideas, arms control helped both the Soviet Union and the United States grow accustomed to MAD.[24]

Admittedly, many observers have concluded that arms control did little to limit defense spending during the Cold War. Agreements simply codified existing procurement goals, often channeling weapons development in the directions preferred by both Soviet and U.S. defense establishments. Agreements that restricted one weapons system often seemed only to spark the accelerated development of some other technology or weapon.[25]

Arms control was best at slowing quantitative growth in arsenals; until the very end of the Cold War, it did little to restrict the qualitative improvement of weapons systems. Bargaining chips, weapons systems primarily justified as a means to induce the Soviets to negotiate, often were not traded away but were instead put into production.[26] The consensus among defense intellectuals is that arms control saved the United States few resources during the Cold War; some would even suggest that the strain of weapons development and procurement proved too great for a corrupt and inefficient Soviet Union, helping to accelerate its collapse.

In response to this conventional wisdom, one could offer the counterfactual argument that without arms control, little other than economic constraints existed to put a brake on expenditures for nuclear arsenals. In all likelihood, MAD still would have emerged in the U.S.-Soviet nuclear relationship but at extraordinarily high force levels. Assessing how much arms control saved U.S. taxpayers also might depend on the way one examines the ledger sheet. Arms control might have saved the United States some resources. If the superpowers had deployed even rudimentary strategic missile defenses of their homelands, the U.S. taxpayer could have been faced with enormous increases in the cost of defensive systems and offensive upgrades. By contrast, expenditures on the U.S. strategic nuclear arsenal remained relatively stable throughout the Cold War: 10 percent of the U.S. defense budget generally was devoted to U.S. strategic nuclear forces. So the overall growth in U.S. defense expenditures was driven largely by qualitative improvements in the U.S. conventional arsenal.[27] In any event, given the relatively small amount spent on nuclear deterrence, economy in strategic nuclear weapons offered relatively little potential savings.

Cold War arms control clearly fostered crisis stability, helped limit the costs of war by reducing its likelihood, and might have even saved both superpowers some defense expenditures. But exactly how did arms control achieve these traditional objectives? Critics would suggest that arms control was irrelevant during the Cold War. The positive results usually attributed to arms control were in reality produced by entirely different developments. Other factors—for instance, the emergence of MAD—could account for crisis stability, the absence of superpower war, or a slowing arms race.[28] For that matter, some observers have suggested that in comparison with other competitive military buildups, the U.S.-Soviet standoff never really produced much of an arms race in the first place.[29] But if one looks at arms control as a process, it appears that the actual conduct of negotiations helped to achieve the overarching goals of arms control—in two rather unique ways.

First, arms control negotiations provided both superpowers with a peaceful and generally nonthreatening way to communicate their intentions and concerns to their primary rival. This was an important development, especially if one considers the likely alternatives to calm communication. By capitalizing on the superpowers' newfound caution, induced by the nearly cataclysmic Cuban missile crisis, arms control helped curtail the 1950s policies of "brinkmanship" and Sputnik diplomacy.[30] In other words, in the absence of arms control negotiations, leaders on both sides of the Cold War divide seemed willing to engage in risky challenges to their competitors following changes in the strategic nuclear balance. Without diplomatic communication about strategic developments, military actions and threats of violence seemed to be preferable to demonstrations of resolve toward one's opponent. Of course, unilateral or nonnegotiated initiatives could have taken on a more benign quality; early arms control advocates often identified the benefits provided by informal arms control initiatives.[31] But bilateral arms control negotiations contain an important element that unilateral initiatives lack: they offer evidence of a willingness on the part of both parties to talk rather than fight. Arms control provided a tangible signal to citizens and leaders of both superpowers that the Cold War would not necessarily terminate in World War III, helping to halt a creeping, and extraordinarily dangerous, fatalism about the inevitability of war.[32] The transition to MAD would have been far more dangerous if each change in the strategic balance prompted a new round of threats, bluster, and bluff between the superpowers.

Second, arms control negotiations facilitated the emergence of a community of concerned individuals that in turn increased the sophistication and political acceptability of the entire arms control enterprise. Over time, a group of people who shared similar expertise about nuclear weapons issues, if not always the same policy preferences, emerged in both the United States and the Soviet Union. This network of professionals played an important role in sustaining interest in a diplomatic approach to restraining the arms race.[33] They helped policymakers communicate clearly about nuclear strategy and intentions. Indeed, the concepts of arms control were produced by a sustained interaction between interested communities in the Soviet Union and the United States. Some analysts even argue that by repeatedly and publicly sharing negative images of nuclear war, this professional network made deterrence possible.[34] Others have argued that this community itself made arms control possible as interest in arms control spread from U.S. scholars and policymakers to Soviet military experts.[35] Arms control was an interactive and evolutionary process that was partially sustained by the involvement of a large community of scholars, soldiers, and policymakers.[36]

The Real Test of Arms Control: The Future

If arms control contributed to U.S. security during the Cold War, what hurdles must it overcome if it is to succeed in the future? A good place to begin this type of assessment is to identify the problems that undermined past arms control efforts. A look at the interwar naval arms control regime, highlighted by the 1922 Washington Conference, the 1927 Geneva Naval Conference, and the 1930 and 1935 London Naval Conferences, would provide a good way to assess the prospects of the post–Cold War arms control enterprise. Generally speaking, parallels exist between the interwar arms control regime and today's ambitious arms agreements: both were sustained efforts to limit what was perceived as the dominant weapons of their day, and, at the high point of their success, both were confronted with a significantly altered international political landscape. Recent appraisals of this post–World War I effort to limit the qualitative and quantitative development of great power navies, however, have produced a cautionary tale for those who entertain high hopes for arms control's future. This scholarship suggests that after a promising start the interwar arms control regime deteriorated until it actually had a profoundly negative impact on the security of those states that attempted to preserve the regime. The lessons offered by the demise of the interwar regime can be summarized in this way: arms control works best when least needed; politics matters; and democracies beware.

Arms Control Works Best When Least Needed

This catchy phrase points to the first potential pitfall confronting the arms control enterprise now that the Cold War is over.[37] According to Colin Gray, arms control rests on a paradox: "If arms control is needed in a strategic relationship because the states in question might go to war, it will be impracticable for that very reason of need, whereas, if arms control should prove to be available, it will be irrelevant."[38] Gray uses the arms control paradox to question the Cold War arms control regime: if the U.S.-Soviet competition was really serious, and Gray believes that it was, arms control did little to improve U.S. security and damaged legitimate U.S. defense efforts. Clearly, Gray is wrong to use the paradox to critique the Cold War arms control regime; arms control proved practicable during the Cold War, even though it yielded agreements that were not to Gray's liking.[39] Arms control negotiations also served as an important forum for communication between the superpowers, a factor that Gray's critique largely ignores. Yet, if one interprets the original notion not as a normative prescription but as an empirical observation, it provides two warnings to arms control advocates.

First, because of the political rapprochement between the United States and the Commonwealth of Independent States (CIS), the value of the Cold War arms control regime has greatly diminished. Arms control does not provide much additional security to states that lack the fundamental grievances or mutually exclusive political goals that could propel them into war. Ironically, START II and the flurry of unilateral arms control initiatives that occurred at the end of the Cold War testify to the decreasing relevance of arms control in the strategic relationship between the United States and the CIS. Even though it is possible to enter into agreements and undertake unilateral initiatives (e.g., de-MIRVing ICBMs, cutting nuclear warheads by 70 percent, taking the U.S. bomber force off of day-to-day alert) that could barely be imagined just a few years ago, these kinds of agreements no longer contribute much to U.S. security. Some would argue that arms control provides an important hedge against an abrupt return to the Cold War. But, if one accepts the proposition that it is unlikely that U.S.-Russian relations will again become extremely confrontational, then superpower arms control long ago reached the point of diminishing returns.

Second, U.S.-Russian arms control runs the risk of becoming ritualized. Policymakers in both Moscow and Washington might be tempted to turn to the arms control arena for a guaranteed quick success to bolster flagging popularity among their constituencies. After all, it is not particularly difficult to get allies or potential allies (states that lack outstanding political grievances; these are the states that populate the extreme ends of the friendship–hostility range outlined in Chapter 2) to agree to mutual force reductions, although these kinds of agreements often add little to one's security. Already, signs of this sort of behavior have emerged in the U.S.-Russian strategic relationship: some arms control advocates continue to lobby for further negotiated cuts in nuclear arsenals. In response, the Clinton administration announced during the fall of 1994 that the United States would first focus on implementing current arms control accords before entering into new negotiations to further reduce its nuclear arsenal.[40]

Especially damaging about this ritualized behavior is that it pegs U.S. force levels and the U.S. defense debate to a rather strange standard. If the U.S.-Russian strategic relationship is allowed to govern defense and arms control policy, then U.S. forces will be developed to match the forces of a state that has, according to most observers, relatively benign intentions toward the United States. The development of U.S. conventional and nuclear forces should not just match the arsenals of friendly countries; it should instead be designed to overwhelm the arsenals of the country's potential enemies.

The concern that U.S. policymakers might become preoccupied with an ever more ambitious and increasingly irrelevant U.S.-Russian arms control agenda might strike some observers as farfetched. But British and U.S. diplomats continued to abide by and even strengthened the interwar naval arms control regime during the second London Naval Conference, even though the Japanese announced in December 1934 that they would stop abiding by the provisions of the Washington Naval Treaty in December 1936.[41] Under these circumstances, arms control simply damaged the military capability of the British-U.S. alliance. According to Gray, "The central luminous fact about the Washington-London system was that its overall net effect was to constrain either not at all or not at all usefully the navies which in a blessedly uncoordinated fashion came close to defeating the guardians of Western civilization in 1940–43."[42] British and U.S. leaders succeeded in limiting each other's arsenals, while their potential enemies were left free to pursue their defense buildup.

Politics Matters

Those in Britain and the United States who continued to develop and abide by increasingly stringent arms control proposals, even though it was clear that several states had abandoned the interwar naval arms control regime, simply forgot that politics matters.[43] Instead of recognizing that the political atmosphere that allowed ambitious arms agreements to emerge in the early 1920s had vanished by the early 1930s, they continued to search for "technical" solutions (restricting the quantitative or qualitative characteristics of arsenals) to fix a deterioration in political relations. Arms control advocates responded to a Japanese decision to pursue their security and territorial ambitions unilaterally with renewed proposals to limit fleet displacement and armament. Since the characteristics of the world's navies had little to do with the Japanese decision to create a co-prosperity sphere by using force if necessary, arms control failed to address the political forces that increased the likelihood of war in the Pacific.[44] In the view of some scholars, technical arms control efforts contribute to security only if they are undertaken in a relatively benign political environment or at least follow a degree of political accommodation among the participants in an arms control regime. Arms control is necessary under these circumstances; arms control is the vehicle that allows states to enjoy the reduction in military efforts that should accompany political détente.

Some analysts would thus assess positively the flurry of arms control activity that accompanied the end of the Cold War. The ambitious arms control agenda laid out by Russian and U.S. leaders is the logical and appropriate outgrowth of the change in the political atmosphere between these former rivals. Weapons that were once deployed to keep a Soviet Union at bay are not needed to deter the relatively pacific states that make up the CIS. But this analysis of the interwar period also suggests two factors that should prompt a reassessment of current arms control activities.

First, even though the United States and the states that make up the former Soviet Union are enjoying cordial diplomatic relations, this political rapprochement cannot be generalized to their relations with the rest of the international community. Once again, there is a danger that arms control advocates might attempt to employ the same kinds of technical solutions, appropriate to U.S.-

Russian relations, to solve far more fundamental political disputes. Recent U.S. efforts to stop the proliferation of nuclear weapons and materials provide a disturbing illustration of this kind of phenomenon. Little criticism was leveled against the Clinton administration for its purchase of weapons-grade uranium from the government of Kazakhstan to help prevent this material from entering the black market. U.S., Kazakhstani, and even Russian leaders share the political objective of stopping the proliferation of nuclear weapons or the use of nuclear materials by terrorist organizations; under these circumstances, the U.S. purchase of the uranium constitutes a face-saving gesture to help the government of Kazakhstan avoid embarrassment over its inability to safeguard this dangerous material.[45] By contrast, much soul-searching and recrimination accompanied the Clinton administration's decision to supply North Korea with light-water nuclear reactors and a 10-year supply of oil in exchange for Pyongyang's pledge to shut down the gas-graphite nuclear reactors that supply weapons-grade material to its nuclear weapons program.[46] Even though the Clinton administration developed similar technical approaches to the nuclear programs in Kazakhstan and North Korea, the absence of a clear political accommodation between Washington and Pyongyang led some observers to label the agreement between the United States and North Korea as a form of appeasement.[47] The U.S.-Kazakhstan operation, by contrast, was welcomed by most people in the United States.

Second, opinions vary about whether the United States and the Soviet Union ever reached the kind of political accommodation or modus vivendi that some would suggest is necessary for constructive arms control.[48] But an important technical restraint existed during the Cold War that facilitated negotiations. MAD, by reducing the value of incremental additions to the superpowers' arsenals, increased the mutual benefit produced by cooperative efforts to limit arms in an otherwise adversarial relationship. Political accommodation was not crucial to Cold War efforts to limit arms. In this instance, useful technical agreements could be reached in the absence of an underlying political consensus because of the "technical" restraints MAD itself placed on politics. Without MAD, or political accommodation, to serve as a catalyst for cooperation, it would be unrealistic to expect that the arms control strategies geared to a Cold War context will succeed in the future.

Democracies Beware

For some scholars, the main lesson of the interwar arms control regime was that democracies are at a distinct disadvantage in negotiating agreements with less democratic rivals. Democratic regimes must be responsive to their constituents' demands for reduced taxes, economy in government, and increased spending on social programs. Antidefense lobbies can demand unilateral concessions on defense matters. Domestic groups also clamor for strict adherence to existing arms control agreements; issues of convenience (equipment replacement cycles, operational readiness, economic considerations) are never allowed to interfere with treaty implementation. Arms control advocates also oversell the potential benefits supplied by treaties, exaggerating the role they actually play in keeping the peace. By contrast, nondemocratic leaders can flaunt arms control provisions with little fear of facing domestic opposition from disgruntled legislators or opposition groups.[49]

What most alarms these analysts, however, is the reluctance of democracies to respond quickly to their opponents' treaty violations or even outright abrogation of agreements. Democratic leaders are loath to abandon the monetary benefits or suffer the domestic political costs entailed in abrogating an arms control treaty. As Robert Kaufman points out, the interwar record is far from reassuring on this point. Before Franklin Roosevelt could justify a U.S. naval buildup (20 percent above treaty limits) in 1938, the Japanese established a record of treaty violations, stated that they would no longer abide by the interwar arms control regime (1934), provoked a full-scale war in China following the Marco Polo Bridge incident (1937), and bombed the U.S. gunboat *Panay* in their march on Nanking (1937).[50] Because of this reluctance to respond to anything short of unequivocal evidence that their rivals are no longer adhering to a treaty, democracies often face the prospect of playing catch-up to their less democratic opponents. In Kaufman's view, even successful arms control runs the risk of eventually providing aggressive states with a substantial head start in an arms race.

Conclusion

By the end of the Cold War, classical arms control had generally lived up to its founders' original expectations. Even though it probably never produced clearly discernible savings in overall defense budgets, it did help the superpowers grow accustomed to MAD, thereby contributing to crisis stability and reducing the costs of a superpower nuclear war to zero. By providing a means of communication other than blunt military action or threats of nuclear violence, it fostered an exchange of ideas about military and political affairs between the superpowers that sustained the hope that it was indeed possible to avoid disaster. In hindsight, what is remarkable is not the extraordinary detail of the Cold War arms control agreements, the years spent wrangling over the military and political impact of hypothetical scenarios made possible by key treaty provisions, or the burst of bilateral and unilateral arms control activity that marked the end of the Cold War. What is remarkable is that arms control occurred at all.

But these Cold War successes should not lead to complacency about the risks of nuclear war or the prospects for future arms control. The technical straitjacket produced by MAD, the vision of mutual nuclear holocaust that motivated the founders of classical arms control, does not characterize nascent nuclear relationships around the globe. This raises doubts about the willingness of other leaders to imitate the U.S.-Soviet effort to control arms. Additionally, not all international disputes possess the modicum of mutual interest or potential for political compromise that makes arms control possible. It is unlikely, for example, that arms control could have done anything to end the savage war in Yugoslavia.

Given this changing technical and political environment, adapting the classical tenets of arms control to a post–Cold War world is a priority project for scholars, policymakers, and students alike. Multilateral arms control initiatives raise special political problems. Because of the wide range of hostility among various participants in the chemical and biological weapons conventions, for instance, it will be difficult to implement the technical provisions of these agreements given the various political agendas embraced by the participants. In other words, multilateral conventions could have a negative impact on specific bilateral disputes because their implementation requires a degree of political compromise absent in relations between some pairs of potential antagonists. The United States must also avoid the temptation to link arms control too closely to the benchmark supplied by Russian forces. The military capability of potential opponents, not the waning capability of former enemies, should drive U.S. defense policy.

Most important, it is imperative that the United States not come to believe that arms control is simply a means to save money or that recent progress is not irreversible. Given that Cold War hostility evaporated in just a few years, it is equally possible that the political climate that facilitates ambitious arms control programs can literally vanish overnight. Arms control will continue to succeed as long as policymakers have the courage and intellect to recognize when arms control is likely to pay dividends and when it is likely to contribute to disaster.

Suggested Reading

Adler, Emanuel, ed. *The International Practice of Arms Control.* Baltimore: Johns Hopkins University Press, 1992.

Kaufman, Robert G. *Arms Control During the Pre-Nuclear Era: The United States and Naval Limitations Between the Two World Wars.* New York: Columbia University Press, 1990.

Krepon, Michael, ed. "Has Arms Control Succeeded?" *Bulletin of the Atomic Scientists,* May 1989.

Jervis, Robert. "Arms Control, Stability, and Causes of War." *Political Science Quarterly,* Summer 1993.

Sagan, Scott D. *The Limits of Safety: Organizations, Accidents and Nuclear Weapons.* Princeton, N.J.: Princeton University Press, 1993.

Schelling, Thomas, and Morton Halperin. *Strategy and Arms Control.* Washington, D.C.: Pergamon-Brassey's, 1985.

Notes

1. The revolutionary, or at least counterintuitive, notion embodied in arms control is that, in Thomas Schelling's words, "one can simultaneously think seriously and sympathetically about our military posture and collaborating with our enemies to improve it." Schelling, "Reciprocal Measures for Arms Stabilization," *Daedalus* (Fall 1960), p. 892. On this point also see Robert Jervis, "Arms Control, Stability, and Causes of War," *Political Science Quarterly* (Summer 1993), pp. 239–242. The Fall 1960 issue of *Daedalus* (in addition to Thomas Schelling and Morton Halperin, *Strategy and Arms Control* [New York: Twentieth Century Fund, 1961; reprinted Washington, D.C.: Pergamon-Brassey's, 1985]) is often cited as the intellectual point of departure for what we now call arms control. The Winter 1991 edition of *Daedalus*, "Arms Control Thirty Years On," contains a fascinating retrospective in which many of the contributors to the 1960 volume evaluate their work. This edition of the journal was also published as Emanuel Adler, ed., *The International Practice of Arms Control* (Baltimore: Johns Hopkins University Press, 1992). For an earlier retrospective on the 1960 issue of *Daedalus*, see Franklin A. Long and George Rathjens, eds., *Arms, Defense Policy and Arms Control* (New York: W. W. Norton & Co., 1975). For other responses to the question posed in this analysis, see Michael Krepon, ed., "Has Arms Control Succeeded?" *Bulletin of the Atomic Scientists* (May 1989), pp. 26–46.

2. For a critical appraisal of the scholarly failure to predict the end of the Cold War, see John Lewis Gaddis, "International Relations Theory and the End of the Cold War," *International Security* (Winter 1992–1993), pp. 5–58.

3. Thomas Schelling, "The Thirtieth Year," in Adler, *The International Practice of Arms Control*, p. 21.

4. Richard Betts, *Nuclear Blackmail and Nuclear Balance* (Washington, D.C.: Brookings Institution, 1987), pp. 62–66. Suez marked the start of a pattern in Khrushchev's behavior during crises that I label "Sputnik diplomacy."

5. Betts, *Nuclear Blackmail*, pp. 66–79; Gordon Chang, "To the Nuclear Brink: Eisenhower, Dulles, and the Quemoy-Matsu Crisis," *International Security* (Spring 1988), pp. 96–123; and H. W. Brands, "Testing Massive Retaliation: Credibility and Crisis Management in the Taiwan Strait," *International Security* (Spring 1988), pp. 124–151.

6. Jerome H. Kahan, *Security in the Nuclear Age* (Washington, D.C.: Brookings Institution, 1975), pp. 30–31; McGeorge Bundy, *Danger and Survival* (New York: Vintage Books, 1988), pp. 334–350; and Walter A. McDougall, *The Heavens and the Earth: A Political History of the Space Age* (New York: Basic Books, 1985), pp. 141–156, 250–262.

7. For a discussion of the strategic imbalance that favored the United States on the eve of the Cuban missile crisis, see Scott D. Sagan, "SIOP-62: The Nuclear War Plan Briefing to President Kennedy," *International Security* (Summer 1987), pp. 22–51. U.S. policymakers, however, were never really confident about the ability of the United States to win a nuclear war. See Richard Betts, "A Nuclear Golden Age? The Balance Before Parity," *International Security* (Winter 1986–1987), pp. 3–32.

8. Albert Wohlstetter, "The Delicate Balance of Terror," *Foreign Affairs* (January 1959), pp. 221–234.

9. At times, the domestic costs of the Cold War were quite high. For an explanation of how the United States kept Cold War domestic threats in check, see Aaron L. Friedberg, "Why Didn't the United States Become a Garrison State?" *International Security* (Spring 1992), pp. 109–142.

10. After the development of thermonuclear weapons in the early 1950s, according to Bernard Brodie, the old question of nuclear scarcity versus abundance evaporated. Technological advances and the availability of nuclear materials led to a situation in which the destructive potential of nuclear arsenals became unlimited. See Brodie, *War and Politics* (New York: Macmillan, 1973), pp. 382–383.

11. Schelling and Halperin, *Strategy and Arms Control*, pp. 10–11.

12. Khrushchev's bluff, "Sputnik diplomacy," was called on 21 October 1961, when Roswell Gilpatric, deputy secretary of defense in the Kennedy administration, announced that the United States no longer was concerned that a missile gap existed; in fact, if a gap existed, it now was in favor of the United States. See Raymond Garthoff, *Reflections on the Cuban Missile Crisis* (Washington, D.C.: Brookings Institution, 1989), p. 45, fn. 74.

13. However, as James Blight argues, the goals embraced by both superpowers changed to avoiding a nuclear showdown as the prospects for nuclear war became clear. See Blight, *The Shattered Crystal Ball: Fear and Learning in the Cuban Missile Crisis* (Savage, Md.: Rowman & Littlefield, 1990). Preemption occurs following indications that an opponent is about to attack. A preemptive strategy implies that a state is not willing to allow its opponent to inflict the first blow; upon receipt of warning that the opponent is gearing up for an attack, the goal is to beat (preempt) the opponent to the punch by firing one's weapons first.

14. Schelling and Halperin, *Strategy and Arms Control*, pp. 137–138. On technological determinism, see Barry Buzan, *An Introduction to Strategic Studies: Military Technology and International Relations* (New York: St. Martin's Press, 1987). For alternative explanations of weapons development, see Herbert York, *Race to Oblivion: A Participant's View of the Arms Race* (New York: Simon & Schuster, 1971); and Matthew Evangelista, *Innovation and the Arms Race* (Ithaca, N.Y.: Cornell University Press, 1988).

15. On the joint pledge and other efforts to prohibit nuclear weapons in space (1963 Limited Test Ban Treaty; UN Resolution of December 1963, "A Declaration of Legal Principles Governing States in the Exploration and Use of Outer Space"; and the 1967 Outer Space Treaty), see McDougall, *The Heavens and the Earth*, pp. 274–275, 417–420.

16. Schelling and Halperin, *Strategy and Arms Control*, pp. 14–17.

17. On this variety of accidental war, see Scott D. Sagan, *The Limits of Safety: Organizations, Accidents and Nuclear Weapons* (Princeton, N.J.: Princeton University Press, 1993).

18. On inadvertent escalation, see Barry Posen, *Inadvertent Escalation: Conventional War and Nuclear Risks* (Ithaca, N.Y.: Cornell University Press, 1991); Joseph F. Bouchard, *Command in Crisis* (New York: Columbia University Press, 1991); and James J. Wirtz, "Strategic Conventional Deterrence: Lessons from the Maritime Strategy," *Security Studies* (Autumn 1993), pp. 117–151.

19. Sagan, *The Limits of Safety,* pp. 156–203.

20. MAD occurs when it is impossible to distinguish winners from losers following a nuclear exchange. See Robert Jervis, *The Meaning of the Nuclear Revolution* (Ithaca, N.Y.: Cornell University Press, 1989), pp. 4–5.

21. Some observers continued to protest the acceptance of MAD as a basis for U.S. strategic nuclear policy up until the conclusion of the Cold War. See Colin S. Gray, "Nuclear Strategy: The Case for the Theory of Victory," *International Security*

(Summer 1979), pp. 54–87; and Colin Gray and Keith Payne, "Victory Is Possible," *Foreign Policy* (Summer 1980), pp. 14–27. For a response to this position, see Robert Jervis, "Why Nuclear Superiority Doesn't Matter," *Political Science Quarterly* (Winter 1979–1980), pp. 617–633; and Charles Glaser, *Analyzing Strategic Nuclear Policy* (Princeton, N.J.: Princeton University Press, 1990), pp. 133–165. For an overview of the debate, see Charles Glaser, "Why Do Strategists Disagree About the Requirements of Strategic Nuclear Deterrence?" in Lynn Eden and Steven Miller, eds., *Nuclear Arguments* (Ithaca, N.Y.: Cornell University Press, 1989), pp. 109–171.

22. On the 1967 Glassboro summit, see John Newhouse, *Cold Dawn: The Story of SALT* (New York: Holt, Rinehart & Winston, 1973), pp. 94–95; and Kahan, *Security in the Nuclear Age*, p. 115. In an odd twist, Ronald Reagan reminded the Soviet delegation to the 1985 Geneva summit of Prime Minister Aleksei Kosygin's and Foreign Minister Andrei Gromyko's spirited arguments in favor of missile defenses. Reagan was attempting to convince the Soviet leadership of the benefits of the Strategic Defense Initiative (SDI). According to Raymond Garthoff, the Soviets found this volte-face disturbing. See Garthoff, *The Great Transition: American-Soviet Relations and the End of the Cold War* (Washington, D.C.: Brookings Institution, 1994), p. 244.

23. In his report to the Supreme Soviet following the conclusion of the November 1985 Geneva summit, Gorbachev spoke out against SDI: "We do not base our policy [toward the United States] on a desire to encroach on the national interests of the USA. I will say more: we would not, for example, want changes in the strategic balance to our favor. We would not want this because such a situation would heighten suspicion of the other side and increase the instability of the general situation. … Things have developed in such a way that both our countries will have to get used to strategic parity as the natural state." Quoted in Garthoff, *The Great Transition*, pp. 242–243.

24. Claims vary about the sophistication of Soviet and U.S. nuclear strategists, measured by a recognition of the limitations imposed by MAD. For example, Stephen Kull found little evidence of sophistication in the analytical positions of the Soviet and U.S. experts he interviewed during the mid-1980s. Alternatively, Steve Weber has noted extensive evidence for relatively sophisticated analyses in Soviet and U.S. nuclear thought by the late 1960s. See Kull, *Minds at War: Nuclear Reality and the Inner Conflicts of Defense Policymakers* (New York: Basic Books, 1988); and Weber, *Cooperation and Discord in U.S.-Soviet Arms Control* (Princeton, N.J.: Princeton University Press, 1991).

25. By the mid-1970s, even supporters of arms control acknowledged these kinds of limitations. See George W. Rathjens, "Changing Perspectives on Arms Control," in Franklin A. Long and George Rathjens, *Arms, Defense Policy and Arms Control* (New York: W. W. Norton & Co., 1975), p. 201.

26. Robert J. Bresler and Robert Gray, "The Bargaining Chip and SALT," *Political Science Quarterly* (Spring 1977), pp. 65–88. For a critique of the bargaining chip argument, see Glaser, *Analyzing Strategic Nuclear Policy*, pp. 344–348.

27. If one embraces the notion of the stability-instability paradox, however, MAD (stability at the nuclear level of conflict) produced instability (conventional war, conventional weapons development, etc.) at lower levels of violence. Thus, arms control, by helping to preserve MAD at relatively low levels of weaponry, might have accelerated a comparatively expensive conventional arms race. On the stability-instability paradox, see Glenn Snyder, "The Balance of Power and the Balance of Terror," in Paul Seabury, ed., *The Balance of Power* (San Francisco: Chandler, 1965), pp. 194–201.

28. Jervis, *The Meaning of the Nuclear Revolution*, pp. 23–45.

29. Grant T. Hammond, *Plowshares into Swords: Arms Races in International Politics, 1840–1991* (Columbia: University of South Carolina Press, 1993).

30. On the notion of brinkmanship, most often associated with the Eisenhower administration, see Betts, *Nuclear Blackmail*, pp. 1–16; Thomas Schelling, *Arms and Influence* (New Haven, Conn.: Yale University Press, 1966), pp. 91–109; Kahan, *Security in the Nuclear Age*, pp. 14–15; and Townsend Hoopes, *The Devil and John Foster Dulles* (Boston: Little, Brown and Co., 1973), p. 407. The U.S. nuclear alert during the 1973 October War and the "war scare" experienced by the Soviets in the early 1980s demonstrate, however, that arms control did not eliminate overt nuclear threat making from the superpower relationship. See Barry Blechman and Douglas Hart, "The Political Utility of Nuclear Weapons: The 1973 Middle East Crisis," *International Security* (Summer 1982), pp. 132–156; and Michael McGwire, *Perestroika and Soviet National Security* (Washington, D.C.: Brookings Institution, 1991), pp. 380–392.

31. Schelling and Halperin, *Strategy and Arms Control*, pp. 77–80.

32. Elite or public perceptions that war is inevitable greatly increase the prospects that states will engage in preventive war or preemption. See Jack S. Levy, "Declining Power and the Preventive Motivation for War," *World Politics* (October 1987), pp. 82–107.

33. Peter M. Haas, "Introduction: Epistemic Communities and International Policy Coordination," *International Organization* (Winter 1992), p. 3.

34. Timothy Luke, "Nuclear Security After the Moscow Coup: Deterrence After the Empire Strikes Back," paper presented at the annual meeting of the American Political Science Association, Chicago, Ill., 3–6 September 1992.

35. Emanuel Adler, "The Emergence of Cooperation: National Epistemic Communities and the International Evolution of the Idea of Nuclear Arms Control," *International Organization* (Winter 1992), pp. 101–145.

36. Steven Weber, "Interactive Learning in U.S.-Soviet Arms Control," in George Breslauer and Philip Tetlock, eds., *Learning in U.S. and Soviet Foreign Policy* (Boulder, Colo.: Westview Press, 1991), pp. 784–824.

37. For analyses that support this position, see Robert G. Kaufman, *Arms Control During the Pre-Nuclear Era: The United States and Naval Limitations Between the Two World Wars* (New York: Columbia University Press, 1990), p. 104; Colin S. Gray, *Weapons Don't Make War: Policy, Strategy, and Military Technology* (Lawrence: University of Kansas Press, 1993), p. 106; and Colin S. Gray, *House of Cards: Why Arms Control Must Fail* (Ithaca, N.Y.: Cornell University Press, 1992).

38. Gray, *House of Cards*, p. 17.

39. The source of Gray's error is that he overestimates the intractability of the political confrontation between the United States and the Soviet Union. If the arms control paradox and Gray's view of the Soviet Union were both correct, then U.S.-Soviet arms control probably should not have occurred. Gray salvages his position by claiming that the arms control that did occur was not very good (but his original formulation of the arms control paradox says little about the quality of arms control). Ibid., pp. 128–159.

40. "Clinton Reportedly Accepts Plan to Retain Bush's Nuclear Policy," *Dallas Morning News*, 22 September 1994, p. 11A. For a fine discussion of the "implementation first" decision contained in the Clinton administration's Nuclear Policy Review, see Chapter 5.

41. Kaufman, *Arms Control*, pp. 174, 181.

42. Gray, *House of Cards*, p. 107.

43. Emily Goldman, *Sunken Treaties: Naval Arms Control Between the Wars* (University Park: Pennsylvania State University Press, 1994), pp. 15–17. According to

Kaufman, "The record of naval limitation suggests strongly that arms limitation will fail without corresponding political *detente*. *Detente* made naval limitation possible during the 1920s, just as Japan's determination to dominate China made failure inevitable during the 1930s." See Kaufman, *Arms Control*, p. 196.

44. Goldman, *Sunken Treaties*, pp. 189–237.

45. Michael R. Gordon, "Move of Kazakhstan Uranium Required Months to Negotiate," *Dallas Morning News*, 24 November 1994, p. 26A.

46. Jim Mann, "Clinton OKs Deal to Stop N. Korea's Nuclear Program," *Los Angeles Times*, 24 November 1994, p. 10.

47. Frank Gaffney, "Whistling Past Galluci Gulch," *Washington Times*, 24 November 1994, p. A20.

48. For a positive description of this political accommodation, see John Lewis Gaddis, "The Long Peace: Elements of Stability in the Postwar International System," *International Security* (Spring 1986), pp. 99–142.

49. Kaufman, *Arms Control*, pp. 197–199.

50. Ibid., p. 183.

PART 3

Preventing the
Spread of Arms

9

Preventing the Spread of Arms: Nuclear Weapons

Virginia I. Foran

Since the first test of a nuclear weapon in 1945 by the United States, efforts to limit the spread of nuclear weapons to additional states have been at the forefront of international arms control. Most frequently referred to as nuclear nonproliferation, these efforts have been largely successful. Over the past 50 years, nuclear nonproliferation has passed through four phases and is at the crossroads of a fifth. The first four phases were international control (1945–1946), nonproliferation by secrecy (1945–1952), the Atoms for Peace program (1953–1960), and the Non-Proliferation Treaty and regime (1961–1995). All four phases were affected by the superpower competition of the Cold War era. With the dissolution of the Soviet Union, a fifth phase is emerging. Its character will depend on an evaluation of the success of past nonproliferation efforts, the current incentives and constraints to proliferation, and whether the international community regards the spread of nuclear weapons on the eve of the twenty-first century as largely inevitable or manageable. Whatever the result, as long as nuclear weapons are regarded as the most dangerous weapons available to humankind, the fifth phase will have important implications for all future arms control efforts.

This chapter will discuss each of the past four phases of nuclear nonproliferation efforts and the challenges to those efforts; it will evaluate the potential components of the fifth phase and the likelihood of its success.

History of Nonproliferation Efforts

*Phases I and II: Failure of International Control
and Nonproliferation by Secrecy*

In the late 1930s, when physicists in France, Great Britain, and the United States began to realize the destructive potential of the atom bomb, they persuaded Pres. Franklin Roosevelt to develop this technology as quickly as possible.[1] In 1942 the U.S. atomic bomb program began under the code name the Manhattan Project. On 16 July 1945, the United States conducted the first test of an atomic device near Alamogordo, New Mexico.[2] Less than one month later, Pres. Harry S Truman authorized dropping two atomic bombs on the Japanese cities of Hiroshima and Nagasaki and forced the unconditional surrender of Japan and the end of World War II.[3]

Soon after the first use of nuclear weapons, U.S. military strategists, scholars, and policymakers began to speculate whether the atomic bomb was fundamentally different from previous types of weapons. The demonstration of atomic weapons on Japan raised questions regarding the potential implications such weapons might have on the nature and conduct of war, especially if they became as commonplace as conventional weapons. Some argued that because it took so few weapons to destroy so much within a very short time, traditional methods of retaliation or defense no longer applied.[4] They questioned whether the United States would be able to defend itself adequately from a nuclear attack and noted how the situation would become even more complex if many states acquired these weapons.

In September 1945, the U.S. Congress responded to these fears by drafting the Atomic Energy Act (AEA). Also known as the McMahon Act, the AEA restricted sharing atomic technology with any nation, even U.S. allies such as Great Britain.[5] The United States hoped that its efforts would prevent it from having to defend itself from a nuclear attack. At the same time, there was a growing consensus that a U.S. monopoly on nuclear technology could not be maintained indefinitely and that additional efforts should be made to place atomic weapons and relevant technology under international control.

In June 1946, after several months of study and debate, the United States proposed a plan to the UN to place all aspects of atomic energy under an independent international authority responsible to the UN Security Council. Known as the Baruch Plan (for U.S. representative to the UN Atomic Energy Commission Bernard Baruch), it required that all states cease production of atomic weapons and deposit all information on the construction of their weapons with an international agency to be called the Atomic Development Authority (ADA).[6] Within a few days, Soviet representative Andrei Gromyko made a dramatic counterproposal calling for a convention prohibiting the production and employment of atomic weapons and requiring all states conducting research on atomic energy to exchange relevant scientific information. The Soviet Union's principal concern was in breaking the U.S. monopoly of the most technically advanced information regarding nuclear weapons.[7] In light of that concern, the Soviet Union insisted that the United States destroy its existing stockpile of nuclear weapons and materials prior to the creation of the ADA. After several months of negotiation, the United States refused to agree to this stipulation, believing that the Soviets were stalling for time to make further progress on their own atomic bomb program. With both sides holding firm to their positions, the negotiations broke down and the first plan for the nonproliferation of nuclear weapons was never implemented.

Meanwhile, Great Britain returned to its own research and development of nuclear weapons. Prime Minister Winston Churchill approached the United States for financial assistance and technical cooperation on the basis of the 1943 Quebec Agreement, the U.S.-British agreement for collaboration on nuclear research. The McMahon Act prohibited the United States from keeping its promise to share information with the British. Concern about continued U.S. access to a major Western supply of uranium—located in the Belgian Congo—led the United States to find a loophole in the act. The United States agreed with Great Britain to "full and effective cooperation in basic research, [but] not in development, design, construction, and operation of [nuclear] plants."[8] Events in 1948 and 1949—such as the takeover of the Czech government by communist-led forces in February 1948, the Soviet-enforced land blockade of Berlin in July of that same year, and the Soviet test of its first atomic device in August 1949—would escalate the Cold War, lead to demands for additional nuclear weapons, and intensify the pressure on the United States to collaborate on nuclear matters with its allies.

The United States was then in the awkward position of trying to reconcile its need to allow allies limited access to U.S. nuclear weapons for the purpose of coordinating defense plans with its ongoing desire to limit the spread of nuclear weapons. A new approach to nonproliferation was needed. A solution was proposed by Pres. Dwight Eisenhower in 1953.

Phase III: The Atoms for Peace Program

Despite U.S. efforts to prevent the spread of nuclear weapons, in October 1952 Great Britain became the third nuclear weapon state by successfully testing a nuclear bomb. By the time Eisenhower became president, the United States was involved in a land war with North Korea and China and hydrogen bomb programs were under way in the United States and the Soviet Union. In addition, Belgium, Canada, France, and Italy had established national nuclear research and development programs. Increasingly, Eisenhower became concerned about the threat of nuclear war and sought to deemphasize the military aspects of nuclear technology in the hopes of lessening the incentives to build nuclear weapons.

In December 1953, after close consultation with his own advisers and discussions with Britain and France, Eisenhower proposed his Atoms for Peace program to the UN. In his speech, Eisenhower acknowledged that despite U.S. efforts to control the technology and raw materials needed for nuclear weapons, several countries had successfully developed their own atomic bombs. If the spread of nuclear technology was inevitable, and with it an increase in the probability of nuclear war, then it was imperative that both superpowers reduce their arsenals and emphasize the peaceful applications of nuclear energy. He stated, "It is not enough to take this weapon out of the hands of soldiers. It must be put into the hands of those who know how to strip its military casing and adapt it to the arts of peace."[9] Eisenhower proposed that an Atoms for Peace program would contribute to this goal by sharing nuclear technology with additional countries on a selective basis, as long as each promised that it was for peaceful purposes. In this way, all states could get the benefits of nuclear technology without the fear that it would someday be used against them.

To support the Atoms for Peace program, the International Atomic Energy Agency (IAEA) was created. The IAEA would serve as the depository of voluntary contributions of fissile material that would be distributed to participating countries for peaceful uses. To enable the United States to contribute fissile material, however, new laws were necessary. The U.S. Congress was supportive, and, in 1954 the outdated McMahon Act was replaced by the Atomic Energy Act.[10] The United States could now join other states in exchanging information in the field of peaceful nuclear energy with other countries.

By the time the final statute for the IAEA was approved by all members of the UN in 1956, the U.S. Atomic Energy Commission had completed more than 22 bilateral agreements for cooperation on nuclear energy, including raw materials and equipment, and was negotiating 27 others. Several other states, including Britain, France, and Norway, had negotiated sales of equipment and raw materials as well. In particular, the United States approved the sale to India of 50 tons of heavy water, used in nuclear reactors that produce plutonium as a by-product, while France secretly agreed to provide Israel with a plutonium-producing reactor.

While the Atoms for Peace program encouraged sharing nuclear technology for peaceful purposes, the final statute of the IAEA did not require verifying the peaceful nature of all sales and programs. Safeguards ensuring that the technology and materials received through Atoms for Peace were not being diverted to nuclear weapon programs were left up to the supplying governments, although the IAEA would assist if requested. In many cases, no safeguards were applied, and most only covered a small portion of the nuclear activity approved by the Atoms for Peace program. These aspects of Atoms for Peace would prove to be its downfall, as the technology and equipment needed for a peaceful nuclear program could be too easily used for nuclear weapons development.[11] It would soon become apparent that nuclear nonproliferation needed to rest on something stronger than a state's declaration that its nuclear program was for peaceful purposes.

Atoms for Peace optimism wanes.   While the Atoms for Peace program emphasized nuclear cooperation, proposals to limit the arsenals of the declared nuclear weapons states by negotiating moratoriums on nuclear testing were being contemplated in other assemblies and the UN. In August 1957, Britain, Canada, France, and the United States submitted the Four-Power Proposal to the UN General Assembly Disarmament Subcommittee. This proposal called for a two-year cessation of atomic tests.[12] In the suspicious atmosphere of Cold War competition, however, these efforts failed, in large part over issues of verification and safeguards. Intrusive inspections to verify compliance with a test ban could also mean access to military secrets.

In February 1960, France conducted its first test of an atomic device, raising the nuclear club's membership to four. At the same time, the United States began to suspect that Israel was developing a nuclear weapon capability at its French-designed nuclear facility in the Negev Desert.[13] This made four declared nuclear weapons states and counting—the nuclear genie was quickly spreading.

Phase IV: The Non-Proliferation Treaty and Regime

The Atoms for Peace program, while well meaning, had not reduced the incentives for proliferation and was potentially providing some of the necessary materials and technology for additional proliferators. In 1961, reflecting growing concern with the worsening proliferation situation, the UN General Assembly unanimously passed a resolution calling on all states to negotiate an agreement for the nonproliferation of nuclear weapons.[14] This resolution provided the basis for the negotiation of the fourth phase in nonproliferation.

By 1963, confidence had risen in nonintrusive means of verification of nuclear testing using satellites. Confidence was still not high enough to resolve the differences for a comprehensive test ban treaty, but it was enough to negotiate a Partial Test Ban Treaty (PTBT), also known as the Limited Test Ban Treaty (LTBT), prohibiting the testing of nuclear devices in the atmosphere, in the sea, and in outer space. In July 1963, while announcing the imminent signing of the PTBT, Pres. John F. Kennedy underscored the importance of nuclear nonproliferation by predicting that by 1970 there could be as many as 25 declared nuclear weapon states unless a nuclear nonproliferation treaty was concluded.[15] The PTBT was only a start in the right direction. With the People's Republic of China's test of its first atomic device in October 1964, and increasing concern about India's nuclear energy program, President Kennedy's prediction appeared to be well on its way to confirmation.

After three years of difficult negotiations, and seven years after the 1961 General Assembly resolution was passed, the Non-Proliferation Treaty (NPT) was signed in July 1968. The NPT would come into force in March

1970, after the minimum number of states (70) acceded to it. The treaty created two categories of states: nuclear weapon states and nonnuclear weapon states. States that conducted a test of a nuclear device before the NPT was signed belonged to the first category, bound by the obligations the treaty specified when they joined the NPT. All states that had not conducted a test by July 1967 would be bound by the obligations set for nonnuclear weapon states when they acceded to the treaty. Once a nonnuclear state acceded to the NPT, it could not become a nuclear weapon state and remain in good standing. (A list of current NPT members is found in Appendix 2.)

The nonproliferation bargain stipulated by the treaty is essentially the same as required by Atoms for Peace, with two crucial additions. First, nonnuclear weapon states party to the NPT agreed to forgo developing or acquiring nuclear weapons in exchange for peaceful nuclear technology from nuclear weapon states; they also agreed to submit their peaceful nuclear programs to inspections by the IAEA. Each nonnuclear weapon state that signs the treaty has 18 months to conclude a "full-scope safeguards" agreement with the IAEA. This agreement requires making a full declaration to the IAEA of all nuclear facilities, including research and development facilities, nuclear power reactors, and sites where raw materials such as natural uranium are mined or prepared. In stark contrast, declared nuclear weapon states are not required to have their facilities inspected by the IAEA but can do so voluntarily.

Second, in exchange for nonnuclear weapon states pledging that they would remain nonnuclear, declared nuclear weapon states party to the treaty agree that they will seek an early end to their own nuclear arms race. Article I of the treaty requires that nuclear weapon states also pledge not to directly or indirectly transfer nuclear weapons or control of such weapons to nonnuclear weapon states and not to assist or encourage nonnuclear weapon states to manufacture or seek control over such weapons. (See Appendix 2 for details of the NPT.)

An imperfect bargain. The NPT bargain was not easily obtained. Interested states pursued a number of competing objectives that required making compromises to the treaty's ideal goals. While all states could agree on the general goal of nonproliferation, they could not agree on how to achieve it. The treaty that resulted reflected the compromises required at the time. Without such compromises, the NPT would not have been concluded.

Many states were reluctant to sign the treaty because it legally perpetuated an imbalance in the military capabilities of nuclear weapon states and nonnuclear weapon states (at least until disarmament was achieved) and because of the inherent asymmetries in inspection obligations. In addition to these imbalances, differences between the obligations of more technically advanced nonnuclear weapon states and other nonnuclear states began to emerge during the final negotiations.[16]

For example, all nonnuclear states sought access to nuclear technology. However, some states already had nuclear programs—begun with assistance from the Atoms for Peace program. At that time, nuclear energy was believed to be an inexpensive resource that would power many states into the twentieth century and help to eliminate some of the vast differences between the First and Third Worlds. On the other end of the spectrum, in one of the rare episodes of Cold War agreement, the United States and the Soviet Union recognized that capping the number of nuclear weapon states at five was in each state's best interest. Both states agreed that inspections of peaceful nuclear activities of nonnuclear states had to be intrusive enough to ensure that no state could convert a peaceful nuclear program into a nuclear weapons program without detection. As a result, the Soviet Union and the United States sought restrictions on certain types of nuclear programs that lowered the threshold between peaceful uses and weapons technology. Plutonium reprocessing and gas centrifuge technology used to enrich uranium fell into this category. Germany, Italy, Belgium, and Japan were concerned that such restrictions would leave their nuclear industries at a disadvantage compared with the declared nuclear weapon states. The Federal Republic of Germany was particularly concerned that its research on plutonium-based fast-breeder reactors would be compromised by the inspectors.[17] To persuade these states to sign the treaty, restrictions on such technology were eased and the states were reassured that safeguards would not interfere with their civil nuclear programs. Underdeveloped states that had yet to develop nuclear programs saw the compromise as indicating a special status for the more advanced nonnuclear weapon states.

The case of India. Another overall weakness with the NPT bargain emerged during negotiations with India to persuade it to become a signatory. Proponents of the treaty argued that adherence to the NPT would benefit all states equally because each state could be assured that one's neighbors (providing they had signed the treaty) had peaceful intentions. On that basis, states would be able to voluntarily forgo developing nuclear weapons. In return, members of the NPT would receive access to peaceful nuclear technology and a promise that declared nuclear weapon states would seek an early end to the arms race. This bargain did not satisfy many concerns—in particular, what did the treaty offer nonnuclear states that were concerned about a nuclear-armed neighbor? For example, how could India agree to adhere to the NPT in perpetuity in the face of nuclear and conventional military threats from China? India argued that for the bargain to be fair, nuclear weapon states either had to be prepared to defend nonnuclear weapon states from nuclear attack or had to agree not to use nuclear weapons against them.

Respectively, these requests came to be known as positive and negative security guarantees.

During the final stage of negotiations over the NPT, India specifically requested a security guarantee from the United Kingdom, the United States, and the Soviet Union for protection in the event of a nuclear attack or the threat of nuclear attack. The response came in June 1968, when the three states offered a joint Security Council resolution promising that they would assist any nonnuclear weapon state party to the NPT that is "a victim of an act or an object of a threat of aggression in which nuclear weapons are used."[18] This response, however, was not satisfactory to India because it was tied to joining the NPT. From the Indian perspective, all nonnuclear weapon states should be encouraged to remain nonnuclear by ensuring their security "regardless of whether or not they sign the nonproliferation treaty."[19]

In the end, India was not persuaded to sign the treaty and has refused to sign ever since. The quest for security guarantees, however, did not end. In September 1968, after the NPT was finalized and opened for signature, the UN sponsored a conference of the nonnuclear nations. Of the 92 states that attended, 81 had already signed the NPT, but all were dissatisfied with the treaty's security guarantees. A proposal for an international convention to negotiate stronger guarantees failed by one vote.[20] Since then, a few nonnuclear weapon states have continued to push for stronger positive and negative security assurances from nuclear weapon states. Other nonnuclear states, less directly threatened by a nuclear-armed or a superior conventionally armed state, thought that the NPT review mechanism would provide some oversight of the declared nuclear weapon states' promises.

The review mechanism. The possibility that it would be only a matter of time before all states had access to the technology and materials needed to produce a nuclear bomb persuaded many nonnuclear states to negotiate an exit option to the treaty in the event of failure of the NPT regime; it also persuaded them to keep the pressure on the declared nuclear states' promise to seek an early end to the arms race. Every five years, for a period of 25 years after the treaty entered into force, states party to the NPT would undertake a review of the obligations of all members of the treaty. At the end of the 25 years, all states party to the treaty would vote whether to extend the treaty indefinitely or for another fixed number of years.

In particular, during these periodic reviews, members evaluated whether the obligations stipulated in Articles IV and VI of the treaty were being met. Article IV stipulates that nonnuclear states party to the treaty receive an adequate supply of material and equipment needed for nuclear energy programs. Article VI calls on all members to "pursue negotiations in good faith on effective measures relating to cessation of the nuclear arms race at an early date and to nuclear disarmament, and on a treaty on general and complete disarmament under strict and effective international control."[21] In addition, during some reviews, a few nonnuclear members have accused the United States and other nuclear weapon states of violating Article I of the treaty, which prohibits aiding or encouraging a nonnuclear weapon state to develop nuclear weapons.

The United States did provide tremendous financial assistance to Pakistan, particularly during the Soviet war with Afghanistan (1980–1989). From approximately the mid-1970s, Pakistan has been suspected of trying to develop its own nuclear weapon. It has been argued that some U.S. dollars indirectly underwrote the Pakistani nuclear program by allowing large portions of the Pakistani domestic budget to be diverted to an undeclared nuclear weapons program.[22] Soviet financial support to India is suspected of making a similar contribution, while the United States has also been accused of acquiescing to Israel's undeclared nuclear weapons program.[23]

Before the first review of the treaty's performance could be conducted, however, the emerging nonproliferation regime was met with a significant challenge—India, a country outside the nonproliferation regime, conducted a nuclear test. In the past, such tests had provided the demonstration of a state's nuclear capability and were usually followed by a declaration of the state's nuclear weapon status. Although India did not follow this course, the test illuminated some of the loopholes in the ability of the nonproliferation regime to prevent the spread of nuclear weapon capability.

The 1974 Indian Test: Closing the Loopholes

In May 1974, only four years after the NPT came into force, the government of India conducted what it termed a "peaceful nuclear explosion." Prime Minister Indira Gandhi insisted that the nuclear test was not a declaration that India was a nuclear weapon state. Yet to most countries in the world, the test was a clear sign that India had the capability of producing nuclear weapons if it wanted to. The event sent shock waves through the new regime. Not only was India not persuaded to join the NPT, but now it was clear that even a developing country could master the technology needed to produce nuclear weapons. To make matters worse, there was ample evidence that India relied on a Canadian-supplied reactor and fissile material from the United States, both acquired under the Atoms for Peace program, to build its first nuclear device. It became clear that any state, even NPT signatories (since they can withdraw from the treaty by providing three months' notice), had the potential to convert nuclear energy technology into a nuclear bomb. How could the NPT, therefore, prevent additional states inside or outside the regime, especially those that had nuclear energy programs, from following in India's footsteps?

Nonproliferation by denial.   To address some of these loopholes, NPT members that were exporting nuclear technology and materials began to augment NPT guidelines with some additional voluntary rules. Article III.2 of the NPT requires that all exports of nuclear materials to nonnuclear weapon states be subject to IAEA safeguards. To implement this requirement of the NPT, member states that engaged in such export activity agreed on a specific list of materials and items that would be covered by the NPT provision. This became known as the Trigger List.[24] The list, however, applied only to exports to NPT members.

After the Indian test, in November 1974, the principal supplying states met again in London to discuss how to better monitor exports of nuclear technology and supplies to states outside the regime and how some of the most sensitive parts of the nuclear fuel cycle should be exported—if at all. This group, known as the London Club and, more formally, the Nuclear Suppliers Group (NSG), adopted a uniform code of conduct for interstate sales of nuclear materials.[25] Since then, the group has met several times to periodically expand its membership and update the list of items under voluntary controls.

In 1992, the NSG agreed to make full-scope safeguards a condition required of every state receiving nuclear-related equipment and supplies. The term *full-scope safeguards* refers to an agreement (INFCIRC 153) with the IAEA to periodically inspect all declared nuclear facilities. Therefore, even states not party to the NPT would have to agree to IAEA safeguards to receive nuclear-related material from outside suppliers. In addition, the NSG created a list of components and materials that could be used both for peaceful nuclear activities and for nuclear weapons that would have the full-scope safeguards requirement. This list of dual-use items was a significant achievement for the nonproliferation regime, as it indicated a willingness to restrict potential commercial sales for the goal of nonproliferation.

The NSG guidelines are very useful in slowing down the spread of nuclear weapons capability to additional states. They force states that do not want to open their nuclear facilities to IAEA inspections to produce everything indigenously, or to purchase what they need clandestinely. Although this may not prevent a state determined to make nuclear weapons from eventually becoming so capable, the NSG rules significantly raise the costs of doing so.

There are several drawbacks to the NSG guidelines. Not all nonnuclear states receiving peaceful nuclear technology or equipment are trying to develop nuclear weapons. The NSG guidelines do not make this distinction. They apply to all nonnuclear states regardless of whether the state is considered a potential proliferator or not. More important, dual-use safeguards increase the inspection obligations on all nonnuclear states while restricting the access to peaceful nuclear technology and equipment that is assured all NPT members by Article IV. Finally, the guidelines are only as effective in slowing or preventing nuclear proliferation as the IAEA safeguards are at detecting weapons-related activities. The discovery of Iraq's nuclear weapon program during the 1991 Gulf War revealed some of the limitations of the IAEA safeguards system.

Limitations of the IAEA Safeguards System

When the NPT went into effect in 1970, the IAEA had already been operating for over 10 years facilitating the Atoms for Peace program. It was clear from the negotiations of the NPT that even the most ardent supporters of nuclear nonproliferation did not want to sacrifice access to nuclear technology and materials for the sake of nonproliferation. The final draft of the NPT increased the scope of safeguards to be applied to civil nuclear programs and made them a requirement for membership, but restrictions on access to technology and materials were minimized. This compromise went forward despite lessons learned from the Atoms for Peace program that certain peaceful nuclear technology could be adapted for weapons purposes.

As a result, while the IAEA was to be the principal verification arm of the NPT, the overall restructuring required was not substantial. The IAEA expanded its responsibilities but did not change the balance of objectives of the original mandate reflected in Article II of the agency's 1957 statute:

> The Agency shall seek to accelerate and enlarge the contribution of atomic energy to peace, health and prosperity throughout the world. It shall ensure, so far as it is able, that assistance provided by it or at its request or under its supervision or control is not used in such a way as to further any military purpose.[26]

To reflect the additional responsibility of the IAEA Department of Safeguards due to the adoption of INFCIRC 153, the number of personnel assigned to the department dramatically increased.[27] Implementation of the full-scope safeguards agreement, however, still relied on the voluntary cooperation and declaration by the participating state of all its nuclear facilities and activities.

The case of Iraq.   Full-scope safeguards are designed to detect undeclared activities at declared sites, but they cannot detect undeclared activities at undeclared facilities. This became widely recognized in early 1991 in the aftermath of the Gulf War, when Iraq's undeclared and surprisingly advanced nuclear weapons research and development activities were discovered by UN inspectors. Ironically, a little more than two months before the war, Iraq had been found by the IAEA to be in compliance with its full-scope safeguards agreement.[28]

Gradually, the picture of Iraq's nuclear program became clear, but only after the UN Security Council authorized a special commission to investigate the program.[29] In retrospect, it is apparent that Iraq bypassed not only the IAEA but also the export control regulations of advanced nuclear suppliers in Asia, Europe, and North America. Iraq also took advantage of Western animosity toward the fundamentalist Islamic regime in Iran when dual-use items were exported to Baghdad without question.[30] It should be noted, however, that getting to the bottom of Iraq's clandestine nuclear efforts would have never been possible by routine IAEA inspections alone. The existence of the UN Special Commission on Iraq (UNSCOM) was due to the unique cooperation of all declared nuclear states investigating the activities of an aggressive state defeated in war.

If the Iraqi discovery was not enough to illustrate the limitations of the IAEA, in February 1993 the IAEA announced that it could not confirm North Korea's initial declaration of its plutonium inventory. To clarify the issue, the agency requested a special inspection of two undeclared nuclear sites. In the months that followed, underscoring the voluntary aspects required of states in order for the IAEA to carry out its responsibilities, North Korea not only refused to allow the special inspections but also threatened to withdraw from the NPT entirely.[31]

The special inspection provision was one of the measures approved by the IAEA board of governors to improve the agency's ability to detect clandestine weapon activities.[32] Since the discoveries in Iraq, the IAEA has taken a number of steps to increase the potential effectiveness of safeguards: making special inspections of undeclared sites, intelligence sharing (for the purposes of detecting undeclared sites), early reporting of design information on new facilities or modifications of existing facilities, and voluntary reporting of export and import of designated nuclear material.[33]

The improvements in the IAEA implementation of safeguards were greatly needed and could enrich the agency's contribution to nonproliferation. However, the cases of both Iraq and North Korea illustrate how the IAEA is constrained, like all other international organizations, by its reliance on the cooperation of states with the agency. Most of the improvements noted here rely even more heavily on this tenuous and unpredictable factor.

Even before the problems in Iraq and North Korea, states sought approaches outside of the NPT to curb the spread of nuclear weapons.

Nonproliferation Efforts Outside the NPT:
Nuclear-Weapon-Free Zones

Despite its imperfections, the NPT is the most widely supported multilateral arms control treaty. Still, there are a number of important states that continue to refuse to sign, including Brazil, Cuba, India, Israel, and Pakistan. Several of these remaining holdouts, however, are currently party to regional nuclear-weapon-free zone (NWFZ) agreements that exist alongside the regime or are contemplating the negotiation of an NWFZ for their specific geographic region.

In general, an NWFZ creates an international legal prohibition against any nuclear weapons within a defined geographic region. This includes prohibiting the deployment of weapons belonging to declared nuclear states. Such agreements are complex because not only do they require all states within the geographic region to agree to participate, but they also require the cooperation of all nuclear weapon states. The advantage of regional agreements and the contribution they make to international nonproliferation efforts is that they can address the specific regional security concerns of states that do not have confidence in the NPT or the IAEA. Frequently, the verification provisions of regional NWFZs are more intrusive than IAEA full-scope safeguards, and they can be carried out by the members of the NWFZ personally. These aspects provide greater confidence that the agreement is being adhered to, thereby increasing trust among members of the NWFZ and helping to eliminate the overall incentives for acquiring nuclear weapons.

There are at least eight NWFZs in some stage of negotiation. The Latin American nuclear-weapon-free zone, governed by the Treaty of Tlatelolco, was created in 1967 after the Soviet Union attempted to deploy missiles in Cuba in the early 1960s. By the end of 1994, all states within this region, except Cuba, had ratified the treaty, although Havana had indicated its willingness to join.[34] The treaty will not go into force until all states in the region have ratified it. Argentina and Brazil, the states with the most advanced nuclear programs, only completed ratification in 1994, after agreement was reached on an additional inspection mechanism formally called the Argentine-Brazilian Agency of Accounting and Control of Nuclear Materials (ABAAC).[35] Confidence in the peaceful intentions of each other's nuclear programs led Argentina to sign the NPT in February 1995, although Brazil's accession remains unlikely in the near future. Still, the regional arrangements have made nuclear proliferation far less likely than before. (See Appendix 3 for Treaty of Tlatelolco details and Chapter 14 for more on Latin America.)

The South Pacific Nuclear-Free Zone (SPNFZ), governed by the Treaty of Rarotonga, was created in 1986 to end French nuclear testing in the Pacific Ocean region. None of the countries in the zone is thought to be developing nuclear weapons, and all have signed the NPT. France, however, has refused to sign the agreement and in June 1995 announced that it would conduct eight more tests before signing a comprehensive test ban treaty.[36]

In addition to these, three other agreements demarcate geographic areas where nuclear weapons have been prohibited: the Antarctic Treaty of 1961, the Outer Space Treaty of 1967, and the Seabed Arms Control Treaty of 1972.

Since the end of the Cold War, efforts to create NWFZs in Africa, the Middle East, Southeast Asia, and South Asia have had varied success. An African NWFZ received a tremendous boost when South Africa, believed to be an undeclared nuclear weapon state during the 1980s, announced in 1993 that it had dismantled all six nuclear weapons it had produced and then formally acceded to the NPT.[37] This was the first case of a nuclear weapon state voluntarily giving up its nuclear capability. South Africa gave its support to creating an African NWFZ and in bringing civil nuclear energy programs to the African region.[38]

Some progress on establishing an NWFZ in the Middle East has also been made since the end of the Cold War. In January 1994, the UN General Assembly adopted a resolution urging states in the region to take the steps required to implement an NWFZ. Israel is reluctant to participate in an NWFZ unless Arab states renounce war as a means of settling the Arab-Israeli conflict and unless a full peace settlement is negotiated. Continued progress on Israeli-Palestinian relations is a key component to any potential peace settlement. In February 1995, Egypt threatened to not support the indefinite extension of the NPT at the 1995 Extension Conference unless Israel agreed to become a party to the treaty. Israel stated clearly that it would not even contemplate signing the NPT until Iran, Iraq, and Libya no longer posed a threat to Israel's existence.[39] In an effort to defuse the issue, Israel proposed that two years after comprehensive peace is reached in the Middle East it would agree to a weapons-of-mass-destruction-free zone (WMDFZ) and sign the NPT.

Southeast Asian nations were also negotiating the final details of a draft NWFZ treaty in 1995.

Since 1991, India and Pakistan have participated in informal discussions to create a nuclear safe zone (NSZ) in South Asia. An NSZ would aim to create a stable deterrent relationship between the two countries while acknowledging that both countries have a nuclear weapon capability. An NSZ agreement is not the ideal nonproliferation agreement because it creates a category of nuclear weapon states outside the disarmament obligations of Article VI of the NPT. However, such an agreement could contribute to the negotiation of additional bilateral agreements (such as an agreement not to use nuclear weapons first) and other agreements that would enhance regional stability and prevent an open-ended nuclear arms race. In time, perhaps both states can be persuaded to develop their own nuclear disarmament goals.

When the membership of the NPT is added to states participating in an NWFZ or considering joining an NWFZ, no nation is left untouched by nonproliferation efforts. This is significant especially for the negotiation of a new nonproliferation bargain, sought in particular by nonnuclear weapon states at the 1995 NPT review conference.

The Search for a New Bargain: Can We Do Better?

If there is so much criticism of the NPT and other international efforts to curb the spread of nuclear weapons, how is it that there are still so few nuclear weapon states compared with President Kennedy's prediction made in 1963? At the beginning of 1995, a worst-case estimate noted that there were five declared nuclear states (Great Britain, China, France, Russia, and the United States), three undeclared nuclear states (Israel, India, and Pakistan), and three states thought to be developing or considering developing nuclear weapons (Iran, North Korea, and Libya) (see Map 9.1). If all states were to declare themselves nuclear weapon states, there would be a total of 11 nuclear weapon states—far fewer than President Kennedy's prediction.[40]

Some positive nonproliferation developments have recently occurred. These include South Africa's renunciation of its nuclear weapons program; intrusive, on-site inspections in Iraq that would not have been possible without joint superpower cooperation; France and China acceding to the NPT, along with Ukraine, Kazakhstan, Belarus, Estonia, Latvia, and 20 other states, all in a period of three years, constituting the busiest accession period since the NPT came into force in 1970.

Perhaps the remaining challenges facing the regime are the most difficult to resolve. Some have characterized the proliferation problem since the end of the Cold War as more dangerous than before. They point out that nuclear materials and know-how are even more prevalent since the dissolution of the Soviet Union in 1991, especially because of the limited ability of the newly independent states of that region to prevent the transfer of nuclear materials, scientists, and technology to nonnuclear states. The availability of nuclear materials and expertise means that the time it takes to develop an indigenous nuclear weapons capability may be much shorter than before—making the IAEA's job of detection even more difficult.[41]

The limitations of the IAEA and its dependence on voluntary openness underscore that the existing regime, even if it is able to raise the economic and political costs of proliferation, cannot prevent a state determined to develop or acquire nuclear weapons from succeeding. For states outside the regime—like India, Israel, Pakistan, and Cuba—the nonproliferation tools available are even more limited. Some argue that nonproliferation efforts have reached their limit and that proliferation is inevitable. Prudence should replace idealism. Consistent with this belief is the counterproliferation initiative proposed by the United States to address the possibility of confronting an adversary armed with nuclear weapons or other weapons of mass destruction.

Counterproliferation

Proposed in December 1993 by the U.S. secretary of defense, the various aspects of a counterproliferation policy were still evolving in 1995. A February 1994 National Security Council memorandum detailing "agreed definitions" defined counterproliferation as

Map 9.1   Nuclear Proliferation 1995

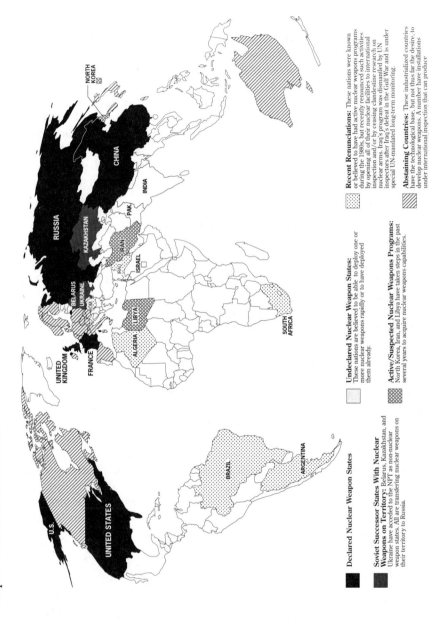

Declared Nuclear Weapon States

Soviet Successor States With Nuclear Weapons on Territory: Belarus, Kazakhstan, and Ukraine have acceded to the NPT as non-nuclear weapon states. All are transferring nuclear weapons on their territory to Russia.

Undeclared Nuclear Weapon States: These nations are believed to be able to deploy one or more nuclear weapons rapidly or to have deployed them already.

Active/Suspected Nuclear Weapons Programs: North Korea, Iran, and Libya have taken steps in the past several years to acquire nuclear weapons capabilities.

Recent Renunciations: These nations were known or believed to have had active nuclear weapons programs during the 1980s, but recently renounced such activities by opening all of their nuclear facilities to international inspection and/or by ceasing clandestine research on nuclear arms. Iraq's program was dismantled by UN inspectors after Iraq's defeat in the Gulf War and is under special UN-mandated long-term monitoring.

Abstaining Countries: These industrialized countries have the technological base, but not thus far the desire, to develop nuclear weapons. A number have installations under international inspection that can produce weapons-grade nuclear material.

Carnegie Endowment for International Peace, *Tracking Nuclear Proliferation,* 1995.

the activities of the Department of Defense across the full range of U.S. efforts to combat proliferation, including diplomacy, arms control, export controls, and intelligence collection and analysis, with particular responsibility for assuring U.S. forces and interests can be protected should they confront an adversary armed with weapons of mass destruction or missiles.[42]

In general, there are two objectives of the U.S. counterproliferation initiative. The first is to reduce the incentive to acquire weapons of mass destruction by removing any strategic advantage the weapons might have. This objective relies on the traditional methods of nonproliferation, such as diplomacy and denial, and, if that is not sufficient, considers active preemption or interdiction of proliferation activities. The second objective is to deter the use or threat of use of nuclear, chemical, and biological weapons by a country that has already proliferated. The method of deterrence has yet to be fully defined. No deterrent was immediately ruled out, although some argued that it should be limited to conventional means of deterrence. The basic approach, however, is to retaliate or threaten to retaliate, and thereby deter the use of weapons of mass destruction in the first place.[43]

During 1994 and 1995, a debate emerged between supporters of the counterproliferation initiative, which NATO appears to be embracing as well, and supporters of traditional approaches to proliferation. Critics of counterproliferation argued that although the new approach might be prudent, the net effect on proliferation might be worse than relying on the traditional approach. For example, while efforts to interdict proliferation activities might slow down states trying to acquire or develop weapons of mass destruction, it is an inherently more aggressive action than, for example, multilateral export controls and therefore more likely to encourage retaliatory action.[44] Furthermore, such action might actually encourage states to seek nuclear weapons as opposed to other weapons of mass destruction as the only way to deter counterproliferation activities—thereby having just the opposite intended effect on proliferation.

Traditional approaches to proliferation have focused on reinforcing the norm of nonuse of weapons of mass destruction in order to reduce the need to acquire them. States that have forsworn such weapons benefit each time another state voluntarily joins the regime. Counterproliferation, on the other hand, does nothing positive to encourage states that have already forsworn proliferation activities to continue to do so and potentially appears as a further example of proliferation prejudice—nuclear states using their military advantage to prevent states from acquiring that same military capability. Furthermore, states that are the targets for counterproliferation activities may be even less likely to voluntarily join the nonproliferation regime than they were before.

Though it seems prudent to have an alternative approach to nonproliferation once diplomatic efforts fail, the question remains whether the counterproliferation initiative, once implemented, would have a positive or negative effect on overall proliferation and would prevent the use of weapons of mass destruction. It was appropriate, however, that new approaches to nonproliferation were being sought prior to the 1995 Review and Extension Conference of the NPT, as it was a period for assessing the effectiveness of strategies born in the Cold War era and for planning future strategies.

The 1995 Review and Extension Conference:
Examining the Balance Sheet

The Review and Extension Conference of the Non-Proliferation Treaty, held in April and May 1995, provided an opportunity to examine the balance sheet of nuclear nonproliferation on the eve of the twenty-first century. As opposed to previous reviews where the evaluation was based on whether the obligations of the treaty were being fulfilled adequately, the 1995 review evaluated whether the treaty was contributing to nonproliferation enough to be maintained, or whether it had outlived its usefulness. Given the amount of criticism that had been levied at the discriminatory structure of the treaty as well as the negative evaluation of the fulfillment of its obligation, the actual decision of the conference to extend the NPT indefinitely and unconditionally was a surprise.

Article X.2 of the NPT required that 25 years after implementation, a majority of the parties would meet to decide whether the treaty "shall continue in force indefinitely, or shall be extended for an additional fixed period or periods." While the requirement for a review conference appeared clear, Article X.2 did not provide adequate guidance as to how different options for extension should be voted on or whether and how amendments to the treaty could be made.[45] Prior to the extension conference, it was not even clear if, should the parties refuse to vote on extension, the treaty would lapse.[46] As a result, many proposals on extension were made, each emphasizing the strengths and weaknesses of the treaty.

Extension options.   There were three principal extension options defined by the treaty. The first was to extend the treaty indefinitely and unconditionally. Just prior to the conference, this option was supported by all of the five nuclear weapon states and at least 75 other states. A simple majority of the 172 parties to the treaty at the time of the conference was required for this option to be adopted.

The second option was to extend the treaty for a single fixed period of time. There were a number of proposals in this category. Some proposals were to extend the treaty for another 25 years; others were for shorter periods. However, some believed that because Article X.2 did not provide for another extension conference the NPT would lapse at the end of the fixed period of time. Other member states disagreed, arguing that Article X.2 did not rule out another extension conference.

A third option would be to extend the treaty for additional fixed periods. This option would not differ significantly from the second option if, for example, the treaty was extended for two or three successive 10-year periods or a single 30-year period. Consistent with the ongoing criticism of the treaty, some nonnuclear states party to the treaty were reluctant to support indefinite and unconditional extension. They were dissatisfied with the progress the nuclear weapon states had made toward fulfilling their Article VI disarmament obligations. In particular, these states noted the failure to conclude Comprehensive Test Ban Treaty or a cutoff in the production of fissile material. Furthermore, even with the START Treaty in place, the United States and Russia still possessed more nuclear weapons in 1995 than they had when the NPT went into force.

As a result, one of the proposals was to tie the extension of the treaty to a specific disarmament timetable. If the nuclear weapon states did not meet those goals, then the treaty would lapse. This proposal, if adopted, would require making an amendment to the treaty—a difficult task. A proposal to extend the treaty only under the condition that it was amended would be essentially equivalent to not extending the treaty at all.

Conference outcomes.   Given the range of extension proposals and legal interpretations of the treaty on the eve of the conference, many member states and proliferation experts were skeptical of a successful outcome. For many of the states supporting indefinite extension of the treaty, a successful outcome included avoiding a divisive vote on any of the extension options. If a majority could be won on an indefinite extension—the only extension option with significant support—putting the decision to a vote would reveal any number of disgruntled states that might feel obligated to leave the regime once the vote was announced.

During the conference proceedings, three basic groups of states emerged. The first and largest group comprised states that openly declared their support for indefinite extension of the NPT. The second most numerous group included states that listed the treaty's weaknesses and called on the nuclear weapon states to meet their disarmament obligations as required by Article VI but that did not reveal publicly their preferred extension option. The third group of states, most notably Indonesia as the leader of the nonaligned NPT members, tried to rally nonnuclear states around the extension option tied to the nuclear weapon states' progress toward disarmament.

Ultimately, the gap between these three groups was bridged by a proposal calling for the strengthening of the treaty's review process and for the conference to agree on a set of principles for nuclear nonproliferation and disarmament. This proposal, together with a draft resolution sponsored by

11 Middle Eastern states that called on Israel to accede to the NPT, became the compromise put to the parties on the second-to-last day of the conference. The proposal became two documents: "Strengthening the Review Process for the Treaty" and "Principles and Objectives for Nuclear Non-Proliferation and Disarmament." Strong objection by the United States to singling out Israel as the prime target of the Middle East resolution led to the resolution being redrafted by the United States, Britain, and Russia. The new "Resolution on the Middle East" called upon all states in the region to take steps toward the goal of an "effectively verifiable Middle East zone free of weapons of mass destruction." These three documents provided a way to address the problems with the treaty and its implementation raised during the conference. Despite the treaty's well-recognized imperfections, there was simply not enough political support or wherewithal among the disgruntled members to either amend the treaty or to relegate it to the arms control dustbin.

A Canadian proposal provided the basis for adopting an extension decision without a vote. The decision simply stated "that as a majority exists among States party to the Treaty for its indefinite extension, in accordance with Article X.2, the Treaty shall continue in force indefinitely."[47] The full conference decided to not consider the only other extension proposal, which called for rolling 25-year extensions with provision for automatic extension unless a majority of NPT parties vote against it. Again, despite criticism of the treaty during the conference, no state voiced objections to prevent adoption of the indefinite extension decision.[48]

The surprise outcome of the conference has led to speculation about why all NPT members ultimately decided to support, albeit to varying degrees, the indefinite extension of the NPT. Some have suggested that many nonaligned states were more concerned about their future financial or nuclear cooperation with certain nuclear weapon states (e.g., Mexico and Egypt with the United States, or Iran with China and Russia) than with standing collectively with other states unsupportive of indefinite extension. Others have suggested that the compromise package actually addressed many of the states' concerns, in particular the enhanced review process and principles and objectives for nonproliferation and disarmament. The contribution the compromise package makes to nonproliferation will be evaluated in the emerging fifth phase of international nuclear nonproliferation efforts.

Phase V: Challenges to the Optimism

The Non-Proliferation Treaty and its members emerged from the review process having endured scathing criticism but with overwhelming support for its regime and its objectives. With only 12 states across the globe refusing to join, at one level there should be significant optimism about the future of nuclear nonproliferation. However, members still disagree about how to achieve the ultimate objectives of the regime. Many of the weaknesses of the regime remain, but a compromise on how to address them was sought instead of negotiating a new nonproliferation bargain. The challenge for the future will be in implementing the compromise well enough to not lose ground with current regime members.

The members, most important the nuclear weapon states and nuclear supplier states, emerged from the conference with a long list of tasks but with little legally binding obligation to actually implement that list. None of the three documents adopted at the conference has the legally binding character of the NPT itself. Yet they are not without influence. In particular, the "Principles and Objectives for Nuclear Non-Proliferation and Disarmament" calls for completion of a comprehensive test ban treaty (CTBT) by no later than 1996. This was perhaps the most important arms control development of the conference and set the first goal to be achieved in this emerging phase of nuclear nonproliferation. Progress toward this goal will be a constant subject of inquiry for the enhanced review process. Principal negotiating states for a CTBT may waiver in their commitment to a fully comprehensive test ban, as indicated by debate within the United States for a test ban treaty that would allow extremely low-level tests (up to one-half kiloton).[49] However, other NPT members will have opportunities in the enhanced review process to collectively insist on a complete test ban.

Similarly, the new principles and objectives prescribe that new nuclear supply arrangements "should require, as a necessary precondition, acceptance of IAEA full-scope safeguards." Hence, what the voluntary Nuclear Suppliers Group agreed to do outside the NPT became a requirement in principle for all NPT parties. If NPT members so choose, this new requirement could have an important impact on, for example, China's suspected exports of missile components to Pakistan.[50]

Finally, a long-awaited opportunity for NPT members to improve negative and positive security assurances arises in the call for "further steps," which "could take the form of an internationally legally binding instrument."[51]

The consequences of the compromise bargain not being fulfilled are difficult to evaluate from this vantage point. Nonetheless, a worst-case scenario could include NPT members (beginning with the states most affected by lack of progress on promises made at the extension conference) defecting or threatening to defect from the NPT, which could encourage additional states to do the same. Nonproliferation optimism could quickly unravel, requiring many states to adopt counterproliferation initiatives.

Ultimately, however, the progress made toward the objectives described in the preamble to the NPT and reiterated in the final document of the 1995 Review and Extension Conference will not be determined by the treaty and documents themselves but by the collective, voluntary political will of the regime members and their individual view of responsibility to the international community.

Suggested Reading

Brodie, Bernard. *Strategy in the Missile Age*. Princeton, N.J.: University Press, 1959. This book and the following one provide the classic arguments for why weapons of mass destruction fundamentally changed the nature of war and military strategy and triggered the need for nonproliferation efforts. The edited volume addresses the implications of nuclear weapons on international politics, in particular U.S.-Soviet relations, and the need for international controls on nuclear weapons. Brodie's volume develops new military strategies employing nuclear weapons. Even though both volumes focus on the U.S. experience, they are essential to understanding the dilemma faced by all states that possess or are trying to acquire nuclear weapons capability.

————, ed. *The Absolute Weapon: Atomic Power and World Order*. New York: Harcourt, Brace and Company, 1946.

Chellany, Brahma. *Nuclear Proliferation: The U.S.-Indian Conflict*. New Delhi: Orient Longman, 1993.

Epstein, William. *The Last Chance: Nuclear Proliferation and Arms Control*. New York: Free Press, 1976.

Foran, Virginia I., ed. *The Making of U.S. Policy: U.S. Nuclear Non-Proliferation Policy 1945–1991*. Alexandria, Va.: National Security Archives and Chadwyck-Healey, 1992.

Frankel, Benjamin, and Avner Cohen. "Opaque Nuclear Proliferation: Methodological and Policy Implications." *Journal of Strategic Studies* 13, September 1990.

Khan, Munir Ahmad. *Nuclear Energy and International Cooperation: A Third World Perception of the Erosion of Confidence*. New York: Rockefeller Foundation and Royal Institute of International Affairs, 1979. Report prepared for the International Consultative Group on Nuclear Energy. Dr. Khan, the chairman of Pakistan's Atomic Energy Commission, presents a Third World perception of nuclear power and proliferation.

Scheinman, Lawrence. *The International Atomic Energy Agency and World Nuclear Order*. Washington, D.C.: Resources for the Future, 1987. Dr. Scheinman's volume focuses on the institutional aspects of monitoring a state's compliance with the Non-Proliferation Treaty and provides a useful characterization of three phases of international nonproliferation efforts—international control, the Atoms for Peace program, and post–Atoms for Peace.

Shaker, Mohamed I. *The Nuclear Non-Proliferation Treaty: Origin and Implementation 1959–1978*, vols. 1–3. New York: Oceana Publications, 1980. These three volumes represent the only comprehensive history of international nonproliferation efforts and the background information necessary for understanding the current problems with the regime.

Spector, Leonard S., with Jacqueline R. Smith. *Nuclear Ambitions*. Boulder, Colo.: Westview Press, 1990. This book is the last of a series of extremely detailed overviews of states thought to be clandestinely developing nuclear weapons. It provides historical background and describes the original motivations for pursuing nuclear weapons, the current status of the nuclear programs, and efforts by the international nonproliferation regime to prevent the state from acquiring nuclear weapons.

Notes

1. France was also undertaking research in nuclear fission, but at that time it was mostly dedicated to developing nuclear energy. France's program ended abruptly with Hitler's invasion in 1940, and most of France's scientists fled to Canada. See Wilfred L. Kohl, *French Nuclear Diplomacy* (Princeton, N.J.: Princeton University Press, 1971), p. 16. Great Britain's ability to develop a nuclear bomb was drastically reduced by its early involvement in World War II. In 1943, however, Roosevelt and Churchill signed the Quebec Agreement, whereby the United States promised to share the results of its research conducted during the war with Great Britain. See Timothy J. Botti, *The Long Wait: The Forging of the Anglo-American Nuclear Alliance, 1945–1958* (New York: Greenwood Press, 1987), pp. 1–5.

2. Two excellent reviews of the Manhattan Project and the individuals involved in the making of the first atomic bomb are Peter Wyden, *Day One: Before and After Hiroshima* (New York: Simon & Schuster, 1984); and Richard Rhodes, *The Making of the Atomic Bomb* (New York: Simon & Schuster, 1986).

3. See *Arms Control and National Security: An Introduction* (Washington, D.C.: Arms Control Association, 1989), p. 18.

4. See *New York Times*, 16 February 1946, p. 17, as cited in Bernard Brodie, ed., *The Absolute Weapon: Atomic Power and World Order* (New York: Harcourt, Brace and Company, 1946), p. 25.

5. The McMahon Act, named for its Senate sponsor, made it nearly impossible for the United States to continue with its obligations to share atomic technology with Great Britain, as specified by the Quebec Agreement. The act was amended in 1954 to implement Eisenhower's Atoms for Peace program. See Richard G. Hewlett and Oscar E. Anderson, Jr., *A History of the United States Atomic Energy Commission: The New World, 1939–1946*, vol. 1 (University Park: Pennsylvania State University Press, 1962), p. 7.

6. The Baruch Plan is based substantially on a report prepared by Dean Acheson and David Lilienthal. See Hewlett and Anderson, *History of the United States Atomic Energy Commission*, pp. 540–549.

7. *Documents on Disarmament, 1945–1949*, vol. 1, p. 17.

8. Botti, *Long Wait*, pp. 20–22, 29.

9. See *Text of Address Delivered by the President of the United States Before the General Assembly of the United Nations, December 8, 1953*, document number 00141, in Virginia I. Foran, ed., *The Making of U.S. Policy: U.S. Nuclear Non-Proliferation Policy 1945–1991* (Alexandria, Va.: National Security Archives and Chadwyck-Healey, 1992).

10. Lawrence Scheinman, *The International Atomic Energy Agency and World Nuclear Order* (Washington, D.C.: Resources for the Future, 1987), p. 65.

11. Ibid., pp. 121–123.

12. See *Public Papers of the Presidents: Dwight D. Eisenhower, 1957* (Washington, D.C.: U.S. Government Printing Office, 1958), p. 627.

13. Avner Cohen, "Most Favored Nation," *Bulletin of the Atomic Scientists* (January/February 1995), p. 46. Regarding the French atomic test, see Kohl, *French Nuclear Diplomacy*, p. 103.

14. See chronology entry of 5 December 1961 in Foran, *Making of U.S. Policy*.

15. See *Public Papers of the Presidents of the United States: John F. Kennedy, 1963* (Washington, D.C.: Government Printing Office, 1964), p. 280.

16. For a comprehensive description and analysis of the negotiating history of the NPT, see Mohamed I. Shaker, *The Nuclear Non-Proliferation Treaty: Origin and Implementation 1959–1978*, vols. 1–3 (New York: Oceana Publications, 1980); and Glenn Seaborg with Benjamin S. Loeb, *Stemming the Tide: Arms Control in the Johnson Years* (Lexington, Mass.: Lexington Books, 1971).

17. Seaborg and Loeb, *Stemming the Tide*, pp. 287–306.

18. See *The Near-Nuclear Countries and the NPT* (Stockholm: SIPRI, 1972), pp. 19–21.

19. Ibid., p. 21.

20. Seaborg and Loeb, *Stemming the Tide*, pp. 381–382.

21. Coit D. Blacker and Gloria Duffy, eds., *International Arms Control: Issues and Agreements*, 2d ed. (Stanford, Calif.: University Press, 1984), p. 395.

22. This perspective is presented in William E. Burrows and Robert Windrem, *Critical Mass: The Dangerous Race of Superweapons in a Fragmenting World* (New York: Simon & Schuster, 1994), pp. 60–90.

23. See Seymour Hersh, *The Samson Option* (New York: Random House 1991), p. 52–58. For an alternative and more accurate historical analysis of the relationship between the United States and Israel on this issue, see Cohen, "Most Favored Nation," pp. 44–53.

24. The initial meeting of states is also referred to as the Zangger Committee for its chairman, Claude Zangger. See Appendix F: Nuclear Suppliers Organizations, in Leonard S. Spector and Jacqueline R. Smith, *Nuclear Ambitions* (Boulder, Colo.: Westview Press, 1990), p. 433.

25. For additional information about the Nuclear Suppliers Group, see Tadeusz Strulak, "The Nuclear Suppliers Group," *Nonproliferation Review* (Monterey, Calif.: Monterey Institute of International Studies, Fall 1993), pp. 2–10.

26. As cited in Scheinman, *International Atomic Energy Agency*, p. 91.

27. Scheinman, *International Atomic Energy Agency*, pp. 111–112.

28. David Albright and Mark Hibbs, "Iraq and the Bomb: Were They Even Close?" *Bulletin of the Atomic Scientists* (March 1991), p. 18.

29. Even four years later, in 1995, details of Iraq's weapons of mass destruction programs were still being discovered, or provided to the UN Special Commission by luck, as when two of Saddam Hussein's close advisers and family members defected to Jordan. R. Jeffrey Smith, "UN Says Iraqis Prepared Germ Weapons in Gulf War: Threat of U.S. Response Is Said to Have Blocked Use," *Washington Post*, 26 August 1995.

30. David Albright and Mark Hibbs, "Iraq's Shop-Till-You-Drop Nuclear Program," *Bulletin of the Atomic Scientists* (April 1992), pp. 27–37.

31. David Albright, "How Much Plutonium Does North Korea Have?" *Bulletin of the Atomic Scientists* (September/October 1994), pp. 46–53.

32. "IAEA to Implement 'Suspect Site' Inspection Powers," *Arms Control Today* (March 1992), p. 27.

33. Roland Timerbaev, "Nonproliferation Organizations and Regimes Beyond 1995," in Joseph Pilat and Robert Pendley, eds., *1995: A New Beginning for the NPT?* (New York: Plenum, 1995), pp. 4–8; and David Albright and Kevin O'Neill, "Jury-Rigged, but Working," *Bulletin of the Atomic Scientists* (January/February 1995), pp. 24–25.

34. Jason Webb, "Cuba Soon to Ratify Nuclear-Free Treaty," *Reuters* (1827), 14 December 1994.

35. For additional information regarding the Treaty of Tlatelolco, in particular the difficulty of gaining Brazil's and Argentina's adherence to the treaty, see Monica Serrano, "Brazil and Argentina," in Mitchell Reiss and Robert S. Litwak, eds., *Nuclear Proliferation After the Cold War* (Washington, D.C.: Woodrow Wilson Center Press, 1994), pp. 231–255.

36. Speech by Ambassador Gerard Errera, 708th Plenary Session of the Conference on Disarmament, 15 June 1995, translation by International Language Institute, Leed, UK.

37. Regarding the evolution of South Africa's nuclear program and what was known about it during the 1980s, see Leonard S. Spector, *Nuclear Proliferation Today* (New York: Random House, 1984), pp. 277–310.

38. See David Fischer, "South Africa," in Reiss and Litwak, *Nuclear Proliferation.*

39. Samia Nakhoul, "Egypt Playing Poker in Nuclear Row with Israel," *Reuters* (0821), 20 February 1995; Jeffrey Heller, "Israel's Peres to Visit Egypt Over Nuclear Row," *Reuters* (0809), 20 February 1995.

40. Leonard S. Spector, Mark G. McDonough, and Evan S. Medeivas, *Tracking Nuclear Proliferation: A Guide in Maps and Charts, 1995* (Washington, D.C.: Carnegie Endowment for International Peace, 1995), p. 9.

41. See *Nuclear Proliferation: Confronting the New Challenges,* Report of an Independent Task Force on Nuclear Proliferation (New York: Council on Foreign Relations, 1995).

42. Zachary S. Davis and Mitchell Reiss, *U.S. Counterproliferation Doctrine: Issues for Congress,* CRS Report for Congress, 21 September 1994, p. 8.

43. See Robert Grant, *Counterproliferation and International Security: The Report of a U.S.-French Working Group* (Arlington, Va.: U.S.-Crest, 1995); and Leonard S. Spector, "Neo-Nonproliferation," *Survival* (Spring 1995), pp. 66–85.

44. Barry R. Schneider, *Radical Responses to Radical Regimes: Evaluating Preemptive Counter-Proliferation,* National Defense University, McNair Paper 41 (Washington, D.C.: Institute for National Strategic Studies, May 1995), pp. v–vi.

45. For a legalistic interpretation of the requirement for NPT extension, see George Bunn, *Extending the Non-Proliferation Treaty: Legal Questions Faced by the Parties in 1995* (Washington, D.C.: American Society of International Law, 1994).

46. See Mitchell Reiss, "The Last Nuclear Summit," *Washington Quarterly* 17, p. 7.

47. *1995 Review and Extension Conference of the Parties to the Treaty on the Non-Proliferation of Nuclear Weapons, Final Document, Part I, Organization and Work on the Conference,* NPT/CONF.1995/32 (Part I), New York, 1995.

48. Several states did, however, note their objections afterward, with four states (Iraq, Libya, Malaysia, and Syria) stating that if there had been a vote they would have voted against indefinite extension. Many other states noted their lingering concerns about the treaty's future implementation but decided to "defer to the wishes of the majority" and not obstruct the extension decision. Conference notes by author; Lewis A. Dunn, "High Noon for the NPT," *Arms Control Today* (July/August 1995), pp. 3–9; and *1995 NPT Review and Extension Conference, Final Document.*

49. Spurgeon M. Keeny, Jr., "The CTB Under Fire," *Arms Control Today* (July/August 1995), p. 2. The Clinton administration announced in August 1995 that the United States would support a zero-yield CTBT, renouncing any intention to carry out low-level tests. See "Statement by the President: Comprehensive Test Ban Treaty" (Washington, D.C.: The White House, 11 August 1995).

50. R. Jeffrey Smith and David B. Ottaway, "Spy Photos Suggest China Missile Trade; Pressure for Sanctions Builds Over Evidence that Pakistan Has M-11s," *Washington Post*, 3 July 1995, pp. A1, A17.

51. *1995 NPT Review and Extension Conference, Final Document.*

10

Preventing the Spread of Arms: Chemical and Biological Weapons

Marie Isabelle Chevrier and Amy E. Smithson

Introduction

Marie Isabelle Chevrier

Chemical and biological weapons (CBWs), together with nuclear weapons, constitute the troika of weapons of mass destruction. One of the guiding principles of arms control, to limit the destructiveness of violent international conflicts, leads inevitably to the exploration of the means to suppress the use of CBWs as instruments of warfare. This search predates modern arms control, yet effective means to eliminate CBWs from the world arsenals are only now within the grasp of the international community.

The spectrum of CBWs ranges from the chemical weapons agents used in World War I, chlorine and mustard gas, to more modern vintage nerve agents (through toxins, which are poisons of biological origin) and bacteria, viruses, and other living biological agents.[1] The weapons become more deadly as one moves along the spectrum. Scientific advances, particularly in the area of biotechnology, have contributed new entries to the list of potential threat agents and have added impetus to arms control negotiations.

Chemical and biological weapons share certain military characteristics. Most important, they affect only living matter. While the weapons could be used to restrict access to airstrips, for example, and thus inhibit the ability to transport troops and material, they do not have the ability to destroy an opponent's other weapons. In contrast to the use of nuclear weapons, the use of CBWs would not significantly retard the retaliatory capacity of the victim nation, except insofar as it incapacitated key personnel and military forces. Second, gas masks and chemical suits that protect troops against CBWs would also prove effective against biological agents and toxins. In addition to these characteristics, which limit the military utility of CBWs, the use of the weapons also shares the contradistinction of being "condemned by the general opinion of the civilized world," as stated in the 1925 Geneva Protocol, which prohibits the use but does not restrict the possession of both types of weapons.[2]

Although these weapons share some important characteristics and are often thought of in concert, since the early 1970s quite different arms control agreements have been developed to govern them. The remainder of this chapter will thus separate the discussions of the two weapons systems. The 1972 Biological and Toxin Weapons Convention (BWC) and the 1993 Chemical Weapons Convention (CWC) differ from other agreements in that both are disarmament treaties. Each requires that parties renounce possession of the weapons and destroy any weapons in their possession. Moreover, there is an area of overlap between the treaties. While all toxins are covered under the BWC, two toxins, ricin and saxitoxin, are also controlled under the CWC (discussed later). The appearance of the two toxins in the CWC underscores the profound difference between the treaties: the CWC has extensive verification provisions, whereas the BWC does not.

The Control of Chemical Weapons

Amy E. Smithson

Breaking the Arms Control Mold

The 1993 Chemical Weapons Convention, which prohibits the development, production, stockpiling, transfer, and use of chemical weapons, breaks the familiar concept of arms control in several respects. Arms control was often a key barometer of the U.S.-Soviet relationship during the Cold War, featuring high on summit agendas but never quite achieving the breakthroughs that its proponents envisioned. Some in the national security community therefore took a less than charitable view of arms control, characterizing it as an idealistic exercise. The CWC, however, has less to do with idealism than with the rigorous business of controlling and destroying weaponry. Gone are the days of vague promises—the CWC is part of a generation of arms control treaties that are complex, technically specific, and implemented with a matrix of provisions designed to monitor and promote adherence.

The CWC was negotiated for more than two decades in the Conference on Disarmament, with 39 nations at the table and almost as many observing (see Appendix 2). Such a negotiating environment was a sharp departure from the customary superpower dominance of the arms control arena. The United States and the Soviet Union (succeeded by Russia) were integral to the treaty's negotiation, but their roles were at times eclipsed by the contributions and actions of states such as Australia, Germany, and France, among others.[3] The truly multilateral nature of the accord was reinforced when more than 155 nations signed the CWC within two years of its being opened for signature in mid-January 1993.

The CWC also departs from the formula used to achieve another key multilateral nonproliferation agreement, the 1968 nuclear Non-Proliferation Treaty (NPT), which offers assistance in the peaceful uses of the atom to states that forgo nuclear weapons programs. No such quid pro quo is involved in the CWC, which aims to establish a level playing field by requiring all signatories to destroy their chemical weapons stockpiles.[4] In contrast, the NPT has instituted a dichotomy of nuclear haves and have-nots.[5]

Another of the CWC's nontraditional dimensions is the integral involvement of industry in the treaty's negotiation and implementation. To rein in the creation of new chemical weapon stockpiles, negotiators had to find a way to impose controls in the difficult and ill-defined area of dual-use materials.[6] For example, chemicals such as thiodiglycol and phosphorus trichloride can be used to make agents or the products that sustain modern daily life—fertilizers, pharmaceuticals, textile dyes, pesticides, ceramics, and ballpoint pen ink, to name a few. Negotiators were forced to conceive of a way to monitor the use of chemicals in a widespread commercial industry. Failure to do so would leave a gaping hole in the treaty's verification protocol.

Midway through the negotiations, representatives of the chemical industry stepped in, formulating positions, providing technical expertise, volunteering facilities for trial runs of inspection procedures, and participating in ad hoc meetings with the negotiators in Geneva.[7] Their focus was on the issues of most concern to industry—namely, confidentiality and reporting and inspection requirements. The outcome of this collaborative process was a treaty that could achieve its objectives while sustaining industry support.

In other words, the CWC was designed to be a living mechanism for achieving cooperative threat reduction. As such, it is less about hopeful trust than about the verified destruction of existing stockpiles, the maintenance of defense preparedness, and monitored transparency in thousands of facilities worldwide. The effort is without parallel.

Having distinguished the CWC from other arms control agreements, subsequent discussion will be devoted to a more in-depth exploration of the treaty's verification provisions and an overview of how the CWC serves U.S. security interests. The subchapter concludes with observations about the implementation challenges that lie ahead.

The CWC's Unprecedented Verification Protocol

The CWC's verification provisions are built upon a rank ordering of chemicals that places them on three lists, or schedules, according to their toxicity and military and commercial utility. Schedule One contains 12 military agents and supertoxic chemicals with very limited commercial use.[8] Schedule Two lists 14 chemicals that have low to moderate utility in the commercial sector but are considered high risk because they can be used as chemical weapons or precursors to the production of chemical agents. Commercial industry uses large quantities of Schedule Three's 17 chemicals, which have also served as chemical weapons or precursors. A fourth, more generic, category captures "other chemical production facilities," notably those that use discrete organic chemicals containing phosphorous, sulfur, or fluorine, which are the building blocks of all chemical agents. The existence of this final category acknowledges that with the appropriate modifications, chemical agents can be manufactured at virtually any commercial facility.[9] The treaty sets mandatory reporting thresholds for the production, processing, consumption, acquisition, import, and export of scheduled chemicals.[10]

With the exception of the monitored use of small amounts of Schedule One chemicals for permitted research, medical, pharmaceutical, and protective purposes, Schedule One chemicals—the weapons—are to be destroyed within 10 years after entry into force.[11] Use of Schedule Two, Three, and other chemicals will continue within the commercial sector and will be subject to routine inspections, conducted on short notice. The number of routine inspections conducted annually worldwide and within each state will depend on the number of governmental and commercial facilities declared. Routine inspections will initially center on chemical weapon storage and production facilities, but as disarmament progresses the emphasis will gradually shift toward industrial sites.

Routine inspections will confirm the consistency of facility operations with the inspected site's data declarations, the absence of Schedule One chemicals, and the nondiversion of scheduled chemicals for prohibited, military purposes. Ostensibly, all areas of a facility are open to the inspection team, but in practice inspections will focus on the areas of a facility where declared activities occur. A standard inspection will include interviewing personnel at the facility, reviewing documentation, photographing items of interest or concern, and sampling from reactor vessels, effluent streams, or bulk storage tanks. A gas chromatograph–mass spectrometer and other analytical equipment will enable on-site sample analysis, but samples can be sealed, tagged, and transferred to approved laboratories if additional analysis is required.

Although data declarations and routine inspections are important, the linchpin of the verification regime is undoubtedly challenge inspections. Any treaty party that suspects another state party of violating the CWC can request a challenge inspection of the suspect site.[12] All treaty parties undertake the explicit obligation to accept challenge inspections. Given no less than 12 hours' notice before an inspection team arrives, the challenged state must transport the inspectors to the perimeter of the suspect site within 36 hours of their arrival, allowing access inside the perimeter within 108 hours after the team's arrival in country.

Challenge inspections will be guided by a concept known as managed access, which, in principle, allows inspectors enough access to determine whether the site is involved in prohibited activity while also permitting the inspected facility to protect sensitive information that is unrelated to the CWC. The extent of access and the exact nature of inspection activities are subject to negotiation. To safeguard sensitive information, host officials can log off computers, shroud items, limit the number of inspectors entering an area, and restrict the screening of samples to the presence or absence of Schedule One, Two, or Three chemicals and their degradation products. In particularly sensitive situations, access can be limited to a percentage of buildings and random areas within those buildings. When compiling their report, inspectors will take into account the caliber of the cooperation encountered during the inspection.

Despite such extensive provisions, challenge inspections are not a guarantee that all troubling situations will be quickly resolved. Inspectors may emerge from an inspection with the smoking gun of proof, but, far more often, uncertainties will remain after challenge and routine inspections.

Whether appropriate action is taken in these instances will depend on the resolve of the international community, which in turn often relies on U.S. political leadership. If the country in question does not rectify its behavior, there is no substitute for international will to take punitive action. Even though definitive evidence of noncompliance may be lacking, what the inspectors do or do not uncover will surely tell the international community more than it previously knew, enabling the appropriate adjustment of export control policies and, possibly, other sanctions.

The CWC and U.S. National Security Interests

Thorough implementation of the CWC is in U.S. security interests for some relatively straightforward reasons. For instance, the United States has decided unilaterally to destroy its aging, deteriorating chemical weapons stockpile, regardless of any treaty commitment to do so.[13] Therefore, it is in the U.S. interest to see that other states also eliminate their arsenals and to prevent the further proliferation of these weapons. The treaty is the lever that will compel and police international chemical weapons disarmament.[14] Approximately three-quarters of the nations believed to possess chemical weapons or harbor the capability to manufacture them have signed the

CWC.[15] Nations with rogue leaderships like Libya, Iraq, Syria, and North Korea, which rarely participate in any international endeavors, regardless of merit, are also holdouts in this instance.

A long time may pass before some states come into the fold. Some states may never do so. Although the CWC will not enjoy universal adherence at the outset, it will nonetheless institute a framework of laws and verification provisions that will be the foundation of an international behavioral norm against chemical weapons. Without the CWC, states can continue to develop and stockpile chemical weapons with impunity because there will be no law against such activities. Universal adherence is the ultimate objective, not an immediate requirement. Lack of universal adherence does not lessen the value of this treaty to U.S. security interests. Implementation of the CWC will undoubtedly reduce the number of chemical weapons worldwide and, thereby, the threat that such weapons pose to U.S. national security.

Critics argue, however, that until universal adherence to the CWC is obtained, the United States must retain chemical weapons to deter their use.[16] Chairman of the Joint Chiefs Gen. John M. Shalikashvili authoritatively refuted this assertion in Senate testimony. Shalikashvili stated that the U.S. response to any future threat or use of chemical weapons "will be predicated upon both a robust chemical weapons defense capability, and the ability to rapidly bring to bear superior and overwhelming military force in retaliation." He referred also to the deterrent effect of former secretary of defense Richard Cheney's announcement that the U.S. response to Iraqi use of chemical weapons during the Gulf War would be "absolutely overwhelming" and "devastating."[17] This new policy, revised from a retaliation-in-kind posture, also reflects the general consensus that chemical weapons are not militarily effective against well-trained and -equipped soldiers and that their use against unprotected civilians is abhorrent.

To encourage the most widespread adherence possible, the CWC contains automatic penalties for states that do not join. Holdouts will lose access to commercial trade in scheduled chemicals if they have not joined within three years of the CWC's entry into force. In addition to economic penalties, states that refuse to adhere to the CWC will find themselves increasingly isolated from the global community.

Outside of the CWC's auspices, a controversial international export cooperative known as the Australia Group will continue to function, despite the opposition of developing countries, which view the Australia Group as discriminatory. This ad hoc coalition was created in 1985 to curb the flow of dual-use chemicals fueling the use of chemical weapons during the Iran-Iraq War. The more than 25 members of the Australia Group voluntarily harmonize their export controls for over 50 dual-use chemicals, evaluating applications for such exports on a case-by-case basis. The Australia Group was intended to be a supplement to, not a substitute for, the CWC.

Another key issue influencing assessments of whether the CWC is in U.S. interests is the verifiability of the agreement. The most immediate temptation is to appraise the CWC's verification provisions by the standards commonly used with nuclear and conventional treaties, where missiles, tanks, and aircraft are the items being monitored. Use of such standards as the yardsticks to measure the CWC verification provisions is erroneous because the status of dual-use chemicals is extremely difficult to track with national technical means of verification. For this very reason, CIA director James Woolsey noted that the intelligence community's ability to assess the chemical weapons threat will benefit from the information made available by the CWC's reporting and inspection requirements. However, he testified that the U.S. intelligence community "cannot state that [it has] high confidence in [its] ability to detect noncompliance, especially on a small scale."[18]

On-site inspections are essential to achieving any amount of confidence in the verifiability of dual-use chemical activities. The CWC's unprecedented challenge inspections will heighten confidence in the ability to detect and deter violations, but Woolsey's statement acknowledges that small-scale cheating will be difficult to catch. Most experts agree, however, that small-scale cheating will not necessarily constitute a militarily significant threat to U.S. forces.[19] Thus, the proper context for this less than perfect state of affairs is in understanding that without the CWC, the United States would be less informed about chemical weapons proliferation and less able to confirm suspicions of cheating. Furthermore, U.S. military forces and citizens would be threatened by all the chemical weapons that the CWC would otherwise eliminate.

The largest chemical weapons stockpile by far is that which Russia inherited from the Soviet Union. Russia signed the CWC and other bilateral agreements with the United States (see Appendix 3) but has had difficulty getting a program under way to destroy its 40,000-metric-ton arsenal.[20] Economic and political upheaval, as well as public distrust of the Russian government's ability to destroy the weapons safely, have contributed to Russia's inability to mount a destruction program. In addition, officials formerly associated with the Soviet chemical weapons program have alleged that a new generation of nerve agent has been developed, produced, and tested.[21]

Given these circumstances, some have argued for a reversion to Cold War behavior—to stonewall the CWC until the Russians fully divulge the status of their chemical weapons programs. Such a strategy, however, will do little, if anything, to assuage U.S. concerns about the situation in Russia. The best way to ascertain the nature of Russia's chemical weapons activities—real, alleged, or imagined—is through the inspection procedures afforded by the CWC, which would also prod the Russians toward a more purposeful destruction program. Just as it is in the U.S. interest to help Russia dismantle its nuclear arsenal, it would behoove the United States and other Western countries to assist Russia's chemical weapons destruction program. Were some of Russia's chemical weapons to fall into the hands of proliferators or terrorists, they could also be used against U.S. soldiers or civilians.[22]

Conclusion

Getting the CWC successfully off the ground will, in and of itself, be a monumental task. First, 65 signatories must ratify the accord. Ratifications have accumulated slowly as states have grappled with the necessary steps. For example, signatories must draft and pass complex implementing legislation.[23] Governments must also establish a national authority to collect data and function as the principal liaison with the new international monitoring agency in The Hague.

Meanwhile, a transitional decisionmaking body composed of all signatories, the Preparatory Commission (PrepCom), was charged with translating the treaty from a legal text to more detailed operational procedures. PrepCom responsibilities included elaborating inspection procedures, selecting and purchasing inspection equipment, and overseeing the formation of a monitoring agency of 450 people, the heart of which is a corps of trained and equipped inspectors.

Most PrepCom participants shared the understanding that their work must facilitate this new agency's ability to fulfill its unique and difficult objectives. However, as with any international undertaking, PrepCom participants that were dissatisfied with the outcome of the treaty negotiations viewed the PrepCom as an opportunity to reshape the CWC's operational procedures in a manner more to their liking. Depending on one's perspective, these efforts were either simple, minor adjustments or a threat to the integrity of the treaty's verification protocol. The extent to which the PrepCom process compromised the inspectorate's verification authority and capabilities may not be truly understood until inspections begin.

No matter what the outcome of the PrepCom process or, for that matter, the date of the treaty's entry into force, the implementation of the CWC will be a pathbreaking exercise featuring on-site inspections in nations that have never hosted such activities. In short, the CWC will transform most states from arms control spectators to arms control participants. No longer will full-fledged implementation of arms control occur only on a superpower or an East-West axis. The involvement of the industrial sector adds another dimension that will no doubt make this treaty's implementation a phenomenon to be watched closely for lessons that may be applicable to other security problems involving dual-use technologies. For instance, the CWC's verification provisions have already been touted as the prototype for overhauling the 1972 Biological and Toxin Weapons Convention, which lacks a verification protocol.

With sufficient national and international political will, the CWC can become the model for cooperative threat reduction in the twenty-first century. To the extent that this essential element is missing, however, the CWC will fall short of achieving its promise as a mechanism for enhancing security through disarmament and for curbing the proliferation of chemical weapons. U.S. leadership will be crucial for ensuring that this treaty lives up to its potential, but the treaty's ultimate success or failure will rest with the international community. Chemical weapons are a global problem, the solution to which lies with concerted global action.

The Control of Biological Weapons

Marie Isabelle Chevrier

Biological Weapons

War and disease have walked hand in hand throughout human history—more people have died of illness during war than from the force of arms.[24] This has occurred even in the general absence of the deliberate spread of disease. Biological weapons are strategic weapons; only nuclear weapons rival them in their ability to inflict large numbers of casualties. Despite their strategic potential, however, biological weapons have never been used in modern warfare.[25] If their use is so rare, why should we be concerned about their international control? The answer lies in their destructive potential, their relative ease of acquisition, persistent allegations of their use, and recent reports of their proliferation.

Biological weapons are living organisms, most commonly self-replicating microorganisms such as bacteria and viruses, deliberately disseminated to cause death or disease in humans, animals, or plants. Toxins are either substances produced by living organisms or synthetically produced analogues of naturally occurring substances that cause death or incapacitation at some dosage level primarily in humans. When biological agents or toxins are equipped with the means to be deliberately disseminated, they become biological or toxin weapons.[26] They could cause extensive casualties if employed deliberately. Using only one biological agent, the bacteria that causes anthrax, as an example, the World Health Organization estimated that an attack on a city by even a single bomber disseminating 50 kilograms of the dried agent in a suitable aerosol form would affect an area far in excess of 20 square kilometers with tens to hundreds of thousands of deaths.[27] In addition to causing primary casualties, the spores of the bacteria that cause anthrax are very hardy and could survive for decades, possibly making the area hazardous for years.[28]

The incentives to acquire biological weapons are well known. It is widely perceived that such weapons constitute a highly lethal, technologically simple, inexpensive, and difficult-to-detect weapon system. The strength of the incentives depends on the unique characteristics of the biological weapons and their attractiveness relative to other weapons systems. Yet each incentive is tempered by a caveat so as not to exaggerate the attraction of these weapons. Although a small quantity of biological weapons, evenly dispersed, could cover a larger geographic area than could chemical weapons, the ability to evenly disperse biological weapons and maintain their potency remains technically problematic. The perception that a country could maintain the clandestine nature of a biological weapons program with relative ease may understate the effort needed to hide such a program. Despite the difficulty of designing a system to detect biological weapons, the U.S. government has uncovered the existence of biological weapons programs in several countries, presumably through intelligence and national technical means. Moreover, relative simplicity and cost does not mean that a fully weaponized system would not tax the resources of many countries, leaving less for other, perhaps more reliable, weapons.

Biological weapons also have a long list of well-recognized drawbacks. Indeed, if they did not, the current list of possible proliferators would be much longer. Several characteristics of such weapons hamper their military utility.[29] First, unlike nuclear and other explosive weapons, biological weapons would not destroy any retaliatory capability of the target nation. Second, victims exposed to biological weapons will suffer effects only after a delay, limiting their use to situations where delayed action would be immaterial or an advantage. Third, biological weapons are subject to a greater level of uncertainty than other weapons of mass destruction—caused by meteorological conditions, the difficulty of predicting human reactions to many biological weapons agents without antipersonnel experiments, and ignorance of a target's level of protection. Finally, there are potential drawbacks to the user, including persistence of some biological agents in the environment and possible infection of the user's troops, population, livestock, and crops.

U.S. Biological Weapons Policy

Throughout and immediately following World War II, U.S. policy mirrored the 1925 Geneva Protocol prohibiting the use of biological weapons even though the United States had not yet ratified it. It consisted of a no first use commitment, coupled with a retaliatory policy if foes used biological weapons against the United States or its allies.[30] By 1956, however, the United States had abandoned its no first use commitment. Based on the perceived threat that the Soviet Union would use biological weapons in any future wars, the United States prepared to initiate the offensive use of such weapons.[31]

The United States conducted research and development on biological weapons agents and munitions during World War II and began construction of a large-scale production plant for such agents and munitions. Throughout the 1950s and 1960s the United States maintained a vigorous biological warfare program that produced biological weapons agents and munitions and conducted numerous tests to determine U.S. vulnerability to a biological attack.[32] Although cloaked in heavy secrecy at the time, the experiments drew heavy criticism when the populace became aware of their existence. Biological weapons agents and toxins could be disseminated or delivered to their targets using any of several types of munitions, including missiles, cluster bombs, spray tanks mounted on aircraft, and bomblet dispensers.[33] The United States also had plans for the employment of these biological munitions in both strategic and tactical operations.[34] In 1969, following an extensive policy review, Pres. Richard Nixon unilaterally renounced U.S. possession of biological weapons, and all U.S. stocks of the weapons were subsequently destroyed.

The Biological Weapons Arms Control Regime

Prior to the advent of modern science, biological, chemical, and toxin weapons were not distinguished from one another and were lumped together under the category of poisons and banned in warfare.[35] Modern international agreements that govern biological weapons are the Geneva Protocol of 1925, which prohibits the use of such weapons,[36] and the Biological and Toxin Weapons Convention (BWC) of 1972 (see Appendix 2). Parties to the BWC pledge "never in any circumstances to develop, produce, stockpile or otherwise acquire or retain" biological or toxin weapons and the means to deliver them.[37] Until the Chemical Weapons Convention enters into force, the BWC stands as the only international treaty that outlaws the possession of an entire class of weapons. The theory behind the BWC is to deprive states of the means to use biological weapons. The regime presumes "to exclude completely the possibility of bacteriological (biological) agents and toxins being used as weapons."[38]

The negotiation of the BWC came rapidly on the heels of President Nixon's announcement that the United States would unilaterally renounce the possession of biological weapons.[39] His announcement was remarkable in several respects. Through it the United States, without a quid pro quo from any other country, renounced the use and relinquished the possession of biological weapons, presumably for all time. The United States said, in effect, that it did not want biological weapons even if other countries had them.[40] Thomas Schelling describes such a policy as a dominant negative preference—"not having the weapon is preferred *irrespective* of whether the other side has it" (emphasis in the original).[41] This preference can describe "an infinity of ridiculous weapons that nobody is interested in having even if the other side is foolish enough to procure them."[42] The most plausible explanation for Nixon's initiative is that he concluded that the United States was better off without biological weapons than with them. As long as the United States chose to possess such weapons, it conferred a legitimacy on the possession of the weapons. A U.S. biological weapons stockpile would have contributed to the perception that the possession of such weapons was desirable, which in turn might lead to the long-term proliferation of those weapons.[43] Only by renouncing the possession of the weapons could the United States hope to convince the world that the weapons were a military albatross.[44]

Compliance and Verification

The BWC describes two methods to resolve compliance problems—an informal cooperation and consultation process among states and a formal complaint procedure in the UN Security Council. There has long been dissatisfaction with these provisions. The convention's negotiators concluded that verification, as we understand it for other arms control agreements, was not possible—at least at that time.[45] France was unwilling to sign the BWC initially because it does not include any satisfactory provision for international control.[46] Other countries in the West, weighing the benefits of an international ban on biological weapons against the likelihood that a country would violate the convention and the military advantage, if any, that they would gain by doing so, chose to accept the limitations of these articles.[47] Other countries were not so sanguine that verification of the BWC was an all-or-nothing proposition. Sweden and other countries made efforts to include verification provisions during the treaty negotiations and at subsequent review conferences.

In the United States, Dr. Fred Iklé, then director of the Arms Control and Disarmament Agency, acknowledged the difficulty of verifying compliance with the BWC during ratification hearings, yet he justified the treaty as being in the U.S. interest on three grounds: the treaty would inhibit proliferation, military utility of the weapons was dubious, and such weapons were morally repugnant.[48] Despite verification problems, Dr. Iklé knew of no objections or opposition to ratification of the BWC in any branch of government.[49]

Allegations of Violations

At the first review conference of the BWC in 1980, the United States first raised allegations of a Soviet violation of the treaty with regard to the 1979 outbreak of anthrax in the Soviet city of Sverdlovsk (now Ekaterinburg, Russia). The United States claimed that the cause of the outbreak was an explosion in a biological weapons production plant and accused the Soviet Union of violating the BWC. The Soviets denied the accusations of wrongdoing; they acknowledged the existence of the epidemic but blamed it on the ingestion of tainted meat. Following years of controversy, Russia's president Boris Yeltsin admitted that the Soviet Union maintained a biological weapons program in violation of the BWC and that Russia had continued the program.[50] This is the only instance of any country admitting a violation of the BWC. Scientists once critical of U.S. evidence have recently concluded that the anthrax outbreak was caused by the release of anthrax from a military facility.[51] In the early 1980s, the United States again accused the Soviet Union of violating the BWC by providing toxin weapons to the Vietnamese for use in Southeast Asia. The so-called Yellow Rain controversy has never been officially resolved. The United States has never retracted its allegations, despite heavy criticism.[52]

The Review Conferences of the BWC

The issue of verification of the BWC has been raised at each of the periodic conferences to review the performance of the treaty. At the second review conference, held in 1986, parties to the treaty agreed to confidence-building measures consisting of a comprehensive exchange of information on biological research, facilities, and outbreaks of diseases. Delegates to the third review conference, in 1991, expanded the measures and established an ad hoc group of government experts to identify and examine potential verification measures from a scientific and technical standpoint. The group, known as VEREX,[53] concluded that some of the measures, especially used in combination, would make the treaty a more effective instrument.[54] Following the submission of the VEREX report, a special conference of the BWC in 1994 considered its findings and established a new ad hoc group to draft and recommend a proposal for a legally binding instrument to strengthen the effectiveness of the BWC, especially concerning the issues of compliance and verification.

Contentious Issues, Supporters, and Detractors

Many issues regarding verification, including whether the very word *verification* should or can be applied to the BWC, continue to divide countries that are parties to the treaty. Discussions of verification are similar to those in other arms control contexts; yet important differences exist. Biological weapons can be developed in much smaller facilities than other weapons of mass destruction. Moreover, facilities capable of developing such weapons would ordinarily house legitimate public health or pharmaceutical activities. Long-standing U.S. policy is that the BWC is not verifiable as it understands that concept for other arms control agreements, and no verification regime can be devised to make it so. For this reason, the United States is opposed to using the word *verification* in the biological weapons context. The United States stands virtually alone on this issue. Several factors influence other countries' positions on verification. First, the VEREX process determined that measures could be used to strengthen the treaty. Second, advances in biotechnology have made it possible to identify biological agents and toxins on-site. Finally, several countries have participated in trial inspections and have been favorably impressed with the ability of inspectors to gather and evaluate information gleaned in inspections.

Regime Intrusiveness and the Protection of Sensitive Information

Parties to arms control treaties recognize inherent trade-offs among the goals of any compliance regime. All parties would like a regime that is able to distinguish between permitted and prohibited activities with a minimum of intrusiveness. Unfortunately, any regime that makes the distinction with reliability is likely to be intrusive. Parties with a large and sophisticated defense establishment worry about the loss of national security information. Parties with a growing biotechnology industry worry about the loss of commercial proprietary information. Negotiators struggled with similar issues in concluding the CWC. The ad hoc group must decide how to balance these competing values.

Objective Criteria for Permitted Activities and Threshold Quantities

The prohibitions in the BWC are purposefully very broad and hinge on the criterion of intent. In Article I parties agree not to possess agents or toxins that have "no justification for prophylactic, protective, or other peaceful purposes."[55] Some countries seek an official interpretation of this language. Developing objective criteria for permitted—or prohibited—activities entails the risk of limiting the treaty's purposely broad and inclusive prohibitions. Thus, perhaps unintentionally, efforts to define prohibited or permitted activities could serve to weaken the purposes of the treaty.

Establishing a threshold quantity of agents could theoretically be one objective way to distinguish between prohibited and permitted activities. A threshold quantity would be either a small quantity, the possession of which would automatically be considered as permitted by the treaty, or a larger quantity, possession of which would automatically constitute a violation of the treaty. Those who oppose threshold quantities worry that a determined country could shield a prohibited biological weapons program behind the mask of thresholds. Moreover, neither a low threshold to define permitted activities nor a high threshold to determine prohibited activities would eliminate the role of determining intent. A range of quantities consistent with both peaceful and violent purposes would constitute a gray area requiring a judgment of the intent of the possessor. Opponents of thresholds also note the ease and speed with which a large quantity of biological agent or toxin could be produced, thereby rendering a threshold quantity ineffectual.

Technical Assistance and the Activation of Article X

Article X of the BWC, which calls for parties to cooperate in the "development and application of scientific discoveries … for the prevention of disease or other peaceful purposes," has never been implemented despite proposals from developing countries to do so. The developed countries have resisted all efforts to make assistance mandatory, preferring voluntary assistance. They stress that the provision of technical assistance is not a part of verification and that discussion of ways to activate Article X diverts attention from the more important problem of verification. Brazil has argued that developing countries need technical assistance to participate effectively in a verification protocol and that implementing Article X would contribute to verification rather than diverting attention from it.[56] Some parties to the BWC are likely to remain adamant that a commitment to technical assistance by the developed countries be a prerequisite to their agreement on a legally binding protocol.

Export Controls and Article X

The Australia Group restricts trade in some equipment, pathogens, and toxins that could be instrumental in the development or production of biological weapons. These restrictions are seemingly at odds with Article X of the convention, which gives parties to the treaty "the right to participate in the fullest possible exchange of equipment materials and scientific and technological information … for peaceful purposes." Countries that are the targets of such trade restrictions want the earliest possible lifting of trade restrictions.[57] They use the "right" established in Article X to bolster their arguments. Since virtually all restricted equipment has legitimate applications in the medical field, countries that have been the objects of the controls could argue that their public health has been and will continue to be adversely affected. In contrast, members of the Australia Group are indisposed to lift restrictions until compliance has actually been demonstrated, perhaps for a considerable length of time. Countries endorsing continued export controls rely on Article III, wherein parties agree "not to transfer to any recipient whatsoever … any of the agents, toxins, weapons, equipment or means of delivery specified in Article I of the Convention" to support their case.

Agent Lists

The function of a list of biological agents and toxins and its potential role in a protocol is also controversial. One alternative is to develop a list of agents and toxins and use possession of any agent on the list as a criterion for declaring facilities that would be subject to visits or inspections under a new protocol to the treaty. A second alternative is to determine characteristics of agents and toxins (e.g., lethal dosage) and require all facilities working with agents having those characteristics to submit declarations and thus be subject to inspection. Those that favor using a comprehensive list of specific agents value the simplicity of a list of agents and toxins. A list would make reporting requirements straightforward and relatively simple to implement. Other countries are concerned with the difficulties of constructing a comprehensive list and keeping it current with developments in biology and biotechnology, opening the way for a determined country to circumvent it.

A compromise on this issue would retain specific agent and toxin characteristics as the criteria for declarations, yet the requirements would include—under each criterion—an extensive list of agents and toxins that fall under that criterion—referred to as an illustrative, rather than a comprehensive, list. The illustrative lists would facilitate the submission of declarations and would provide consistency across countries. At the same time, the characteristic criteria would make it difficult for a country to establish a clandestine biological weapons program and to hide behind the protective cover of a list in regard to its reporting obligations.[58]

On-Site Visits

Central to the ad hoc group's task will be a decision as to which on-site measures will be most useful in establishing compliance. Several complementary issues are at stake. First, when people from one country arrive at another to examine biological facilities and activities taking place therein, what do we call it? *Information visits, validation visits, routine inspections, short-notice inspections, challenge inspections, on-site inspections,* and *fact finding missions* are all candidates. At issue is more than a matter of semantics; each name has somewhat different implications for policy. To the extent that declarations establish data on facilities of concern, at least some visits/inspections will likely take place at declared facilities. Because a biological weapons program could be hidden relatively easily at an undeclared site, some type of inspection would of necessity include undeclared facilities. Similarly, any inspection of an undeclared facility would be of the short-notice variety. The international community must choose from a limited menu of visits/inspections that entail trade-offs among costs, intrusiveness, probabilities of detecting violations, and strength of deterrence.

Other concerns about on-site visits persist. First, should there be more than one type of visit? Second, what will inspectors do when they arrive? Which of the on-site measures will be available to inspectors at each type of visit? In other words, what will be the operational distinctions among different types of visits? Third, who will select facilities for inspection, and what criteria will they use? Fourth, how much will on-site visits cost, and how will those costs be distributed? Each of these issues is likely to be contentious as the details of a protocol are hammered out.

Strengthening the convention includes improving compliance with its provisions and resolving suspicions of noncompliance. Therefore, an agreement on certain principles must serve as the foundation for any protocol. One principle is the connection between on-site measures and the detection of violations. How frequent (or how great is the likelihood of a site being selected) and how intrusive do on-site measures need to be to detect violations of the treaty? Similarly, how high does the likelihood of detection need to be to deter violations? What kinds of inspections will convince those who suspect others of violating the treaty that no violations are taking place? Countries that worry most about others cheating place a high value on short-notice inspections to detect and deter violators. Those most concerned with demonstrating their own compliance prefer visits whose purpose is to validate information in declarations, whereas those most concerned with protecting confidential security and commercial proprietary information favor infrequent, nonintrusive visits. The resolution of these issues will critically influence the protocols' effectiveness.

The Biological Weapons Proliferation Problem

The proliferation of biological wapons remains a problem in spite of the BWC.[59] In February 1993, the director of the CIA and his assistant revealed the following information regarding specific countries in testimony before the U.S. Senate:

> Iraq ... has an advanced bw [biological weapons] program which has not been seriously degraded by the Gulf war or United Nations inspections following the war.... Iran ... could have operational bw now.... A bw program capability may exist in China.... Egypt has a bw program.... Taiwan ... has done work in biological warfare but does not have a weaponized program.... North Korea ... has research efforts underway in biological warfare.[60]

In addition to these six countries, the testimony disclosed that "most countries that have had an advanced chemical weapons program have also looked into a biological weapons program."[61]

The connection between chemical weapons proliferation and biological weapons proliferation is elaborated in Table 10.1, comparing states that have, probably have, and possibly have these weapons. It demonstrates that every country that the United States (or, in the case of South Korea, Russia) suspects of having some sort of biological weapons program is also suspected of having a chemical weapons program. The table reveals that with a few notable exceptions—Ethiopia, India, Myanmar (Burma), Pakistan, and Vietnam—the countries that are probable chemical weapons states also appear on at least one biological weapons list. Notably, the table also shows that only two of the 13 countries listed as possible chemical weapons states are also listed as having a biological weapons program—Cuba and South Africa.[62]

It is essential to recognize the importance of geography in this list. Six of the 11 biological weapons suspect countries are in the Middle East or North Africa: Egypt, Iran, Iraq, Israel, Libya, and Syria. With the exception of Russia—which has committed to the destruction of its biological weapons capability—all the rest are in East Asia: China, North Korea, South Korea, and Taiwan. That the present biological weapons proliferation problem is concentrated in these two areas suggests that international policy to alter incentives to acquire biological weapons must also take into account the political military situations in these two volatile areas. The extent of the problem in the Middle East suggests that any policies specific to biological weapons will be secondary to a comprehensive Middle East peace and agreements on all weapons of mass destruction in the Middle East. East Asia represents a different challenge. If the 1994 agreement between the United States and North Korea proves to be successful in eradicating North Korea's nuclear weapons capability, thereby reducing hostilities in the region, each Korea may be willing and able to demonstrate its compliance with the BWC.

In the case of biological weapons, efforts to counter proliferation can be directed to countries in three categories. One can develop policies tailored to encourage countries that are suspected of already having a biological weapons program to relinquish it. Simultaneously, policies need to be developed and implemented to prevent states from pursuing an interest in offensive biological weapons in the first place. Finally, antiproliferation policies could be directed at prohibiting countries with embryonic biological weapons programs from developing them further. Of particular concern among the set of countries in the second category are those that may be the most likely to turn to biological weapons. In the spirit of being aware of "the dog that didn't bark," policymakers may learn more about preventing biological weapons proliferation from those probable and possible chemical weapons states that have not demonstrated any discernible interest in biological weapons than from those that have. Probable chemical weapons states that are not on the biological weapons list are India, Pakistan, Ethiopia, Myanmar (Burma), and Vietnam.

Table 10.1   The Connection Between Chemical and Biological Weapons Proliferation

Chemical Weapons Program Estimate	CWC Status	Biological Weapons Program Estimate	Source of Biological Weapons Data[a]
Known			
Iraq		Has an advanced program	CIA
Former Soviet Union	Signed	Admitted	
United States	Signed	Program canceled	
Probable			
China	Signed	Probable capability	CIA/HASC
Egypt	Signed	Possible program	CIA/HASC
Ethiopia	Signed		
India	Signed		
Iran	Signed	Probable program, could be operational	CIA/HASC
Israel	Signed	Possible program	HASC
Libya		Possible program	HASC
Myanmar (Burma)	Signed		
North Korea		Probable program, research efforts under way	CIA/HASC
Pakistan	Signed		
South Korea	Signed	Signals that it is conducting research	Russia
Syria		Probable program	HASC
Taiwan		Probable program, has done research	CIA/HASC
Vietnam	Signed		
Possible			
Angola			
Argentina	Signed		
Bulgaria	Signed		
Cuba	Signed	Possible program	HASC
Czech Republic	Signed		
France	Signed		
Indonesia	Signed		
Laos	Signed		
Poland	Signed		
Romania	Signed		
Somalia			
Saudi Arabia	Signed		
Slovakia	Signed		
South Africa	Signed	Possible program	UN
Thailand	Signed		

Note: a. CIA: Senate testimony of Adm. R. James Woolsey and Mr. Gordon Oehler. See U.S. Congress, Senate, Committee on Government Affairs, "Proliferation Threats of the 1990s," Committee Report, 24 February 1993.

(*continues*)

Table 10.1   *(continued)*

HASC: U.S. House Armed Services Committee, "Countering the Chemical and Biological Weapons Threat in the Post Soviet World," Report of the Special Inquiry into the Chemical and Biological Threat, 102d Cong., 2d sess. (Washington, D.C.: U.S. Government Printing Office, 1993), p. 13.

Russia: "Russian Foreign Intelligence Service Report on the Proliferation of Weapons of Mass Destruction," summary and excerpts prepared by Committee on Governmental Affairs, U.S. Senate, 24 February 1993. Also "A New Challenge After the Cold War: The Proliferation of Weapons of Mass Destruction," report prepared by the Foreign Intelligence Service of the Russian Federation, Moscow, 1993, translated by Foreign Broadcast Information Service, February 1993.

UN: The biological weapons information on South Africa is quite dated and may no longer be accurate. It is contained in the 1984 UN General Assembly report "Military Activities and Arrangements by Colonial Powers in Territories Under Their Administration Which Might Be Impeding the Implementation of the Declaration Granting Independence to Colonial Countries and Peoples," A/AC.109/781, 31 July 1984, p. 12. Cited in W. Seth Carus, *The Poor Man's Atomic Bomb? Biological Weapons in the Middle East,* Policy Paper No. 23 (Washington, D.C.: Washington Institute for Near East Policy, 1991), p. 27.

The appearance of Vietnam and Myanmar on this list suggests the importance of ascertaining why these two states have apparently shown no interest in biological weapons while nearby Asian states have. It is also possible, that having shown an interest in chemical weapons, these states may be the ones most likely to look with interest at biological weapons in the future. Thus, determining whether these countries have deliberately rejected biological weapons, and if so, why, would be valuable. The same is true for India and Pakistan. With the exception of Cuba and possibly South Africa, none of the possible chemical weapons states are listed as possible or even doubtful biological weapons states.

Given the apparent strong, positive connection between chemical and biological weapons proliferation, how is the CWC likely to affect biological weapons proliferation? As Seth Carus suggests, "The prevention of chemical warfare programs provides an important—perhaps even essential—firebreak against biological weapons proliferation."[63] The CWC may have the desired effect of not only making the acquisition of chemical weapons less likely but also reducing the likelihood that a nation will seek a biological weapons capability.[64] Unfortunately, the possibility also exists that countries stymied in the process of acquiring chemical weapons may switch to biological weapons, which are governed by a treaty lacking the intrusive inspection regime of the CWC.

Conclusion

U.S. policy since 1969 has been that it is better off without biological weapons than with them even if other countries choose to possess such weapons. Nevertheless, U.S. security would be enhanced if other countries rejected these weapons as well. The BWC has been successful in reinforcing the international norm against the use and possession of these weapons of mass destruction, yet it has not successfully assured parties that their treaty partners are living up to their obligations. At the time the BWC negotiations were completed in 1972, an intrusive regime to confirm compliance would not have been politically possible. Achievements in other arms control arenas have demonstrated that nations are willing to endure intrusive inspections in order to achieve a higher level of security. In the next few years, nations will reveal whether they are willing to extend the concept of openness to biological facilities and activities. This test of political will is likely to determine the fate of biological weapons in the twenty-first century. Will the BWC become a quaint remnant of détente, or a solid barrier against the deliberate spread of disease?

Suggested Reading

Chemical Weapons

Burke, Gordon M., and Charles C. Floweree. *International Handbook on Chemical Weapons Proliferation.* New York: Greenwood Press, 1991. Presents a generic and a country-by-country assessment of chemical weapons proliferation, as well as a list of alternatives to control the proliferation threat.

Lundin, S. J., ed. *Verification of Dual-Use Chemicals Under the Chemical Weapons Convention: The Case of Thiodiglycol.* Oxford: Oxford University Press and the Stockholm International Peace Research Institute, 1993 and 1991.

Roberts, Brad, ed. *Chemical Disarmament and U.S. Security.* Boulder, Colo.: Westview Press and the Center for Strategic and International Studies, 1992. Gives an overview of the treaty's components and its role in enhancing U.S. and international security.

Spiers, Edward M. *Chemical Weaponry: A Continuing Challenge.* New York: St. Martin's Press, 1989. Provides a thorough history of chemical weapons, defenses, tactics, and their use.

Trapp, Ralf. *Verification Under the Chemical Weapons Convention: On-Site Inspection in Chemical Industry Facilities.* Oxford: Oxford University Press and the Stockholm Peace Research Institute, 1993 and 1991. Offers in-depth discussions of the challenges of monitoring dual-use chemicals.

U.S. Senate. 103d Cong., 1st sess., Treaty Doc. 103-21. *Message from the President of the United States Transmitting the Convention on the Prohibition of Development, Production, Stockpiling and Use of Chemical Weapons and on Their Destruction.* Washington, D.C.: 23 November 1993. Contains the U.S. government's official description of the treaty and its provisions, including background information and article-by-article analysis.

Biological Weapons

Chevrier, Marie Isabelle. "Deliberate Disease: Biological Weapons, Threats, and Policy Responses." *Environment and Planning C: Government and Policy* 11, 1993, pp. 395–417.

———. "From Verification to Strengthening Compliance: Prospects and Challenges of the Biological Weapons Convention." *Politics and the Life Sciences,* August 1995.

————. "Impediment to Proliferation: Analysing the Biological Weapons Convention." *Contemporary Security Policy,* August 1995, pp. 72–102.

Lacey, Edward J. "Tackling the Biological Weapons Threat: The Next Proliferation Challenge." *Washington Quarterly,* Autumn 1994, pp. 53–64.

Roberts, Brad, ed. *Biological Weapons: Weapons of the Future?* Significant Issues Series. Washington, D.C.: Center for Strategic and International Studies, 1993.

Rosenberg, Barbara Hatch. "North vs. South: Politics and the Biological Weapons Convention." *Politics and the Life Sciences,* February 1993.

Wright, Susan. "Prospects for Biological Disarmament in the 1990s." *Transnational Law and Contemporary Problems,* Fall 1992, pp. 453–485.

————, ed. *Preventing a Biological Arms Race.* Cambridge, Mass.: MIT Press, 1990.

Notes

1. Graham S. Pearson, "Biological Weapons: The British View," in *Biological Weapons: Weapons of the Future?* Brad Roberts, ed., *Significant Issues Series,* vol. 15, no. 1 (Washington, D.C.: Center for Strategic and International Studies, 1993), pp. 10–11.

2. Thirty-five nations reserved the right to retaliate with weapons prohibited by the protocol if another country used the weapons first. The Netherlands and the United States, however, restrict the reservation to retaliate with respect to chemical weapons only. For full texts of the reservations, see Dietrich Shindler and Jiri Toman, *The Laws of Armed Conflict,* 3d ed. (Dordrecht, Netherlands: Nijoff, 1988).

3. Australia tabled a greatly revised version of the rolling text in the spring of 1992 that became the basis for the last stage of the negotiations. Under German chairmanship, the Australian and French governments, among others, worked diligently to compel the negotiations to a close that fall.

4. India and Iran headed a group of developing countries concerned that the CWC would formalize discrimination in export control of chemicals that can be traded, but it will be monitored under the CWC. This group sought unimpeded trade, the abolition of the Australia Group, and an explicit pledge of assistance for their fledgling chemical industries, similar to the NPT's nuclear assistance programs. The CWC encourages the full and free exchange of chemicals, equipment, and scientific and technical information for nonprohibited purposes. However, such activities will not be governed or carried out by an international body, as the IAEA does with assistance in nuclear research and power. See pp. 37–39 of Trevor Findlay's *Peace Through Chemistry: The New Chemical Weapons Convention* (Canberra: Australian National University, 1993); and Hassan Mashhadi, "How the Negotiations Ended," *Chemical Weapons Convention Bulletin* (September 1992), pp. 28–30.

5. The United States, the Soviet Union, France, Britain, and China, which possessed nuclear weapons at the time the treaty was signed, kept their arsenals in exchange for pledging to refrain from assisting states attempting to proliferate nuclear weapons and to progress toward the deep reduction and complete elimination of nuclear weapons. *Arms Control and Disarmament Agreements: Texts and Histories of the Negotiations* (Washington, D.C.: U.S. Arms Control and Disarmament Agency, 1990), pp. 98–100; also see Chapter 9.

6. The term *dual-use* describes items that have peaceful and military applications. Other dual-use items include computers, nuclear fuel, some types of machine tool equipment, and electronic guidance systems.

7. Trade associations from the United States, Europe, Canada, and Japan, which have the most developed chemical industries, played the most prominent roles, but industry representatives from such countries as Brazil, Peru, Iran, and Mexico also tracked developments in Geneva closely. Industry became directly involved to see that the treaty impinged as little as possible on corporate productivity, trade, operations, innovative capability, competitiveness, and profitability. Also, the chemical industry did not want to be tarred erroneously by association with the manufacture of chemical weapons, which is normally a government activity. See Will Carpenter, "The Perspective of Western Chemical Industry," in *Chemical Weapons Convention: Shadows and Substance*, Benoit Morel and Kyle Olson, eds. (Boulder, Colo.: Westview Press, 1993), pp. 114–126.

8. Two basic types of chemical agents exist. Blister agents, such as mustard gas, attack the skin, respiratory system, and eyes, causing blistering, blindness, and death. Exposure to even minute quantities of nerve agents such as GB or VX can cause vomiting, loss of bladder control, blindness, convulsions, coma, and death.

9. Manufacture of chemical agents at a commercial facility would entail risks to the health of workers and the public, especially if the appropriate pollution abatement and safety equipment were not employed. Use of such equipment and the presence of unusual levels of security are some of the telltale signs of possible illicit chemical weapons production. See pp. 15–70 of *Technologies Underlying Weapons of Mass Destruction* (Washington, D.C.: U.S. Office of Technology Assessment, U.S. Government Printing Office, December 1993).

10. For example, production of as little as 100 grams of a Schedule One material must be reported, whereas the threshold for reporting production of Schedule Three chemicals is 30 metric tons.

11. Treaty parties are allowed to produce 1 metric ton of Schedule One chemicals annually for activities such as the development of vaccines and antidotes against chemical agents and the testing of protective equipment, like gas masks.

12. The director of the international inspectorate must initiate the challenge inspection without delay, but a 41-member international governing body will have 12 hours to review and reject the challenge inspection request by a three-quarters vote if it is deemed frivolous, abusive, or beyond the scope of the CWC.

13. Public Law 99-145, November 1985, orders the destruction of all U.S. chemical weapons using unitary agents. A 13 May 1991 statement by Pres. George Bush committed the United States unconditionally to the destruction of the entire U.S. stockpile, including those weapons utilizing binary agents. Unitary agents are toxic to humans as the weapons sit in storage, while binary agents must be mixed as the weapon is delivered to make them toxic. Under the revised policy, the United States would forswear use of chemical weapons for any reason, including retaliation against any state, upon entry into force of the CWC. The CWC stipulates that the irreversible destruction of chemical weapons take place in a manner that is safe for humans and the environment. For more, see Amy E. Smithson with the assistance of Maureen Lenihan, *The US Chemical Weapons Destruction Program: Views, Analysis, and Recommendations* (Washington, D.C.: Henry L. Stimson Center, September 1994).

14. The 1925 Geneva Protocol prohibits only the use of chemical weapons. The CWC rolls back the threat by also banning their development, production, and stockpiling.

15. See Table 10.1. While only the United States and Russia have publicly declared possession of chemical weapons, after the Gulf War, Iraq's chemical weapons were destroyed under the supervision of the UN Special Commission.

16. See the testimony of Frank Gaffney and Amoretta M. Hoeber before the Senate Foreign Relations Committee, *Hearings on the Chemical Weapons Conven-*

tion, 103d Cong., 2d sess., S. Hrg. 103-869 (Washington, D.C.: U.S. Government Printing Office, 1994), pp. 119–130. Debate on this point may continue indefinitely.

17. See the testimony of Gen. John M. Shalikashvili, Chairman of the Joint Chiefs, in Senate Armed Services Committee, *Military Implications of the Chemical Weapons Convention,* 103d Cong., 2d sess., S. Hrg. 103-835 (Washington, D.C.: U.S. Government Printing Office, 1994), pp. 37–86. Article X of the CWC specifically provides states the right to maintain chemical defenses.

18. Testimony of James Woolsey, director of Central Intelligence, before the Senate Foreign Relations Committee, *Hearings on the Chemical Weapons Convention,* p. 162.

19. Although small amounts of nerve agents can be lethal, the effectiveness of a chemical attack can be quickly degraded by weather conditions and counteracted by properly equipped troops that are trained to operate in a chemical environment. Therefore, hundreds and even thousands of tons of chemical agent may be required to mount an effective chemical attack. U.S. national technical means should be able to detect such large-scale cheating. See *Proliferation of Weapons of Mass Destruction: Assessing the Risks* (Washington, D.C.: U.S. Office of Technology Assessment, U.S. Government Printing Office, August 1993), pp. 46–62.

20. In September 1989, the United States and the Soviet Union signed a Memorandum of Understanding to initiate a series of data exchanges and trial on-site inspections. Phase I went off smoothly soon afterward, but the more elaborate Phase II activities did not proceed until 1994. In a June 1990 agreement, which has yet to enter into force, both states agreed to stop producing chemical weapons and to reduce their respective stockpiles to no more than 5,000 agent tons. The Bilateral Destruction Agreement and the CWC complement each other and can be separately ratified and implemented.

21. For an overview of the situation in Russia, see Walter L. Busbee, "Now for the Heavy Lifting: Destroying CW Stockpiles in the United States and Russia," and Amy E. Smithson, "A Commentary on the Russia Factor," in *Ratifying the Chemical Weapons Convention,* Brad Roberts, ed. (Washington, D.C.: Center for Strategic and International Studies, 1994), pp. 105–115, 101–104, respectively.

22. The United States has already offered technical and financial assistance to Russia, signing an agreement to that effect on 30 July 1992 and setting aside $55 million in funds to aid the Russian destruction program. More funds will be needed to complete the job.

23. This legislation conveys the treaty's obligations to corporations and individuals, establishes criminal and civil penalties for treaty violations (e.g., a private company's purposeful delay of an inspection or sale of prohibited chemicals to a nontreaty party), and creates the domestic framework for data declarations, inspections, and reform of export control laws, if needed.

24. William H. McNeill, *Plagues and Peoples* (New York: Doubleday, 1979).

25. Allegations have been made that one side or the other used biological weapons during the two world wars and the Korean War. The allegations of German use of biological weapons during World War I principally involve animal, not human, pathogens. Much more extensive evidence exists about the Japanese biological weapons program in China from 1939 to 1945. Japan allegedly used biological weapons in experiments employing Chinese, Russian, British, and U.S. prisoners of war and Chinese civilians as subjects, as well as against Chinese troops and the civilian population. Sporadic allegations or rumors that the United States, Britain, and the former Soviet Union have used biological weapons or toxins against smaller states highlight one of the most pernicious aspects of the problem of such weapons: their use can be

alleged with very little if any evidence, and disproving allegations is an almost impossible task. Thus an enormous amount of uncertainty surrounds nearly all of the allegations of biological weapons use.

26. United Nations, *Chemical and Bacteriological (Biological) Weapons and the Effects of Their Possible Use*, United Nations Report No. E. 69, I. 24 (New York: United Nations, 1969), pp. 5–6. The term *biological weapons* is commonly used to include both biological and toxin weapons, and I have also done so here.

27. World Health Organization, "Health Aspects of Chemical and Biological Weapons," *Report of a WHO Group of Consultants* (Geneva: World Health Organization, 1970), p. 19.

28. See W. Seth Carus, "'The Poor Man's Atomic Bomb?' Biological Weapons in the Middle East," *Policy Papers Number 23* (Washington, D.C.: Washington Institute for Near East Policy, 1991); Graham S. Pearson, "Biological Weapons: The British View," and W. Seth Carus, "The Proliferation of Biological Weapons," in *Biological Weapons: Weapons of the Future?* Brad Roberts, ed. (Washington, D.C.: Center for Strategic and International Studies, 1993), pp. 22–24; and Marie Isabelle Chevrier, "Deliberate Disease: Biological Weapons, Threats, and Policy Responses," *Environment and Planning C: Government and Policy* 11 (1993), pp. 395–417.

29. See Chevrier, "Deliberate Disease," pp. 395–417; and Kathleen C. Bailey, *Doomsday Weapons in the Hands of Many: The Arms Control Challenge of the '90's* (Urbana and Chicago: University of Illinois Press, 1991), pp. 87–88.

30. Samuel I. Rosenman, comp., *The Public Papers and Addresses of Franklin D. Roosevelt, 1943: The Tide Turns* (New York: Harper and Brothers, 1950).

31. *US Army Activity in the US Biological Warfare Programs*, vol. 1 (Washington, D.C.: U.S. Department of the Army, 24 February 1977), p. 4-2.

32. *US Army Activity in the US Biological Warfare Programs*, vols. 1 and 2 (Washington, D.C.: U.S. Department of the Army, 24 February 1977).

33. *Employment of Chemical and Biological Agents*, Army Field Manual No. 3-10; Naval Warfare Information Publication No. 36-2; Air Force Manual No. 355-4; and Marine Corps Manual No. 11-3 (Washington, D.C., 1966), p. 45.

34. Marine Corps Manual No. 11-3, p. 48.

35. John Ellis van Courtland Moon, "History of the Taboo Against the Use of Chemical and Biological Weapons," unpublished paper, 1989.

36. Thirty-five nations reserved the right to retaliate with weapons prohibited by the protocol if another country, whether it is a signatory to the protocol or not, uses the weapons first. The Netherlands and the United States, however, restrict the reservation to retaliate with respect to chemical weapons only. Both countries bind themselves not to use biological weapons under any circumstances, even if they are used against them. Any use of biological weapons by a party to the treaty, even in retaliation, would be considered a violation of the BWC.

37. *Arms Control and Disarmament Agreements: Texts and Histories of Negotiations*, Publication 105 (Washington, D.C.: U.S. Government Printing Office, 1980), p. 124.

38. Ibid.

39. In 1970, Nixon extended the renunciation to toxin weapons.

40. Among Nixon's policy options: renounce first use of biological and chemical weapons only; renounce first use and suspend the production and/or modernization of biological weapons stockpiles, yet retain possession of a quantity of biological weapons as a deterrent to the use of such weapons and as a retaliatory capacity (or even as a bargaining chip for later arms negotiations); or renounce any use of biological weapons, destroy existing stocks, and convert existing production facili-

ties to peaceful purposes. He chose the third option. It is commonly believed that one of the primary reasons the Nixon administration renounced biological weapons was their limited military utility. However, this is not a sufficient explanation for this action. If military utility was the only force driving the decision, any one of the less radical policy alternatives could have been chosen. It was unnecessary to renounce the possession of biological weapons for all time. The military utility of such weapons, after all, could change.

41. Thomas C. Schelling, *Choice and Consequence* (Cambridge, Mass.: Harvard University Press, 1984), p. 244.

42. Ibid., p. 253.

43. Elisa D. Harris, "The Biological and Toxin Weapons Convention," in *Superpower Arms Control,* Albert Carnesale and Richard N. Haass, eds. (Cambridge, Mass.: Ballinger, 1987), pp. 191–213.

44. For additional arguments, see Han Swyter, "Political Considerations and Analysis of Military Requirements for Chemical and Biological Weapons," Symposium on Chemical and Biological Warfare, *Proceedings of the National Academy of Sciences* (January 1970), p. 266.

45. The representative from Britain said in submitting a draft of a biological weapons convention, "I recognize that the greatest difficulty we have to face is that of verification. ... The principal difficulty arises from the fact that almost all the material and equipment with which we are trying to deal here have legitimate peaceful purposes; and it would be wrong to inhibit work of real value to humanity in combating disease, for example, and impracticable to inspect every laboratory in every country. We must accept, therefore, that no verification is possible in the sense of the term as we normally use it in disarmament discussions." U.S. Arms Control and Disarmament Agency, statement by the British disarmament minister (Mulley) to the Eighteen-Nation Disarmament Committee, 6 August 1968, *Documents on Disarmament 1968* (Washington, D.C.: U.S. Government Printing Office, 1968), pp. 561–562.

46. U.S. Arms Control and Disarmament Agency, statement by the French representative (Taittinger) to the First Committee of the General Assembly, 2 November 1972, *Documents on Disarmament 1972* (Washington, D.C.: U.S. Government Printing Office, 1972), p. 758.

47. Harris, "The Biological and Toxin Weapons Convention," p. 198.

48. U.S. Senate, Committee on Foreign Relations, *Prohibition of Chemical and Biological Weapons,* 93d Cong., 2d sess. (Washington, D.C.: U.S. Government Printing Office, 1974), pp. 15–16.

49. Ibid., p. 18.

50. J. Dahlburg, "Russia Admits It Violated Pact on Biological Warfare," *Los Angeles Times,* 15 September 1992, p. A1.

51. Matthew Meselson et al., "The Sverdlovsk Anthrax Outbreak of 1979," *Science,* 18 November 1994, pp. 1202–1208.

52. Julian Robinson, Jeanne Guillemin, and Matthew Meselson, "Yellow Rain in Southeast Asia: The Story Collapses," in *Preventing a Biological Arms Race,* Susan Wright, ed. (Cambridge, Mass.: MIT Press, 1990); and Elisa D. Harris, "Sverdlovsk and Yellow Rain: Two Cases of Soviet Noncompliance?" *International Security* (Spring 1987), pp. 41–95.

53. VEREX is not, strictly speaking, an acronym. It is simply the name of the ad hoc group.

54. United Nations, *Summary Report, Ad Hoc Group of Governmental Experts to Identify and Examine Potential Verification Measures from a Scientific and Techni-*

cal Standpoint, Fourth Session, Geneva, BWC/CONF.III/VEREX/8, 13–24 September 1993, pp. 1–20.

55. *Arms Control and Disarmament Agreements: Texts and Histories of Negotiations* (Washington, D.C.: U.S. Arms Control and Disarmament Agency, 1980).

56. "Strengthening the BWC: Elements for a Possible Verification System," *Special Conference of the States Parties to the Convention on the Prohibition of the Development, Production and Stockpiling of Bacteriological (Biological) and Toxin Weapons and on Their Destruction.* BWC/SPCONF/WP.4, United Nations, 1994, p. 3.

57. See, for example, "Working Paper by China, India, Iran," *Special Conference of the States Parties to the Convention on the Prohibition of the Development, Production and Stockpiling of Bacteriological (Biological) and Toxin Weapons and on Their Destruction.* BWC/SPCONF/WP.15, United Nations, 1994, p. 2.

58. This compromise has been recommended; see Federation of American Scientists Working Group on Biological and Toxin Weapons Verification, *Beyond VEREX: A Legally Binding Compliance for the Biological and Toxin Weapons Convention* (Washington, D.C.: Federation of American Scientists, 25 July 1994), pp. 3–4, 11–14.

59. There are major problems to overcome in the examination of the data concerning biological weapons proliferation. Much of the U.S. data concerning such proliferation is classified and not open to public or academic scrutiny. Moreover, different sources may not share the same definition of *proliferation.* Finally, the quality of the information regarding such proliferation may not be reliable. See Elisa D. Harris, "Chemical Weapons Proliferation: Current Capabilities and Prospects for Control," in *New Threats: Responding to the Proliferation of Nuclear, Chemical and Delivery Capabilities in the Third World* (Lanham, Md.: University Press of America and Aspen Strategy Group, 1990).

60. U.S. Senate Committee on Governmental Affairs, "Proliferation Threats of the 1990's," Committee Report, 24 February 1993.

61. Ibid.

62. The source of the information on South Africa's possible biological weapons program may be dated. It appears in Carus, "The Poor Man's Atomic Bomb?" p. 27.

63. Carus, "The Poor Man's Atomic Bomb?" p. 29.

64. This point of view gives rise to another question: How well will the CWC prevent chemical warfare programs? To the extent that chemical weapons proliferators who are also among those suspected of having an interest in a biological weapons program have not signed the CWC, the desirable firebreak will be at best incomplete. Table 10.1 also shows whether each state of concern has signed the CWC. Four countries among the 11 suspected of having some interest in biological weapons have not yet signed the CWC: Libya, North Korea, Syria, and Taiwan.

11

Preventing the Spread of Arms: Delivery Means and Conventional Weapons

Jo L. Husbands

Finding the means to limit violence as the transformation of the international system from the Cold War era unfolds is one of the primary security challenges for the decade, and controls on arms transfers (sales and aid) could be part of this effort. The classical goals of arms control—to reduce the risks of war, to reduce the costs of preparing for war, and to reduce the damage should war occur—lie at the heart of efforts to control arms transfers. During the Cold War, the United States and the Soviet Union used gifts or sales of weapons as essential tools in their competition for influence in the Third World. Limiting arms transfers, like one goal of nuclear arms control, offered the hope of creating some type of rules of the road to avoid the risks of destabilizing competition between the superpowers.

Arms transfers remain an appropriate focus for arms control in the post–Cold War period. Today's wars are being fought almost entirely with imported weapons. The conventional weapons that could be used to deliver weapons of mass destruction (WMD) are a significant component of the proliferation problem. Arms are not a direct cause of conflict, but they can enable combat to continue; certain weapons can make the conflict more intense and more deadly to both combatants and civilians; and on occasion particular weapons can significantly influence the tide of battle.

This chapter is divided into two major parts. The first reviews the current state of international arms transfers and, briefly, of arms production. In particular, it tries to sort out longer-term trends from Cold War legacies to provide a context for discussing approaches to control. The second part examines a range of options to control or limit arms transfers, including controls by suppliers, such as the Missile Technology Control Regime (MTCR); controls on the demand side, such as regional arms limitation; and confidence-building and transparency measures, such as the new UN arms register.

Starting Points: Arms Trade Fundamentals

The Size of the Market

The international arms market, at least for major military equipment, continues to shrink. Since the mid-1980s, developing and developed countries have been spending less in real terms on their militaries, for imports of major weapons, and for overall defense expenditures as well.[1] According to the U.S. Arms Control and Disarmament Agency (ACDA), in 1993 the world arms trade reached its lowest level since the early 1970s. The $22 billion in deliveries represented a 70 percent drop from the trade's near record of $74 billion in 1987.[2]

The decline in the market began before the end of the Cold War and was clearly tied to the worldwide recession and the fall in oil prices. The Iran-Iraq War masked this trend, as did a series of large, well-publicized arms purchases after the Gulf War. And there are exceptions: the states of East and Southeast Asia increased their military spending during much of the last decade, sparking fears of new regional arms races. The (at least temporary) settlement of conflicts clearly tied to the Cold War and the disappearance of the Soviet Union as a major arms supplier thus only accelerated a trend that was already under way.

To the extent that these economic conditions persist, the market will not revive. But this also means that declining arms transfers result as much from diminished capacity to buy as from any fundamental shift in demand. Better economic times could mean renewed growth in arms imports.

In addition, the size of the arms market, which reflects primarily the trade in advanced conventional weapons, is not necessarily the best guide to its impact on conflict. First, with obvious and important exceptions, most of the 120-plus wars since World War II were fought with relatively unsophisticated and inexpensive weapons.[3] Second, the spread of democracy in regions such as Africa, Latin America, and Central Europe, which many believe will reduce conflict between nations, is not well reflected in arms trade statistics. Latin America and Africa were never significant components of the trade in major weapons, and in Central Europe it is hard to sort out the effects of democracy from those of the economic woes that would make new arms purchases difficult. What weapons are available to whom and from whom means more to the future of conflict than the sheer volume or relative dollar value of sales. Yet the declining market has important implications for both suppliers and recipients and for hopes of controlling the arms trade.

The Shape of the Market

Both the supply and demand sides of the arms market have always been highly concentrated. Among recipients, a few nations and regions account for most of the weapons imported into the Third World. Arms transfers to the Third World were negligible in the 1950s, since most U.S. military assistance went for the reconstruction of Europe and because the Soviet Union did not begin a military assistance program to the Third World until late in the decade. In the 1960s most transfers went to Asia, especially to Southeast Asia during the war in Indochina. Since the mid-1970s, 60–75 percent of all arms exports to the Third World, and the vast bulk of the most sophisticated arms, have ended up somewhere between North Africa and South Asia. On the supplier side, the five permanent members of the UN Security Council—the United States, France, China, Great Britain, and Russia—account for 80 percent or more of the arms exported to the Third World.[4]

More than weapons are being transferred; technology and production capabilities are spreading steadily from the developed to the developing world. How much actual knowledge is being transferred varies widely, since some of the arrangements involve little more than the assembly of finished components. But these cooperative arrangements helped create a number of new Third World arms exporters, such as Israel, Brazil, and China. The new producers sought their own military industries for reasons of national pride, self-reliance, independence from the major suppliers, and in some cases as part of a strategy of national economic development. Their role and impact is the subject of debate, but at present they are all having a hard time competing with exports from the bigger suppliers.

In addition to the open trade, the arms market includes gray and black components. The gray market refers to equipment or components that are sold for ostensibly civilian purposes but then used by the military. The black market is clandestine and includes weapons supplied by governments as part of covert assistance programs. Not surprisingly, no one has a solid estimate of the size of these markets. Most of the supplies to nonstate actors such as terrorists or insurgency groups come through these channels, as does much of the technology for developing biological, chemical, and nuclear weapons capabilities. This trade, along with the open trade in so-called light arms, is attracting increasing attention from those concerned with preventing or controlling civil and ethnic violence.

The Implications of Technological Diffusion

The spread of advanced weapons technology has a number of apparently contradictory effects. Most of the estimated 20–30 million casualties from the conflicts of the post–World War II period were not caused by sophisticated weapons.[5] The impact of sophisticated weaponry on combat in the Third World is uncertain. For example, exports of advanced fighter aircraft often spark controversy, but most of them have yet to be used in combat. And with the exception of the Arab-Israeli conflicts, aircraft that have seen combat generally performed below their advertised capabilities.

Nonetheless, as already mentioned, the introduction of particular technologies may have an important impact on the tide of battle or the outcome of war. And technological sophistication and its impact are relative. Allied air power completely dominated the Gulf War in 1991, yet the much maligned Iraqi air force was able to turn its helicopter gunships on its own rebellious citizens with devastating effect. This leads some to argue that the focus should be on controlling key destabilizing technologies, such as ballistic missiles, long-range strike aircraft, or shoulder-fired rockets such as the U.S.-made Stinger. Others argue that the trade in sophisticated weapons, although a drain on resources, has limited effect on most conflicts.

Three Cold War Legacies

Industrial overcapacity. An ironic peace dividend from the Cold War is the substantial overcapacity of military industries in the West and the East as military forces are restructured and procurement budgets are cut. Budget authority for U.S. defense procurement declined 71 percent in real terms between fiscal years 1985 and 1996.[6] Russia was much harder hit. By one estimate, Russian defense procurement declined over 80 percent between 1990 and 1993.[7] No major nation can now sustain its current industrial base solely through purchases for its own forces, and reduced budgets also mean less trade among the developed states. In the absence of significant conversion strategies for these industries, all the states face potent economic pressures to export weapons to ease the transition. Even if conversion is acknowledged as inevitable, exports are seen as a means to cushion the immediate pain.

Military spending cuts are coming in conjunction with, and accelerating, other important trends in the defense sector. For example, the trend in Europe has been toward fewer major firms and greater transnational ownership and cooperation. The consolidation of the European market in 1992 has worked against the previous determination of most nations to have their own national industries. In reality, only the United States and the Soviet Union could ever have sustained their defense industries with internal demand. Economic pressures to export are thus nothing new to the Europeans, but the intensity has increased significantly.

Mergers and acquisitions are a primary path to the consolidation of defense industries. By the end of the century, some analysts predict that major weapons systems such as fighter aircraft, large naval vessels, and main battle tanks will be produced in small numbers by a small number of firms. If this were so, and if the political will were there, in principle the export of advanced weapons systems or platforms could be controlled by agreement among this small group of suppliers.

The nature of defense production is changing in other ways as well. A key trend is the increasingly dual-use nature of military technology. Many innovations now come from the civilian sector to the military, and commentators expect this to be the continuing trend. It also appears that components will increasingly come off the shelf rather than being specially designed to military specifications. This is particularly true for communications and information processing, two areas that emerged from the Gulf War with the potential to transform conventional warfare. In the future, with the exception of complete advanced weapons systems, it will be increasingly difficult to distinguish between many kinds of civilian and military goods, particularly in areas such as telecommunications.

These trends have sparked efforts to find new patterns for export controls to replace the outmoded Cold War regimes such as NATO's former Coordinating Committee (COCOM). Some experts argue that the trends make export controls futile. Others argue that in the future controls will have to be based on significant international cooperation, on transparency and shared information rather than on denial.

The dominance of the United States.   The United States has emerged from the Cold War as the largest arms supplier in the world. Since the early 1990s, it has accounted for at least half of all the world's arms sales. In 1993, U.S. arms sales agreements worth $14.8 billion were 73 percent of all agreements with the Third World.[8] The United States also maintains the only remaining military assistance program of any significance. No state will be able to challenge that primacy for the rest of the decade. How the United States conducts its arms transfers, and whether it seeks and supports multilateral cooperation and restraints, will thus have an immense impact on arms control.

In the executive branch and Congress, discussions of arms export policy are dominated by concerns for U.S. jobs and the U.S. defense industrial base. During the 1992 presidential campaign, Pres. George Bush announced a sale of F-16s to Taiwan at the factory where the fighters would be produced. The Clinton administration is giving nonproliferation a high priority, but this concern is confined primarily to weapons of mass destruction and ballistic missiles. At present, promoting arms transfers as a means of retaining economic competitiveness dominates U.S. policy.

The disappearance of the Soviet Union.   The final legacy involves the elimination of the Soviet Union as one of the two leading suppliers and the uncertain future of Russia. From the early 1970s until the end of the Cold War, the Soviet Union was the world's largest supplier of military hardware.[9] In

1993, Russian sales agreements with the Third World totaled $2.8 billion, a far cry from a record high of $25 billion in 1987.[10] The virtual disappearance of the military assistance that sustained much of the former Soviet Union's arms transfers is the primary reason its exports have declined so sharply. This eliminated a number of countries, such as Cuba, Angola, and Vietnam, from the ranks of major arms importers.

Russian leaders up to the level of Pres. Boris Yeltsin have declared their hopes for arms exports: the arms trade is "an enforced necessity for us today. It is a source of foreign currency, which is currently in extremely short supply. It is also a condition for supporting defense sectors."[11] The Russians have been seeking markets in many countries; so far, however, they have met with limited success. Many Western experts doubt that Russian exports will prove attractive in the current, intensely competitive market, even though the Russians are apparently willing to sell their most sophisticated conventional weapons and production technology. The Gulf War both enhanced the aura of Western military equipment and tarnished the image of Russian hardware. Some experts also question whether the Russians can maintain their current low prices if conversion genuinely takes hold and the defense sector has to compete for materials with the rest of the economy.

Western governments have responded to Russian efforts with criticisms of particular agreements, such as the sale of advanced submarines to Iran, but also with considerable sympathy for the enormous challenge posed by conversion. Proliferation concerns have also prompted the United States and other Western governments to offer assistance for the creation of export control systems.

The impact of the legacies. The single greatest effect of the end of the Cold War is the end of the political rivalry between the United States and the Soviet Union, which influenced almost every aspect of arms transfers in the post–World War II period. Taken together, the legacies point out the importance that economic factors—preserving jobs, lowering unit costs, easing the pain of conversion—have assumed in shaping supplier policies. They clearly color the prospects for achieving meaningful controls on transfers of conventional weapons.

Controlling Arms Transfers

The Pros and Cons of Arms Trade Controls

The debate over the feasibility and desirability of attempting to control conventional arms transfers has gone on for many years. For most nations, access to conventional weapons is directly tied to fundamental issues of national sovereignty and the right of national self-defense enshrined in the UN charter. North-South issues of access to technology and developing countries' resentment of the tendency of industrialized nations to believe that they know what is right for the developing world are inextricably linked to arms transfers. Yet many nations, both developed and developing, are uneasy about the steady proliferation of weapons and weapons technology and about the impact that arms flows can have on particular conflicts. The urge to control arms transfers is part of a broader wish to find ways to control and ameliorate conflict. But it runs up against an equally strong desire to help—or at least permit—friends and allies to acquire the weapons they believe they need to ensure their national security.

These tensions are reflected in the continuing arguments over U.S. policy. Jimmy Carter made limits on U.S. arms exports a theme of his presidential campaign. In 1977 the White House announced a restraint policy, listing 11 purposes that limiting arms sales would serve.[12] Four years later the Reagan administration put a different emphasis on arms transfers, reflecting its concern with the East-West conflict and the support that arms transfers could provide to Third World allies in that struggle. The 1981 White House statement gave seven other reasons for using arms transfers as a foreign policy tool.[13]

In addition, discussions of the merits or fallacies of arms transfers restraint always face questions of feasibility. Achieving significant controls can appear to be an overwhelming task, particularly as one moves down the ladder of technological sophistication from the high-performance weapons, such as fighter aircraft and main battle tanks, that are still produced by only a few suppliers. On some level, every nation in the world participates in the arms trade. Unilateral export restraint, even by the United States, may prove ineffective if former customers can find new suppliers. The record to date for multilateral restraint is not encouraging. Yet modest successes have occurred in spite of the daunting challenges, and there is a wide variety of potential means to try to control arms transfers. For example, there are at least four arenas for efforts to encourage restraint.

• *The international realm.* This category includes international humanitarian law, such as that dealing with some classes of cruel and inhumane weapons, and norms that encourage restraint. The international community may use confidence-building measures, such as the new UN Register of Conventional Armaments, which encourages greater openness about imports and exports. The international community may also seek to cut off the flow of weapons to countries it considers rogues or outlaws, such as South Africa under apartheid, or to affect the course or outcome of a war.

• *Multilateral supplier restraints.* Since exports of major weapons remain highly concentrated, comprehensive supplier controls could have a significant impact. A second approach focuses on particular technologies; the MTCR, for example, seeks to inhibit the spread of ballistic and cruise missiles.

• *Regional approaches.* These could incorporate limits on weapons imports and exports as part of broader regional security arrangements. Regional initiatives are receiving more attention and study. At least in principle, they appear to represent a promising avenue that avoids the arguments about discrimination that hamper supplier restraints.

• *Unilateral state actions.* These remain a major tool for regulating the arms trade. Some states are tightening their export legislation, if only to have better control over their own activities. U.S. restraint would obviously have a major impact but is unlikely to be seen without signs that such leadership would yield broader international efforts and cooperation.

International Approaches

Fostering transparency—the UN Register.   The UN Register of Conventional Armaments is one of a growing number of international and regional efforts to foster transparency and openness about military spending, arms production, and arms imports and exports. Transparency is not control; instead the hope is that greater openness and knowledge will build trust and encourage restraint. The work of the Conference on Security and Cooperation in Europe (CSCE) is perhaps the best example of a web of confidence-building measures such as prior notification of military maneuvers as part of a regional security strategy.

The idea for an international register to report arms imports and exports emerged in the late 1980s. In 1988 the UN General Assembly passed a resolution to create a group of government experts to study ways to promote transparency and openness about conventional arms transfers. The end of the Cold War and the revelations after the Gulf War about Iraq's arms programs increased interest in preventing weapons proliferation, and advocates thought that increased transparency would support international nonproliferation efforts. The expert group's report formed the basis for a General Assembly resolution in December 1991 to create a register.

The register is a limited exercise, requiring countries to report their arms imports and exports for the preceding year in seven major categories—battle tanks, armored combat vehicles, large-caliber artillery systems, combat aircraft, attack helicopters, warships, and missiles and missile launchers. Its creators hoped the information would encourage governments to cooperate and coordinate their policies and would provide knowledge to the public so that citizens would become more active in urging their governments to limit imports or exports.

In its first two years of operation the register received mixed reviews. About half of the total General Assembly membership submitted reports the first year (1992) and a few less took part in the second round. Some important countries—Saudi Arabia, Syria, and Iran, for example—did not submit reports. For some areas, in particular sub-Saharan Africa, the kinds of weapons reported in the register are irrelevant to the arms trade in the region. And the data provided by exporters and importers did not always match. Nonetheless, the register has so far succeeded in tentatively establishing a norm of transparency about international arms transfers and has provided a trove of fascinating data for arms trade experts. Moreover, many countries also submitted additional information about their arms export policies or more detailed information about their purchases than required.

The issue now is the future of the register, especially efforts to expand its scope to include other categories of weapons. Many fear that the register must grow or die, but there is only limited consensus on what the growth should be. Some countries propose adding holdings and production, so that the developed countries' arsenals are better reflected in the data made available. Others have proposed adding weapons of mass destruction. Still others have suggested requiring reports on transfers of smaller weapons, including land mines, since these are the weapons most likely to be actually used in combat.

Another problem is getting key nations such as Saudi Arabia to submit reports. One suggestion is that the major suppliers should require all their trading partners to submit reports as a condition for purchasing arms. If all the permanent members of the Security Council put such a condition on their exports, participation in the register would almost certainly rise and would capture most of the trade in major weapons.

It is too soon to tell how much the information the register provides will enhance attention to arms transfers as a security issue. But getting the UN General Assembly to address arms transfers at all was a significant achievement. For many years developing countries charged that any mention of the issue was an attempt by the developed states, and especially the nuclear powers, to divert attention from the far greater problems posed by weapons of mass destruction. If, as intended, the register is coupled with other UN initiatives to promote regional and cooperative security, it could be the beginning of important efforts to address the problems of arms transfers.

Cruel and inhumane weapons/land mines.   Even if war seems uncontrolled and uncontrollable, people have sought ways to limit its effects through the creation of a body of norms and international law. These are the laws of war, also referred to as international humanitarian law. Controlling or proscribing the use of certain weapons that are considered too indiscriminate or unnecessarily injurious is part of this effort. In 1868 the St. Petersburg Declaration outlawed the use of a newly invented bullet designed to explode and shatter on contact with a soft surface, such as the human body, and the Hague Conventions of the early 1900s went on to ban other weapons.

Today the primary focus of these efforts is on finding a way to cope with the millions of antipersonnel land mines sown in the course of conflicts around the world. The U.S. State Department estimates that 80–110 million land mines are still in the ground in countries such as Angola, Afghanistan, Cambodia, Nicaragua, and Somalia.[14] Parts of some countries are genuinely infested with mines, which are increasingly used as weapons of terror to make territory uninhabitable. Cheap to buy and easy to plant, they are dangerous and expensive to clear, and they make it far more difficult for countries to rebuild and return to a normal life once conflicts are over. Returning refugees to their homes may become impossible if villages, roads, and fields are too dangerous to inhabit. Those who survive land mine explosions often lose limbs, placing additional burdens on already overloaded health care systems. UN land mine experts estimate that many mines cost as little as $3–25, whereas clearing a single mine may cost $300–1,000.

The international human rights and humanitarian community has responded by seeking a global ban on the production, transfer, stockpiling, and use of antipersonnel land mines. The primary international convention on cruel and inhumane weapons includes a protocol that deals specifically with land mines, but this governs only use—not production or stockpiling.[15] Ban advocates generally regard the protocol as too weak and too sympathetic to the military uses of land mines to be successfully reformed.

The ban campaign has attracted substantial attention from governments and the press, but the test of its ultimate success is years away. Several industrialized countries, including the United States, have imposed moratoriums on land mine exports. Some see the efforts to ban land mines as a model for other efforts to control particularly dangerous weapons. Yet it is not clear how readily other weapons could be stigmatized, since the characteristics that make land mines particularly repugnant—that they linger long after conflict is over to kill and maim unwary civilians—are not shared by most weapons.

Embargoes.   From time to time the international community has sought to enforce arms embargoes on certain states, such as the ban on transfers to the former Yugoslavia during its civil war and the embargo on exports to South Africa during apartheid. Supplies of weapons can be a significant factor in sustaining adversaries' abilities to continue to fight. Suppliers have used controls on the resupply of weapons to affect the outcome of war or to force an early halt to fighting.

Critics of embargoes cite several reasons for their dislike of the approach. Many consider embargoes ineffective. South Africa was able to acquire significant amounts of military equipment and build up an impressive indigenous industry during the years it was under a UN embargo. During the Iran-Iraq War, 34 countries supplied arms to the combatants, 29 of them to both sides, even though several national and international efforts to limit the flow of weapons were in place. Although embargoes are imposed on all sides in a conflict, the effects are usually not neutral. They may convey significant advantages on one side, as in the case of Bosnia. Yet others respond that arms suppliers may also consciously seek to affect who wins and loses a war, so differential impact is not a reason to reject an arms embargo if the international community wants to at least take a stand.

Multilateral Supplier Restraints

Past efforts at negotiating multilateral controls were largely unsuccessful, with the exception of the agreement in the 1950s among the United States, Great Britain, and France to limit transfers to the Middle East. That effort fell apart, however, in the wake of the Six Day War in 1967.

The most significant recent attempt at multilateral supplier controls came during the Carter administration. The administration initiated the Conventional Arms Transfers Talks (CATT) with the Soviet Union in late 1977, but after a series of experts' meetings CATT foundered in late 1978 on the increasing tensions between the superpowers and disputes within the U.S. government about whether cooperation or confrontation should dominate U.S. policy toward the Soviet Union. Each side wanted to put limits on transfers it saw as most dangerous for its key allies in the Third World, which the other side tended to see as essential to sustaining the security of an important friend. It was never settled whether to begin with regions where it might be possible to reach agreement but where agreement would not have much impact on global arms transfers (e.g., Latin America or sub-Saharan Africa) or to tackle the most difficult problems (the Middle East or South Asia) in hopes of the greatest rewards. A number of U.S. policymakers took the CATT experience as a lesson in the folly of attempting multilateral controls.

Suggestions for new attempts at supplier restraint revived from time to time in the 1980s (such as when an Exocet missile sold to Argentina by France sank a British ship during the Falklands/Malvinas Islands conflict), but there was never sufficient interest to sustain a serious effort. That changed after the Gulf War, when revelations of the arsenal that Iraq had accumulated prompted the United States to suggest that the permanent members of the Security Council should develop common guidelines and mechanisms of consultation to govern their transfers to the Middle East. (The story of that failed effort is related in Chapter 13.) The Clinton administration made no effort to revive the talks, and, without active leadership from the dominant supplier, there is no hope of significant efforts at multilateral controls.

Delivery means—the Missile Technology Control Regime.   Chapter 6 describes the growing number of countries that have achieved or are pursuing ballistic missile programs. Of the various advanced conventional weapons that are spreading throughout the Third World, ballistic missiles are singled out for three reasons.

The first reason is the lack of effective defenses. Of all the potential delivery vehicles, only ballistic missiles face no effective defenses at present. The apparent initial successes of the Patriot antimissile system against the Iraqi Scuds proved to be exaggerated, although the actual results will probably never be known fully. Antiaircraft systems can be overcome successfully, but for a nation with only a limited arsenal of WMD, the enhanced certainty of penetration that missiles offer—providing they perform as designed—is clearly attractive. Also attractive is the political and psychological advantage conferred by possession of a weapon against which one's adversary is defenseless.

Second, ballistic missiles are significantly faster than other delivery vehicles, especially over middle-range and long distances. This offers the possibility of surprise and diminishes the chances that an adversary could mount effective civil defense. The latter is important for reducing the potential casualties from an attack using WMD. Most of the ballistic missiles outside the possession of the acknowledged nuclear powers do not provide the accuracy attainable with manned aircraft. But accuracy is not a prime requirement for missions using nuclear and biological weapons—and to a lesser extent using chemical weapons—against cities or major military installations.

Third, missiles promise psychological and political effects. Ever since the German V-1 cruise missile and V-2 ballistic missile attacks in World War II, missiles have carried a special psychological power. In many cases this power exceeds their actual military impact. According to one source, Iraqi Scuds caused a total of just over 30 deaths and 300 injuries during the Gulf War.[16] Yet the attacks transfixed a worldwide audience as the missiles exploded in Israel, and they sparked renewed interest in defenses against tactical missiles. The prestige of missiles may also be increased by their clear connections to space programs, a link that makes control efforts susceptible to charges of discrimination and of attempts to deny legitimate access to technology.

The United States launched the MTCR in 1987. Modeled on other suppliers' arrangements to govern exports related to nuclear and chemical weapons proliferation, the regime initially included seven countries—the United States, Canada, France, West Germany, Italy, Japan, and Great Britain—and focused on controlling exports of missiles and missile technology for systems with payloads over 500 kilograms and ranges over 300 kilometers. The MTCR has now grown to include an additional 16 full members among the industrialized countries. Perhaps more important, MTCR has gained pledges from Argentina, China, Hungary, Israel, Romania, South Africa, and the Soviet Union/Russia to abide by its guidelines.

The MTCR is controversial. It is a good example of Trevor Taylor's concept of arms control for others (see Chapter 2) in several ways. For one, in conception and operation the MTCR is a classic export control regime based on denial by suppliers. As such, it is subject to the same dual criticisms that all such regimes confront—discrimination on the one hand and insufficient scope and effectiveness on the other. In addition, with the United States and some other industrialized countries increasingly interested in defenses against theater missiles, critics charge that the MTCR is an effort to improve the chances that those defenses will be effective. This is the kind of arms control, they contend, that is designed primarily to make it safer and easier for the industrialized states to intervene in the developing world.

Other arguments over MTCR concern its effectiveness, particularly in response to the threat of WMD. Critics point out that, in practice, almost anything from a small boat to an intercontinental ballistic missile could be used to deliver WMD. Terrorism scenarios rely heavily on "bombs in a suitcase" rather than sophisticated means of delivery. When it comes to the possible use of WMD by nations, most scenarios involve advanced delivery systems, but even then missiles are only one of several possible delivery vehicles. Concentrating on missiles could give a false sense of security that one is doing something significant about WMD, especially if there is no comparable effort to address other potential delivery means.

Another dispute centers on whether the MTCR can seriously inhibit the spread of missile technology. Some analysts believe that it has dampened some countries' efforts, particularly those indigenous production programs that depend heavily on imported technology. Critics respond that this is a delay at best, and they question how much outside assistance a determined nation requires. (Experts generally agree, however, that it is a significant technical challenge to produce a workable WMD warhead for the missile.)

Finally, even if the MTCR works, critics question whether its success is worth the strain the regime puts on relations among suppliers or between suppliers and recipients. The MTCR has caused tension in U.S. relations with a number of its European allies and with the former Soviet Union and China. Others, however, including some of the other authors in this volume, regard the MTCR as the prototype of new arms control approaches based on cooperative responses to emerging threats. One's view of MTCR depends on whether one sees the effort as serving general international goals or U.S. national security interests. The Clinton administration was firmly committed to the MTCR and saw it as an essential part of its efforts to control the spread of WMD.

Regional Approaches

With the end of the Cold War and the collapse of the East-West security structure, there is far greater interest in regional arrangements to control arms transfers. In principle, limits on weapons imports and exports could be part of broader security agreements, and regional initiatives appear to be the most promising avenue for attempts to restrain the trade in smaller or less sophisticated weapons. But at present there are more intriguing ideas than evidence that such ideas work.

The logic behind this approach is as strong as the theoretical case for multilateral approaches to restraining the trade in major weapons. Arms trade controls have little chance of long-term success without changing the demand for weapons, and most of the demand arises from the patterns of conflict within regions. Arms flow may affect the dynamics of regional security relationships, increasing insecurity by fostering suspicion and mistrust or by enhancing the military capabilities of rival or aggressor nations. The security dilemma discussed earlier in this volume is readily apparent in the impact of arms imports on conflict-prone regions.

Trying to address the problem leads to classic chicken-and-egg dilemmas. Is it possible to reduce arms transfers without first removing the underlying causes of conflict that made countries seek arms in the first place? Could tensions be reduced and the prospects for peace improved if countries slowed the pace of their arms imports or avoided acquiring new weapons their adversaries found particularly destabilizing, especially if this were done cooperatively? Not all arms supplies are destabilizing, but how does one decide which will have negative effects?

And there is no guarantee that a peace process will have solely peaceful consequences. Settlements may lead to commitments by allies to provide significant new arms supplies to ensure security in the aftermath of war. The Camp David Accords, brokered by Pres. Jimmy Carter between Egypt and Israel in 1978, provide a particularly good example of this phenomenon. Allies may also provide significant supplies of arms as a war winds down or as it formally ends, to try to tip the balance if peace fails and new fighting breaks out.

Despite the obstacles, nations that fear the negative consequences of arms races have attempted to initiate regional restraint. The Declaration of Ayacucho, signed in December 1974 by eight Latin American nations, is one example. The initiative sought to encourage limits on military spending and arms imports to free resources for economic development. The process of dialogue and experts' meetings created by the declaration collapsed within a few years. But it nonetheless served as an example for later attempts to limit arms imports and promote conflict resolution within Latin America, such as the Contadora peace process initiated by the leaders of several Central

American nations, which played a key role in helping to settle the conflicts in that region in the late 1980s.

The Ayacucho example points up the fact that some of the impulse for arms transfer controls may come from governments that would prefer to use scarce resources for other purposes, such as economic development, rather than for arms purchases. Regional approaches could make such resource shifts easier, by providing "cover" for civilian leaders in nations where the military establishment plays a powerful role in politics. Some arms imports have more to do with the political power of a country's military than with any objective security threat, and unilateral restraint may not be possible without the assistance of outside commitments.

The regions where, to an outside observer, arms trade restraint—for either major or light weapons—would be most desirable show little interest in such arrangements. But there are important peace and security-building arrangements under way in some areas, notably the Middle East, so the current dim prospects do not eliminate hope for the future. This is an area where far more study and creativity are needed to turn logic into initiatives that might have a chance of success.

A special case—the light weapons problem.   Regional approaches, to the extent they provide conflict resolution strategies and mechanisms, are one of the more promising venues for attempts to limit the trade in so-called light weapons. These weapons, which range from guns and rifles to any arms that can be carried by a light truck, are extraordinarily difficult to control. The sheer number of suppliers and recipients dwarfs the trade in major weapons, and the range of markets—legal, gray, and black, including covert assistance by governments—demands a daunting range of control efforts. In addition, there is little publicly available information about the trade. Limited approaches are inevitable, since tackling the entire trade would come close to attempting universal disarmament.

Regional approaches offer the prospect of tying control strategies more closely to the conflicts in which these weapons are likely to be used. Conflict, broadly defined, lies at the heart of most people's concern with the light arms trade. Most of the wars since the end of World War II have been relatively low-tech affairs fought primarily with light weapons. Most were civil wars, in which civilian casualties typically outnumber those of formal combatants. If one uses a generous definition of *conflict* to include a government's repression of its own people, as well as insurgencies or terrorist acts, these rely almost entirely on light arms. Light arms are thus intimately tied to conflict in a way that major, high-technology weapons systems need not be. Attempting to control the light arms trade connects naturally with thinking about preventing and controlling conflict.

One approach for regional controls on light weapons would be to develop tools that could be applied at various stages in a conflict. A simple division would be those measures that could be used before conflict breaks out or in its early stages; those that could be employed while conflict is under way; and those that could be used once conflict is over.

The spate of civil and ethnic conflicts since the end of the Cold War has created considerable interest in obtaining early warning of such conflicts, in hopes that prevention measures might be applied before serious fighting breaks out. Although not strictly a control mechanism, monitoring the flow of light arms to regions of tension can be a useful measure of incipient conflict. Disclosing light arms acquisitions could be an important transparency measure if taken independently or, better yet, as part of broader regional security arrangements. An even more ambitious measure would involve agreements for regional consultations prior to weapons purchases.

Once fighting has broken out, limits or outright embargoes on arms supplies are an obvious control mechanism. Although embargoes are often international measures, as discussed earlier, successful implementation depends on the cooperation of neighboring states. This makes them relevant to regional initiatives as well.

When the fighting stops, provisions for disarmament and demobilization as part of peace settlements offer another opportunity to control light arms. Almost all recent cease-fire agreements and peace settlements seem to include some provisions to disarm the combatants, either as a separate measure or as part of broader demobilization. Again, neighboring states can have an important impact on the prospects for a lasting settlement.

A focus on the stages and processes of conflict provides a way to array a wide variety of potential policy tools for regional efforts to control the flow of light weapons. Countries and regional organizations in both Central America and sub-Saharan Africa are currently exploring some of these approaches, although it is too early to assess how successful their efforts will be.

Unilateral Approaches

The general problem of export controls.   Weapons are not refrigerators or television sets. One need not make moral judgments about their existence or possible use to appreciate the argument that governments may want to have knowledge of and control over the flow of weapons across their borders. Even the most zealous and laissez-faire exporter may have an interest in tracking where exports go. Many governments care about what arms are coming into their countries, particularly when this includes weapons destined for insurgency groups or criminals. There may be strong reasons not to want to share that knowledge with outsiders—or one's own citizens—but the information may be important and worth some effort to collect.

The simple tracking of arms flows is likely to be the job of border police or customs services. Gray or black market transfers generally fall within the mandate of these services as well. Policy issues arise when the question becomes whether to have some broader controls over weapons transfers, to pick and choose among potential recipients. Most industrial states and many developing country suppliers have export control policies, with understandably wide variation in their comprehensiveness and level of enforcement among them.

The situation becomes even more complicated when the issue is control over dual-use items or components with potential military applications. If countries attempt export controls in this area, there are likely to be overlapping jurisdictions and conflicts among agencies with different priorities. In the United States, for example, the Defense and Commerce Departments often spar over export promotion versus restrictions on the export of sensitive technologies.

U.S. policy on arms exports has varied over the years. Foreign policy considerations have always been more important than economics, although individual companies or members of Congress routinely try to promote favorable sales decisions because of the economic benefits that will accrue. When the Carter administration was attempting to limit U.S. transfers, policymakers tried to move the point of decision to the early stages of the sales process, since once discussions begin potential sales may take on a life of their own that makes them difficult to turn down.

The United States has periodically tried to limit exports of particular weapons and technologies. From the Johnson administration in the mid-1960s until the 1980s, the United States generally avoided selling advanced fighter aircraft to Latin America. For a number of years, the United States prohibited any sales of portable antiaircraft missiles because of fears they would fall into terrorist hands. The Reagan administration reversed that policy, supplying Stinger missiles to the anti-Soviet rebels in Afghanistan. The recent rise of new democratic states emerging from repressive rule has led the United States to abandon its previous refusal to provide equipment and training to improve the quality of police forces, which it undertook in the 1970s after discovering that a disturbing percentage of U.S.-trained police were engaging in serious human rights violations.

U.S. arms transfer policy is currently governed by the Arms Export Control Act, which was passed in 1976 in response to congressional concern about rising U.S. arms sales to the Middle East. Because of the political importance of weapons exports, arms sales are treated as part of overall U.S. security assistance policy and are subject to congressional review. Most arms sales take place on a government-to-government basis; these are called foreign military sales, or FMS. Some kinds of equipment can be sold only via FMS. The U.S. government arranges the deal, buys the military hardware from the U.S. company, and then resells it to the foreign government. Many foreign governments prefer this arrangement, since the U.S. government will assemble the entire package deal, including spare parts and service. It is also possible for foreign governments to buy weapons directly from U.S. manufacturers, although this requires approval of an export license by the State Department and, in some cases, interagency review.

Whether or not the United States is engaged in significant efforts to limit its own arms exports, there is a strongly held conviction that it is in the best interests of the United States to exercise some level of control over arms transfers to ensure that they serve foreign policy goals. Even in times of relatively enthusiastic export promotion, U.S. arms transfers are treated as more than commodities and are subjected to policy review—and, in some cases, to restrictions.

Unilateral initiatives. The slow pace and daunting obstacles to negotiated arms control have prompted a number of analysts to suggest an alternative strategy of unilateral initiatives.[17] To them, the obstacles to developing multilateral supplier controls are so great that there is little point in undertaking unilateral initiatives in hopes of sparking reciprocity. Nonetheless, it is worth considering whether the United States, as the largest supplier nation, might be able to use unilateral initiatives to achieve some arms trade reductions or to encourage other states to limit supplies to particular countries. The latter seems the more promising course. An obvious candidate would be Russia and its sales to Iran. The United States could offer to restrain its sales in the lucrative Asian market, opening the way for Russian sales there, with a clear if unstated expectation that in return Russia would refrain from sales to parties that worry the United States. Recipient countries could be expected to resent having their choices curtailed, and other suppliers, notably the British and the French, might try to move in to replace the U.S. sales. If the United States is seriously concerned about particular exports to particular countries, however, such market-sharing initiatives could be one policy tool.

Conclusion

To date, the record of attempts to control the spread of conventional weapons is relatively bleak. Arms transfers are intimately tied to international, regional, and national politics, so overcoming one barrier to limits leaves a host of others. The economic pressures to export are so strong for producers today that it is hard to envision where the initiative for supplier restraint would come from. And a case can be made that in an anarchic world, where nations remain ultimately responsible for the security of their citizens, arms transfers serve the cause of peace and stability. If the resources of governments to pursue nonproliferation are limited, do conventional weapons deserve much attention?

In reality, the choices are not so stark. An international effort by suppliers to put significant restraints on their exports is unlikely in this decade unless some shock forces a substantial change in priorities. But individual suppliers will continue to regulate their exports to ensure that they meet national goals. In addition, there may be continuing efforts like the MTCR to restrain the spread of particular technologies. Regional efforts have not yielded much in the past, but recent years have seen significant efforts from within regions, including those where many would have argued indigenous peace efforts were impossible. Arms transfer restraint may be part of those processes at some stage. Transparency measures like the UN Arms Register may increase the amount of attention arms transfers receive.

Taken together, these various individual efforts will not satisfy those for whom the arms trade is immoral and who want sweeping international controls and reductions. But arms transfer problems will remain on the arms control agenda and will almost certainly be part of any systematic effort to address weapons proliferation.

Suggested Reading

Boutwell, Jeffrey, Michael T. Klare, and Laura W. Reed, eds. *Lethal Commerce: The Global Trade in Small Arms and Light Weapons.* Cambridge, Mass.: American Academy of Arts and Sciences, 1995.

Cahn, Anne Hessing, and Jo L. Husbands. "The Conventional Arms Transfer Talks: An Experiment in Mutual Arms Trade Restraint," in Thomas Ohlson, ed., *Arms Transfer Limitations and Third World Security.* New York: Oxford University Press for the Stockholm Peace Research Institute, 1988.

Chalmers, Malcolm, Owen Greene, Edward J. Laurance, and Herbert Wulf, eds. *Developing the UN Register of Conventional Arms.* West Yorkshire, U.K.: Department of Peace Studies, University of Bradford, 1994.

Krause, Keith. *Arms and the State: Patterns of Military Production and Trade.* New York: Cambridge University Press, 1992.

Laurance, Edward J. *The International Arms Trade.* New York: Lexington Books, 1992.

Notes

This chapter represents the views of the author as an individual and does not represent conclusions or official positions of the National Academy of Sciences. Portions of this chapter were presented at the 44th Pugwash Conference on Science and World Affairs, Kolymbari, Crete, Greece, 30 June–6 July 1994, and the 7th International Amaldi Conference of Academies of Science and National Scientific Societies, Warsaw, 22–24 September 1994.

1. The two primary sources for arms transfers data are the yearbooks of the Stockholm International Peace Research Institute (SIPRI) and the annual reports of the ACDA. The most recent are *SIPRI Yearbook 1994: World Armaments and Disarmament* (New York: Oxford University Press, 1994) and *World Military Expendi-*

tures and Arms Transfers [*WMEAT*] *1993–1994* (Washington, D.C.: U.S. Government Printing Office, 1995). A third source, compiled by Richard Grimmett from the Congressional Research Service, uses the same data as the ACDA but generally provides it more quickly. His most recent report is *Conventional Arms Transfers to the Third World, 1986–1993* (Washington, D.C.: Congressional Research Service, 29 July 1994).

2. *WMEAT, 1993–1994*, p. 9. Imports by developing countries continue to account for over 57 percent of total arms imports, with the Middle East, and increasingly East Asia, the most important customers.

3. Ruth Leger Sivard, *World Military and Social Expenditures 1989* (Washington, D.C.: World Priorities, 1989), p. 23.

4. *WMEAT, 1993–1994*, p. 139; author's calculations.

5. Ruth Leger Sivard, *World Military and Social Expenditures 1991* (Washington, D.C.: World Priorities, 1991), pp. 22–25.

6. William J. Perry, *Annual Report to the President and the Congress* (Washington, D.C.: U.S. Government Printing Office, 1995), p. 271. Note that 1985 was the high point of the Reagan administration's intense procurement efforts, so the decline predated the end of the Cold War. The new U.S. five-year defense plan calls for real increases in procurement funding of 47 percent, but in an era of huge deficits and efforts to balance the federal budget one can question whether those increases will materialize.

7. Kevin P. O'Prey, *The Arms Export Challenge: Cooperative Approaches to Export Management and Defense Conversion*, Brookings Occasional Paper (Washington, D.C.: Brookings Institution, 1995), p. 25.

8. Grimmett, *Conventional Arms Transfers*, p. 6. This was up from 56 percent the previous year. Arms sales can fluctuate significantly from year to year; the 1993 increase, for example, was largely the result of big new contracts from Saudi Arabia and Kuwait.

9. *WMEAT, 1966–1975*, pp. 72, 74; *WMEAT, 1972–1982* (1984), pp. 86, 91; *WMEAT, 1993–1994* (1995), p. 145.

10. *WMEAT, 1995*, p. 151.

11. Quoted in Peter Almquist and Edwin Bacon, "Arms Exports in a Post-Soviet Market," *Arms Control Today* (July/August 1992), p. 12.

12. *Arms Transfer Policy*, Report to the Congress for Use of Committee on Foreign Relations, U.S. Senate (Washington, D.C.: U.S. Government Printing Office, 1977), pp. 12–13.

13. *Changing Perspectives on U.S. Arms Transfer Policy*, Report Prepared for the Subcommittee on International Security and Scientific Affairs of the Committee on Foreign Affairs, U.S. House of Representatives, by the Congressional Research Service, Library of Congress (Washington, D.C.: U.S. Government Printing Office, 1981), p. 127.

14. U.S. Department of State, *Hidden Killers: The Global Landmine Crisis* (Washington, D.C.: U.S. Government Printing Office, 1994), p. 1.

15. This is the UN Convention on Prohibitions or Restrictions on the Use of Certain Conventional Weapons Which May Be Deemed to Be Excessively Injurious or to Have Indiscriminate Effects. The convention entered into force in December 1983. Over 60 nations, including the United States, are currently parties to the convention. A review conference took place in the fall of 1995.

16. Stanford University Center for International Security and Arms Control, *Assessing Ballistic Missile Proliferation and Its Control* (Stanford, Calif.: Stanford University CISAC, 1991), p. vii.

17. Edward J. Laurance, "Reducing the Negative Consequences of Arms Transfers Through Unilateral Arms Control," in Bennett Ramberg, ed., *Arms Control Without Negotiation: From the Cold War to the New World Order* (Boulder, Colo.: Lynne Rienner Publishers, 1993).

PART 4

Regional Issues

12

Regional Arms Control

Gregory J. Rattray and Jeffrey A. Larsen

With the passing of the Cold War, arms control increasingly takes place in regional as opposed to bipolar or global settings. To deal with the relationship between regional issues and arms control, this part takes a very different approach from those preceding it: it presents three short case studies rather than a theoretical discussion or review of a certain type of arms control.

Importance of Regional Factors

We believe students of arms control need to be aware of the wide variety of perspectives that parties can bring to the negotiation and implementation of cooperative security arrangements. Whereas the rest of the book concentrates mainly on general principles and functional areas as a means to analyze arms control issues, in this part we provide another type of lens by bringing out regional perspectives.

Past discussions of arms control in the Cold War focused almost exclusively on the U.S. and Soviet record in managing the East-West strategic balance. Yet most of today's states have very different security considerations. Regional concerns and domestic political contexts vary widely. Geography, history, and religion create different incentive structures and approaches. Other nations will rank order among security concerns and, as a result, arms control objectives in new ways. The sources of conflict have changed as well. While the superpower confrontation focused on political and ideological differences, the nationalist and ethnic divisions driving today's conflicts may require new kinds of arms control efforts. In all cases, those analyzing arms control efforts must recognize the pitfalls of ethnocentrism and force themselves to understand concerns other than those driven by technology.

Arms Control and Regional Security

Some successes in reducing regional conflict have occurred after the Cold War. In Southwest Africa, Namibia has held free elections and outside powers have withdrawn from Angola. The level of conflict has declined with the peace settlement in Cambodia. The Central American region has seen progress in Nicaragua, El Salvador, and Guatemala. While tensions on the Korean peninsula have waxed and waned, important agreements have been reached that provide real hope for reducing the chance of war. Efforts toward a comprehensive peace in the Middle East continue, if haltingly at times. In some areas, international organizations such as the UN and the International Atomic Energy Agency (IAEA) have played key roles.

Obviously, however, troubles remain. The conflicts in the former Yugoslavia remain seemingly intractable. The level of violence and degree of suffering as a result of ethnic hatred and civil wars in Rwanda and the Sudan have shocked the world. Even the generally tranquil security environment in South America has been disturbed by border clashes between Ecuador and Peru.

What is the role for arms control in stemming these conflicts and improving regional security? The end of the East-West rivalry has changed the dynamic of regional security balances. The superpowers are generally less concerned with trying to achieve regional ascendancy. Without ideological competition, there is seemingly less pressure to export weapons and related technologies to allies and client states. At the same time, the United States and others remain concerned about regional instabilities. The United States and Russia can can provide examples of the synergistic impact of successful arms agreements in reducing security tensions between possible competitors. Additionally, those involved in East-West arms control can draw on a wealth of expertise in efforts to assist regional arms control in areas such as verification procedures and technologies.

As a result, regional powers cannot rely on superpower competition as leverage for buying armaments from these states. Other outside powers and international organizations can more easily assume the role of honest brokers in disputes. Also, the security hierarchies of almost all states have changed, raising the importance of economic concerns. These factors may allow a more vigorous application of the arms control lessons learned during the Cold War.

Prospects for arms control in regional settings remain mixed. Many places around the globe are still under the shadow of war. Peace in such areas must come first. Many regions contain nations with uncertain intentions and programs regarding weapons of mass destruction. Domestic factors, especially concerns regarding defense industries, can cause mixed sets of incentives and behavior for the United States and others in pursuing regional security solutions.

Realistic expectations will remain central to any real progress through arms control. In the short term, focusing on confidence-building measures rather than weapons reduction may prove necessary. Over the long term, movements toward making structural arms control agreements and encouraging holdouts to join global regimes can become possible. As always, arms control will remain a means to the end of state security. While the objectives a state may pursue through arms control are applicable across the globe, the utility of arms control approaches will vary from region to region and state to state.

Case Studies

To analyze and illustrate arms control's contribution in regional settings, three case studies were chosen. The regions covered include the Middle East, Latin America, and South Asia. Our purpose in selecting these studies is to illustrate how the underlying principles of arms control and the lessons of Cold War arms control have been applied in different contexts. The regions selected provide variety in the types of weapons discussed, the cultures involved, and the levels of success achieved.

The regional case studies presented in this part provide the reader with some specific examples, from a non-U.S. perspective, of the key concepts outlined in Part 1 of the book. In particular, the studies highlight a number of important aspects of the international and domestic contexts within which arms control is pursued.

Each author selected a particularly valuable case to illustrate the dynamics of arms control. Christopher Carr begins with an analysis of the 1991 Middle East Arms Control Initiative (MEACI), outlining the difficulties the major powers confronted in reducing their own contributions to regional instability through conventional arms transfers. In analyzing the failure of the MEACI, he also holds out hope for future progress in this area depending on the results of the larger Middle East peace process.

Cynthia Watson looks at the positive results in improved security through arms control that have been achieved in Latin America, particularly in reducing the significance of the Argentine-Brazilian nuclear rivalry. In examining this rivalry, she demonstrates how different conceptions of the path to ensuring sovereignty and economic well-being between military and civilian regimes resulted in nuclear convergence between the two states.

Peter Lavoy concludes by examining the factors underlying nuclear tensions in South Asia. He analyzes the different approaches to disarmament, nuclear ownership, and bargaining in India and Pakistan, two states that he believes are only beginning to learn the utility of arms control in managing their mutual security.

The possibilities for arms control are highly dependent on the relationship between the states involved in the endeavor, as discussed by Trevor Taylor in Chapter 2. The level of conflict or cooperation that exists influences
both the course of negotiations and the prospects for compliance with agreements. Christopher Carr shows that certain events, particularly the sale of
U.S. warplanes to Taiwan, caused trust to break down and states to withdraw from the MEACI process. Yet he holds out hope for the initiative if the
Middle East peace process makes substantial progress in reducing regional
tensions. Cynthia Watson describes how the parallel emergence of democratic regimes in Argentina and Brazil fostered trust and provided a crucial
enabler in securing cooperation to stop the pursuit of nuclear weapons in
Latin America. Peter Lavoy outlines how the perpetual state of impending
conflict between India and Pakistan prevents these states from reaching
meaningful arms control agreements in South Asia.

The case studies show the significance of domestic factors, such as strategic culture (outlined by Jennifer Sims in Chapter 3), in determining how
successful arms control efforts will prove to be.[1] For example, Watson argues that government change in Latin America produced changes in the
way national security was viewed by Brazil and Argentina. Previous military
regimes in these states viewed security as a competitive pursuit. However,
recent democratic governments see economic improvement as a central goal,
and thus they value cooperation in achieving security. Lavoy highlights the
barriers to viewing arms control as a legitimate means of ensuring security
that are evident in the deeply suspicious strategic cultures of India and Pakistan. He believes improvement in the situation is possible if the national
security establishments of these two states can learn lessons from the series
of crises that have characterized the South Asian version of the Cold War.

The part as a whole demonstrates the differences and similarities that
characterize arms control efforts around the globe. No single arms control
context is the same. Even when similar objectives (such as the control of
emerging nuclear weapons programs) are present, the arms control process
proceeds differently in different regions. Yet these chapters also shows students of arms control the value of understanding key concepts that appear
in arms control agreements across regional environments.

Note

1. The concept of strategic culture emerged primarily in the late 1970s and
early 1980s by those analyzing the U.S.-Soviet nuclear relationship. Two key works
outlining these concepts are Colin S. Gray, *Nuclear Strategy and National Style*
(Latham, Md.: Hamilton Press, 1986), and Carl G. Jacobsen, ed., *Strategic Power:
USA/USSR* (New York: St. Martin's Press, 1990), particularly Chapter 1 by Jack Snyder
and Chapter 8 by Ken Booth.

13

False Promises and Prospects: The Middle East Arms Control Initiative

Christopher D. Carr

The political and strategic dimensions of the Middle East are dictated principally by regional conflicts and rivalries rather than by global conditions or by great power competition. The Arab-Israeli dispute and the omnipresent tensions in the Gulf have not been completely devoid of external involvement, but for the most part that involvement has been peripheral rather than central. Only on the matters of Israel, oil, and arms has the outer world been drawn directly into the conflict in the Middle East. These factors, either in combination or separately, have dictated the extent and type of involvement by external powers and have served as the basis for such arms control activity as has taken place within the region.

Even at the height of the Cold War the Middle East failed to fall neatly within the concept of spheres of influence. Although many states in the region were considered to be proxies of the superpowers, in reality these countries (including Egypt, Syria, Iran, Iraq, and Saudi Arabia) were for the most part exploiters of the balance-of-power game rather than active participants. They demanded a price for their nominal allegiance to one side or the other, and that price was most often paid for in arms. Thus, for nearly half a century the history of arms control in the Middle East was not about regimes of restraint or regulation but about managing the flow of arms into the region to maintain the allegiance of the recipients.

As a result of this activity there have been very few attempts at formal arms control within the Middle East. The recipients of arms were consumed with acquiring weaponry either because of their role in the Arab-Israeli dispute or because, like Iran and Iraq, they were primarily interested in maintain-

255

ing a balance between themselves in respect to local disputes. The suppliers, principally the United States, the Soviet Union, Britain, and France, were for the most part relegated to fulfilling the demands of the regional powers, either for political reasons or to sop up the petrodollars.

To excuse the reactive nature of supplier policies, the concept of balancing powers within the region was formulated. This strategy proposed that arms were transferred because by maintaining a balance of power between Iran and Iraq or Israel and the Arab frontline states a politico-military equilibrium could be attained and maintained within the region. This concept reached its purest form as part of the Camp David Agreement, signed between Israel and Egypt in 1978. As an incentive to both sides (but principally to an increasingly isolated Egypt), the United States added a codicil to the agreement whereby it guaranteed to provide (and almost completely underwrite) enough weaponry to ensure that a balance of military hardware was maintained between the two signatories. As a result of this commitment, the United States provided more than $30 billion in arms to Egypt and Israel between 1979 and 1990.[1]

Apart from this balancing procedure and the need to pay for the allegiance of local states, the external suppliers of arms to the region have been motivated in their actions by the presence of oil-rich states that desired to acquire large arsenals of state-of-the-art weaponry, for which they were prepared to pay cash. These sales were originally motivated by a desire to minimize the impact of the oil crisis of 1973–1974. Later, other rationales, including surplus U.S. capacity at the end of the Vietnam War and the need for European states to maintain their defense industrial bases, provided the basis for an unrestrained approach to Saudi Arabia and the other Gulf states. The Soviet Union was itself not immune to the glimmer of petrodollars and indulged in major sales to Iraq and Libya during the 1970s and 1980s.[2]

It was only when a bitter and destructive conflict erupted between Iraq and Iran in 1980 that the supplier states began to question the advisability of a consumer-dominated free market in arms. Most observers believed that the suppliers to Iran and Iraq had, wittingly or not, contributed to an arms race in the Gulf. When the Iranian revolution had served to destabilize the balance between itself and Iran, Baghdad seized the opportunity to take an ascendant position by attacking in the south of Iran. Unable to achieve a fatal blow, the Iraqis then settled down to a war of attrition with the Iranians, which in tactics and strategy looked much like World War I.[3]

Apart from some manifestations of guilt over the death toll in the Iran-Iraq War, the observers/suppliers were also concerned about the wider ramifications of the conflict. The impact on oil supplies, the breaching of the chemical weapons threshold by Iraq, and the role of secondary and tertiary arms suppliers served to focus the attention of the United States, Western Europe, and the Soviet Union on the conflict. However, aside from the maintenance of a loose embargo, very little attempt was made to impose any international intervention in the region, and the war was allowed to continue until both antagonists were exhausted by eight years of war. In terms of arms control, the conflict was important in that it demonstrated a worst-case scenario for what might occur if such intervention were absent and did not provoke any major arms control initiative either during or immediately after the cessation of hostilities.

It would take two almost contemporaneous events, the end of the Cold War and Desert Storm, to motivate the major powers to consider the institution of a multilateral arms control policy for the Middle East. The end of the Cold War allowed for the possibility of including all the major global actors in such an undertaking; Desert Storm, with the latent if unfulfilled possibility of a dangerous, high-technology confrontation, provided the subjective impetus behind such a proposal.

The Middle East Arms Control Initiative

On 29 May 1991 Pres. George Bush announced the Middle East Arms Control Initiative (MEACI) in a commencement address at the U.S. Air Force Academy. Although the announcement was made unilaterally, the initiative itself was designed to be a multilateral endeavor. The initiative was directed particularly to the five permanent members of the UN Security Council (the United States, Russia, China, Britain, and France). Since this group of states controlled 78 percent of all arms sales to the Middle East, it was reasoned that, if sufficiently motivated, they could collectively establish controls over the most destabilizing aspects of transfer of arms to the region.[4]

As originally envisaged by President Bush, the MEACI would cover all of the region from Morocco to Iran and from Syria to the states of the Gulf Cooperation Council. The basis of the initiative would be that of supplier restraint, with the participants pledging themselves to a series of commitments that would be given substance in a series of high-level meetings within the group. Foremost among these commitments would be the observation of a general code for responsible arms transfers, the avoidance of destabilizing transfers, and the establishment of effective domestic export controls on the end use of arms. In the pursuit of transparency, the suppliers were to notify each other in advance about certain sales, meet regularly to consult on arms transfers, and consult if they believed that the guidelines were not being observed. They would also provide data for an annual report on the transfers that they had made into the region.

While the supplier-constraint proposals were the core of the initiative, President Bush also linked his regional approach with general arms control proposals covering ballistic missile technology and chemical and biological weapons. This simply reiterated the already widely expresed desire to ensure that weapons of mass destruction (WMD) would not proliferate in the unstable environment of the immediate post–Cold War era.

The first meeting on the MEACI occurred in Paris on 8–9 July 1991. The communiqué that was issued after this meeting was more a statement of future intent than the inception of any definitive policy, but it did include a careful intimation that the participants were not establishing an exporters' cartel but were trying to achieve "a common standard by which (the suppliers) could judge arms transfers."[5]

The group next met in London in October 1991. It had been proposed that the London meeting would be more substantial than the Paris convocation and should result in the identification and categorization of weaponry and behavior that might contribute to instability in the Middle East. In essence, the London meeting was designed to establish the definitional parameters within which the group, as arms suppliers, would act in the future.

On the matter of avoiding the injection of destabilizing systems into the region, the participants identified eight categories of concern during the London meeting:[6]

1. Arms that would prolong or exacerbate existing conflicts
2. Arms that would increase tension in the region
3. Arms that would in themselves create bilateral or multilateral instability
4. Arms that would contravene established embargoes or other restraints to which the participants subscribed
5. Arms that were clearly beyond the legitimate self-defense needs of the recipients
6. Arms that might be used to support terrorist acts
7. Arms that might cause interference in the internal affairs of a sovereign state
8. Arms whose acquisition would place an economic strain on the recipient state

In addition, seven categories of weaponry were identified as subject to the information/transparency process: tanks, armored combat vehicles, artillery, military aircraft, military helicopters, naval vessels, and "certain missile systems."

As Reggie Bartholomew, the U.S. representative at the talks, was later to relate, the London guidelines "are not a formula for determining who gets what. Again we are not trying to create an international arms cartel. Rather, the guidelines give us wide berth to question and be questioned on such matters. This is exactly what we intended when we proposed the guidelines."[7]

Unfortunately, the London meeting would be the high point of the MEACI—when the group next met, in February 1992, the fine words and good intentions were replaced by bickering and division.

At the second London meeting the group had been able to reach a consensus on broad definitions. However, during the 1992 Washington meeting it became obvious that there were deep differences over some of the fundamental and necessary specifics.[8] For example, the participants in Washington could not agree on a definition for *weapons of mass destruction*. While ballistic missiles appeared to clearly fit into this category, it was arguable that certain types of more conventional surface weapons and advanced aircraft might also be accorded this distinction. The group split on this issue and did not reconcile the problem in Washington.

There was also disagreement on which types of fixed-wing combat aircraft would be included in the group that required prior notification of sale. The period of advance notification was itself a matter of contention. The Chinese in particular wanted to limit the period to 30 days at the most and were not very sanguine about any notification period. In contrast, the United States was in favor of a 2–3-month notification period. This agreement would also remain unsettled at the end of the Washington meeting.

After the Washington gathering, the Middle East Arms Control Initiative would deteriorate into a series of bureaucratic exchanges, becoming perfunctory and largely meaningless by the end of the Bush administration. It had taken less than 18 months for a major, presidentially sponsored foreign policy initiative to move from public announcement to private demise. But why this initiative failed and what lessons can be drawn from its failure remain important.

Evaluating the MEACI

The MEACI was killed by certain realities. These can roughly be divided into three categories: domestic U.S. problems that were specific to the time of the MEACI process (1991–1992) and generic in respect to arms transfers to the Middle East; global realities that were predicated upon conditions created by the evolution of a so-called new world order; and conditions in the Middle East that both threatened the MEACI and detracted from its impact.

That the MEACI was a U.S. presidential initiative was initially a strength, but it became a liability during the election year of 1992. As George Bush became more desperate to attract votes, he made pledges to arms manufacturers that were plainly at odds with both the spirit and the letter of the MEACI. The most destructive of these commitments was to allow the sale of F-16 aircraft to Taiwan, an act which so alienated the mainland Chinese government that it almost immediately withdrew from the MEACI process. For Bush, the political and economic value of the sale ($5–8 billion and 3,000 jobs in Fort Worth, Texas) was, in September 1992, worth far more than saving the MEACI.

Economic realism played a wider role in the eclipse and demise of the MEACI. Between May 1991, when George Bush announced the initiative, and May 1992, when the policy began to dissipate, the United States made arms sales to the Middle East that were worth $8.5 billion.[9] This activity was partly the result of the technological impact of Desert Storm. Systems such as the Patriot air-defense missile and the M-1 Abrams tank had received such favorable press during the conflict that many states, particularly in a Gulf region that still felt threatened by the Iraqi regime, felt an imperative to acquire them in large numbers. For example, the Kuwaiti government bought 236 Abrams tanks to reequip its army. With the market for such high-cost matériel being largely restricted to the Middle East oil states, the United States felt that to place restrictions on this bonanza of orders was to deny U.S. defense manufacturers the right to freely compete in the arms market-place. Naturally, when Washington's MEACI partners became aware that the United States appeared to be preaching restraint through the MEACI but was making large sales to states in the region, there was some recognition that the Bush administration was less than committed to its own arms control policy.

In a wider sense, the end of the Cold War had created a crisis within the defense industries of all the MEACI states. France had 235,000 jobs in the defense industrial sector, and 65 percent of all the products of French arms manufacturers went to overseas customers. With double-digit unemployment in France in 1992, any commitment to a policy that would throw more French out of work would have been highly unpopular. The same situation existed in Britain, where it was estimated that the Kuwaiti decision to buy U.S. tanks had on its own jeopardized 2,000 British jobs.[10]

The collapse of the Soviet/Russian economy also placed great strains on that member of the group. By 1992 Russia was desperate for any export commodity that would provide hard-currency support for the ruble. Soviet-pattern armaments still had a value-for-money, utilitarian attraction to many Middle Eastern states in the early 1990s, and with states such as Iran willing to pay cash for military hardware the lure proved too much for Moscow. The international community was not surprised, therefore, when it learned that the Russians had sold submarines for use by the Iranian navy.[11] Unfortunately, such a sale was directly contrary to at least five of the restrictive categories agreed upon in London.

Far from releasing the major arms-producing states from their obligation to produce armaments, the end of the Cold War had made them, in the face of drawdowns and cancellations by their own governments, all the more desperate to promote arms sales to maintain the integrity of their own defense industries. This reality, more than any other factor, served to undermine the security rationales that were the basis of the MEACI.

Apart from domestic political and economic intrusions into the arms control process, certain events taking place within the Middle East also served to displace the MEACI as a priority. The most important of these was the burgeoning rapprochement between Israel and the PLO, which two years later would metamorphose into the accord that established a Palestinian homeland. Given the complexity of these discussions, any multilateral activity that might complicate or confuse the issues was deemed extraneous, and the MEACI could have been viewed in that light. Also, it was recognized that the external powers might need to use arms transfers as a bargaining chip, and the United States in particular did not want to be hampered by any pledge to constrain itself.

In addition to the Israeli-PLO negotiations, the continuing instability in the Gulf tended to undermine the restraint resolve of the MEACI states. With Saddam Hussein still in power in Iraq (albeit at the helm of a crippled military and an embargo-burdened economy), the states of the Arabian peninsula needed constant reassurance regarding external political and military support. Many felt that to have imposed the MEACI constraints on these vulnerable countries would have sent the wrong message to the rulers of the region, including Hussein. It would therefore again be ironic that an arms control initiative born of concerns raised by the U.S. role in Desert Storm would be at least partly sabotaged by the unfinished business left over from that conflict.

To a greater or lesser extent, all arms control activity is affected by the type of realities that terminated the MEACI. It takes a fearless (and perhaps foolhardy) political leadership to promote a multilateral arms control policy without consideration of the impact on the domestic audience or the local economy. In the case of the MEACI, George Bush was to learn in November 1992 that any goodwill or impetus that might have been provided by Desert Storm had dissipated almost overnight; the lessons of Desert Storm would not be as clear as the president had thought they were in May 1991. Bush had particularly underestimated the impact of the post–Cold War drawdown on key political constituencies in the United States. When he was forced to recognize this, it was tantamount to an abrogation of the MEACI principles.

Future Prospects for Middle East Arms Control

Two emerging realities might serve to resurrect the spirit of restraint sometime in the future: the impact of the now-consummated Israeli-Palestinian accord and the ongoing economic troubles of some of the Gulf states, most prominently Saudi Arabia. Regarding the latter issue, if the oil-state recipients of arms were forced to self-restrict their acquisitions on the basis of cash-flow problems, then to institute a supplier-constraint regime would be less painful than it appeared in 1992.

It is also plausible that if the Israeli-Palestinian peace plan were to succeed, then the overall level of tension in the Middle East might be reduced and the area might be more susceptible to the kind of restraint embodied in the MEACI. This assumes, however, that a constant flow of arms is not required, as in the past, to fine-tune local balances of power. It also assumes that other tensions, such as the continuing resurgence of Islamic fundamentalism, will not create their own set of demands for arms transfers into the region.

The Middle East has been a zone of conflict for the past 45 years. As such, it should have received particular attention in terms of both the qualitative and the quantitative aspects of arms control. However, the net effect of oil money, the local definitions of *security* and *need for weaponry*, and the role of weaponry in the Arab-Israeli dispute have led to an almost unconstrained policy of arms transfers into the region. It has also encouraged Israel to acquire nuclear weaponry and states such as Egypt and Iraq to experiment with chemical agents. The net results of this profligate policy have been wars of increasing lethalness and increasingly costly periods of peace. The commercial and political benefits for the suppliers have fueled this lack of constraint, and in the post–Cold War era pressures to make sales of high-technology, high-cost armaments are likely to increase.

The prospect of peace between Israel and all the frontline Arab states allows for the possibility of either viable supplier-restraint arms control proposals or regional accords based on agreed qualitative and quantitative limits, or a combination of the two activities. If the peace is sufficiently persuasive to allow Israel to reduce its state of arms, then the Arab states, on the basis of economic rationales alone, will likely follow. Supplier proposals, based on the spirit if not the letter of the MEACI, could then be used to retard such practices as preemptive selling or the insertion of escalatory or unbalancing weaponry into the area.

Conclusion

The MEACI was not inherently infeasible or inappropriate. Instead, it was crippled at birth by certain exigencies of a global, regional, local, and domestic nature that conspired against it coming to fruition. Many of these problems had already been mitigated less than 18 months after the initiative had been de facto abandoned. Perhaps the important lesson of the MEACI is that such proposals should be fostered and maintained even when their moment appears to have passed because, given the volatility and prospects afforded by a rapidly changing political environment, their time might yet come again.

Suggested Reading

Stockholm International Peace Research Institute. *World Armaments and Disarmament Yearbook.* Oxford: Oxford University Press, 1993.
Strategic Survey. London: International Institute for Strategic Studies, 1993.
U.S. Arms Control and Disarmament Agency. *World Military Expenditures and Arms Transfers.* Washington, D.C.: U.S. Government Printing Office, 1992.

Notes

1. *Foreign Military Sales, Foreign Military Construction Sales, and Military Assistance Facts,* Department of Defense, Security Assistance Agency, 30 September 1991, pp. 10–11.
2. *World Military Expenditures and Arms Transfers* [*WMEAT*] *1988,* U.S. Arms Control and Disarmament Agency (Washington, D.C.: U.S. Government Printing Office, 1989), pp. 21–25.
3. A. Cordesman and A. Wagner, *The Iran-Iraq War* (Boulder, Colo.: Westview Press, 1990).
4. Stockholm International Peace Research Institute, *Yearbook 1992* (Cambridge: Oxford University Press, 1992), pp. 308–311.
5. *WMEAT, 1992–1993.*
6. Ibid.
7. "Statement Before the Subcommittee on Arms Control, International Organization and Science," House Foreign Affairs Committee, Washington, D.C., 24 March 1992, *U.S. Dept. of State Dispatch,* 30 March 1992.
8. *WMEAT, 1992–1993.*
9. *Foreign Military Sales, Foreign Military Construction Sales, and Military Assistance Facts,* September 1994.
10. *Arms Control Today* (January/February 1993), pp. 23–34.
11. *Aviation Week and Space Technology,* 9 November 1992.

14

Arms Control in the Late Twentieth Century: The Latin American Perspective

Cynthia A. Watson

Two preconditions are key to understanding the role of arms control in the Latin American context. First, Latin America, unlike the Middle East or South Asia, has no deep-seated national rivalries that threaten the survival of neighboring states of the region. While tensions between states have existed, the region has had none of the types of disputes that characterize other regions. Second, the persistent concern about outside intervention, particularly by the United States, has made Latin American states willing to sign multilateral agreements intended to restrain more powerful states. Paradoxically, these same states are reluctant to sign on to any international agreements that might be interpreted as discriminatory. Brazil sees international control over nuclear power or the environment as intervention in their affairs and their path of growth.

Latin America has been involved in international arms control since the 1950s. Brazil was heavily involved in the early international moves toward nuclear disarmament prior to the 1964 military coup, which greatly changed the orientation of the country's economic development toward advocating technological growth at all costs. Similarly, various civilian governments in Argentina during the 1950s and 1960s flirted with arms control; however, the Buenos Aires juntas (which lasted from the 1960s through 1983) were more suspicious of such activities by the time the strategic arms control agreements of the 1970s were signed. Other arms control measures, particularly the Antarctic Treaty, have pertained to Latin American states and remain integral to the region's stability today.[1]

The Treaty of Tlatelolco

Latin America is the only region in the world with an existing nuclear-weapon-free zone for states in the region. In the early 1960s, the Brazilian government, with rhetorical support from Pres. Fidel Castro's anti-U.S. government in Havana, advocated a regional approach to maintaining Latin America as a nuclear-free zone. When its developmentalist military seized the government, Mexico assumed the leadership of the movement. This reflected concern over possible ramifications from the Cuban missile crisis (October 1962). Mexico's proximity to the United States, with possible fallout from a U.S.-Soviet nuclear exchange, was clearly a motivating factor for this perspective, but Mexico was also seeking to take an independent path that would allow it to remain outside of U.S. control. Mexico, in cooperation with several South American leaders, argued that the region would not benefit from any deployment or development of nuclear weapons but that the right to engage in peaceful nuclear explosions should be reserved. The movement to endorse a nuclear-free area for the region, from Tierra del Fuego north to the Caribbean Basin and the Rio Grande River, occurred simultaneously with UN efforts to develop the global nuclear Non-Proliferation Treaty (NPT).

The Latin American Nuclear-Free Zone (LANFZ) differed from the NPT in several significant ways. The Free Zone agreement, known formally as the Treaty for the Prohibition of Nuclear Weapons in Latin America (also known as the Treaty of Tlatelolco for its signing in a suburb of Mexico City), called for an inhabited[2] region with no nuclear weapons. Signatories were not to test, use, manufacture, acquire, possess, deploy, or install nuclear weapons. Member states were to put their allowed peaceful activities under the safeguards of the International Atomic Energy Agency (IAEA). Latin America had to come to grips with nonmember states either deploying weapons in the region by bringing the weapons through in transit (such as on warships going through the Panama Canal or around Cape Horn) or locating weapons in colonial areas. As a result, the treaty had two significant protocols.

In the first protocol, states such as Britain, the Netherlands, and the United States agreed not to deploy nuclear weapons in their territories in the region; France signed but did not ratify this protocol. Questions arose about the U.S. role in Puerto Rico and the Panama Canal Zone, but the United States maintained its traditional unwillingness to comment on where its ships might carry nuclear weapons. As a result, the United States delayed ratification of the protocol until 1981.

The second protocol related to the known nuclear states observing the treaty by not bringing their weapons into the region. The acknowledged nuclear powers, including the French and Chinese, signed and ratified this protocol. During the South Atlantic conflict of 1982, many Argentines believed that this protocol was violated by the United Kingdom in deploying nuclear-weapons-carrying vessels to the Falklands/Malvinas area.

Three key states held significant reservations that the treaty would infringe on their sovereignty in "internal development." Cuba reserved the right to protect itself against any treaties that the United States might be using to "enslave" the region. The Argentines and Brazilians voiced considerable skepticism of each other's intentions. Argentina did not ratify the treaty until the early 1990s; its neighbors, Chile and Brazil, ratified the agreement but held reservations until Argentina fully acceded to the accord. Argentina and Brazil were key to the LANFZ's long-term success because they were the only two states with advanced nuclear programs that could have created weapons. An examination of the dynamics of the Brazilian and Argentine nuclear programs follows. Without the prospect of nuclear weapons programs in either state, the Treaty of Tlatelolco would never have been tested as a successful regime and possible model for other regions.

The Argentine-Brazilian Nuclear Rivalry

As noted elsewhere in this volume, nuclear programs have sprung up around the world in an action–reaction cycle, with civilian power programs often serving as the basis for potential weapons development. The same held true in Latin America. Mexico briefly entertained ideas of a civilian nuclear program but abandoned the effort by the early 1970s. The program was too costly and not likely to lead to a truly autonomous Mexican national program. Further, Mexico could in no way justify a nuclear weapons program when neighboring one of the two superpowers; the imbalance made such a prospect absurd. The major petroleum finds of the 1970s completely obviated even a civilian nuclear power program for financial reasons since the vast new supply made petroleum so much cheaper.

Argentina and Brazil have historically seen each other as rivals for prominence in South America. But they have never fought against one another and have had no outstanding border disputes, refugee problems, or other likely reasons to fear one another. Yet the two states have chafed at the idea that their positions as significant powers in the world have been ignored by the international community. Both states suffered from the decline in terms of trade of their exports (for Brazil, coffee and rubber; for Argentina, wheat and beef) because of fluctuations in international markets. The desire to establish an ability to govern their own growth (i.e., to be sovereign) existed throughout Latin America, but especially in these two states.

Argentina

At the end of the 1920s, Argentina had one of the dozen-highest standards of living in the world, with a strong agricultural export economy and a high attraction for European immigrants to the relatively underpopulated country. It was rich in natural resources, and Argentines saw themselves as the most cultured, developed state in Latin America, if not the Western Hemisphere. But the Great Depression cut into Argentina's economic and political stability, fueling a feeling that the country was vulnerable to external manipulation.

The nationalist government of Juan Domingo Perón (1946–1955) took a step in the early 1950s that bred long-term concern about Argentine nuclear intentions. Perón had supported the Axis Powers throughout World War II but claimed after the war to take a *justicialista* (a "third position," which accepted neither U.S. nor Soviet dominance). In May 1951, Perón announced that the Argentines—not the United States or the Soviet Union—had managed to create "a controlled thermonuclear device." Exposed within days as a hoax and a national embarrassment, the affair had two long-lasting effects on Argentina's nuclear aspirations. First, it made the rest of the world suspicious of Perón's interest in developing any sort of nuclear program. Second, the political establishment worked to create a professional agency to control any nuclear program in Argentina.

The Argentines managed to keep the world guessing about their nuclear intentions. The reactor system they chose was a heavy-water system using natural uranium, which seemed to be a means of evading outside control over the production of plutonium and the enrichment of uranium. By the late 1970s, a brutal "national security" dictatorship ruled in Buenos Aires, and three heavy-water nuclear reactors were either operating or under construction. The regime also had a published plan for another dozen reactors by the twenty-first century. This government showed no interest, however, in signing the Treaty of Tlatelolco or in agreeing to outside monitoring through the NPT.

Brazil

The Brazilians were stunned at the implications of the Argentines developing a nuclear capability. They recognized Argentina as a major state but saw their role as that of the primary regional power. The country had a significantly higher population, greater resources and landmass, and tremendous potential for global prowess. As a result of regional goals and potential global aspirations, the Brazilians, in the late 1950s, began working on a nuclear program.

Nuclear activity in Brazil accelerated under the military regime that took power in 1964. This new leadership sought to emphasize the technological development of Brazil and saw nuclear growth as a way to make its mark in the international system. Additionally, the 1973–1974 Organization of Petroleum Exporting Countries (OPEC) price increases hit Brazil hard because the country had to borrow money to buy increasingly expensive petroleum, thus initiating the debt crisis. Creation of a nuclear energy grid to reduce imports of petroleum was an obvious way to enhance national security and to avoid vulnerability to the political and economic whims of outsiders.

In an attempt to avoid the growing international concern about nuclear proliferation following the Cuban missile crisis, the Brazilians pursued a parallel nuclear weapons program to accompany the open nuclear power industry. Brazil created international concern when it bought a complete nuclear fuel cycle from the West Germans in 1975. Coming a year after India's peaceful nuclear explosion, this Brazilian-German deal was a motivating force for the United States to orchestrate the creation of the London Suppliers Club to control nuclear technology (see Chapter 9).

In the early 1980s, events seemed to indicate that the nuclear rivalry was accelerating. The nuclear program in Argentina had been controlled for much of its existence by the navy. The junta in Buenos Aires began discussing the idea of a nuclear-powered submarine at the time when its perceived aggression against Britain in the Falklands/Malvinas war (1982) raised concern that this was a covert weapons program. The Brazilian military reacted by trying to increase its indigenous nuclear capability while also working on a parallel program for weapons. The programs became important sources of national pride for the ruling military regimes.

The Evolution of Nuclear Cooperation

Both nuclear programs were pared back dramatically by budget woes that hit in the mid-1980s, following civilian resumption of power in both states. But even prior to that dramatic change, the militaries in Brasília and Buenos Aires had actually begun a dialogue on their nuclear programs, which involved sharing information on the indigenous technologies under development in the two states.

The Argentine president, Raúl Alfonsín (1983–1989), sought to restrain much of the military's extreme nationalism, including that related to nuclear issues, but he refused to agree to the NPT because of its discriminatory nature.[3] The president did, however, become an active participant in several initiatives to discuss curtailing nuclear weapons, such as the Four Continents Initiative of the mid-1980s, which aimed at banning nuclear testing. Largely because of Alfonsín's positions, Argentina is also a part of the Australia Group to limit the export of biological and chemical weapons (see Chapter 10).

Building on these ties, the civilian presidents began a series of summits in the mid-1980s, with heavy emphasis on nuclear discussions. These initial confidence-building meetings led ultimately not only to nuclear cooperation but also to Argentina's decision to ratify the Treaty of Tlatelolco. Additionally, these meetings were crucial to the creation of Mercosur, the Southern Cone free market of Uruguay, Argentina, Brazil, and Paraguay. This market had built trust and stability, which made any chances of backing out of the nuclear cooperation less likely. The overwhelming desire on the part of Brazil and Argentina to promote economic integration through Mercosur has done much to overcome historic suspicion in the two states, including that dealing with nuclear affairs.

The one chilly moment in the relationship occurred in 1989 when Brazilian president Fernando Collor de Mello announced that he had discovered the scope of the military's secret weapons development programs. His announcement indicated that the parallel weapons program had not ceased in the mid-1980s, as the nuclear summits between José Sarney, then president of Brazil, and President Alfonsín of Argentina had indicated.

Nuclear programs still exist in Argentina and Brazil, but they are significantly smaller and are now genuine civilian power programs. Economic integration and increased trust have paid off. In November 1994, both states agreed to consider signing the NPT. Each has become somewhat more sensitive to the overall global emphasis on international regimes, such as that for nonproliferation under the auspices of the NPT.[4] Argentina became a full member of the NPT in December 1994, but Brazil still will not join on sovereignty grounds. The remainder of Latin America, with Cuba and a handful of Caribbean island-states as exceptions, is already party to the NPT and remains firmly committed to this arms control measure.

The complete implementation of the Latin American Nuclear-Free Zone and the nuclear accommodation between Brazil and Argentina represent important evolution in the region. The entire area has shown remarkable transformation as civilian, popularly elected regimes have moved simultaneously to ease nuclear tensions. The nuclear-free zone regime of Latin America is unique—the region is the only area of the populated world that abolished nuclear weapons before these weapons were ever developed or deployed in the region. But the lessons for the rest of the world are that economic integration and civilian regimes go hand in hand with the desire for joining international regimes to enhance nuclear arms control.

Lessons for Arms Control

One cannot grasp the role of arms control in Latin America without considering its position in the international community.[5] In the post–Cold War world,

Latin America faced a tremendous debt, much of which was owed to U.S. banks. Carlos Menem's Argentine government, like virtually all others in the region, no longer could try to play off U.S. economic proposals against those of the Eastern bloc as a manner of getting economic benefits. The United States and its economic system represent the only model that is currently appealing to states desperate to achieve stability, economic growth, and development. Policies such as cooperating with renegade Iraq would threaten the relationship with the states from whom Argentina wants economic concessions and freer trade. It is difficult to overstate the vulnerability under which Latin America has been operating over the past decade due to the depths of the debt crisis. This is a region that has been subjected to frequent military regimes, which often assumed power because they seemed more able to run the government and the economy. The new civilian governments remain keenly aware of the need to succeed, which means not taking on positions that will threaten economic growth. Should the market model disappoint Latin Americans, however, old policies and antagonisms would likely revive.

This region of the world appears less likely to arm because few traditional national security threats exist, but the 1995 Ecuador-Peru conflict was a chilling reminder that wars can occur. It must be remembered, however, that national security can take on a broader role than merely defending borders. Governments are increasingly asked to improve the standard of living as a part of national security. The traditional issues associated with arms control may no longer apply in this area of the world. This does not mean that conflicts will not result, but states may use a different calculus in resolving them.

Latin American states are moving toward complete participation in various global arms control regimes. One important caveat, however, remains. These commitments have grown when democratic, popularly elected governments were in power. While democracy seems to be more permanent than it has in the region for generations, the reality is that the governments remain in power only so long as they provide economic, social, and political benefits to the whole of their societies.

Suggested Reading

Atkins, G. Pope. *Latin America in the International Political System*. Boulder, Colo.: Westview Press, 1989. This is one of the best treatments of Latin America's relationship to international arms control regimes.

Milenky, Edward. *Argentina's Foreign Policies*. Boulder, Colo.: Westview Press, 1978. While dated, this is a good text on how Argentina has developed its relationships with the world and with the rest of the region. Particularly useful in understanding why this republic was for so long hostile to U.S. views on arms control.

Spector, Leonard S., and Jacqueline Smith. *Nuclear Ambitions*. Boulder, Colo.: Westview Press, 1990. Last in a series (supported by the Carnegie Endowment) on developments in arms proliferation around the world. Discusses shifts in the Argentine and Brazilian views on nuclear proliferation and adherence to arms control regimes.

UN Department for Disarmament Affairs. *Nuclear Weapons: A Comprehensive Study.* New York: United Nations, 1991. Good primer on the development of nuclear weapons in states around the world.

Watson, Cynthia Ann. "Nuclear Development in Argentina: Capabilities and Intentions." Unpublished dissertation. University of Notre Dame, Ind., 1984. Laid out the Argentine nuclear program in detail, addressing the civilian options that allowed the international community some concern during the South Atlantic conflict of 1982.

Notes

Thanks to Etel Solingen and Anna Roque. The views expressed here are those of the author alone, not the National War College, National Defense University, Department of Defense, or any branch of the U.S. government.

1. Latin America has been an important part of the Antarctic regime. Chile and Argentina are two states that consider their claims on the Antarctic to be an aspect of national sovereignty. As two of the original signatory states, these Latin American countries agreed not to militarize the continent. In an era of increased nationalism relating to other claims in the South Atlantic, the military government in Buenos Aires did not renege on its Antarctic commitment. Any revisions of the Antarctic Treaty (1959) would generate considerable interest throughout Latin America, however, as other states are increasingly interested in potential resources of the area.

2. The Antarctic Treaty actually was the first treaty to denuclearize (and demilitarize) an area of the world, but the Antarctic region has no permanent population.

3. Part of the reason that Alfonsín was fundamentally different as an Argentine leader was that he rejected many of the positions that the military had on nuclear proliferation. Rather than feel constrained by the possibility of the armed forces seizing power from him, as had happened to many civilian regimes between 1930 and 1983, Alfonsín could take an independent position. His personal history of resisting the military on human rights, along with his status as the first elected civilian president after the military had discredited itself, were keys to his new power.

4. Newly elected Brazilian president Fernando Henrique Cardoso expressed more caution than did his Argentine counterparts, who seemed to have abandoned prior concerns about the discriminatory nature of the NPT. Foreign Broadcast Information Service, *Latin America*-94-215 (Washington, D.C.: U.S. Government Printing Office, 7 November 1994), p. 29.

5. Latin American states have bought a relatively modest number of conventional arms sold in the past 50 years. Indigenous arms industries in Chile, Argentina, and, in particular, Brazil have produced arms for domestic use as well as for export. The end of the Cold War, however, proved devastating for these industries as the more traditional arms merchant states (such as the United States and Europe) were confronted with excess capacity and a desire to export; Latin American exporters could not compete with the more sophisticated weaponry.

15

Nuclear Arms Control in South Asia

Peter R. Lavoy

Having already fought three wars and more than once having flirted with a fourth, India and Pakistan are often viewed as the two states most likely to wage a nuclear war. This may be an exaggeration. The risk of nuclear conflict in South Asia is significant, but it can be controlled with the effective application of arms control to stabilize nuclear deterrence between India and Pakistan.

This chapter examines existing Indian and Pakistani efforts to manage their nuclear competition. It argues that a durable nuclear peace in South Asia rests on the ability of these adversaries to overcome a formidable array of political, psychological, and bureaucratic obstacles to establishing an effective nuclear arms control regime in the region.

Washington and Moscow regulated the dangers of their global nuclear rivalry through a series of unilateral actions, reciprocal measures, and formally negotiated agreements to establish stable political and military relations. This nuclear arms control process took place over several decades.[1] It is not surprising that India and Pakistan have been slow to develop a stable nuclear order in South Asia. In response to recent military crises, Indian and Pakistani leaders have learned to conduct military operations more cautiously (they have concluded several confidence-building measures [CBMs] on issues of marginal military importance), but they do not yet accept arms control as a way to enhance military security and stabilize strained political relations. With both states engaged in costly defense preparations, fears of surprise attack, military escalation, and even nuclear conflict loom over the subcontinent.

Although fashioned first to stabilize the nuclear competition between the superpowers, nuclear arms control is now suitable for South Asia. Arms control and CBMs can help India and Pakistan avoid a war that neither side wants, minimize the costs and risks of their arms competition, and curtail the scope and violence of conflict should it recur in South Asia.[2] Regional arms control is important because each side engages in coercive strategic behavior—provocative troop movements and military exercises near tense borders, alleged support for militant groups in unstable regions of the other country, and cross-border firing along the line of control in Kashmir (the de facto India-Pakistan border)—and yet both governments know they cannot afford escalation to full-scale combat, much less nuclear conflict. Here we analyze the opportunities, incentives, and obstacles for a specific set of concepts and practices created by the superpowers during the Cold War to operate in the strategic and cultural context of contemporary South Asia.

Neither India nor Pakistan has openly manufactured nuclear forces, but both nations have nuclear bomb programs and could, on short notice, assemble and use nuclear weapons. India has a large quantity of bomb-grade plutonium, and few doubt the ability of Indian scientists to make nuclear weapons following the country's 1974 "peaceful nuclear experiment." On the other side of the border, Pakistan's enrichment plant at Kahuta is believed to have produced enough weapons-grade uranium for several nuclear bombs. Because of concerns about ongoing Pakistani efforts to develop these weapons, the U.S. government terminated all economic and military assistance to Pakistan in October 1990. Pakistan and India each have aircraft capable of delivering nuclear weapons to targets inside the other's territory; and both states are developing, or seeking to obtain, ballistic missiles that might also be able to deliver nuclear warheads.

Several confidence-building measures have been proposed for India and Pakistan: a regional cutoff of fissile material production, a regional nuclear test ban, safeguards on new and existing nuclear facilities, extension of the nuclear no-attack pledge to cover population centers, enhanced international security assurances, regional risk reduction centers, upgraded hotlines between military and political officials, and regular exchanges of military personnel. However, even the best ideas cannot succeed in the absence of a stable arms control culture.

Effective and durable arms control requires India, Pakistan, and the United States—the only outside power capable of facilitating regional arms control—to develop the institutions and attitudes required for nuclear stability. Five obstacles impede efforts to establish this culture in South Asia: (1) the diplomatic preoccupation with nuclear disarmament to the detriment of modest but feasible nuclear restraint measures; (2) reluctance to acknowledge the military purposes of Indian and Pakistani nuclear programs, precluding a realistic debate about reasonable limits on nuclear forces and strategies; (3) an unwillingness of either state to pursue arms control as a vital source of national security; (4) an inability to transform the India-

Pakistan strategic dialogue from tacit to explicit bargaining; and (5) the persistence of resentment and defiance among India, Pakistan, and the United States. These obstacles are examined below.

Inertia of Disarmament Diplomacy

A major barrier to new thinking about nuclear deterrence and arms control in the region is the persistence of the long-espoused ideas of disarmament and denuclearization among the three key actors involved: India, Pakistan, and the United States. Traditional diplomatic postures on regional nuclear issues are firmly entrenched in the foreign policy bureaucracies of each state. Continued calls for the elimination of nuclear arms at the global level by New Delhi, and regionally by Islamabad and Washington, inhibit new thinking about arms control. Winds of change are blowing in South Asia (experts in all three states argue for regional arms control over disarmament) but this new thinking does not enjoy wide support among policy elites.

India: Global Disarmament

India has long been an outspoken opponent of nuclear deterrence and arms control. Even before independence, Jawaharlal Nehru campaigned to ban nuclear weapons. Like Mahatma Gandhi, Nehru argued that nuclear violence could not be countered by threats of nuclear retaliation; this would spell suicide for humanity. Every Indian prime minister since has viewed deterrence as immoral and as an irrational basis for national security in the nuclear age. This opinion was expressed clearly in the Delhi Declaration of Rajiv Gandhi and Mikhail Gorbachev in 1986 and in India's 1988 Action Plan on nuclear disarmament. In welcoming the 1993 START II agreement, India urged the "nuclear weapon states to re-examine doctrines of nuclear deterrence which have been used by them in (the) past to justify expansion of their nuclear arsenals."[3]

India makes a sharp distinction between disarmament and arms control, rejecting the latter as an incomplete and diversionary response to the nuclear danger.[4] Largely ritualistic from the 1940s through the 1970s, India's support of nuclear disarmament grew stronger in the 1980s. Despite mounting evidence of Pakistan's efforts to acquire the bomb in that decade, the string of political benefits Islamabad gained through its espousal of regional denuclearization, mounting global pressures on India to embrace regional arms restraint, and increased domestic pressure for India to declare itself as a nuclear weapon power, New Delhi still advocated global nuclear disarmament. This policy remains intact even as world attention has shifted from East-West arms control to regional nonproliferation. Having long viewed horizontal proliferation (rise in the number of nuclear-armed states) and vertical proliferation (expansion and modernization of existing nuclear arsenals) as two sides of the same coin, India is more outspoken about the latter and insists that both problems must be solved simultaneously. Stressing the importance of equity in global non-proliferation efforts, Indian officials still see the global elimination of nuclear forces as the only fair and effective way to curb the spread of nuclear capabilities. Popular support for this policy line, the bureaucracy's resistance to rethink it, and the reluctance of political leaders to revise it are three factors that sustain India's disarmament diplomacy.

Pakistan: Regional Disarmament

As India stresses global denuclearization, the idea of regional disarmament preoccupies Islamabad. Pakistan did not participate actively in the global debates on nuclear arms during the 1950s. When Pakistan became alarmed about India's nuclear potential in the 1960s, however, Islamabad initiated a campaign to draw international attention to the military implications of India's civil nuclear program and to raise the diplomatic costs to India of developing nuclear arms. Although the policy means have changed over time, these aims still guide Pakistan's nuclear diplomacy.

During the 1960s and 1970s Pakistan sought to prevent India from go-ing nuclear by encouraging international measures to stop the spread of military nuclear capabilities to all nonnuclear weapon states. Pakistan was an early backer of a nuclear nonproliferation treaty; in 1962 Pres. Mohammad Ayub Khan urged the world community to devise "a treaty to outlaw the further spread of nuclear weapons."[5] While acknowledging the need to con-trol vertical proliferation, Pakistani diplomat Agha Shahi said that the top priority was to curb horizontal proliferation (a problem he saw as a greater security threat to nonnuclear weapon states) and insisted that "to tie the question of non-proliferation of nuclear weapons to other measures restrict-ing the nuclear arms race could only result in an impasse."[6] In the end, Paki-stan refused to sign the NPT because it was not binding on India, which refused to sign, and because it contained no mechanism for assuring the security of Pakistan and other nonnuclear weapon states.

Shortly after the NPT failure, and less than a year after Pakistan's loss in the 1971 war, Islamabad launched a two-track policy to match and contain India's growing nuclear might. In early 1972, Prime Minister Zulfikar Ali Bhutto se-cretly directed his top scientists to start work on a nuclear bomb program. Sev-eral months later Bhutto initiated the second track—a bid to obtain Indian denuclearization through a diplomatic campaign to rid South Asia of nuclear weapons. Originally announced at the unveiling of a Pakistani nuclear reactor in late 1972, a South Asia Nuclear-Weapon-Free Zone plan was submitted by Pakistan to the UN in November 1974, six months after India's nuclear test.

Pakistan continued to pursue each policy track in the 1980s. As part of his diplomatic offensive against India, Gen. Zia ul-Haq proposed six measures for regional disarmament: mutual renunciation of nuclear arms; inspection of each side's nuclear facilities; simultaneous acceptance of IAEA full-scope safeguards; joint accession to the NPT; a bilateral nuclear test ban; and a multilateral conference under UN auspices on nuclear nonproliferation in South Asia.[7] Prime Minister Nawaz Sharif added another proposal in 1991 when he called for five powers (the United States, Russia, China, India, and Pakistan) to discuss the nuclear issue in South Asia. India has rejected all of these regional nuclear disarmament proposals.

The United States: Nuclear Nonproliferation

As part of its global nonproliferation policy, the United States advocates nuclear disarmament for India and Pakistan. U.S. efforts to curb the bomb's spread rest on the premise that new nuclear forces are inherently dangerous. While nonproliferation has been a steady goal, Washington has changed its strategy for controlling the bomb's spread globally and in South Asia.[8] Breaking with early U.S. efforts to pressure India and Pakistan to join the NPT, the Clinton administration has urged these nuclear holdouts first to cap, then over time to reduce, and finally to eliminate their nuclear arms capabilities. In pursuit of this policy, Washington stresses nonproliferation in bilateral discussions with New Delhi and Islamabad; it urges them to stop producing fissile material for weapons purposes; it withholds economic and military aid from Pakistan until nonproliferation progress is verified; it supports high-level Indo-Pakistani talks on regional security and nonproliferation; it presses China not to aid Pakistan's nuclear or missile efforts; and it engages other states (Russia, Britain, France, Germany, and Japan) to hold bilateral nonproliferation discussions with India and Pakistan.

Through early 1995, Washington had little to show for these efforts. Despite improved relations with both countries, particularly after the 1994 visit of Prime Minister P. V. Narasimha Rao to the United States and the January 1995 visit to the region by Secretary of Defense William Perry, tensions over the nuclear issue remain high between Washington and the South Asian states. But as U.S. officials come to accept that nuclear disarmament may no longer be a feasible goal for this region, Washington appears gradually to be pushing for India and Pakistan to practice arms control. Secretary Perry suggested as much in a January 1995 speech: "I recognized that the nuclear ambitions of India and Pakistan flow from a dynamic that we are unlikely to be able to influence in the near term. We might be able to (gain) influence over the long haul, but only if in the meantime we can prevent the tension from flaring into another conflict."[9]

Washington's pragmatic line is finding supporters in surprising places. Conceding that nuclear disarmament is beyond reach globally and in South

Asia, and convinced that current diplomatic approaches are counterproductive, a new group of Indian and Pakistani defense specialists back arms control as a means to enhance national security and to avoid nuclear war. Indian military experts K. Subrahmanyam and Gen. K. Sundarji accept the permanence of nuclear forces in the region and stress the need for India and Pakistan to learn to live peacefully in such an environment.[10] Although the Indian government still pushes global nuclear disarmament and is not prepared to act on the nuclear realist perspective, it is showing greater flexibility and pragmatism. After the 1990 military crisis over Kashmir, New Delhi embraced the concept of confidence building with Pakistan; several CBMs were negotiated and implemented by the two sides over the next three years (e.g., a ban on flights within 5 kilometers of the line of control in Kashmir, prenotification of military exercises on either side of the border, restrictions on the size and location of military exercises).[11] In Pakistan, too, there are isolated signs of willingness to move beyond the traditional policy of regional denuclearization to stabilize regional security. For example, retired general K. M. Arif has urged the Indian and Pakistani governments to consider turning the region into a "nuclear safe zone (that is, a region where nuclear deterrence is stable)."[12] No government yet accepts this plan, but the tide is turning: officials in Washington, New Delhi, and Islamabad now seriously consider various nuclear arms control proposals if they do not yet embrace them.

Nuclear Opacity

The common reluctance of India and Pakistan to openly discuss their force capabilities and intentions poses two problems for regional nuclear security. The first complication concerns the strategic instabilities arising out of covert nuclear forces. The second problem is that nuclear opacity impedes Indian and Pakistani efforts to openly propose, negotiate, and accept nuclear arms control agreements.[13] This opacity leads policymakers to work out in private measures that would be politically unpopular if publicized in either country.

Strategic Stability

Many experts believe that secrecy concerning nuclear capabilities, force employment doctrines, targeting plans, and escalation thresholds weakens deterrence and creates other political and military problems. Shai Feldman argues that covert nuclear bomb programs entail closed decisionmaking without wider scrutiny, dominance of the military in the formulation of doctrine, biases toward offense and preemption, and strained crisis management and nuclear signaling.[14] Sundarji sees two strategic problems of nuclear opacity for South Asia: the first due to the possibility of a war between India and Pakistan being triggered through miscalculation of each other's nuclear status, as well as ignorance of the nuclear doctrines that the two countries are likely to go by, which would culminate in a tragic nuclear exchange; and the second due to the difficulties of ensuring the safety of nuclear warheads and the prevention of unauthorized use when in a clandestine state.[15]

On the other hand, nuclear opacity probably is required to preserve nonweaponized deterrence between India and Pakistan. George Perkovich and others contend that a condition of mutual deterrence deriving from the power of India and Pakistan to assemble nuclear arms quickly can be a steady source of regional security.[16] These analysts recognize, however, that the stability of nonweaponized deterrence requires Islamabad and New Delhi to undertake a demanding set of confidence-building measures to assure each other and the international community that they have not built weapons and that they seek a situation of mutual security.

Arms Control

In South Asia, nuclear arms have a meaning that extends well beyond their value as military and strategic bargaining instruments. Large portions of the region's informed population see civilian and military nuclear programs as components of, and indeed symbols for, national sovereignty and security. Thus it is difficult for Indian and Pakistani politicians to make public concessions on nuclear issues. If New Delhi and Islamabad move to embrace nuclear arms control, it will be difficult for them to cultivate popular support for measures that are understood by very few citizens owing to years of government secrecy. Opaque nuclear proliferation in South Asia may have constrained a regional arms race and provided policymakers flexibility in negotiations, but it has done so at the cost of preventing Indian and Pakistani leaders from cultivating domestic constituencies for nuclear arms control and from identifying the precise nuclear security problems that are in the most need of control.

Existing Agreements and Limitations

Neither India nor Pakistan has accepted limits on military activities that either country realistically might wish to pursue at some point in the future. Past and existing Indo-Pakistani treaties and confidence-building measures have helped to reduce tensions and resolve troublesome disputes but have not significantly altered the sources of military rivalry, stabilized nuclear security, nor seriously constrained the strategic behavior of either country. Arms control does not yet play a central role in South Asian military and nuclear affairs.

Islamabad and New Delhi concluded their most consequential military pacts after their three wars. The costs of conflict forced them to negotiate measures for troop disengagements and to make minor territorial adjustments along disputed borders; but neither side treated these settlements as conclusive since they did not solve basic problems—especially those underlying the Kashmir dispute.[17]

India and Pakistan jointly observe several military confidence-building measures. Driven to avoid another violent conflict in the aftermath of the second India-Pakistan war, the two states agreed in 1966 to provide prior notification of border exercises. In 1982 they established the Indo-Pakistan Joint Commission. Designed to facilitate normal relations between the two states by creating a forum for bilateral cooperation in communications, consular affairs, cultural exchanges, trade, smuggling, and, more recently, drug trafficking, the commission convened several formal sessions at the foreign minister level and more sessions at lower levels.

As separatist violence in Indian-held Kashmir accelerated in 1990, Indian and Pakistani troops fought armed skirmishes along the line of control. The heightened risk of a fourth India-Pakistan war quickly focused government attention in Islamabad and New Delhi, and even more so in Washington, on the need for military confidence-building measures. After a year of little progress, the foreign secretaries of Pakistan and India met in New Delhi in April 1991 and signed two major agreements, one pledging nonviolation by military aircraft of each other's airspace and the other requiring each side to provide advance information about any military exercises and troop movements along common borders. India and Pakistan subsequently established a formal line of communication (hotline) between their military commanders.

Despite this impressive paperwork, few regional CBMs operate according to plan. Both sides violate no-fly zones for combat aircraft and helicopters to map terrain across the border. The agreement on prior notification of military exercises reportedly has been violated. Abuses of the military hotline also are reported: after opening fire and inflicting casualties on enemy troops in Kashmir and on the Siachin glacier the attacking party can call the enemy on the hotline to prevent hostilities from widening. Military and civilian officials in the region remain skeptical of arms control as a means to enhance national security.

Bargaining

In the 1980s India and Pakistan enjoyed strong political leaders who had sufficient maneuvering room at home and the confidence needed to engage the other side and to deescalate crises. It is not obvious that the tacit bargaining that worked well in the 1980s can be managed as effectively in the present era. Religious revivalist outbursts, spy scandals, communal rioting and bombings, and low-intensity conflict in Kashmir have disrupted the political dialogue. The transformation of domestic politics in each country, marked by the rise of the religious right and the erosion of national leadership, makes it necessary to formalize arms control negotiations.

The effectiveness of tacit bargaining depends on the current state of relations between India and Pakistan and on the strength of each side's political leaders. Unfortunately, India and Pakistan have had weak and unstable governments for several years, and there are no signs that political conditions are improving in either country. In response to a July 1993 call for bilateral tension-reducing talks by Pakistan's interim president, Wasim Sajjad, for example, Indian foreign minister Salman Khursheed stated: "India wants to ease these tensions, but there is a period of uncertainty in Pakistan. For the present let us wait and watch."[18] This attitude remains. Unilateral restraint and tacit CBMs are important in any adversarial relationship, especially when the threat of nuclear war is involved. But arms control must be formally negotiated and ratified if it is to garner widespread domestic support and survive sudden changes in political leadership, popular sentiment, and international events.

Strategic Understanding and Reciprocity

The final barrier to creating a viable arms control regime in South Asia is the prevalence of resentment and defiance among India, Pakistan, and the United States. Specific conflicts have confounded amicable relations among these countries, but, more important, each state often acts with moralism and sometimes hypocrisy. The lack of trust and understanding between India and Pakistan is well known; neither side is willing to initiate a relationship of reciprocated good gestures. The animosity created by differences over the nuclear issue between Washington and India and Pakistan is also destructive. U.S. nonproliferation pressure inhibits open discussions between India and Pakistan on regional nuclear security. Pakistanis resent the imposition of the 1985 Pressler amendment (the U.S. legislation banning economic and military aid to Pakistan because of Pakistan's nuclear weapons activities), which they see as discriminatory, and Indians object as strongly to U.S. pressure on New Delhi to join the NPT and curb space and missile activities. As a result, much Indian and Pakistani diplomatic energy goes to diverting U.S. pressure rather than thinking about and proposing creative ideas to promote regional nuclear security.

At a deeper psychological level, the sense of U.S. and collective Western pressure on nonproliferation perpetuates anti-Western feelings. Such sentiments could produce a situation far more serious than that created by the "nuclear nationalism" that presently exists in India and Pakistan. Despite

fragmentation of the domestic fabric in both nations, the defense of national sovereignty, which the nuclear programs symbolize, is a strong rally-
ing cry. In a colonial region that has a long history of anti-Western popu-
lism, the U.S. strategy of technology denial and punitive actions has the
potential to trigger a new round of anti-Western activism.

Conclusion

The advent of nuclear weapons capabilities in South Asia poses new risks for
India and Pakistan. The United States and the Soviet Union were able to manage similar risks during the Cold War, but not easily. After several dangerous
episodes (the Cuban missile crisis in particular), Washington and Moscow eventually learned to bring their foreign policy practices, defense programs, and
military behavior in line with the requirement of avoiding nuclear war. India
and Pakistan are now on the verge of undergoing a similar learning process.
The outcome remains to be seen, but this chapter suggests that the risk of nuclear
war in South Asia can be controlled with the effective application of arms control measures by India, Pakistan, and the United States to stabilize the emerging
nuclear deterrence on the subcontinent.

Suggested Reading

Cohen, Stephen P. *The Indian Army: Its Contribution to the Development of a Nation.*
    Berkeley: University of California Press, 1971.
————. *The Pakistan Army.* Berkeley: University of California Press, 1984.
Krepon, Michael, and Amit Sevak, eds. *Crisis Prevention, Confidence Building, and
    Reconciliation in South Asia.* New York: St. Martin's Press, 1995.

Notes

1. See Chapters 1 and 5 for elaboration on this point.
2. These are the three arms control goals that Thomas C. Schelling and Morton
H. Halperin identified in *Strategy and Arms Control* (New York: Twentieth Century
Fund, 1961), p. 1.
3. Indian press statement, 12 January 1993; reprinted in FBIS-NES-93-008,
13 January 1993.
4. For more on the distinction between disarmament and arms control, see
the Introduction of this volume.
5. President Ayub Khan's statement to the UN General Assembly is quoted in
Hameed A. K. Rai, *Pakistan in the United Nations* (Lahore: Aziz Publishers, 1979), p.
241.
6. Quoted in *Documents on Disarmament, 1967* (Washington, D.C.: U.S. Government Printing Office, 1968), p. 671; and *Documents on Disarmament, 1968*, p.

318.

7. Ali Sarwar Naqvi, "Pakistan: Seeking Regional Peace and Progress in Non-Nuclear South Asia," *Arms Control Today* 23, no. 5 (June 1993), p. 11.

8. Peter R. Lavoy, "Learning and the Evolution of Cooperation in U.S. and Soviet Nonproliferation Activities," in George W. Breslauer and Philip E. Tetlock, eds., *Learning in U.S. and Soviet Foreign Policy* (Boulder, Colo.: Westview Press, 1991), pp. 735–783.

9. Quoted in *Defense News* (6–12 February 1995), p. 16.

10. K. Subrahmanyam, "An Indo-Pak Nuclear Restraint Regime," *Economic Times*, 30 September 1992 and 1 October 1992; "No First Use Policy," *Economic Times*, 26 May 1993; and Gen. K. Sundarji, "The Nuclear Threat," *India Today*, 30 November 1990, "Nuclear Realpolitik," *India Today*, 31 August 1991, and "A New Equation," *India Today*, 31 October 1991.

11. For a thorough discussion of these measures, see Michael Krepon, Dominique M. McCoy, and Matthew C. J. Rudolph, eds., "A Handbook of Confidence-Building Measures for Regional Security," Handbook No. 1 (Washington, D.C.: Henry L. Stimson Center, 1993).

12. See Gen. Khalid Mahmud Arif's articles in *Dawn* (Karachi): "The New Global Scenario," 3 February 1992, and "The Nuclear Tussle," 30 December 1992.

13. *Nuclear opacity* is the term used to describe the nuclear policies of India, Pakistan, Israel, and possibly other emerging nuclear states. Opaque nuclear states deny possession of nuclear weapons, do not make direct nuclear threats, do not deploy nuclear weapons, and do not openly debate nuclear plans. For further discussion, see Avner Cohen and Benjamin Frankel, *Opaque Nuclear Proliferation*, Benjamin Frankel, ed. (London: Frank Cass, 1991), pp. 14–44.

14. Shai Feldman, *Israeli Nuclear Deterrence* (New York: Columbia University Press, 1982).

15. K. Sundarji, "Former Military Chief Discusses Nuclear Options," *India Express*, 20 December 1992.

16. Perkovich, "A Nuclear Third Way in South Asia," *Foreign Policy*, no. 91 (Summer 1993); see also *Preventing Nuclear Proliferation in South Asia* (Asia Society Study Report, 1995).

17. Douglas C. Makeig, "War, No-War, and the India-Pakistan Negotiating Process," *Pacific Affairs* 60, no. 2 (Summer 1987), p. 272.

18. Quoted in "No Talks Until Stable Government in Pakistan: India," *Nation*, 28 July 1993.

PART 5

Conclusion

16

The Evolving Nature of Arms Control in the Post–Cold War World

Jeffrey A. Larsen

Arms control is an evolutionary concept. Throughout its lifetime it has continually changed emphases and moved into new areas of consideration. This is especially true of the metamorphosis seen since the end of the Cold War. Arms control has been a core intellectual pursuit of national security theorists for over 40 years, and it is one that is unlikely to disappear as the result of changed relationships between great powers. Indeed, as several of this book's authors point out, arms control is likely to become more important and relevant in the post–Cold War era than it was earlier.

Gregory Rattray's broad definition of arms control has served us well throughout the course of this book: "Arms control is a process involving declared steps by a state to enhance security through cooperation with other states." As we examined past efforts at arms control and looked ahead at the likely direction such efforts will take in the future, we saw that arms control steps can be unilateral, bilateral, or multilateral; cooperation can be implicit as well as explicit. This definition will continue to work as we make the transition into the post–Cold War era and find new ways to achieve arms control through its myriad aspects. In attempting to address the negative effects of the security dilemma between states, arms control attenuates those effects and hastens the understanding between political entities. Reducing and possibly eliminating such military efforts gets to the core of solutions to the security dilemma. Arms control shall remain a useful package of tools in the grab bag of a state's political capabilities to influence other states and ensure its own security.

There is value to the process of arms control that transcends agreements and treaties. The synergies that arise out of arms control negotiations and implementation can create new levels of trust and cooperation between international actors. This finding, while not new, needs to be given due consideration by critics of the arms control process and to be publicized by advocates of closer international links and continued negotiations.

Review of the Book's Major Findings

We began our study with a group of chapters that collectively laid out the basic underlying principles of this concept called arms control. Kerry Kartchner reminded us that the early pioneers of the field of arms control developed basic assumptions that explained why we "do" arms control. Arms control must, first and foremost, be a means to the end of greater national security, rather than an end in itself. It can pursue one or more of three objectives: reduce the likelihood of war, save money and resources otherwise spent on defenses, and reduce the consequences of war should one break out. These basic goals underlie all the discussion that follows the first chapter and are accepted as valid by all the authors of this book.

Part 2 turned to arms control's role during the Cold War. The 45-year confrontation between the world's two superpowers resulted in each side amassing huge stocks of weapons. Preventing or controlling their use, limiting the effects thereof, saving money by not buying more than necessary to maintain deterrence, and eventually abolishing many of these weapons as political relations warmed were all goals taken directly from arms control. Arms control negotiations, implementation, verification, and compliance were pivotal aspects of the bipolar relationship of the Cold War, and each of our authors examined one aspect of this history and the legacy for the future.

Parts 3 and 4 turned to the future of arms control and the way it can deal with threats like proliferation and regional conflict. We looked at the role and usefulness of arms control in the areas of nuclear proliferation, conventional arms transfers, and chemical and biological weapons and in the context of regional competition.

This book covered a lot of ground, from the conceptual basis for arms control to the different types and areas of arms control emphasis. Arms control accomplishes many different objectives, but it also fails regularly, for a number of reasons. It is most successful when those involved in the process recognize the nuances of the context for a particular initiative. Despite this situational uniqueness, there are nevertheless various recurring themes and trends in arms control, which are identified in this book. Among these are the following:

• *The U.S.-Russian strategic balance is no longer the preeminent arms control concern.* The end of the Cold War and the diminished threat from the former Soviet empire means that the imperative to manage the strategic nuclear balance between the superpowers has disappeared, or at least diminished. Strategic nuclear weapons are no longer the major issue facing arms controllers—new concerns have replaced this core fear.

James Wirtz showed us that arms control did succeed during the Cold War—a remarkable outcome. Past results, however, should not lead to complacency over the future. Threats still abound in the post–Cold War world, and in different guises than both sides grew accustomed to during the superpower rivalry. Whether arms control can meet these new challenges is an open question, one that scholars and practitioners of national security policy must address in order to adapt the traditional tenets of arms control to this new world. The United States, in particular, must be wary of thinking of new threats only in terms of the benchmark provided by Russian forces. National security policy must meet the actual threat posed by the military capabilities of current opponents, not the waning capability of former enemies. Nor should the United States be lulled into false security by believing that recent progress in arms control is irreversible. Policymakers must recognize when arms control can help one's national security and when it must be abandoned.

• *The validity of Cold War agreements is, in some cases, in question.* A question arises over the validity of old agreements in this new world. To what extent does an agreement signed by the Soviet Union still hold legal or moral weight in an international arena where the Soviet Union has disappeared? Do superpower agreements focused on controlling large weapons systems distract policymakers from dealing with new, different security concerns, such as the smuggling of nuclear materials? How valid is an agreement such as the CFE Treaty, negotiated between NATO and the Warsaw Pact in a divided Europe, when none of the starting assumptions still hold? These are unanswered but critical questions.

• *The legacy of the Cold War lives on in the emphasis placed on the control and dismantlement of the strategic arsenals of the formerly antagonistic superpowers.* Forrest Waller reminded us that Cold War strategic arms control "began boldly and badly, but finished well." He postulated alternative directions that strategic arms control might take. The United States may choose to simply emphasize the implementation of existing arms control agreements. This would be an easy option; the desire to implement the START Treaties is nearly universal. Or, the United States could pursue deeper reductions in the residual nuclear arsenals of both superpowers. This option is more controversial and would require a reassessment of current nuclear doctrine—one that goes beyond the 1993 U.S. Nuclear Posture Review.

• *Bilateral negotiations will be supplanted by multilateral/global discussions or unilateral announcements.* Bilateral relationships have been superseded by multilateral discussions and unilateral pronouncements. The halcyon days of U.S. and Soviet negotiators sitting at a table in Geneva or Vienna for months on end, haggling over details of a nuclear agreement, are gone. The new model visualizes large groups of nations meeting irregularly to conclude large-scale agreements. Alternatively, the major powers may come to quick agreement over a handshake between their leaders, as executive agreements supplant negotiated treaties and simultaneous unilateral decisions replace hard-fought bargaining at the conference table. In either case, we can expect arms control efforts of the near future to be more multilateral and/or more informal than during the Cold War. This does not imply that the usefulness or value of arms control, whether process or results, will be diminished in the near term, only that it will look different.

• *Without showing some reciprocal efforts at disarmament, the major powers will no longer be able to dictate to the rest of the world their preferred version of an international system or to achieve consensus on nonproliferation regimes.* As Virginia Foran pointed out in her chapter on nuclear proliferation, the former Third World is no longer willing to abjectly surrender to major-power views of how the world should look or operate in the realm of nuclear weapons policy. The 1995 NPT Review Conference made it clear that the nuclear weapons states must be willing to show resolve toward reducing their own stockpiles and undertake associated actions, including a comprehensive nuclear test ban, before their smaller but more numerous UN partners will acquiesce to the great-power desires for an NPT regime. Similarly, nonsuperpower concerns were a major part of debate over the Chemical Weapons Convention and can be expected to influence any future verification protocol for the BWC. These trends buttress the first, that the superpowers no longer control the game board.

• *There is growing value and acceptance of the need for effective verification, including intrusive measures.* Joseph Pilat rightly stressed the value of verification to the success of any agreement. "Trust but verify" was a popular slogan of the early 1980s not only because President Reagan liked it but because the concept makes such good sense. The United States has always seen verifiability as a crucial, albeit not the only, criterion for entering into an arms control agreement. In the post–Cold War era, as verification efforts have become more intrusive, technologies have had to keep up with the requirements—as has public acceptance of such visits. The debate over verification and compliance has not focused on the need for such measures; these are understood by all parties. Rather, questions have arisen over the degree to which verification can be effective in ensuring compliance. The ultimate measure for this effectiveness must, in the end, be national security.

Virginia Foran reminded us that the acceptance of verification has gone hand in hand with successful efforts to stem nuclear proliferation. The failure of early attempts (international control of nuclear weapons and materials and attempts at stemming proliferation through secrecy) led to the Atoms for Peace program in the 1950s. This, too, failed, largely because of inadequate safeguards and verification. These disappointments, coupled with advances in verification technology, led to a more robust nonproliferation regime in the 1960s based on the Limited Test Ban Treaty and the nuclear Non-Proliferation Treaty.

Trevor Taylor found that arms control can actually promote improved relations between states—but only if one side is willing to accept asymmetric cuts in hopes of long-term returns or benefits. The level of trust required to do that is necessary before trust can be developed as an outcome of the arms control process itself. So we have a bit of a conundrum: how to create that first level of trust. Taylor referred us to international relations theory to explain how this might occur. An idealist would point out the inherent perfectibility of humankind and his or her desire to move the world forward through unilateral, and hopefully reciprocated, efforts; the realist would explain it via the basic economics of a rational actor using a cost-benefit analysis. Either explanation may suffice to offer hope of improved relations.

The CWC, in particular, has an unprecedented verification protocol involving intrusive inspections that raise, for some, questions of the constitutionality of such agreements.

• *There is growing difficulty in confirming compliance with arms control accords.* This difficulty stems from several causes: the cost of intrusive verification, new manufacturing techniques, the miniaturization of electronic components, and so on. Weapons development programs and weapons capabilities are becoming easier to hide.

Marie Chevrier described current and potential verification provisions for the BWC, one of the oldest arms control regimes still in existence but one that has serious compliance and verification shortcomings. The ease of producing these biological agents, and the possibility for their proliferation, gives us pause, especially given that nearly all of the potential new biological weapons states are located in two regions—the Middle East and East Asia.

Joseph Pilat also pointed out that the creation of an international verification organization is unlikely. Coercive verification, such as practiced by the IAEA in Iraq following the Gulf War, is unlikely to be the way of the future because of its negative connotations of a defeated power. On the other hand, increased openness, transparency, and confidence-building measures may substitute for verification in areas such as control of fissile materials, which is essentially unverifiable anyway. These instruments developed and matured during the Cold War and are much more sanguine in their approach. The lines between these measures are not altogether clear, but there are certainly synergisms in the relationship involving verification, transparency, and confidence building. The high costs and political difficulties involved with intrusive verification, however, imply that less formal approaches—such as openness, transparency, and confidence-building measures—will become more prevalent in future arms control agreements.

• *The nature and scope of arms control have grown as a result of the end of the Cold War.* Areas of primary concern include proliferation of weapons of mass destruction and regional conflicts. As Gregory Rattray pointed out in his introduction, both the forums and scope of negotiations have expanded as a result of the end of the Cold War. According to Kerry Kartchner, the traditional goals of arms control are still relevant; their objectives transcend the changes to the international system witnessed since the late 1980s. Nevertheless, the process is only relevant if driven by the national security agenda, rather than as an end in itself.

New issues are coming to the fore in the realm of arms control. The definition continues to expand and encompass new areas. Certainly one of the most serious issues is the spread of weapons of mass destruction and their delivery means. Proliferation in all its many forms promises to keep the attention of the civilized world focused on arms control and its capabilities for years to come. There are both demand side and supply side issues to contend with, muddying the waters for students of international security and proliferation.

Conventional arms control may be creating new goals beyond the three traditional ones described by Kartchner. It may actually help settle traditional disputes between states or ethnic quarrels that reappeared after the end of the Cold War. Despite the acknowledged difficulties in getting states to agree to limitations on their national power and freedom of movement, Jeffrey McCausland posited that the larger benefits of arms control may persuade states to agree to those restrictions. Here he buttressed Taylor's findings in Chapter 2 about states agreeing to arms control for reasons of synergistic future benefits.

More concern will also be paid to regional conflicts. The potential for such localized conflicts to spread to neighboring regions, or even across the globe, makes it difficult to be unconcerned about even seemingly remote conflicts. In an era when nuclear weapons are easier than ever to acquire, and chemical and biological weapons remain simple to produce, one must be increasingly concerned with encountering weapons of mass destruction on the battlefield.

Jo Husbands concluded that the record of attempts to control the spread of conventional weapons is bleak, for several understandable reasons. States face strong domestic pressures to export military goods. Regional animosities drive purchases because of the security dilemma outlined by Rattray in his introduction. Arms transfers may actually be a force for peace and stability in some cases, since states are ultimately responsible for the protection of their citizenry in an anarchic world. The Missile Technology Control Regime has been relatively successful in stemming the flow of one type of technology; other such regimes are possible, particularly in areas of public concern, such as land mines.

Arms control must become simultaneously more global in its interests and more localized in its ability to limit the spread of weapons into a region and the spread of conflict out of a region.

• *Arms control faces challenges from public perceptions that it is no longer needed.* In some states the public will demand a withdrawal from the Cold War emphasis on security issues and call for a return to domestic issues. Similarly, some will decide to focus on global problems of a transnational nature, such as pollution, population, or crime, rather than traditional defense issues. This may affect arms control if the requisite support and funding are not there to ensure that the state's security interests are being met in the most cost-effective manner.

Jennifer Sims concluded her chapter with several gloomy forecasts for arms control within the U.S. domestic context—she believes that the imperative for arms control is weakening. At the same time, government downsizing and reduced budgets, particularly in the intelligence community, will likely hurt future arms control efforts. Finally, the growing importance of economics within the arms control equation may discourage involvement in increasingly expensive multinational, broad spectrum regimes.

The Middle East Conventional Arms Initiative, a presidential foreign policy initiative of the early 1990s, collapsed within two years under the pressure of certain realities. In links to earlier chapters by Taylor and Sims, Christopher Carr showed that the MEACI was the victim of domestic U.S. politics in an election year, as well as economic pressures from industry; global issues in the new world order, which also include increasing interest in exports; and regional conditions specific to the Middle East, such as the ongoing Arab-Israeli dispute, which drives the regional security dilemma.

• *Nevertheless, the arms control enterprise in and of itself is no longer controversial; it has been "domesticated."* James Wirtz pointed out that the concept of arms control was revolutionary when first introduced in the late 1950s and early 1960s. Today, however, most major actors on the international stage accept arms control as a valid, beneficial tool for their national security, and the arms control successes of the Cold War years continue to be in force. Nevertheless, there are hurdles to overcome if arms control is to continue to be as important and successful in the future.

• *Disarmament may be returning to the realm of legitimate arms control goals.* Disarmament, after a 20-year hiatus, seems to be coming back into vogue. Going as it does beyond the often narrowly focused fields of traditional arms control, disarmament seeks the total elimination of certain categories of weapons, particularly weapons of mass destruction. Several authors mentioned disarmament efforts in their chapters. For example, both the Chemical and Biological Weapons Conventions target the existence of these weapons, denying a state the right to develop, produce, or stockpile such weapons. This goes well past the early arms control efforts of the Geneva and Hague Conventions, which sought simply to limit or prevent the use of such weapons on the battlefield. Early calls for international control of nuclear weapons could be heard echoing through demands by the "have not" countries in negotiations over the 1995 extension of the nuclear Non-Proliferation Treaty, discussions that often led to calls for a comprehensive test ban and bans on production of fissile materials.

Forrest Waller suggested an approach that would use the opportunity presented by the end of the Cold War to deconstruct the nuclear threat entirely by reducing arsenals to levels of minimum deterrence. Arms control could play a major part in this effort, by increasing the level of understanding and trust between the five nuclear weapons states to accomplish this ambitious goal. A new understanding of what arms control can offer may also help; the Cooperative Threat Reduction program may be the first example of this new way of thinking about security. Finally, a logical extension of this argument would involve pursuing complete global nuclear disarmament. Given the nature of today's world, however, and the potential for rogue nations to acquire weapons of mass destruction, this last option has few proponents.

Final Thoughts

The central theme of this book bears repeating once more. The authors represented in this work believe that while the negotiating methods, regions of concern, and weapons involved may be changing, the underlying principles and objectives of arms control remain relevant in the post–Cold War world. Because of the broadening scope and complexity of negotiations and agreements, arms control may in fact affect national security more than it has in the past. The value of arms control, in other words, is growing in the new world, as states attempt to implement treaties already in place, stem the illegal proliferation of weapons to rogue nations or groups, and meet the security needs of states in a more multipolar, interdependent world. Arms control, we argue, is here to stay.

Appendixes

Appendix 1 Arms Control Time Line

	▲ Baruch Plan
1945	
1950	
	▲ UN Disarmament Commission Founded
	▲ Atoms for Peace proposal
1955	
	▲ Open Skies proposal
	Conference of Experts ▲
	▲ International Atomic Energy Agency
	Antarctic Treaty ▲
	"Spirit of Camp David" ▲
	Surprise Attack Conference ▲
1960	
	Test Ban Talks
	▲ ACDA founded
	Limited Test Ban Treaty
	U.S.-Soviet Hotline ▲
1965	
	Outer Space Treaty ▲
	Latin American Nuclear-Free-Zone Treaty ▲
	NonProliferation Treaty ▲
	Glassboro summit ▲
1970	
	Biological Weapons Convention ▲
	SALT Talks
	SALT I and ABM Treaty ▲
	India-Pakistan Hotline ▲
	Seabed Treaty ▲
	Prevention of Nuclear War Agreement ▲
	Risk Reduction Treaty ▲
	TTBT ▲
	Vladivostok Accord ▲
	CSCE talks
	ABM Protocol ▲
	MBFR Talks
1975	

Timeline of arms control agreements and negotiations, 1975–1995

PNET
Environmental Modification Convention
ASAT Talks
SALT II
SALT Talks
Helsinki Final Act
CSCE Talks
CWC Talks
CTB Talks
Conventional Arms Transfer Talks
MBFR Talks

INF Talks
Soviet walkout after INF Deployed
START Talks
U.S. cancels CTB Talks
Star Wars speech

Geneva summit
Reykjavik Summit
INF Agreement
MTCR
Nuclear and Space (START) Talks
CWC Talks
Stockholm Document
Soviet ASAT moratorium
CDE Agreement
ABM Treaty reinterpretation
Soviet testing moratorium
MBFR Talks

Bilateral CW
START I
Vienna 90
CFE 1A Treaty
CFE Treaty
Open Skies Treaty
Argentina, Brazil end nuclear programs
South Africa ends nuclear program
Conference on Disarmament

Fissile Material Cutoff Talks
Presidential initiatives
Tri-lateral BW
UN Arms Register
OSCE Formed
START II
CWC Treaty
FSC formed
Vienna 92
U.S., U.K. testing moratorium
CTB Talks
Russia testing moratorium
US Counterproliferation Initiative

1975   1980   1985   1990   1995

Appendix 2

Existing Arms Control Treaties

Treaty Banning Nuclear Weapon Tests in the Atmosphere, in Outer Space and Under Water, also called Partial Test Ban Treaty (PTBT) and Limited Test Ban Treaty (LTBT)

Brief Description

The signatories agreed not to carry out any nuclear weapon test explosion in the atmosphere, in outer space, under water, or in any other environment that would cause radioactive debris to spread outside the territorial limits of the state that conducted the test.

Key Dates/Signatories

Signed: 5 August 1963
Ratified: 7 October 1963
Entry into Force: 10 October 1963
Duration: Unlimited
Original Parties: United States, United Kingdom, Soviet Union
125 Follow-on Parties

Treaty on the Principles Governing the Activities of States in the Exploration and Use of Outer Space, Including the Moon and Other Celestial Bodies, also called Outer Space Treaty

Brief Description

This treaty, negotiated primarily between the United States and the Soviet Union, serves to limit the militarization of outer space and celestial bodies. The treaty prohibits any state from placing weapons of mass destruction in outer space or deploying them on celestial bodies. In addition, all celestial bodies are to be used solely for peaceful purposes and may not be used for military bases, fortifications, or weapons testing of any kind.

Key Dates/Signatories

Signed: 27 January 1967
Ratified: 25 April 1967
Entry into Force: 10 October 1967
Duration: Unlimited
115 Parties

Treaty on the Non-Proliferation of Nuclear Weapons, also called Non-Proliferation Treaty (NPT)

Brief Description

The nuclear Non-Proliferation Treaty (NPT) obligates nuclear weapon states party to the treaty (originally the United States, the Soviet Union, and the United Kingdom) to three main principles: not to transfer nuclear weapons or control over such weapons to any recipient, directly or indirectly; not to assist, encourage, or induce any nonnuclear weapon state to manufacture or otherwise acquire such weapons or seek control over them; and to actively work toward complete nuclear disarmament. Additionally, the nuclear weapon states are required to assist the nonnuclear weapon states in the use of nuclear energy for peaceful purposes, including the benefits of peaceful nuclear explosions.

Nonnuclear weapon states also agree to several provisions. They may not receive the transfer of nuclear weapons or control over them. They are also prohibited from manufacturing, seeking help in manufacturing, or otherwise obtaining nuclear weapons.

All states must accept the safeguards negotiated with the International Atomic Energy Agency (IAEA) to prevent the diversion of nuclear energy from peaceful purposes to nuclear weapons. The IAEA is tasked as the treaty's implementation and compliance body; it meets in Vienna.

At the 1995 Review and Extension Conference in New York, the treaty parties adopted three decisions and one resolution. The treaty review process was strengthened, and review conferences will continue to take place every five years. A set of principles and objectives for nuclear nonproliferation and disarmament was agreed to, including the goal of achieving a comprehensive nuclear test ban by 1996. The treaty was extended for an indefinite period by consensus of the parties. Finally, the conference called upon the states in the Middle East to agree to the creation of a zone free of weapons of mass destruction.

Key Dates/Signatories

Signed: 1 July 1968
Ratified: 24 November 1969
Entry into Force: 5 March 1970
Duration: Extended indefinitely 11 May 1995

Nuclear State Parties

United States, Soviet Union (Russian Federation assumes successor status), United Kingdom, France (March 1992), China (September 1992)

Nonnuclear State Parties

Afghanistan[a]	Bulgaria[a]	Republic[a]	Honduras[a]
Albania[b]	Burkina Faso	Ecuador[a]	Hungary[a]
Algeria	Burma	Egypt[a]	Iceland[a]
Antigua and	(Myanmar)	El Salvador[a]	Indonesia[a]
Barbuda	Burundi	Equatorial	Iran[a]
Argentina	Cambodia	Guinea	Iraq[a]
Armenia	Cameroon	Eritrea	Ireland[a]
Australia[a]	Canada[a]	Estonia[a]	Italy[a]
Austria[a]	Cape Verde	Ethiopia[a]	Jamaica[a]
Azerbaijan	Central African	Fiji[a]	Japan[a]
Bahamas	Republic	Finland[a]	Jordan[a]
Bahrain	Chad	Gabon	Kazakhstan[c]
Bangladesh[a]	Chile	Gambia[a]	Kenya
Barbados	Colombia[b]	Georgia	Kiribati[a]
Belarus[c]	Comoros	Germany	People's Demo-
Belgium[a]	Congo	Ghana[a]	cratic Repub-
Belize	Costa Rica[a]	Greece[a]	lic of Korea
Benin	Côte d'Ivoire[a]	Grenada	Republic of
Bhutan[a]	Croatia	Guatemala[a]	Korea[a]
Bolivia	Cyprus[a]	Guinea	Kuwait
Bosnia and	Czech Republic[a]	Guinea-Bissau	Kyrgyzstan
Herzegovina	Denmark[a]	Guyana	Laos
Botswana	Dominica	Haiti	Latvia
Brunei[a]	Dominican	Holy See[a]	Lebanon[a]

(*continues*)

(*continued*)

Lesotho[a]	Nepal[a]	San Marino	Togo
Liberia	Netherlands[a]	São Tomé and	Tonga
Libya	New Zealand[a]	Principe	Trinidad and
Liechtenstein[a]	Nicaragua[a]	Saudi Arabia	Tobago
Lithuania	Niger	Senegal[a]	Tunisia[a]
Luxembourg[a]	Nigeria[a]	Seychelles	Turkey[a]
Macedonia	Norway[a]	Sierra Leone	Turkmenistan
Madagascar[a]	Palau	Singapore[a]	Tuvalu[a]
Malawi	Panama	Slovakia	Uganda
Malaysia[a]	Papua New	Slovenia	Ukraine[c]
Maldives[a]	Guinea[a]	Solomon Islands	United Arab
Mali	Paraguay[a]	Somalia	Emirates
Malta[a]	Peru[a]	South Africa[a]	Uruguay[a]
Marshall Islands	Philippines[a]	Spain[a]	Uzbekistan
Mauritania	Poland[a]	Sri Lanka[a]	Vanuatu
Mauritius[a]	Portugal[a]	Sudan[a]	Venezuela[a]
Mexico[a]	Qatar	Suriname[a]	Vietnam[a]
Micronesia	Romania[a]	Swaziland[a]	Western Samoa[a]
Moldova	Rwanda	Sweden[a]	Yemen
Monaco	St. Kitts and	Switzerland[a]	Zaire[a]
Mongolia[a]	Nevis	Syria	Zambia
Morocco[a]	St. Lucia[a]	Taiwan	Zimbabwe
Mozambique	St. Vincent and	Tajikistan	
Namibia	the Grena-	Tanzania	
Nauru[a]	dines	Thailand[a]	

Notes: a. NPT safeguards agreements that have entered into force as of 1992.
b. Non-NPT full safeguards agreement.
c. Agreed to sign as a nonnuclear state under the START I Lisbon Protocol.

Biological and Toxin Weapons Convention (BWC)

Brief Description

Building on the Geneva Protocol of 1925, which bans the use of biological weapons in war, the Biological and Toxin Weapons Convention (BWC) bans the development, production, stockpiling, and acquisition of biological weapons and the delivery systems of such agents.

An ad hoc group met in several sessions between March 1992 and September 1993 to identify, examine, and evaluate potential methods of verification. Twenty-one potential verification measures, including on-site inspections, were identified and evaluated. An effective verification regime would have to rely on several different measures. The need to protect sensitive commercial property and intellectual information was also identified.

Although the United States declared that it had destroyed all of its biological weapons by 26 December 1975, it has become increasingly clear that the Soviet biological weapons program violated the BWC. In September 1992, trilateral negotiations between the United States, the United Kingdom, and the Russian Federation began in an effort to resolve compliance concerns and improve verification methods (see Appendix 3).

Key Dates/Signatories

Signed: 10 April 1972
Ratified: 26 March 1975
Entry into Force: 26 March 1975
Duration: Unlimited
139 Parties

Treaty Between the United States of America and the Union of Soviet Socialist Republics on the Limitation of Anti-Ballistic Missile Systems, also called Antiballistic Missile (ABM) Treaty

Brief Description:

The basic premise of the ABM Treaty is stated in its preamble: "Effective measures to limit anti-ballistic-missile systems would be a substantial factor in curbing the race in strategic offensive arms and would lead to a decrease in the risk of outbreak of war involving nuclear weapons." The purpose of the treaty is stated in Article I, which prohibits the deployment of an ABM system for "the defense of the territory" or the provision of "a base for such a defense." The former prohibition includes a nationwide defense, whether on land or sea or in air or space; the latter encompasses items such as powerful, large phased-array radars (LPARs), which are the long-lead-time items of a deployed land-based ABM system.

An ABM system is defined for treaty purposes as a system "to counter strategic ballistic missiles or their elements in flight trajectory." An ABM system is described as "currently consisting" of three components: ABM launchers, ABM interceptor missiles, and ABM radars. The word *strategic* was included to preserve the option to deploy antitactical ballistic missiles (ATBMs). The word *currently* makes clear that the treaty encompasses all ABM systems, whether based on current or future technology; the 1972-era components listed in the treaty are illustrative only.

ABM components are defined as either "constructed and deployed for an ABM role" or of "a type tested in an ABM mode." These definitions are linked with treaty prohibitions against the testing in an ABM mode of non-ABM systems such as surface-to-air missile systems (SAMs).

The treaty limited each side to two ABM deployment sites (later reduced to one site by the 1974 protocol). The authorized deployment area, with a radius of 150 kilometers, must be centered either on the national capital area or on an ICBM field; each side has the right to switch the site one time. All deployed ABM components must be located within the designated deployment area, and they must be fixed and land-based. The United States chose to locate its site at the Grand Forks, North Dakota, ICBM fields, while the Soviet Union selected Moscow.

Provisions for ABM test ranges prohibit, among other things, ABM deployments in various locations around the country under the guise of test facilities. The numerical limitation of 15 launchers at an ABM test range reinforces this purpose. The United States has two ABM test ranges from which fixed land-based ABM components may be tested: White Sands, New Mexico, and Kwajalein Island in the Pacific.

The treaty prohibits space-based, air-based, sea-based, and mobile land-based ABM systems and components. The ban covers development and testing as well as deployment. No restraints are placed on research that precedes field testing.

The treaty imposes a ceiling of 100 ABM launchers and 100 ABM missiles at launch sites in the ABM deployment area. It prohibits certain capabilities of fixed land-based components, such as automatic, semiautomatic, or rapid-reload ABM launchers and launchers that could launch more than one ABM interceptor missile at a time. Agreed Statement E extends these prohibitions to ABM interceptors with more than one independently guided warhead. There are no limits on the range or velocity of the ABM interceptors.

During the ABM Treaty negotiations, the U.S. government was concerned about the Soviet Union's potential for upgrading its extensive SAM systems to give them ABM capabilities. Article VI(a) prohibits non-ABM systems, such as SAMs, from having "capabilities to counter strategic ballistic missiles" or from being "tested in an ABM mode."

The treaty limits the location of ABM radars to authorized ABM deployment areas or ABM test ranges. Early warning radars constructed after the treaty entered into force must be located on the periphery of the country and oriented outward. The periphery requirement assumed that a radar so located was vulnerable to military attack and therefore not strategically effective. The outward orientation was intended to prohibit the over-the-shoulder coverage necessary for an effective ABM radar providing coverage of incoming ballistic missiles within territorial boundaries. The explicit exceptions to these rules are radars for space tracking or for national technical means (NTM), which are not limited in terms of power, location, orientation, or other factors.

Space-based sensors and LPARs raise many similar treaty compliance issues, since both can perform many different functions. The U.S. negotiators understood that some space-based sensors were akin to early warning or NTM radars, and their deployment in space was fully consistent with the purpose and letter of the treaty. On the other hand, although not then available, space-based sensors capable of substituting for ABM radars are banned.

Provisions of the treaty are to be verified solely by NTM; each party agrees not to interfere with the other's NTM and not to use deliberate concealment measures that would impede verification by NTM.

The Standing Consultative Commission addresses compliance issues and ongoing problems and challenges. It meets in Geneva, Switzerland.

Key Dates/Signatories

Signed: 26 May 1972
Ratification
  Advised by
  U.S. Senate: 3 August 1972
Entry into Force: 3 October 1972
Duration: Unlimited, with five-year reviews
Parties: United States, Soviet Union

A resolution was signed in Bishkek, Kyrgyzstan, on 9 October 1992 that obligated the members of the Commonwealth of Independent States (CIS) to abide by the treaty. This agreement did not include Azerbaijan, which refused to sign, nor the Baltic states nor Georgia, which were not CIS members. However, the Russian Federation signed a bilateral agreement in March 1994 with Latvia, allowing the Russians to retain control of the radars there for four years, after which they will be dismantled.

**Interim Agreement Between the United States of America
and the Union of Soviet Socialist Republics on
Certain Measures with Respect to the
Limitation of Strategic Offensive Arms,
also called Strategic Arms Limitation Treaty I (SALT I)**

Brief Description

The interim agreement, like the ABM Treaty, was the result of the first series of Strategic Arms Limitation Talks, which lasted from November 1969 to May 1972. The agreement freezes the number of strategic ballistic missile launchers and prohibits the conversion of older launchers to accommodate modern heavy ICBMs. An increase in SLBMs was allowed provided an equal number of land-based launchers was destroyed. The United States was authorized up to 710 SLBMs, while the Soviet Union was allowed 950. Mobile ICBMs were not covered by the agreement.

The agreement was perceived as a holding action, and its duration was limited to five years in the hope that a more comprehensive agreement would be reached. The U.S. Congress passed a joint resolution supporting the agreement, instead of the Senate passing ratification.

Key Dates/Signatories

Signed: 26 May 1972
Joint Resolution
    Passed: 30 September 1972
Entry into Force: 3 October 1972
Duration: Five years
Parties: United States, Soviet Union

Treaty Between the United States of America and the Union of Soviet Socialist Republics on the Limitation of Underground Nuclear Weapons Tests, also called Threshold Test Ban Treaty (TTBT)

Brief Description

This treaty prohibits signatories from the underground testing of nuclear weapons with a yield greater than 150 kilotons at declared testing sites. Because of U.S. concerns about possible Soviet violations of the treaty, negotiations were undertaken from 1987 to 1990 to strengthen the methods of verification and to address the possibility of accidentally exceeding the 150-kiloton limit. The resulting protocol requires notification of explosions and provides various options for measuring the yield of the explosions, including on-site inspection for tests with a planned yield greater than 35 kilotons.

The United States has only one declared testing site, located in Nevada. The former Soviet Union maintained two testing sites, one within the Russian Federation and the other in Kazakhstan.

Key Dates/Signatories

Signed: 3 July 1974 (treaty)
                        1 June 1990 (protocol)
Duration: Five years, with five-year extensions

Ratified: 11 December 1990
Entry into Force: 11 December 1990
Parties: United States, Soviet Union (Russian Federation assumes
                    successor state status)

Treaty Between the United States of America and the Union of Soviet Socialist Republics on Underground Nuclear Explosions for Peaceful Purposes, also called Peaceful Nuclear Explosions Treaty (PNET)

Brief Description

The Peaceful Nuclear Explosions Treaty (PNET) between the United States and the former Soviet Union was signed in 1976. As with the TTBT (see separate entry), its protocol on the verification of compliance was not completed until 1990. The treaty allows peaceful nuclear explosions outside declared testing sites but prohibits any individual explosion exceeding a yield of 150 kilotons. Group explosions are limited to a yield of 1.5 megatons, provided that each individual explosion's yield can be verified and does not exceed 150 kilotons. The protocol for PNET requires notification of explosions and allows for on-site inspections and other methods of measuring the yield of the detonation.

Key Dates/Signatories

Signed: 28 May 1976 (treaty)
                    1 June 1990 (protocol)
Ratified: 11 December 1990
Entry into Force: 11 December 1990
Duration: Five years, with five-year extensions
Parties: United States, Soviet Union (Russian Federation assumes
                    successor state status)

Treaty Between the United States of America and the Union of Soviet Socialist Republics on the Limitation of Strategic Offensive Arms, also called Strategic Arms Limitation Treaty II (SALT II)

Brief Description

The SALT II talks lasted from November 1972 until 18 June 1979, when the treaty was signed in Vienna. The treaty places limits on ballistic missiles and their launchers but does not require the reduction of such items. Each country was limited to 2,250 launchers, with a sublimit of 1,320 launchers for MIRVed missiles. MIRVed ballistic missiles were limited to 1,200, of which only 820 could be ICBMs. In addition, new ICBMs and ASBMs were limited to 10 warheads, while SLBMs were allowed to carry up to 14 warheads. The treaty prohibited spaced-based nuclear weapons, fractional orbital missiles, and rapid reload missile launchers.

A protocol to the treaty was signed at the same time and was to remain in effect until 31 December 1981. The protocol prohibited the deployment of GLCMs and SLCMs with a range of over 600 kilometers, as well as ASBMs and mobile ICBMs. Additionally, MIRVed GLCMs and SLCMs with a range of over 600 kilometers could not be tested.

President Carter submitted the treaty to the Senate immediately following the signing, but because of political considerations and the Soviet invasion of Afghanistan he was forced to remove it from consideration. Since the treaty was never ratified, it became a politically, not legally, binding agreement. On 27 May 1986, President Reagan, after citing Soviet violations, declared that the United States would no longer abide by the limits of the SALT agreements.

Key Dates/Signatories

Signed: 18 June 1979
Submitted to
   Senate: 22 June 1979
Withdrawn from
   Senate: 3 January 1980
United States
   Exceeds Limits: 28 November 1986
Parties: United States, Soviet Union

Treaty Between the United States of America and the Union of Soviet Socialist Republics on the Elimination of Their Intermediate-Range and Shorter-Range Missiles, also called Intermediate-Range Nuclear Forces (INF) Treaty

Brief Description

This treaty provided for the complete elimination of all U.S. and Soviet intermediate-range (1,000–5,500 kilometers) and shorter-range (500–1,000 kilometers) ground-launched ballistic and cruise missiles. Although the final elimination of missiles was completed by 1 June 1991, the on-site inspection regime will continue until the year 2001 to ensure compliance with the treaty. This includes continuous monitoring of the missile final assembly facilities at Magna, Utah, and Votkinsk, Soviet Union (now in the Russian Federation). Additionally, on-site inspections of former missile operating bases and missile support facilities are allowed at a rate of 15 per year until 1996 and 10 per year until 2001. Some of these facilities are now located in successor states other than the Russian Federation (Belarus, Ukraine, Kazakhstan, Uzbekistan, Turkmenistan, Lithuania, Latvia, and Estonia) and states of the former Warsaw Pact. The Special Verification Commission is tasked with overseeing verification and compliance; it is based in Geneva, Switzerland.

Key Dates/Signatories

Signed: 8 December 1987
Ratified: 27 May 1988
Entry into Force: 1 June 1988
Duration: Unlimited (13 years for the inspection regime)
Parties: United States, Soviet Union (Russian Federation assumed
                    successor state status); Belarus, Kazakhstan, and Ukraine
                    have also accepted inspections

Treaty on Conventional Armed Forces in Europe (CFE)

Brief Description

The CFE Treaty was originally signed by the 22 members of NATO and the former Warsaw Pact on 19 November 1990. However, due to the breakup of the Soviet Union and other changes in Europe, 30 states are now parties to the treaty. The area of application (AOA) for the CFE Treaty is commonly referred to as the Atlantic to the Urals, or ATTU (see Map A2.1). For countries that do not fall within this area, such as the United States and Canada, or those that have territory extending outside of the AOA, such as Russia, Turkey, and Kazakhstan, the limits apply only to forces stationed in the ATTU zone. However, an agreed statement requires Russia to destroy 14,500 pieces of equipment that were moved east of the Urals during the negotiations. The treaty only limits the amount of equipment in the AOA; troop limits were addressed in follow-on negotiations, which resulted in the CFE 1A document (see separate entry).

The treaty divides Europe into two groups: the North Atlantic Treaty Organization (NATO) and the members of the former Warsaw Treaty Organization (WTO), imposing conventional arms limitations equally to both. Each of the groups' total holdings are limited in five major categories: tanks, artillery pieces, armored combat vehicles (ACVs), combat aircraft, and attack helicopters. Three of these categories were further defined as follows:

Map A2.1 Atlantic to the Urals

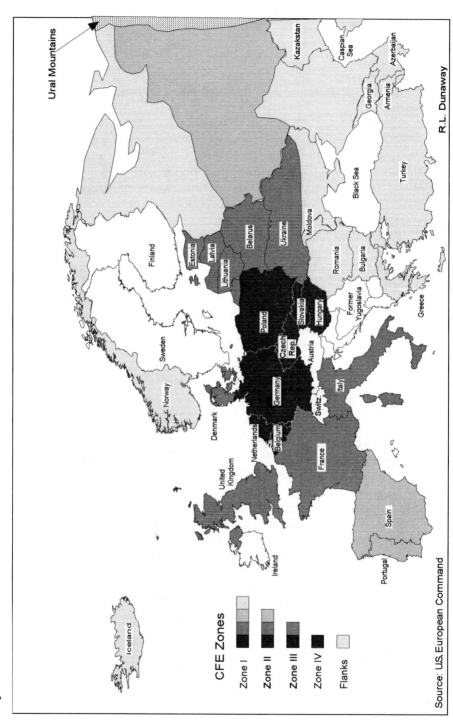

CFE Zones

Zone I

Zone II

Zone III

Zone IV

Flanks

Source: U.S. European Command

R.L. Dunaway

- Artillery: guns/howitzers, mortars, and multiple-launch rocket systems
- ACVs: armored personnel carriers, armored infantry fighting vehicles, and heavy armament combat vehicles
- Helicopters: specialized attack and multipurpose attack

Sublimits were also placed on the most threatening ACVs, including armored infantry fighting vehicles and heavy armament combat vehicles. An additional group of equipment is not limited by the treaty yet is still subject to the treaty. The equipment in this category includes trainer aircraft, combat support and transport helicopters, river bridging vehicles, and armored vehicle look-alikes, all of which are subject to operational constraints and information exchanges.

Four nested zones were also created, each one encompassing the preceding zone plus adjacent territory or districts, resulting in a Russian *matryoshka* doll effect (see Map A2.1). Specific limits are placed on the ground equipment allowed in each zone, the smallest of which is the central zone (see Table A2.1). These limits allow for free movement away from, but not toward, the center of Europe, thus decreasing the threat of a surprise attack. Aircraft and helicopters, while limited in the AOA, are not affected by the zoning limits. Additionally, there were limits put on the number of forces that could be stationed in the so-called flank zone. This zone includes Armenia, Georgia, Azerbaijan, and Moldova, as well as the southeastern third of Ukraine and the Leningrad and northern Caucasus military districts in the Russian Federation. This was done to prevent the Soviet Union from repositioning its forces previously located in Central Europe to the borders of Turkey and Norway, forcing them instead to be moved deep within Russia. In the northern sector of this zone, a portion of the Soviet Union's forces had to be allocated to designated permanent storage sites (DPSSs).

Although each group was left to decide the equipment levels allotted to each country, limits on the amount a single country could possess are stated in the treaty (see Table A2.1). These single party limits, roughly one-third of the total allowed for the AOA, stress the importance of no one nation being able to dominate the continent. Additionally, restrictions were placed on the amount of equipment that one state could station on the territory of another. Before signing the treaty at the November 1990 summit meeting in Paris, both groups met separately to develop individual country limits. While the results of NATO's meeting in Brussels remain relatively unchanged (see Table A2.2), political events have significantly altered the agreement reached by the countries of the former Warsaw Pact in Budapest (see Table A2.3). In May 1992 the eight members of the Commonwealth of Independent States (CIS) that had territory within the AOA met in Tashkent to decide how to divide the former Soviet Union's allotment of equipment. Russia and Ukraine

Table A2.1   CFE Equipment Limits by Zone

Treaty-Limited Equipment	Overall	One Country	Central Zone	Expanded Central Zone	Extended Zones	Flank Zones
Tanks[a]	20,000	13,300	7,500	10,300	11,800	4,700
Artillery pieces[a]	20,000	13,700	5,000	9,100	11,000	6,000
Armored combat vehicles[a]	30,000	20,000	11,250	19,260	21,400	5,900
Combat aircraft[b]	6,800	5,150				
Attack helicopters[c]	2,000	1,500				

Source: CFE Treaty.
Notes: a. As a result of an agreement anounced on 14 June 1991, equipment assigned to naval infantry or costal defense forces are counted against the total authorized.
b. No state is permitted to maintain more than 400 permanently land-based naval aircraft; no group total is to exceed 430 aircraft.
c. No state is permitted to maintain any permanently land-based naval helicopters.

also agreed to sublimits within the flank zone, including percentages for active and permanently stored ground equipment. The Russian Federation is now permitted to place 600 tanks, 400 artillery pieces, and 800 ACVs in DPSSs along the northern portion of the flank zone. Kazakhstan pledged not to station any of its forces west of the Ural River, thus in the AOA. Russia assumed responsibility for the former Soviet Union's forces outside the CIS, such as in Poland, Germany, and the Baltics. In a separate agreement, signed on 5 February 1993 in Prague, the Czechs and Slovaks agreed to a 2:1 split of the equipment allocated to the former Czechoslovakia.

Implementation of the treaty is divided into four phases: baseline validation, 0–120 days after entry into force (concluded November 1992); reduction, three years after baseline validation phase; residual-level validation, 120 days after reduction phase; and residual, which is indefinite because it covers the remaining life of the treaty. Within the reduction phase, a schedule for reduction was established to ensure that each country would reach its reduction limits 40 months after entry into force. The timetable has three parts, each with a corresponding percentage of the parties' reduction requirement that must be completed: 25 percent after 16 months (September 1993), 60 percent after 28 months (September 1994), and 100 percent by 42 months (17 November 1995). All the equipment must be destroyed except for a very limited number that can be decommissioned, converted to trainers or target drones, or converted to nonmilitary uses.

The treaty allows for several methods of ensuring compliance, including national/multinational technical means, information exchanges, and on-site

Table A2.2   CFE Equipment Limits by State (NATO)

States	Tanks	Artillery	Combat Vehicles	Attack Helicopters	Combat Aircraft
Belgium	334	320	1,099	46	232
Canada	77	38	277	13	90
Denmark	353	553	316	12	106
France	1,306	1,292	3,820	352	800
Germany	4,166	2,705	3,446	306	900
Greece	1,735	1,878	2,534	18	650
Italy	1,348	1,955	3,339	142	650
Netherlands	743	607	1,080	69	230
Norway	170	527	225	0	100
Portugal	300	450	430	26	160
Spain	794	1,310	1,588	71	310
Turkey	2,795	3,523	3,120	43	750
United Kingdom	1,015	636	3,176	384	900
United States	4,006	2,492	5,372	518	784
Total	19,142	18,286	29,822	2,000	6,662
Treaty limits	20,000	20,000	30,000	2,000	6,800

Source: CFE Treaty.

Table A2.3   CFE Equipment Limits by State (Former WTO)

States	Tanks	Artillery	Combat Vehicles	Attack Helicopters	Combat Aircraft
Armenia[a]	220	285	220	50	100
Azerbaijan[a]	220	285	220	50	100
Belarus[a]	1,800	1,615	2,600	80	260
Bulgaria	1,475	1,750	2,000	67	235
Czech Republic[b]	957	767	1,367	50	230
Georgia[a]	220	285	220	50	100
Hungary	835	840	1,700	108	180
Kazakhstan[a]	0	0	0	0	0
Moldova[a]	210	250	210	50	50
Poland	1,730	1,610	2,150	130	460
Romania	1,375	1,475	2,100	120	430
Russian Federation[a]	6,400	6,415	11,480	890	3,450
Slovakia[b]	478	383	683	25	115
Ukraine[a]	4,080	4,040	5,050	330	1,090
Total	20,000	20,000	30,000	2,000	6,800
Treaty limits	20,000	20,000	30,000	2,000	6,800

Source: CFE Treaty.
Notes: a. As a result of the Tashkent agreement, 15 May 1992.
b. As a result of the Prague agreement, 5 February 1993.

inspections, all of which are supervised by the Joint Consultative Group, based in Vienna. There are several types of inspections described in the treaty: announced inspections of declared sites, challenge inspections within a specified area (a country may refuse, but then a reasonable assurance of compliance is required), and inspections to verify the destruction or reclassification of equipment. The number of allowed inspections is based on percentages and varies depending on the type of inspection and the current phase of implementation.

The treaty makes an important distinction between objects of verification (OOVs) and declared sites. OOVs are units holding conventional armaments subject to the treaty, while declared sites are where the units are located, usually a military base or facility. Announced inspections require only that the site be announced, thus the team could wait until arrival to decide which one of the several units that might be located at the base would be inspected.

Key Dates/Signatories

Signed: 19 November 1990
Ratified: 15 November 1991
Entry into Force: 9 November 1992 (17 July 1992 is the date used to determine the timing of all treaty rights and obligations)
Duration: Unlimited; review after 46 months and five-year intervals thereafter
Parties:

Armenia[a]	France	Luxembourg	Russia[a]
Azerbaijan[a]	Georgia[a]	Moldova[a]	Slovak Republic
Belarus[a]	Germany	Netherlands	Spain
Belgium	Hellenic Republic	Norway	Turkey
Bulgaria	Hungary	Poland	Ukraine[a]
Canada	Iceland	Portugal	United Kingdom
Czech Republic	Italy	Romania	United States
Denmark	Kazakhstan[a]		

Note: a. Part of the former Soviet Union that is located in AOA.

Treaty Between the United States and the Union of Soviet Socialist Republics on the Reduction and Limitation of Strategic Offensive Arms, also called Strategic Arms Reduction Treaty I (START I)

Brief Description

The START I Treaty, which was signed on 31 July 1991, will reduce U.S. and former Soviet Union strategic offensive arms (SOAs) (ICBMs, SLBMs, and heavy bombers) to 1,600 and attributed warheads (an agreed-upon number of warheads that are associated with each weapon system) to 6,000. There are additional sublimits for attributed warheads: 4,900 warheads on deployed ballistic missiles and 1,100 warheads on deployed mobile ICBMs. The former Soviet Union is also limited to 154 deployed heavy ICBMs (down from 308 before the treaty), each carrying 10 warheads. In addition, an aggregate limit of 3,600 metric tons was placed on ballistic missile throw weight. The treaty also provides for the right to reduce (download) the number of warheads attributed to three existing types of ICBMs and SLBMs. No single type may have more than 500 downloaded warheads, with a sublimit of four warheads downloaded per missile. Overall, no more than 1,250 warheads may be downloaded at any one time.

Warheads carried by heavy bombers, including those in long-range, nuclear air-launched cruise missiles (LRNAs), will be counted at a discount rate. Especially significant is the discounted rate for penetrating bombers, which count as only one warhead regardless of how many missiles they are capable of carrying. Politically binding side agreements will also limit the number of deployed nuclear sea-launched cruise missiles (SLCMs) and the number of Soviet Backfire bombers.

An extensive series of on-site inspections and an exchange of locational and technical data for all systems, with regular updates, will complement each party's national technical means (NTM) to monitor compliance with the treaty. An additional important verification measure is the agreement to exchange telemetric information from all test flights of ICBMs and SLBMs, including the equipment necessary to interpret the data. The Joint Compliance and Inspection Commission (JCIC) is tasked with monitoring compliance with the treaty and has been meeting in Geneva, Switzerland, since 1991.

Although the Russian Federation assumed successor status to the treaty after the breakup of the Soviet Union, a significant number of SOAs were also located in Belarus, Kazakhstan, and Ukraine (see Table A2.5).

On 23 May 1992, a protocol was signed in Lisbon that makes START I a five-nation, multiparty treaty instead of a bilateral treaty. The protocol and appended presidential letters would also obligate three of those parties (Belarus,

Table A2.5 Systems Deployed Outside the Russian Federation at Signature

State	ICBMs/Warheads	Heavy Bombers/ Warheads	Total: SOAs/ Warheads
Belarus	81/81		81/81
Kazakhstan	104/1,040	40/320 (370)[a]	144/1,360 (1,410)[a]
Ukraine	176/1,240	42/336 (596)[a]	218/1,576 (1,836)[a]

Source: START I.
Note: a. Number in parentheses is based on maximum number for which the bomber is actually equipped. The preceding value is START I discount attribution number.

Table A2.6   START I and NPT Ratification Dates

	United States	Russian Federation	Kazakhstan	Belarus	Ukraine
START I	1 Oct 1992	4 Nov 1992	2 Jul 1992	4 Feb 1993	3 Feb 1994
NPT	5 Mar 1970	5 Mar 1970 (Soviet Union)	14 Feb 1994	23 Jul 1993	16 Nov 1994

Source: Arms Control Reporter (Cambridge, Mass.: Institute for Defense and Disarmament Studies, 1995).

Kazakhstan, and Ukraine) to become nonnuclear state parties to the Non-Proliferation Treaty (see separate entry). This provision was also mandated by the U.S. Senate's START I ratification bill. The Ukraine parliament (*Rada*), while conditionally ratifying the START I Treaty, proved hesitant in declaring Ukraine a nonnuclear state under the NPT. On 14 January 1994 in Moscow, the presidents of Ukraine, the Russian Federation, and the United States signed the Trilateral Agreement, which promised Ukraine financial and security assistance as a means of persuading the *Rada* to unconditionally ratify START I and the NPT. Finally, on 3 February 1994 the *Rada* unconditionally ratified START I, and on 5 December 1994 Ukraine deposited its instruments of ratification for the NPT, allowing START I to enter into force.

Key Dates/Signatories

Signed: 31 July 1991
Ratified: See Table A2.6
Protocol to
  Obligate Soviet
  Union Successor
  States: 23 May 1992
Entry into Force: 5 December 1994
Duration: 15 years with option to extend at five-year intervals
Parties: United States, Soviet Union (but now the following successor states: Belarus, Kazakhstan, Russian Federation, Ukraine)

Treaty on Open Skies

Brief Description

The Open Skies Treaty was signed in Helsinki on 24 March 1992 by members of NATO and the former Warsaw Pact. Each participating state will have the right to conduct, and the obligation to receive, overhead flights by unarmed fixed-wing observation aircraft. Each aircraft will be authorized to carry the following equipment: panoramic, still-frame, and video cameras; infrared scanning devices; and side-looking synthetic aperture radars. The inspecting party will provide the aircraft used in the overflight; however, the host nation may impose the "taxi option," which requires the host aircraft to be used in the overflight. Prior to their use, all aircraft and sensor suites must undergo certification inspections.

The number of flights each country can conduct and must receive is limited on the basis of negotiated annual quotas. The U.S. quota is 42 overflights per year; however, during the first three years only 31 are permitted annually. Any states may acquire the data from any overflight.

Key Dates/Signatories

Signed: 24 March 1992
Ratified: 3 November 1993
Provisional
  Period of
  Application: Initially 24 March 1992–March 1993 (extended to February 1995)
Estimated Entry
  into Force: 60 days after deposit of 20 instruments of ratification (expected in 1996)
Duration: Unlimited, with initial review after three years after entry into force and at five-year intervals thereafter
Parties:

Belarus	Georgia	Luxembourg	Slovak Republic
Belgium	Germany	Netherlands	Spain
Bulgaria	Greece	Norway	Turkey
Canada	Hungary	Poland	Ukraine
Czech Republic	Iceland	Portugal	United Kingdom
Denmark	Italy	Romania	United States
France	Kyrgyzstan	Russian Federation	

The Concluding Act of the Negotiation on Personnel Strength of Conventional Armed Forces in Europe, also called Conventional Armed Forces in Europe 1A (CFE 1A) Treaty

Brief Description

The CFE 1A Agreement is a politically, not legally, binding document and therefore is not subject to ratification. The goal of the agreement is to limit and/or reduce personnel levels in the AOA of the CFE Treaty. Each state sets

Table A2.4   CFE 1A Troop Limits

North Atlantic Treaty Group			Budapest/Tashkent Group		
	Ceilings	Holdings		Ceilings	Holdings
Belgium	70,000	68,688	Armenia	not reported	32,682
Canada	10,660	1,408	Azerbaijan	not reported	56,000
Denmark	39,000	29,893	Belarus	100,000	92,664
France	325,000	332,591	Bulgaria	104,000	98,930
Germany	345,000	314,688	Czech		
Greece	158,621	163,705	Republic	93,333	92,893
Italy	315,000	290,224	Georgia	40,000	not reported
Netherlands	80,000	66,540	Hungary	100,000	75,294
Norway	32,000	26,100	Kazakhstan	0	0
Portugal	75,000	42,534	Moldova	20,000	11,123
Spain	300,000	168,346	Poland	234,000	269,670
Turkey	530,000	575,963	Romania	230,000	230,000
United			Russian		
Kingdom	260,000	192,547	Federation	1,450,000	1,110,578
United States	250,000	137,271	Slovakia	46,667	54,223
			Ukraine	450,000	495,156

Source: CFE 1A Treaty.

its own limits. These are open to discussion but not subject to negotiation (see Table A2.4).

The personnel counted against the limits fall into several categories: (1) land or air forces (including ground-based air defense) and the command and staff for these units; (2) other forces that hold equipment limited under the CFE Treaty, including land-based naval aircraft and naval infantry forces, as well as coastal defense units; and (3) reserve personnel called up for full-time service for more than 90 days. Exempted are sea-based naval personnel, internal security units, and forces serving under UN command.

Additional stabilizing measures are also listed in the agreement. A 42-day advance notification is required to increase the personnel strength of any ground force unit by more than 1,000, to increase any air force unit by more than 500, or to call up more than 35,000 reservists (except call-ups made in response to emergency situations such as natural disasters). Additionally, any personnel reassigned to a unit not subject to limitation will still be counted for one to two years.

The national ceilings declared by each state must be reached within 40 months after entry into force. Personnel information is provided during preinspection briefings for CFE declared site inspections or in response to inspectors' requests during a CFE challenge inspection.

Key Dates/Signatories

Signed: 17 July 1992
Ratified: Not required

Entry into Force: 17 July 1992
Duration: Unlimited; initial review after six months, then at five-
                 year intervals
Parties:

Armenia[a]	Denmark	Kazakhstan[a]	Russian
Azerbaijan[a]	France	Luxembourg	Federation[a]
Belarus[a]	Georgia[a]	Moldova[a]	Slovakia
Belgium	Germany	Netherlands	Spain
Bulgaria	Hellenic Republic	Norway	Turkey
Canada	Hungary	Poland	Ukraine[a]
Czech Republic	Iceland	Portugal	United Kingdom
	Italy	Romania	United States

Note: a. Part of the former Soviet Union that is located in AOA.

Treaty Between the United States of America
and the Russian Federation on Further Reduction
and Limitation of Strategic Offensive Arms,
also called Strategic Arms Reduction Treaty II (START II)

Brief Description

In 1991 and 1992, Presidents Bush and Gorbachev made a series of presidential initiatives (see Appendix 3) reducing nuclear stockpiles and lowering the alert status of several weapon systems. These set the foundation for the signing of a Joint Understanding at the June 1992 summit between President Bush and Russian Federation president Yeltsin in Washington. The Joint Understanding called for the elimination of all MIRVed ICBMs and deep cuts in SLBMs, forming the basis of the START II Treaty. This treaty was signed at the January 1993 Moscow summit by Presidents Bush and Yeltsin. It relies heavily on START I for definitions, procedures, and verification and, as such, cannot legally enter into force before START I.

The eliminations are to take place in a two-phase process (see Table A2.7). By the year 2000, each side must reduce its deployed strategic forces to 3,800–4,250 attributed warheads, within which the following sublimits apply: 1,200 warheads for MIRVed ICBMs, 650 warheads for heavy ICBMs, and 2,160 warheads for SLBMs. Phase II limits must be reached by the year 2003 (or by the year 2000 if the United States can contribute to the financing of the destruction or elimination of strategic offensive arms in Russia). At that time, each party must have reduced its deployed strategic forces to 3,000–3,500 attributed warheads, within which the following sublimits apply: zero

Table A2.7   START I and II Limits and Completion Dates

	START I	START II Phase 1	START II Phase 2
Reduction completion date	Seven years after entry into force	2000	2003
Total attributed warheads	6,000	3,800–4,250	3,000–3,500
Ballistic missile warheads	4,900	3,800–4,250	3,000–3,500
MIRVed ICBMs	not addressed	1,200	0
Heavy ICBMs	1,540	650	0
Mobile ICBMs	1,100	1,100	1,100
SLBMs	not addressed	2,160	1,700–1,750

Source: START II Treaty.

warheads for MIRVed ICBMs, 1,700–1,750 total warheads for SLBMs, and elimination of all heavy ICBMs.

To reach the lower warhead ceilings, the downloading procedures identified in START I (see separate entry) have been modified. The Russian Federation is allowed to download 105 SS-19 ICBMs by five warheads, leaving only one warhead per missile (all other downloading is still limited to four warheads per missile). Additionally, the overall ceilings on the aggregate numbers of downloaded warheads were removed. As a result, any missile that was previously equipped with six warheads or more, except the SS-19s, must be destroyed, while those equipped with five or fewer may be retained, provided they are downloaded to only one warhead.

Since the treaty eliminates the entire class of heavy ICBMs (SS-18), special provisions were made regarding the reuse of that hardware. All the missiles and their launch canisters may be converted to space launch vehicles, while up to 90 of the silos may be converted to launch single-warhead ICBMs. Any nonconverted equipment must be destroyed.

The treaty also has several provisions regarding bombers. The B-2 must now be exhibited and will be inspectable, whereas under START I, the B-2 was subject to neither condition unless it was tested/equipped with long-range nuclear ALCMs (LRNA). A one-time reorientation of up to 100 nuclear heavy bombers to a conventional role is allowed without adhering to the START I conversion procedures as long as they were never accountable as LRNA heavy bombers. The United States chose this option for its B-1 fleet. Additionally, conventional and nuclear bombers must be based separately and crews must be separately trained, and bombers must have differences observable by NTM and visible during inspection. The treaty also removes the "discount" provisions from START I bomber warhead counting rules but allows an increased number of bombers to be retained. START II also specifically provides the right to change the number of nuclear warheads the treaty attributes to a bomber, if there is a visible change in the plane's configuration. Approximately 1,300 warheads may be attributed to bombers in each country, depending on the number of ICBMs and SLBMs retained by each party.

Although this treaty builds on START I, some additional verification measures are included. START II significantly increases the number of on-site inspections, mostly relating to the retention of converted Russian heavy ICBM (SS-18) silos and the conversion of heavy bombers. The compliance regime is governed by the Bilateral Implementation Commission, which meets in Geneva, Switzerland.

Key Dates/Signatories

Signed: 3 January 1993
Ratified: Not yet ratified
Estimated Entry
  into Force: 1996
Duration: As long as START remains in force
Parties: United States, Russian Federation

Chemical Weapons Convention (CWC)

Brief Description

The Chemical Weapons Convention (CWC) is a multilateral agreement to ban the production, possession, transfer, and use of chemical weapons by all parties to the convention. It was negotiated by the 39 nations (with 36 additional nations in observer status) of the Conference on Disarmament (see separate entry). Initial treaty signature was in Paris on 13 January 1993, when 130 nations signed the convention. While the number of signatories continues to grow, very few countries have ratified the treaty. Both the United States and the Russian Federation, whose bilateral agreements provided the impetus for the talks, have yet to ratify the treaty.

The convention bans the development, production, stockpiling, transfer, acquisition, and both retaliatory and first use of chemical weapons. It also prohibits a state from aiding any other state, regardless of whether they are a party to the convention, in the pursuit of treaty-banned activities, which effectively institutes a nonproliferation regime. Additionally, parties are required to declare all chemical weapons and facilities no later than 30 days after entry into force and to destroy all chemical weapons within 10 years of entry into force. The convention will also require declarations on the production of other types of precursor and dual-purpose chemicals.

The verification regime will include routine, intrusive on-site inspections of declared government chemical weapons facilities, as well as civilian facilities that use certain chemicals that could be used or converted to make weapons. In addition, challenge inspections may be conducted at any facility where a party suspects illegal activities. These inspections will be on short notice. Inspectors will be allowed to visit the site and investigate whether banned activities are taking place. The CWC will be implemented by the Organization for the Prohibition of Chemical Weapons (OPCW), in The Hague, Netherlands.

Key Dates/Signatories

Signed: 13 January 1993
Ratified: Not yet ratified
Entry into Force: 180 days after 65th ratification
Duration: Unlimited
159 Parties

Appendix 3

Ongoing Arms
Control Negotiations

Fissile Material Cutoff Talks

The idea of a fissile material production cutoff gained prominence from 1956 through 1969, when it became the basis for U.S. arms control negotiations. Limited success was realized in 1964 when the United States, the United Kingdom, and the Soviet Union announced reductions in the production of weapons-grade fissionable materials. The success of superpower arms control initiatives, a U.S. halt in production of fissile material, and President Clinton's speech to the UN in September 1993 provided the impetus for a cutoff convention.

The Conference on Disarmament began preliminary discussions on a fissile material cutoff convention during its 1994 session. Ambassador Gerald Shannon, Canada's representative to the CD, was appointed special coordinator for the talks. In tandem with these negotiations, technical discussions were held in Vienna, with IAEA assistance, to address technical and verification issues. The format and scope of the talks have yet to be determined. While the nuclear weapon states want to address only future production of fissile material, many nonnuclear weapon states, including the Group of 21 "nonaligned" nations, wish to include limits on existing stocks of weapons-grade nuclear material.

Conference on Disarmament (CD)

The Conference on Disarmament (CD), which before 1983 was called the Committee on Disarmament, is the independent negotiating body of the UN for arms control treaties. It is one of three international disarmament forums (with the UN Disarmament Commission and the UN General Assembly First Committee) but the only body that negotiates treaties. The conference consists of 32 members, including all five nuclear weapon states. Additionally, numerous nations are allowed to participate as nonmembers. Although they maintain an open agenda, participants normally discuss weapons of mass destruction, conventional weapons, reduction of military budgets and armed forces, and confidence-building measures. Most of the work on these topics is accomplished in ad hoc committees. The CD is located in Geneva, Switzerland.

Comprehensive Test Ban Talks

The concept of a comprehensive test ban can be found in the Preamble to the Limited Test Ban Treaty, signed in 1963. Later negotiations resulted in more restrictions on testing, such as those in the TTBT and PNET (see separate entries). Trilateral negotiations among the United States, the United Kingdom, and the Soviet Union from October 1977 to November 1980 on a comprehensive ban ended without result. A reopening of the talks was then delayed until the verification issues of existing treaties could be resolved. Currently, four of the five nuclear powers (excluding China) have enacted unilateral testing moratoriums. The Chinese continued to conduct nuclear tests into 1995. In addition, in mid-1995 France resumed testing in the South Pacific. The U.S. moratorium was initiated by Congress on 4 September 1992 and was extended until September 1995 by President Clinton.

After initial consultation between the five nuclear powers, the First Committee of the UN General Assembly on 19 November 1993 approved a resolution by consensus that advocated a global treaty to ban all nuclear weapons tests. As urged by the UN resolution, the Conference on Disarmament created the Nuclear Test Ban Ad Hoc Committee, which held several negotiating rounds during 1994. The result was the creation of a "rolling text," which contained agreed treaty text as well as bracketed disputed text, which will be the basis for a final treaty. The verification regime may include a global network of seismic stations and radionuclide sensors and the right to conduct on-site inspections. The verification oversight agency has not been selected.

The 1995 NPT review conference called on all nuclear weapon states to sign a CTBT no later than 1996, which all five nuclear weapon states agreed to do.

Nuclear-Free Zones

There have been several efforts by both international and regional organizations to ban or limit the use of nuclear material in specific regions of the world. Three separate treaties, which have been signed by almost all the nations of the world, prohibit nuclear materials from being stored or tested in outer space, on the seabed floor, and in Antarctica. Additionally, efforts are currently under way to establish nuclear-free zones in the Middle East, South Asia, Northeast Asia, and Africa. Two regional nuclear-free zones, in Latin America and the South Pacific, have already been established through treaties.

South Pacific Nuclear-Free Zone

The South Pacific Nuclear-Free Zone, created in 1986, is a multilateral treaty that bans the stationing, manufacturing, testing, and dumping of nuclear weapons or nuclear waste within the zone. The issue of ship and aircraft traffic is left up to individual countries. There are 11 parties to the treaty, including Australia and New Zealand. There are three protocols to the treaty that are open for signature to the nuclear weapon states. The first bans the manufacturing, testing, and storing of nuclear weapons in areas for which the state is responsible. The second bans the use or threatened use of nuclear weapons against parties to the treaty. The third bans nuclear testing in the region. China and the Russian Federation have signed the second and third protocols, while the United States, the United Kingdom, and France have refused to sign any of the protocols.

Latin American Nuclear-Free Zone

The Latin American Nuclear-Free Zone was formalized in the Treaty of Tlatelolco, signed on 14 February 1967. The treaty bans the storage and testing of nuclear weapons within the signatory countries but allows for the peaceful use of nuclear material. The treaty has two protocols: one that obligates states with colonies to adhere to the treaty and another that calls for nuclear weapon states to recognize the zone. All Latin American states except Cuba have ratified the treaty.

Confidence- and Security-Building Measures (CSBMs)

As opposed to structural arms control measures designed to limit, reduce, or eliminate numbers of weapons systems, CSBMs are intended to foster transparency and trust through purposely designed cooperative measures. CSBMs are intended to help clarify states' military intentions, reduce uncertainties about potentially threatening military activities, and constrain opportunities for surprise attack or coercion. Specific examples of CSBMs in the European context are provided next.

The Conference on Security and Cooperation in Europe (CSCE)—as of December 1994 the Organization on Security and Cooperation in Europe (OSCE)—established a series of agreements and procedures designed to increase the security of members through increased military transparency and cooperation. The Helsinki Final Act, signed in 1975, was the first of these measures. It was signed by the United States, Canada, and all European nations except Albania. In addition to recognizing existing borders and the need for economic cooperation, the act required advance notification of military maneuvers involving more than 25,000 troops. This agreement set the foundations for the complicated and increasingly intrusive measures that followed.

The CSCE later formed a subcommittee named the Conference on Disarmament in Europe (CDE), which met from 1984 to 1986. One of the results of this conference was the Stockholm Document, which entered into force in January 1987 and expanded the requirements for notification and provided for observation of military activities. Members of the CSCE met from March 1989 to November 1990 to strengthen the existing CSBMs in line with the Stockholm agreement. The result was the Vienna Document 1990, which entered into force on 1 January 1991. The Vienna Document 1992, negotiated between 26 November 1990 and 4 March 1992, supplemented these measures and entered into force on 1 May 1992.

The following is a summary of existing measures within the OSCE's confidence-building regime, as established by the Vienna Documents:

- Forty-two-day advance notification of ground exercises involving more than 9,000 troops or 250 tanks, or more than 3,000 airborne or amphibious assault troops
- Observation rights to all countries for ground maneuvers involving more than 13,000 troops or 300 tanks or more than 3,500 airborne or amphibious assault troops
- Limits the number of exercises a country can conduct with more than 40,000 troops or 900 tanks to one per two years
- Limits the number of exercises a country can conduct with 13,000–40,000 troops or 300–900 tanks to six per year, of which only three can involve more than 25,000 troops or 400 tanks
- Each party may be inspected by any other party but is only obligated to accept three short warning inspections and 15 information verification inspections each year
- Exchanges of military information by 15 December that will be accurate for the following year, including the location, manpower levels, major weapon systems employed, and commanding organizations for any unit at or above regiment/brigade level
- Invitations to air bases and demonstrations of new weapons and equipment

At the July 1992 Helsinki summit meeting of the CSCE, a decision was made to form the Forum for Security Cooperation (FSC). This organization, which meets weekly in Vienna, is tasked with carrying out follow-on negotiations to CFE/CFE 1A and the Vienna CSBMs. Additionally, this body oversees implementation, implementation assessment, discussion, and clarification of existing CSBMs.

Missile Technology Control Regime (MTCR)

In April 1987 the United States, Canada, France, West Germany, Italy, Japan, and the United Kingdom created the Missile Technology Control Regime (MTCR) to restrict the proliferation of missiles and missile technology. The MTCR is the only multilateral missile nonproliferation regime. It is a voluntary arrangement, not an international agreement or a treaty, among countries that have an interest in stopping the proliferation of missile technology. The regime develops export guidelines that are applied to a list of controlled items and is implemented according to each nation's procedures. In January 1993 the MTCR guidelines were expanded to restrict the spread of missiles and unmanned air vehicles, with a range of at least 300 kilometers, capable of delivering a 500-kilogram payload or a weapon of mass destruction. The guidelines are sensitive to the fact that ballistic missile and space launch vehicle technology are virtually identical. They are designed not to impede a nation's space program as long as it does not contribute to the delivery of weapons of mass destruction. Membership in the MTCR is open to any country that commits to the principles of nonproliferation and has a record of effective export controls. The MTCR currently has 25 members.

Bilateral Chemical Weapon Agreements

The United States and the Soviet Union entered into two bilateral agreements regarding chemical weapons to facilitate the Chemical Weapons Convention (see separate entry). The Memorandum of Understanding, signed at Jackson, Wyoming, in 1989, called for two phases of data exchanges and visits/inspections of facilities. Phase I was completed in December 1989, when the United States and the Soviet Union declared that they had 29,000 and 40,000 agent metric tons, respectively. Phase II called for more detailed exchange of information and more thorough inspections. The second agreement is the Bilateral Destruction Agreement (BDA), signed in June 1990. The BDA bans chemical weapons production, provides a schedule for the destruction of all chemical weapons, and allows for on-site inspections.

In a series of summit meetings between President Yeltsin and Presidents Bush and Clinton, several advances were made. Yeltsin committed Russia to abide by the existing agreements and signed implementing documents, including a time line, for Phase II of the Wyoming memorandum. Additionally, the BDA schedule was altered to delay reduction to 5,000 agent tons until December 2004. Financial assistance to help Russia meet these deadlines was provided by the United States under the Nunn-Lugar Act. An additional agreement signed at Tashkent by some CIS states (Azerbaijan, Armenia, Kazakhstan, Kyrgyzstan, Moldova, Russian Federation, Tajikistan, Turkmenistan, and Uzbekistan), commits these parties to similar goals regarding chemical weapons and the CWC.

While the Russian implementation of the Wyoming memorandum has been problematic, the United States attributes this to substantive differences within the Russian government on how to handle the chemical weapons data declaration; the United States continually presses the Russian Federation for complete compliance. The United States is technically ready to destroy chemical weapons and is required to do so under a congressional mandate; however, it faces opposition from environmental groups.

Presidential Initiatives

Between September 1991 and January 1992 a series of presidential initiatives were announced by the presidents of the United States and Russia that significantly affected the nuclear force structure. Some of the measures were simply accelerations of those mandated by START I, while others were incorporated into START II (see separate entries). However, additional binding actions are not addressed in either treaty.

September/October 1991

On 27 September 1991, President Bush announced the following U.S. actions:

- All U.S. strategic bombers and 450 Minuteman II ICBMs removed from day-to-day alert
- All tactical nuclear weapons on surface ships, attack submarines, and land-based naval aircraft removed for destruction or central storage
- Nuclear short-range attack missile (SRAM II), Peacekeeper Rail Garrison ICBM, and mobile portion of small ICBM (SICBM) canceled
- Elimination of all MIRVed U.S. and Soviet ICBMs proposed
- Discussions on nonnuclear ABM systems requested

On 5 October 1991, President Gorbachev declared the following similar reductions:

- Heavy bombers and 503 ICBMs remained off alert
- All tactical nuclear weapons on surface ships, attack submarines, and land-based naval aircraft removed for destruction or central storage
- Bomber nuclear arms and rail-mobile ICBMs placed in storage
- SRAM, small mobile ICBM, and rail-mobile ICBM modernization and expansion programs canceled
- Seven SSBNs decommissioned
- Nuclear arsenal reduced to 5,000 warheads (below START I limit of 6,000 warheads)
- Reduction of strategic offensive arms by approximately one-half suggested
- Discussions requested on nonnuclear (ABM) systems
- One-year moratorium on nuclear testing

28–29 January 1992

In his State of the Union Address to the U.S. Congress on 28 January 1992, President Bush announced further reductions in the U.S. strategic forces to include the following:

- B-2 bomber production limited to 20
- Advanced cruise missile production limited to 640
- Small ICBM and production of Peacekeeper missiles and W-88 warhead for Trident missiles canceled

Additionally, he stated that if Russia were to eliminate all MIRVed ICBMs, the United States would take the following actions to cut strategic nuclear warheads to approximately 4,700:

- Peacekeeper missiles eliminated
- Minuteman III missiles reduced to one warhead per missile
- Trident submarine warheads reduced one-third
- Large number of strategic bombers converted to primarily conventional use

Russian Federation president Yeltsin (who stated that his remarks had been prepared in consultation with other leaders of the CIS) responded in a televised speech in Moscow on 29 January 1992. He stated Russia's intention to abide by all arms control agreements signed by the Soviet Union, as well as his support for the NPT, MTCR, CTBT, and the fissionable material cut-

off talks. He then made public the following reductions in CIS strategic offensive forces:

- Approximately 600 ICBMs and SLBMs off alert
- Advanced bombers, LRAs, and nuclear SLCM production and devel-
  opment halted
- Strategic bomber exercises with more than 30 heavy bombers elimi-
  nated
- 130 ICBM silos and six SSBNs eliminated/prepared for elimination
- SSBN combat patrols cut in half
- Strategic nuclear weapons in Ukraine to be dismantled earlier than
  planned
- Extension of nuclear testing moratorium
- Weapons-grade plutonium production reduced by 1993, halted by
  2000

Lastly, he proposed the following U.S.-Russian reciprocal actions:

- Eliminate all SSBN patrols
- Reduce strategic nuclear warheads to 2,000–2,500
- Retarget strategic offensive forces away from one another
- Reach START limits three years early
- Long-range nuclear SLCMs and new LRNAs eliminated

Cooperative Threat Reduction (CTR) Program

In the fall of 1991, conditions in the disintegrating Soviet Union created a
global threat to nuclear safety and stability. The U.S. Congress, having recognized a window of opportunity to materially reduce the threat from nuclear
weapons in the former Soviet Union and the proliferation potential they
represented, enacted the Soviet Nuclear Threat Reduction Act—also called
the Nunn-Lugar legislation. Subsequently, the program has expanded to
include all weapons of mass destruction (WMD), assistance for defense conversion, and facilitation of military-to-military contacts.

The CTR program currently provides assistance to reduce or eliminate
the threat posed by the thousands of existing WMD and associated infrastructure remaining in the former Soviet Union. Primary program objectives are to accelerate WMD dismantlement and destruction while ensuring
a strong chain of custody for fissile material transport and storage. These
objectives also foster compliance with the START agreement, the Lisbon
Protocol, the NPT, the CWC, and the January 1994 Trilateral Statement. As
of December 1994, the United States had authorized over $1.2 billion for

the program, and agreements were in effect in Russia, Ukraine, Belarus, and Kazakhstan.

Trilateral Biological Weapon Talks

The trilateral working group was initiated because of U.S. concerns that the Russian offensive biological weapons program inherited from the Soviet Union was in violation of the BWC. The first meeting was in September 1992, when delegations of the United States, the United Kingdom, and the Russian Federation met in Moscow to review steps taken to resolve compliance concerns regarding the former Soviet Union. The result was the Trilateral Statement, in which Russia listed the steps taken to resolve BWC compliance concerns. The statement further called for Russia to allow unrestricted access visits to nonmilitary sites, which were to be followed by reciprocal Russian visits to the United States and the United Kingdom.

In April 1994, Russia submitted its annual BWC data declaration to the UN, pursuant to voluntary confidence-building measures adopted at past BWC review conferences. However, the declaration provided no more information than the 1992 declaration on past Russian offensive biological weapons activities. In mid-1994 the trilateral working group met in Vienna to assess the status of the Trilateral Statement implementation process. The countries' commitment to the process was underscored by a statement at the September 1994 Washington summit by Presidents Yeltsin and Clinton on the importance of continued implementation of the Trilateral Statement.

Appendix 4

Acronyms

ABAAC	Argentine-Brazilian Agency of Accounting and Control of Nuclear Materials
ABM	antiballistic missile
ACDA	Arms Control and Disarmament Agency
ACM	advanced cruise missile
ACV	armored combat vehicle
AEA	Atomic Energy Act
AIFV	armored infantry fighting vehicle
ALCM	air-launched cruise missile
ALPS	Accidental Launch Protection System
AOA	area of application
ASAT	antisatellite
ASBM	air-to-surface ballistic missile
ASEAN	Association of Southeast Asian Nations
ATBM	antitactical ballistic missile
ATTU	Atlantic to the Urals
BCC	Bilateral Consultative Commission
BDA	Bilateral Destruction Agreement
BIC	Bilateral Implementation Commission
BMD	ballistic missile defense
BMDO	Ballistic Missile Defense Organization
BMEWS	Ballistic Missile Early Warning System
BW	biological weapons
BWC	Biological and Toxin Weapons Convention
CATT	Conventional Arms Transfer Talks
CBWs	chemical and biological weapons
CD	Conference on Disarmament
CDE	Conference on Disarmament in Europe
CFE	Conventional Armed Forces in Europe
CIS	Commonwealth of Independent States
COCOM	(NATO) Coordinating Committee

CSBMs	confidence- and security-building measures
CSCE	Conference on Security and Cooperation in Europe
CTB	comprehensive test ban
CTBT	Comprehensive Test Ban Treaty
CTR	cooperative threat reduction
CW	chemical weapons
CWC	Chemical Weapons Convention
DOD	Department of Defense
DOE	Department of Energy
DST	Defense and Space Talks
EIF	entry into force
FSC	Forum for Security Cooperation
GLCM	ground-launched cruise missile
GPALS	Global Protection Against Limited Strikes
GPS	Global Protection System
IAEA	International Atomic Energy Agency
ICBM	intercontinental ballistic missile
INF	intermediate-range nuclear forces
INSS	Institute for National Security Studies (U.S. Air Force)
IRBM	intermediate-range ballistic missile
ISMA	International Satellite Monitoring Agency
JCC	Joint Consultative Commission
JCG	Joint Consultative Group
JCIC	Joint Compliance and Inspection Commission
JCS	Joint Chiefs of Staff
LANFZ	Latin American Nuclear-Free Zone
LPAR	large phased-array radar
LRA	long-range air-launched cruise missile (ALCM)
LRNA	long-range nuclear ALCM
LRNNA	long-range nonnuclear ALCM
LTBT	Limited Test Ban Treaty
MAD	mutual assured destruction
MBFR	Mutual and Balanced Force Reduction
MEACI	Middle East Arms Control Initiative
MIRV	multiple independently targetable reentry vehicles
MRBM	medium-range ballistic missile
MSR	missile site radar
MTCR	Missile Technology Control Regime
NACC	North Atlantic Cooperation Council
NATO	North Atlantic Treaty Organization
NFZ	nuclear-free zone
NMD	national missile defense
NNWS	nonnuclear weapons state

NORAD	North American Air Defense Command
NPR	Nuclear Posture Review
NPT	Non-Proliferation Treaty
NSG	Nuclear Suppliers Group
NST	Nuclear and Space Talks
NSZ	nuclear safe zone
NTM	national technical means
NWFZ	nuclear-weaponfree zone
NWS	nuclear weapon state
OOV	object of verification
OPCW	Organization for the Prohibition of Chemical Weapons
OSCE	Organization on Security and Cooperation in Europe
OSIA	On-Site Inspection Agency
OSCC	Open Skies Consultative Commission
PAR	perimeter acquisition radar
PNE	peaceful nuclear explosions
PNET	Peaceful Nuclear Explosions Treaty
PTBT	Partial Test Ban Treaty
RV	reentry vehicle
SALT	Strategic Arms Limitation Talks/Treaty
SAM	surface-to-air missile
SASC	Senate Armed Services Committee
SCC	Standing Consultative Commission
SDI	Strategic Defense Initiative
SDIO	Strategic Defense Initiative Organization
SFRC	Senate Foreign Relations Committee
SICBM	small intercontinental ballistic missile
SLBM	submarine-launched ballistic missile
SLCM	sea-launched cruise missile
SNDV	strategic nuclear delivery vehicle
SNF	short-range nuclear forces
SPNFZ	South Pacific Nuclear-Free Zone
SRAM	short-range attack missile
SRBM	short-range ballistic missile
SSBN	nuclear-powered ballistic missile submarine
SSCI	Senate Select Committee on Intelligence
START	Strategic Arms Reduction Talks /Treaty
THAAD	theater high-altitude air defense
TLE	treaty-limited equipment
TMD	theater missile defense
TTBT	Threshold Test Ban Treaty
UN	United Nations
UNSCOM	UN Special Commission on Iraq

WMD   weapons of mass destruction
WMDFZ   weapons-of-mass-destruction-free zone
WTO   Warsaw Treaty Organization

The Contributors

Christopher D. Carr teaches political science at the Center for Public Policy and Contemporary Issues, University of Denver, and at the University of Southern Colorado.

Marie Isabelle Chevrier is assistant professor of political economy at the University of Texas at Dallas.

Virginia I. Foran is an analyst at the Carnegie Endowment for International Peace, Washington, D.C., where she is research director of the Security Assurances Project.

Sidney N. Graybeal is chief scientist in the National Security Systems and Studies Group, Science Applications International Corporation, McLean, Va., and a member of the Defense Policy Board of the Department of Defense.

Jo L. Husbands is director of the Committee on International Security and Arms Control of the U.S. National Academy of Sciences, Washington, D.C.

Kerry M. Kartchner is representative of the U.S. Arms Control and Disarmament Agency to the Joint Compliance and Inspection Commission, Geneva, Switzerland.

Jeffrey A. Larsen is the first director of the U.S. Air Force Institute for National Security Studies and a senior associate professor of national security studies at the U.S. Air Force Academy in Colorado Springs, Colo.

Peter R. Lavoy is an assistant professor of national security affairs at the U.S. Naval Postgraduate School, Monterey, Calif.

Ronald F. Lehman is assistant to the director, Lawrence Livermore National Laboratory, Livermore, Calif. He recently chaired the advisory panel for the Project on Countering Proliferated Weapons of Mass Destruction for the Congressional Office of Technology Assessment, and was appointed by President Clinton to the President's Advisory Board on Arms Proliferation Policy. He is a former director of the U.S. Arms Control and Disarmament Agency.

Jeffrey D. McCausland is director of European studies, Department of National Security Studies, at the U.S. Army War College, Carlisle, Pa.

Patricia A. McFate is senior scientist in the National Security Systems and Studies Group, Science Applications International Corporation, McLean, Va., and a consultant to the UN Group of Outside Experts on Verification.

Joseph F. Pilat is a research analyst with the Nonproliferation and International Security Division of Los Alamos National Laboratory, Los Alamos, N. Mex.

Gregory J. Rattray is a U.S. Air Force officer and a research associate at the Institute for Foreign Policy Analysis in Cambridge, Mass.

Jennifer E. Sims is deputy assistant secretary of state for intelligence coordination in the Bureau of Intelligence and Research, U.S. State Department.

Amy E. Smithson is a senior associate at the Henry L. Stimson Center in Washington, D.C., where she directs the Chemical Weapons Convention Implementation Project.

Trevor Taylor is professor of international relations at Staffordshire University and an associate fellow of the Royal Institute of International Affairs in London.

Forrest Waller is assistant vice-president and division manager, Science Applications International Corporation, McLean, Va.

Cynthia A. Watson is professor of national security at the National War College, Fort McNair, Washington, D.C.

James J. Wirtz is an associate professor of national security affairs, Naval Postgraduate School, Monterey, Calif.

Index

ABM. *See* Antiballistic Missile Treaty
Accidental Launch Protection System
(ALPS), 127
ACDA. *See* Arms Control and Disarmament Agency
Acheson, Dean, 64, 197*n6*
AEA. *See* Atomic Energy Act
Afghanistan, 49, 105, 183, 237, 244
Agency for the Prohibition of Nuclear
Weapons in Latin America (OPANAL),
87
Agreements: asymmetrical, 42, 49, 139,
180; bilateral, 84, 324–325; binding,
56, 71; chemical weapons, 6; congressional-executive, 75*n10;* constitutional
framework for, 61–70; formal, 24, 56,
57; full-scope safeguards, 184, 195;
intergovernmental, 35; monitoring of,
63; multilateral, 4, 79, 84, 94; "no first
use," 110, 112, 117*n22,* 222*n2;*
nonnegotiated, 160; nuclear, 5;
presidential, 75*n10;* president's role,
61–62; tacit, 56; unilateral, 24, 107,
117*n15,* 141, 160, 287, 325–327; verbal,
24; violations of, ix
Alamogordo (New Mexico), 100, 176
Alfonsín, Raúl, 268, 269, 271*n3*
Alliances: defensive, 39
ALPS. *See* Accidental Launch Protection
System
American Physical Society, 127
Angola, 237; biological weapons in,
219*tab;* chemical weapons in, 219*tab*
Antarctic Treaty (1959), 102, 187, 264,
271*n1,* 271*n2,* 294*fig*
Antiballistic Missile (ABM) Treaty
(1972), 2, 11, 40, 42, 57, 83, 116*n9,*
119, 120, 121–136, 295*fig,* 300–302;

compliance issues, 128–129; implementation, 123–124; and national
missile defense, 124–128; Russian
facilities, 135*fig;* Standing Consultative
Commission, 123; and theater missile
defense, 129–132; treaty scope, 122–
124; verification, 123
Anticommunism, 59
Argentina, 5, 13, 39, 187, 254, 264–270;
arms production, 271*n5;* biological
weapons in, 219*tab;* chemical weapons
in, 219*tab;* in Missile Technology
Control Regime, 240; nuclear
capabilities, 266–267
Argentine-Brazilian Agency of Accounting and Control of Nuclear Materials,
187
Armenia, 147, 148; in Conventional
Forces in Europe Treaty (1990, 1992),
310*tab,* 311
Arms: competition, viii, 20; delivery, 36;
embargoes, 237–238; exports, 44–45,
234, 235; imports, 247*n3;* production,
138–139, 235, 271*n5;* reductions, 80;
transfers, 228–246
Arms control: advocacy groups in, 60–61;
alternative directions for, 111–114;
Cambridge approach, 60; changing
focus, 108; during Cold War, 2–4, 10,
156–160, 287; Congress's role in, 65–67;
contemporary, 106–109; conventional,
11, 138–152; costs of implementation,
ix, 108; defining, vii, 7–9; deterrence as
goal of, 25; disarmament of aggressors
in, 8; discrimination in, 13, 44, 271*n4;*
domestic context, 55–74; economic
impact, 72–73; evolution of, 100–106;
future course of, 12, 108–111, 160–163,

335